Woman with a Voice

Woman with a Voice

Daring to Live Authentically Ever After

Vicki Hannah Lein

Copyright © 2005 by Vicki Hannah Lein.

Library of Congress Number: 2005903735
ISBN: Hardcover   1-4134-9366-1
                Softcover   1-4134-9365-3

All rights reserved. No part of this book may be reproduced or transmitted in any form or by any means, electronic or mechanical, including photocopying, recording, or by any information storage and retrieval system, without permission in writing from the copyright owner.

This book was printed in the United States of America.

To order additional copies of this book, contact:
Xlibris Corporation
1-888-795-4274
www.Xlibris.com
Orders@Xlibris.com
23999

Contents

Acknowledgments 13

Introduction 15
    Follow Your Bliss; Poem: My Intention for My Home and This Book; Poem: Taking the Dare; Poem: Woman with a Voice; Song: Sing My Song; Your Turn

Part I: Embracing Our Authentic Voice

Chapter 1: Listening for the Muse 35
    Poem: Trust Your Muse; Poem: Pull Back the Curtain; Poem: Taking Myself Wherever I Go; Your Turn

Chapter 2: Taking a Stand for Who We Are and What We Believe 44
    Poem: What I Believe; Poem: I'd Rather Be Real; Song: Take a Stand for Love; Poem: I am a Poet, by God!; Poem: If You Want to Be Happy; Happiness Tips; Your Turn

Chapter 3: Loving Ourselves First 55
    Song: I Deserve to Be Loved; Impeccable Self-Care; Your Turn

Chapter 4: Increasing Our Response Ability 61
    E+R=O: Event Plus Response Equals Outcome; Levels of Response; Shift Happens; Story: Fake It Until You Make It; Story: "Father, Forgive Them."; Story: KKK Transformation; Key Points for Using the Levels of Response; Getting Hooked on Creating the Big "O" of

Our Lives; Crazymakers; Story: Weeding Crazymakers out of Your Sacred Garden; Song: Crazymaker, Crazymaker; Two Strategies for Shifting Your Responses; Your Turn

Chapter 5: Creating Powerful Stories for Ourselves 86
Story: Matthew Entertains a New Idea; Story: Not a Happy Physics Party; Poem: My True Voice; Song: I Feel Fifty; Your Turn

Chapter 6: Falling in Love with Truth 101
Song: Truth Rap; Falling in Love with Truth; Story: My Illusion of Control Falls in the Lake; Poem: I Am a Greedy Bitch; Poem: I'm the One Who Smells the Rat; Your Turn

Chapter 7: Choosing Courage 109
Comfort Zones; Story: "That's Not Funny, Dad!"; The Courage to Be Disliked; Song: WarriorBabe; Song: "Come to the Cliff," She Said; Your Turn

Chapter 8: Listening for Possibility 118
Poem: Listening is Dangerous; Poem: Good Listening is Not Interrupting (Except When It Is); Story: Courageous Listening With Martin; Your Turn

Chapter 9: Living in Integrity 125
Poem: Promises are Sacred; Song: "Sorry" Doesn't Work Here Anymore; Murray Teaches Vicki to Make Requests; Your Turn

Chapter 10: Unpacking Our Personal Baggage 134
Story: It Will Never Happen to Me; Poem: My Killer Wail; Hiding in Beige; Poem: Just an Electric Skillet; Poem: If It's Not Personal . . .; Story: How Our Inner Baby Tyrannosaurus Wrecks Love; Song: Menopause!; Poem: Little Girl in Gray; Your Turn

Chapter 11: Taking on Shame and Jealousy 156
   Shame: The Mistake that Defines Us; Poem: The Massacre of Magic; Poem: Anguish on Stage; Jealousy: Shame's Green-Eyed Partner; Your Turn

Chapter 12: Loving Our Bodies "As Is" 168
   Poem: Body Confessions; Song: Tiny Boobies; Poem: Body Freedom; Story: The Love Diet; Song: All Women Are Beautiful; Your Turn

Chapter 13: Grieving as We Go 178
   Song: Ode to Blindness; Story: No More Stars; Poem: Despair? Again Today?; Sadness, Where Are You Hiding?; Martin and His Mom in Europe; Poem: The Call of the Grave; Poem: She's the One Who Didn't Die; Guided Writing: Meeting a Bear; Poem: A Fallow Field; Your Turn

Chapter 14: Speaking Our Appreciation and Gratitude 211
   Song: Well Done; Poem: Murray is My Hero; Story: Bus Stop Epiphany; Song: Still a Rose; Song: Gratitude; Your Turn

Part II: Loving in Harmony

Chapter 15: The Heart of the Matter: Men and Women are Different 229
   Man School; Story: What It's Like To Be Murray; Tips for Men; Poem: How to Spot a Real Man; Poem: How to Spot a Good Woman; Song: Song for Men; Your Turn

Chapter 16: Agreeing to Couple Well 247
   Write Your Love Down While It's Hot; Poem: Why I Love Murray; Murray and Vicki's Holy Agreements; Your Turn

Chapter 17: Agreement #1: Don't Say "Yes" When You Mean "No" and then Blame Me 251
Avoiding Martyr Hell; Poem: What I Can and Can't Control; Story: Doggie Do's and Don'ts; Your Turn

Chapter 18: Agreement #2: Love Yourself Well 257
Seeing the Gift in Asking for Help; Song: Crazy; Your Turn

Chapter 19: Agreement #3: Love Each Other Well 261
Story: Murray and the Ketchup; Your Turn

Chapter 20: Agreement #4: Own Your Own Farts 263
Story: "You Ate My Mint!"; Story: The Ginger Pig; Poem: In My Stuff; Story: Finger-Holding Confessions; Your Turn

Chapter 21: Agreement #5: Take Turns 274
Poem: Wordlessness; Your Turn; Your Turn, Again

Chapter 22: Fighting the Good Fight 278
Poem: When Confrontation Is Hard and Easy; Conflict Prevention; Poem: How Can I Disagree with You Without Getting Defensive?; Starting Difficult Conversations; The Art of Getting Angry; Poem: Too Hot; Story: Hot Anger with Martin and Dave Barry; Story: "Mom, I'm Not a Kid Anymore."; Helpful Hints for Doing Anger "Just Right"; Your Turn

Chapter 23: Gracious Extrications from Difficult Situations 295
Story: Murray, the Thermostat, and Do-Overs; Authentic Apologies; Story: "Vicki, I Need to Talk to You"; Your Turn

Chapter 24: Pulling Back the Curtain on Some Great Fights 301
Story: Murray and the River Panic; Story: Puerto Vallarta Fight; Story: Suitcase Fight; Murray Off and On; Poem: A Fight to the Death; Your Turn

Part III: Loving Family and Friends

Chapter 25: Family: A Divinely Human Yearning 325
The Art of Invisible Mothering; Your Turn

Chapter 26: Kathleen Rebecca 332
Poem: To My Daughter, Katie; Story: An Unsent Letter: Did I Break You?; Note in Katie's High School Yearbook; Story: Katie's Heart; Song: Repo Man; Poem: Grizzly Mother; Poem: Before and Now; Letter: Katie Turns Twenty-One; Poem: Sweet Agony; Letter: A Challenge; Poem: My Daughter Left Today; Letter: Mother's Day; Letter to the Boyfriend; Epilogue; Your Turn

Chapter 27: Martin James 370
My First Poem to Martin; Story: Martin and Self-Esteem; Letter: Martin's 14th Birthday; Martin and the Piano Picture; Story: Martin and Hypocrisy; Story: "Martin, It Works Both Ways"; Poem: Martin, It's Finally Your Turn; Martin's Poem for Me; Your Turn

Chapter 28: Shirley May 385
Poem: Beatrice Lela; Gramma's House; Story: Still Mom; Poem: What Kind of a Mother Have You Been?; Story: The Breaking of a Family; Poem: Sitting by the Fire; Poem: Shirley Living and Dying; Poem: The Breathing; Poem: The Delivery; Guided Writing: Is This Heaven?; Guided Writing: Heaven: This Time for Sure; Song: My Mommy is an Angel; Epilogue; Your Turn

Chapter 29: My Daddy is a Stranger 417
Telling the Truth; Level Three Forgiveness; Story: "Dad, Are You an Alcoholic?"; Letter to My Dad, 1989; Another Letter to My Dad, 1991; Poem: Sometimes My Daddy Is . . .; My Last Letter to My Dad, 1992; Guided Writing: A Walk with My Wound; Poem: A Few Good Men; Poem: Ju-Ju's Daddy is Not a Stranger; Your Turn

Chapter 30: Friends: Our Family of the Heart 437
> On Friendship; Friendship Chronicles; Poem: A Funny Story; Poem: Belaboring the Obvious; Embracing the "Obvious"; Poem: Why I Like You, Jan Bateman; Being Friends with Purpose; Poem: What She Knew Without Being Told; Poem: For Denny Bateman of the Great Heart; Letter to Vicki: Adventuring through the Book; The Dissolution of a Friendship; Poem: Sadie, A Friend Worth Having; Vicki and Sadie's Friendship Repair Kit; Poem: Sadie and Vicki: A Celebration; Epilogue; Your Turn

Part IV: Saying Aloha

Chapter 31: That's All For Now! 471
> Story: The Joy of Writing?; Poem: What If?; Story: Creating the Song Beauty Like a Rock; Song: Beauty Like a Rock; Poem: Africa Singing; A Final Poem: As It Turns Out; Your Turn

Glossary 481

Soul Resources 493

More Soul Resources 495

DEDICATION

Dedicated to Bethany and Shaen;
to Kathleen Rebecca and Martin James,
my fabulous children and two of my best teachers;
to Shirley May,
my beloved mother; whose love beacon kept my spirit alive;
and
to Murray Norman Lein,
my husband and fellow traveler and cosmic trapeze artist.

Here is the best of what I know as a blessing on your lives.

Acknowledgments

Jan Bateman, for editing this book and for contributing to the chapter on Friendship. I can never thank you enough for sharing this journey with me;

Sara Mehlenbacher, copyeditor and proofreader (she is fast and good!);

Karen Bowers and Effie Clendenon for allowing me to include their writing in Part IV;

Andrew Ayers and Valerie Bowen at Fulltone Studio, for their help and encouragement recording my songs,

Stephanie Long, for reading early drafts of this manuscript to me and for giving me the heart to continue;

Barbara Gladstone, for her blunt, brilliant editing feedback;

Carrie, Sarah, Jan, Kathie, and Claire—
my Big Group buddies who got me writing on a regular basis;

Suzannah Doyle for sharing her musical genius so generously with me;

Lea, Nancy, Barbara, Maryanne, Lola, Lynda, Sarah, Mary Betts, Mary, Ellen, and all the other angels in my life who have picked me up when I have fallen;

Bekki Levien for creating the gorgeous cover for this book;

And, finally, to everyone who has the courage
to keep walking through the dark times,
healing the world one heart at a time.

Thank you!

Introduction

*"The band of life is playing.
What song are you waiting to hear before you begin to dance?"*

Follow Your Bliss

I believe we are all born with our highest purpose cradled in our bellies. Our purpose whispers to us, and it is our job in this life to listen to its subtle inklings and nudges. If we trust what we hear and have courage, our greatest gift will make itself known to us. In fact, if we don't follow our bliss, as Joseph Campbell so wisely counseled, I believe our gifts will pursue us, stalk us even, until we let go of our self-limiting stories and commit to becoming who we were meant to be.

This book is a collage of poetry, stories, reflections, and songs. Many of these writings are very personal, but I believe they contain universal themes. In each selection I hope to have my own experiences resonate so clearly in me that anyone reading my words will feel their humanity resonate in them as well. In Part I, I write about qualities of living I have come to embrace: listening, courage, and integrity, to name a few. Part II deals specifically with our most intimate relationships and how we can prevent problems and extricate ourselves when we stumble. Part III is an autobiographical pastiche of my children and parents, with one chapter devoted to the challenge of deep friendship. Part IV contains a glossary of terms that have emerged from my writing, speaking, playing, singing, and fighting.

I doubt that many readers will sit down with *Woman With a Voice* and read it straight through. I'm hoping that different sections will appeal to different readers and that poems and stories will get dog-eared as they get shared. Writing this book has been an act of faith and courage for me. In some ways, this book has created me as much as I have created it.

About the Author

I grew up in Oregon in a family with too much drinking and violence. I have been a high school English teacher, and elementary school counselor, and worked in a drug and alcohol treatment center. Ten years ago the eye disease I inherited from my mother resulted in the destruction of my central vision. I lost my marriage, my ability to read and drive, and my job as a school counselor within a two-year period. The combination of grief and terror that flooded my body drowned my hope and brought me to my knees.

A decade later I am co-creating a robust second marriage, have raised two terrific children, lived through my mother's death, and somehow gotten myself to Europe and Africa as an educational consultant. Some of my work has been translated into Spanish, French, German, and Ukrainian. Songs I have written, in spite of a voice in my head that told me my melodies and lyrics were trite and embarrassing, are now sung all over the world.

These facts completely amaze me. Since I am the first person in my extended family to earn a Master's degree, and one of a very few to go to college at all, I am still astounded that I have dreamed myself into a life as an international motivational speaker/singer/songwriter. I am living a charmed, magical life and I make no apology, but I am drenched in a gratitude that almost overwhelms me some days.

Some people might think the loss of my vision has been my greatest challenge, but they would be wrong. Blindness has been an amazing gift and learning experience that I did not asked for, and some of this book is about how I have managed to "keep on swimmin'."

Perhaps surprisingly, my greatest opponent, though invisible and subtle, has been the voice of doubt that lives inside my head. Every day, all day, I choose: do I listen to the voice of Limitation and Scarcity? ("Who do you think you are, anyway? What makes you think you have anything worth writing down, much less publishing?") Or will I listen to the voice that beckons me to a greater, more dangerous, more unpredictable life: ("Write the song you are hearing in your head right now and some day you will teach it as a gospel celebration of life.")

I have learned to trust what I hear, even when I don't understand exactly what it means or how it is going to happen. I don't get to know the where and when. **Note:** The song I heard was *Beauty Like a Rock* and I did teach it at a conference in Senegal six years after I obeyed the urge to write it. I tell this story in Part IV.

My husband Murray and I both listened to the call of our Muses eight years ago and quit our secure jobs to follow our dreams. I had two children in college and a tenured job with a school district, but I knew my body and soul needed me to jump off the cliff of security into self-employment. I left monthly salary, paid health care, and regular retirement deposits and traded them for the chance to discover and embrace my magnificence. Murray left his job as an occupational therapist at a hospital to work on a contract with a school district that is renewed yearly.

We have never looked back. Though sometimes I will go for a month with no paid work and Murray's salary alone is not enough to pay our bills, we live happily, for the most part. Murray was born to work with children and now he gets to develop his genius instead of needing to recover from a job that sucked his energy and joy. I get to write poems and songs and travel all over the world helping people laugh and cry and dream bigger for their lives. We both work part time, so we have plenty of energy to yum up our house and our garden and visit with friends.

Our creativity keeps flowing and expanding and we keep recreating ourselves and our relationship. Neither of us could go back to our old lives even if we wanted to. Our bodies wouldn't let us. (My Predator Voice is saying. You are bragging! You will turn people off. You are calling destruction upon yourself. That other shoe is dangling over your head as you speak. Who wants to hear about your happiness?" "Maybe so," I say, "but what I have written is true and it is why I want to share what we have learned.")

I wrote this book in the hope that I could provide examples of finding voice and living authentically. I believe if I am able to strike a universal chord within myself, every reader will automatically experience more of their own creativity—a type of delicious, cosmic, sympathetic vibration. Deciding which poems and stories to include and which to save for later has involved listening and choosing, listening and choosing. Since this is the process I am encouraging you to embrace, it is perfect that I have had to practice what I preach.

I am walking my talk, trusting the process, and letting go of outcome. This is "simple" work, yet it requires faith and encouragement and that is why I have had the audacity to write this book. (**Note:** Since I am legally blind I cannot read this book. My computer reads it to me, hence the references to "listen.")

Woman with a Voice is a celebration and a road map, of sorts, for living a rigorous, joyful life. What I offer in these pages, written from my soul, is hard-won wisdom and heart. Creating an authentic life is not for wimps. You must be willing to go everywhere inside yourself and to know everything about yourself, no matter how scary this truth might be. This is a heroic journey that not every individual, couple, family member or friend attempts.

No Holy Grail, no state of perfect love and enlightenment, no "happily ever after" exists for anyone. No matter how much organic food we eat or how much exercise we get, we cannot inoculate ourselves against Life. But the journey, ah the courageous, authentically-ever-after journey! It is alive! It is life! It is juicy and fraught with peril. It is a road less traveled and worth every bone-crunching step.

Poem: My Intention for My Home and This Book

Stating our intentions clearly is like placing an order with the Cosmic Waitress. "This is what I want," we declare and our desires are telegraphed to the stars. Forces mysteriously begin that create "coincidences" and support appears from sources we could never have imagined. Our dreams move forward effortlessly. Not to worry, though, if you believe in hard work. There is hard work aplenty in this process. It's just a different kind of hard work.

Living in faith is challenging because we are walking through a swamp of fear every day. Listening to subtle urgings that defy what we think is logical, practical, and possible is a workout that develops muscles of spirit. It is a paradox that we must envision and dream, state our intentions with no reservations, and then be willing to release how it all turns out. We must also be willing at all times to do the work placed in front of our noses. This way of living is simple, complicated, easy, arduous, mystifying, enlightening, magical and outrageously funny all at the same time.

So it takes courage to give ourselves permission to even think about what we really want, much less proclaim it to the universe. With that in mind I boldly state my intentions for my home and my intentions for every reader of this book.

I want my home and this book
to be inviting, welcoming.
I want my readers,
my guests,
to feel deeply at home, in my words and in my stories,
so deeply at home
that they are willing to entertain new ideas about their possibilities.

I want my home and this book
to be a place where courage and truth are nurtured,
where fierceness isn't terrifying,
where there is a remembering and an honoring
of all the flavors and seasons of Transformation.

I want my home and this book
to be a place where perpetual curiosity is nourished,
where even depression and discouragement are interesting,
essential steps of the journey.

I want my home and this book
to be a place of belly laughter,
where we bend over in gleeful agony,
tears streaming down our faces,
as we joyfully surrender to that untamed Cosmic Sense of Humor,
which might just whack us with The Joke until we Get It.

I want my home and this book
to be a place where my guests do not feel
they need to be anyone but themselves,
where our desire is not for perfection,
but for a delightful, courageous exploration of what is
and what could be.

I want my home and this book
to be a place where family and friends gather
to celebrate and enjoy each other's company,
where sharing is common but not demanded.

I want my home and this book
to be a place of healing,
where the energy of love and truth and courage
permeate and rejuvenate our souls.

When people are in my home or reading this book,
I want them to entertain fabulous, outrageous ideas of possibility.
I want my guests and my readers to let themselves say:
"Maybe I am an artist!'
or "Maybe I am beautiful!"
or "Maybe I can sing!"
or "Maybe I do deserve to be fully alive and happy!"

I want my home and this book
to be a safe harbor
and a trampoline
and an oasis
and a launch pad
and a feather bed
and the inside of the most delicious piece of fruit in the Garden.

I want my home and this book
to connect us to the Deep Home,
a place where we can cool our weary feet,
restore our resolve,
and reconnect to all that is Holy.

And I want my home and this book
to be a place where love grows like dandelions,
spreading effortlessly in the wind.

I want to share the Dandelion Love between my husband Murray and me,
full of a yellow cheerfulness,
with hungry ears and hearts.

Did I mention free-flowing creativity and service to the world?
Unbounded hope?
Delicious naughtiness?
Delightful, life-tilting revelations?

This, and more, is what I want in my home and in this book.

Poem: Taking the Dare

"Daring to live authentically ever after" did not come naturally to me. I am a recovering coward. I used to be afraid of everything: making people mad, disappointing people, making mistakes. Once my authentic voice began making itself known to me, though, I decided to start practicing courage, getting a little braver every day. I "took the dare," as it were, to become all of what I might become.

I hear my magnificence calling me.
But this call is only an inkling,
a tiny nudge from my Possibility.

Can I take this leap into what might be oblivion
or humiliation?
My lungs and my courage freeze.
I can barely breathe.
My dreams spin away from my yearning fingers
as I fall through thorns of fear and shame.

"Just who do you think you are!" the voice of doubt,
a voice as old as the dinosaurs,
bellows in my head.
"Sit down and shut up," it snarls.
"Don't breathe more than your fair share of oxygen.

Never make a mistake.
Never fail.
Never disappoint anyone."
The crushing weight of this Voice
wants me to live in a grave of "No's."

Instead, I take the dare.
From my Cosmic Belly,
I proclaim a "Yes!"
"Yes to the adventure of life!
Yes to falling!
Yes to making a fool of myself!
Yes! and Yes! again!"

My life is a melody,
sometimes harmonious,
sometimes dissonant,
but this is my life,
a true life,
a life where I dare
every day
every moment
to take the dare.

I will take a stand for full catastrophe living.
I will take my lumps.
I will cultivate the courage to be disliked,
the courage to be misunderstood.
I will have the courage to turn out to be who I really am.

I will not die with nooks and crannies of myself unexplored,
denied,
giving off the stench of regrets.
I will not die with "It might have been" dripping off my lips.
I will not die with my song unsung,
with all my music inside me.

I will die with my torch completely burned.
I will die being the most me I can be.

I will dare, every day,
to take the dare.

Poem: Woman with a Voice

Vicki recording *Daring to Sing* at Fulltone Studio.
Photo: Valerie Bowen

When we resonate in our truth and in our unique genius, we are living within an authentic voice. Voice cannot be copied or faked. I should know because in the past I tried that often enough. When we are living with Voice, our lives are adventures, not always easily understood by ourselves or others. The more we live in our Voice, the more dissonant our pretending becomes. We will hear artifice more clearly in others and ourselves, whether we want to or not.

The saying "Be careful what you pray for because you just might get it" is true. If you lean into finding your voice, you might topple into yourself even if you want to stop when it gets scary. When we reach the "critical mass" of enlivening our every cell, we cannot stop the change. It's just like when two mixtures are combined and nothing happens until that final drop is added. New colors emerge, aromas fly, and we have a new substance that cannot return to the parts we started with. At some point our bodies will not let us consider trying to live in the shell that was once us. We will turn into a pillar of salt at the thought of trying to regain the life we have chosen to leave.

This poem tells the story of my voice calling to me and of my learning to listen and trust what I have been hearing my whole life. This story is a fractal of the message of this book, the importance of listening and choosing, which is the essence of finding our voice and daring to live authentically ever after.

I am a child hearing my voice for the first time.

I am five years old.
Daddy brings home a magic machine that doesn't just play records.
It MAKES them.
Mommy comforts my baby brother as Daddy connects the wires.
We are in our living room, huddled around the microphone.
My sister Lee, Daddy, and I sing.
We are a family singing, a singing family.

When we finish our song, Daddy carefully sets the needle
on the record we have created.
My family quiets and listens,
even my two-year-old brother.
And I marvel at the scene,
almost exploding in kindergartener delight,
as I watch the record turn,
the black vinyl record that now has the grooves of our voices etched in
    it forever.

I listen with wonder to my family sing, my voice mingled with theirs.
A profound chord is struck deep in my belly.

A true Vicki note is rung.
Singing and recording
seem as natural to me as laughing when my daddy tickles me.
My five-year-old body resonates with a simple truth:
I was born to sing.
Singing and recording would be the most marvelous way to spend my life.
But even though I am not yet in first grade,
I am pretty sure my singing dream is impossible.

I am a child searching for my voice.

I am nine years old.
My elementary school has a talent show
and I decide I want to try out.
I can't talk any of my friends into joining me,
So I decide to go it alone.
I pick a record from the stack of 45's stored in our stereo cabinet,
And walk in circles around the living room
memorizing the words to "Blue Moon."
I ask my dad, who sings and plays the guitar,
if he will accompany me.
(I have this vague notion
that singers should have music playing along with them.)
He replies with a dead, flat "No."
Not, "Sorry, Sweetie, I just can't swing that. I would love to help you though."
He just says "No."

I decide to audition anyway.
I have no idea where I find this courage.

I stand in the middle of the stage in the cafeteria,
wearing a print dress with capped sleeves and a white collar.
My skinny legs and bony ankles don't seem strong enough to hold me up.
I sing a cappella for the music teacher, whom I love.
I sing from the center of the stage,

and the center of my heart,
remembering, to my amazement,
all of the words.

It is just me and my voice and we are a great team.

I do not get picked for the talent show.
I decide I must not be a singer
and I do not belong on stage.

I am a teenager in love.

I am seventeen, a senior in high school.
My boyfriend and I walk into the auditions
for the first musical our school has ever produced,
I try out only because he is trying out.
I'm sure I'm not good enough to get a part.

I get the lead, Rosie in "Bye, Bye Birdie."
My boyfriend is cast as Albert, the male lead.
Being in this musical takes every bit of courage I have,
And it is the grandest experience of my life so far.
"I didn't know you could sing," my mother tells me, amazed.
"You have talent," my history teacher tells me, somewhat casually, as if
    I already knew.
"You're not half bad as a singer," the director tells me, a perfectionist,
and I know his words are high praise.

The acting had been challenging but fun.
The dancing had been fun and terrifying.
But the singing,
oh, the singing—
the singing had transported me outside of myself and my approval-
    obsessed life
for a few, brief, shining moments.

Maybe I am a singer, I dare to think.

I go to college, buy a cheap guitar, and teach myself chords
from the back of a Joni Mitchell songbook.
I write simple folk songs.
When I marry at twenty-six,
I put my guitar and my singing away.
Sometimes I wonder where my singing went.

I am a woman with a rage.

I am thirty-two.
I am seeing a counselor
to keep myself from passing my childhood pain to my children.
My counselor asks me to keep a journal,
and, for the first time,
I write what is in my heart without censoring anything.
I write to find out what is true inside me.
I hold back nothing.
I find my voice in my writing,
finally,
and She has never left me.
I am now a woman with a voice on the page.

I am a woman whose singing is still calling to her.

It is my fiftieth birthday.
I have been singing for three solid days
with a karaoke machine a friend has loaned me.
I sing for hours every day,
every song I know.
I sing until I am hoarse and can sing no more.

> The phone rings and I think, "The neighbors are calling to tell me to
> shut up."

I am amazed that this belief still lives so deeply and secretly inside me,
the belief that my innocent singing needs to be stamped out,
that I need to be stamped out because I am not good enough.

I decide to take a stand for my singing,
to lean into my voice without a safety line.
I decide to let my singing become whatever it wants to become
without judging its worth,
my worth.
I am fifty and it is about time.

I am finally a woman with a voice.

As I write this I am a month away from being fifty-three.
I am recording a CD with my singing group The Free Range Chix.
(One of our songs has been played on national radio.)
I am also recording CDs to accompany this book.
I have written a chapter for a book titled *Wise Woman Speak*.
I have been asked to speak at an international conference in Africa,
(and,
by the way,
to sing at the banquet.
Take that! Dinosaur Voice!)

I am, by God and by Muse, a woman with a voice.

Song: Sing My Song
(*from the CD* Daring to Sing*)*

> *This song takes a stand for my speaking voice, my singing voice and the voice of my deepest truth.*

I've found it's the little bumps in life that make me mute.
I cannot seem to speak my mind.
Then I hide behind the lame excuse that I'm just trying to be kind.
    (What a crock!)

Chorus:
I need to sing my song. I need to find my voice.
I need to listen deep for my truth inside.
Then I'll make my choice.
'Cuz if you haven't stepped on anyone's toes,
you haven't been for much of a walk.
If you haven't stepped on anyone's toes,
You haven't been for much of a walk.
Not much of a walk.

I'm working hard to find the courage to be disliked,
to be at peace when we disagree.
For if I'm seeking to please instead of seeking truth
I know I never will be free.

Chorus

Jolting Joe DiMaggio had a slump in '41.
Everyone's advice just made him weak.
So he decided he'd just listen to himself.
Then he had a fifty-six game hitting streak.

He had to sing his song.
He had to find his stance.
He had to listen deep for his truth inside,
and then he took a chance.

So it comes down to this:
we have to listen for our own bliss.
So it comes down to this: you've got to listen for your own bliss.

You've got to sing your song.
You've got to find your voice.
You've got to listen deep for your truth inside
and then make your choice.
'Cuz if you haven't stepped on anyone's toes,

you haven't been for much of a walk.
If you haven't stepped on anyone's toes,
You haven't been for much of a walk.
Not much of a walk.

Note: Thanks to Barbara Kingsolver for sharing advice from her grandfather in *High Tide in Tucson*: "If you haven't stepped on anyone's' toes, you haven't been for much of a walk."

Your Turn

At the end of each chapter you will find a "Your Turn" section where I invite you to ponder some questions. You might want to keep a journal to write your responses. Reading this book with a friend or a group of friends or your lover might increase your joy and insights. Or you can email me at vicki@joyworks.us. I would be delighted to hear from you.

So let's get started already!

Do you have a story about finding your voice? About losing it? When do you notice yourself holding back from speaking your truth? If you were to sing or hum as you walked down the street, as people used to do all the time, would you keep humming if you met another pedestrian or would you shut up? Why would you shut up? Who is harmed by your singing, even if you are "terrible?"

What intentions do you have for your home? You might want to ask your friends how they feel when they come to visit you. What intentions do you think operate in the homes where you feel most comfortable? In the homes where you feel you must be on your best behavior? Murray and I have three "Welcome" signs and aromatic flowering plants for people to enjoy before they get to our front door. What messages are you sending people as they approach your home? Are they the messages you want to send? What could you do to be even more explicit about how you want people to experience your home?

Blessings to all of you who put your feet and your hearts on this path with us.

Vicki Hannah Lein

Three CD's accompany this book.
They are available on my website: *www.joyworks.us.*

Alive, Alive: Songs that Lift You Up, Dust You Off, and Set You Free
Daring to Sing
Daring to Be a Poet

Part I

Embracing Our Authentic Voice

"To be nobody but yourself in a world doing its best night and day to make you everybody else, means to fight the hardest battle any human can fight and never stop fighting."

ee cummings

Chapter 1

Listening for the Muse

Poem: Trust Your Muse

Listening to our Muse is the single most important habit to cultivate if we want to live and love authentically ever after. I believe everyone has a Muse inside of them., Our Muse is always full of juicy ideas, and is smarter than we are. I believe our thinking will only get us so far and that when we surrender to our Muse, we open ourselves to our deepest truths.

I believe the Muse and the Dinosaur Predator inside of us battle all day long for our hearts and minds. "You could be a graphic artist!" our Muse might say. "That's a stupid idea!" says the Dinosaur. "Don't you know there are already too many graphic artists in this world and your dad won't like it and you aren't smart enough anyway? And besides that you have no artistic talent? You need to give up before you start."

If we choose the Dinosaur, our life shrinks, but if we listen to our Muse, our life is an exciting adventure that keeps creating and recreating itself every day. Your Muse will keep you busy and take you places you never dreamed you would go. How do you think I got myself to Africa?

I hope this poem haunts you—in a good way.

"Trust your Muse,"
she said.

"Let your Muse lead you.
Follow with eagerness.
Let your Muse be the boss.

"Don't listen to the Dinosaur Voice
that wants to silence you,
keep you tied to a stake,
or run a stake through your heart.

"This voice doesn't love you,"
she said.

"Over-thinking is illegal," she said.
"Don't trust the voice
that wants you to stop
and plan
so you can get it all perfect
before you begin.

"Don't trust the voice
that belittles you,
telling you
your ideas are boring
or stupid
or worthless.

"Trust your Muse,
the voice that says,
with a quiet insistency,
'This!'

"Trust a gentle idea
that wanders into your mind's meadow
like a deer.
It is a dear idea.
Believe it.
Respect it.
Honor it.

"Trust that your Muse is always full
of more than you could ever imagine.
Trust that you are always full
of more than you could ever imagine.

"You are powerful beyond measure.
You are brilliant,
gorgeous,
talented,
and magnificent.

"You are dust from the stars,
golden,
and your job on this earth
is to manifest your greatest gifts
for the world's greatest needs.

"Your job is to be happy
and to leave the world
a little better
for your having been in it.

"Trust your Muse
to take you to the stars,
to take you home,
again
and again,
and again,"
she said,
and you felt a tiny spark of belief,
a tiny spark of your "impossible" dream,
ignite.

You became an unquenchable fire.
You finally emerged
into what your life has eternally beckoned you to become.

Poem: Pull Back the Curtain

At her wedding shower, Bethany, my daughter Katie's best friend, accidentally got this book started by asking her mom's friends to give her advice about relationships as our gift, and, boy, do I love giving advice. I wrote this poem as an attempt to share the cornerstone of my relationship with Murray. "Pulling back the curtain" is a daily practice, which will help us find our true voice and live our lives authentically.

Keep pulling back the curtain,
telling the truth every minute about who you are,
if you want to save your love.

Keep pulling back the curtain,
though you aren't ready.
though it isn't pretty,
always,
all those thoughts and emotions that rampage through you,
unbidden.

But keep pulling back the curtain, anyway.
Keep speaking what is true for you,
though you wish you didn't think it or feel it,
though sometimes you are ashamed
that a being as glorious as you could be so petty,
so jealous,
so vindictive,
so despicable—
so divinely human.

Keep pulling back the curtain
if you want your love to grow
because to hide behind the curtain
will surely suffocate it.

Your marriage may look like it sails on placid waters,
but the truth that lies in the deep will not be denied,
and,
like a monster from those dark depths,
your truth will surge to the surface when it is most inconvenient,
when your children are born,
or when they leave home,
or when you lose a job,
or when your hair starts to turn gray,
or when some new man touches your hand
and your cells fill with a fire you thought hopelessly dead.

Then the truth you have kept hidden behind the curtain
will demand its fee.
Now you will pay your debt
for pretending,
making nice,
keeping the peace,
and avoiding pain.

The truth, my dear,
will set you free,
but first it might scare you to your DNA
and overwhelm you with doubt and dread.

To speak the truth means risking losing everything
everyday.
But to deny yourself and your lover access to your truth
is to smother love
one cell at a time,
a slow death you can ignore until it starts to take you down with it.

No, pull back the curtain,
And, in love, confess who you really are
at just this moment.
Now,
and now again.

Develop the habit of pulling back the curtain on what is true for you,
and you will get good at it—
good at knowing who you really are,
moment to moment—
good at sharing who you are,
moment to moment.
You will learn to share your authentic self with your beloved,
the one the stars picked for you to make this life with.

Let your lover in on the secret of you.
Let your lover hold you
as you open yourself to the buried places inside you
that you can barely risk glimpsing yourself.

As your lover's tender caress envelops you,
as you uncover and reveal your naked unfinished soul—
as you commit this act of great faith—
a trust will be born between you.
Cradled in a truth this deep,
your trust will steady you through turbulent emotional storms,
will anchor you in your love
when the vicissitudes of life squeeze you,
making you bleed and cry out with hot, unintelligible pain.

Practice revealing,
unveiling,
the brave, the cowardly,
the bold, the timid,
the generous, the stingy—
You.

Pull back the curtain, sweet one,
because there is nothing else you can do
to deepen your love,
to expand your love,
to save your love.

Pull back the curtain.

Poem: Taking Myself Wherever I Go

"The advantage of telling the truth," Fat Albert told us, "is on accounta you can remember what you said." The advantage of taking yourself wherever you go is that you will always have someone with you that you can count on.

I take myself with me wherever I go.
How about that?

I live from inside the truth of me
wherever I am,
whomever I'm with.

My feet are firmly planted on solid ground,
the solid ground of my belly and my deep inner listening.
Solidly planted,
but light on my feet—
that's me.

I'm alive in my daily life,
aware of old familial patterns still stuck in my heart,
yet I fully surrender to the power of my in-dwelling God.

I take myself with me wherever I go.

I used to leave myself behind.
Going to an interview?
Leave the real me at home.
Guess at who this stranger expects
and give her that ideal applicant.

Going to dinner with new friends?
Guess what will fit into their world
without rocking it too much.
If I am a Perfect Friend,
if I can become this mythical concoction of my desperate brain,
perhaps they will include me.

Oops! I blew it again!
I misjudged what might rock their boat.
Now this friendship is overboard!

Now, instead of being afraid of drowning,
I prefer to swim.
I swallowed lots of salt water
before I learned how to dance atop the waves.
Mastering all these different strokes took time,
and patience,
and courage.
And I did it.

I take myself with me wherever I go,
singing like I don't need the money,
dancing like nobody's watching,
and loving like I'll never get hurt.

I take myself with me wherever I go.

Your Turn

How does your Muse speak to you? When have you listened and when have you ignored its inklings and nudges? What does your Dinosaur Voice say to you when it is trying to get you to give up? What would happen if you turned to that Voice and said, with a French accent, "Ptooie! I spit on you!"

What would your life be like if you knew how to "pull back the curtain" and let people know who you really are, warts and all? Where are you pretending in your life, pretending you are happy, pretending that something doesn't bother you, pretending that you aren't bored out of your mind? Keep a journal and write down every day the truth of how you are feeling and what you are thinking. If you don't practice telling yourself what is authentically going on with you, you will have no chance of sharing your real self with anyone else.

What compliments have you received in your lifetime? Make a list of all that you can remember. This may be painful. Pay attention to what your Dinosaur Voice does to you as you write out this collection. Practice saying, "Thank you" when someone gives you a compliment. Entertain the idea that maybe they are right about you and see what happens to your body and your hope.

Chapter 2

Taking a Stand for Who We Are and What We Believe

"To thine own self be true."
Shakespeare, Polonius' advice to Hamlet

I would add to this fine advice: "And know what you stand for; what you believe." If you are to authentically connect with yourself or anyone else, you must know who you are and what your most important values are.

I begin this chapter with a poem about what I have come to believe, hoping that you will be inspired to write something similar for yourself.

Poem: What I Believe

I believe there is genius in everyone.
Now more than ever,
the world needs all of us to have the courage to let our glory shine.
The time has passed for hiding our brilliance under bushels!

I believe whatever we practice we become,
and we either practice getting braver,
or we practice being afraid.

I believe, as Marianne Williamson says in her book, *Return to Love*,
"Our deepest fear is not that we are inadequate.
Our deepest fear is that we are powerful beyond measure."

I believe it is not what happens to us that matters;
it is rather the story we tell ourselves,
the stories we chant to ourselves,
that determine whether we create more pain and despair in the world
or more hope.

I believe, though I am over fifty,
I am not even close to being old.
I believe being old is a state of mind,
and I plan to wave the torch of my living
as long as there is one spark left.

I believe there are forces that try to dishearten us,
to kidnap us from our hearts.
And if we do not have the heart to continue,
we are defeated before we begin.

I also believe there are forces that encourage us,
inviting us to be our best.
I believe when we listen deeply to these voices,
these Muses,
we change the world.

I believe we also change the world every time we choose faith over fear,
every time we choose courageous action over self-destructive escape,
every time we choose love over hate.

I believe the world is not too big to change.
I believe the world is ripe for change.

I believe everyone can write and everyone has something important to say.
I believe everyone can sing.
The world needs all of our voices,
and our lives need to be sung.

I believe logic is a wonderful tool
but a terrible god.
I believe giving our lives away to a fear of embarrassment
is a waste of vitality.
Every time we shrink so that others will not feel insecure around us
we sin against ourselves and the divinity living in all of us.

I believe the time to build community is now
and that we build community block by block.
We must keep at it
and not give up
until we have failed three thousand nine hundred and ninety-nine times.
And then we pause only to catch our breath
and launch back in
for another four thousand tries.

I believe each of us has a significant part to play in the healing of the world,
whether any other person recognizes our gift or not.

I believe we should paint our genius on the canvas of our lives,
day after day,
whether we're appreciated or not,
whether we are recognized or not.
(Remember Van Gogh!)

I believe if we don't live out our genius,
if we don't follow our bliss,
it will pursue us.
If we shrink from the responsibility of living our magnificence,
I believe our brilliance will get septic and rot within us.
And,
no matter how much we may drink or smoke or try to buy our way out
    of our misery,
our Bliss will never set us free
until we agree to live it
every day,
every moment.
Small, courageous steps toward our destiny
will save us
and the planet.

This I believe.

Poem: I'd Rather Be Real

When we take a stand for being authentically who we are, we risk losing those we love. I am not talking about letting every thought that is in your head stream out in the name of honesty. I am talking about remaining true to ourselves, and not compromising our essence, even when we feel everything is at stake.

I'd rather be real—
even if it breaks our love,
than pretend to be someone I am not,
someone smaller and grayer than I truly am.

I'd rather be real—
even if it shakes the foundations,
than pretend to be standing on something solid
when it's only yellow jellybeans.

I'd rather be real—
even if it's scary,
even if I feel a rip that threatens to tear
and might rend it all—
than pretend we are wearing fine clothes
like those of the naked emperor.

I'd rather be real—
and have my face swell
and my body stink with panicked sweat—
than pretend to believe a lie.

I'd rather be real—
even if people leave me when my ragged truths are spoken,
than pretend I don't feel what I feel
or see what I see
or know what I know.

I'd rather be real
because I can't be anything else.
I don't want to be anything else.

Song: Take a Stand for Love
(from the CD *Daring to Sing*)

In the spring of 2004 for one brief, shining moment, the Commissioners of Benton County, Oregon legalized the right of two people who love each other to marry. Period. This right was later rescinded, but it prompted me to write a song.

When people have lived together for years, sharing love, finances, and the raising of children perhaps, I cannot find it in my heart to deny them the benefits of Social Security and inheritance because their love came in the same gender package. This is a difficult idea for some people to entertain, but I think our culture must find some loving solution that celebrates the humanity and divinity of every human being.

Chorus:
Take a stand, take a stand, take a stand for love.
Take a stand, take a stand, take a stand for love.
Take a stand, take a stand, take a stand for love.
Let love be the stand that you take.

Take a stand for love. Don't worry about the gender.
Take a stand for love. All love is legal tender.
Judge not lest ye be judged, don't you know?
Let's loosen our grip on the stones that we throw.

Chorus

Take a stand for love of democracy.
Take a stand for listening and curiosity.
Keep your dogma in your yard, for heaven's sake!
Please, let's not burn anyone at the stake.

Chorus

Take a stand for the love of family.
Take a stand for soulful activity.
Our children need music and art in their schools.
Let's not raise a generation of corporate fools.

Chorus

Take a stand for being as brilliant as you are.
Take a stand for reaching for the highest star.
Surf the flow of your magical creativity.
Don't settle for safety and mediocrity.

Poem: I am a Poet, by God!

I take a stand, a brave one, for myself as a poet. How outrageous! How pretentious! How remarkably self-deluding! Oh well.

Hi there, stars! I'm a poet!

Really.

I am a poet because
I swirl in language,
leaning into the danger of speaking an unpopular truth.

I am a poet, and ee cummings is one of my patron saints.
He cheated
and got away with it.
Big Time.
He taught me I could trust my heart.
He taught me a poem could be a rocket ship
or a lily pad (step into this poem and you will get your feet wet).

He taught me the poet is boss,
not the red pencil
or the pinched look.

Sweet Emily Dickinson taught me that the whole world lives in my garden.
She taught me NOW is enough.
Most of her poems languished in a trunk until after she died.
She didn't write poems to become famous
or to make a living.
She wrote poems because she saw the world as a poem.
She was a Van Gogh of words,
not needing the world's approval,
desiring only her faith in the exquisite joy of putting a shape to her world,
her dreams,
her loves.
She wrote almost every day to please no one but herself.

And she had never even heard of ee cummings' words:
"it takes courage to grow up and turn out to be who you really are."
Yes, it does.

I am a poet because I write poetry,
because poetry is my springboard,
long and thin,
but wide enough,
high up in the clear air of spirit and truth and adventure.
I step on my life board of poetry,
bounce a few times,
and jump into the purple sky.
Using the stars to navigate,
I dive,
plummeting sometimes,
into whatever needs knowing,
into dark prickly places, sometimes,
but into sweet, invigorating pools of Yum, when I'm lucky.

I dive into the place that wants knowing,
even as it threatens to destroy all that I thought I already knew.

I dive because I am a life poet,
a poem myself,
wanting to articulate myself,
to become an image,
to try it on like a coat and see how it feels.

I want to wear a T-shirt
with my poet's logo in wide, indigo letters that announce to the world:
"I AM A POET!"
Or maybe I will wear a button
with tiny, magenta letters that say:
"If you can read this button then you are sniffing a poet."

I want someone to come up to me as I am typing this poem in this
    coffee shop
and ask me what I do.
"Why do you ask?" I will say.
She will look up to her right as she thinks about what drew her over to
    me.
"Pheromones," she will say, smiling.
"Ah," I will say. "You smelled the poet."

How do you get a job as a poet?
You don't!
You become a poet,
you are a poet,
I am a poet,
because how else can I manage the wonder and energy
that tickles through my body and soul and spirit and dreams?

I am a poet
and a poem.
Syntax be damned.

Poem: If You Want to Be Happy

Finally, when all is said and done, happiness is a choice. To paraphrase Abraham Lincoln: "People are about as happy as they make up their minds to be." Unhappiness can be a familiar, seductive home, and Lord help anyone who tries to pull a miserable person out of his pain.

You don't have to be happy, you know.
Happiness is scary.
Like good writing, it is wild and precious
and may lead you to unexpected places
and bring you face to face with uncomfortable truths.

Happiness is dangerous,
which is why so many people avoid it,
even though they believe their lives are spent in pursuit of it.

So, go ahead and be unhappy if you want.
I won't try to wrestle your problems away from you.
That's too much fun for you
and too frustrating for me.
You can nurse those grudges,
cuddling them at your breast,
feeding them with your precious life force.
You can chant those stories to yourself and others
about how life is horrible, awful, unfair and terrible,
about how you are the victim in your heroic journey.

You don't have to be happy.
You can be right
or in control,
(so you think!)
or safe,
(so you think).

So relax!
No one can make you happy.
Your unhappiness is all yours
For as long as you need it.

Whew! What a relief!
For both of us.

Happiness Tips

If you do want to be happy, I have a few happiness tips that have worked for me.

- **Under-schedule.** Whatever you think a full schedule is for you, do half of it for a month and see what happens. You will have to say no to fun events. Your children won't be able to go to all the parties and lessons and movies and shopping trips they want, but that will be good for them anyway. They could use a little down time, creating their own entertainment.
- **Be an easy laugh.** Delight in the unexpected. Laugh at your mistakes. Trust everyone until you have reason to distrust them.
- **Make every stranger you meet smile or laugh:** grocery clerks, waitresses, door-to-door salesman. This is easy to do because people doing these kinds of jobs are ready to laugh or smile at just about anything. Try it for a week and see if it doesn't significantly change your life.
- **Over-tip.** Let that abundance flow through your fingers and into someone else's. Have you ever worked in a restaurant? If so, you will over-tip the rest of your life.
- **Clean out a closet or a drawer every week and throw stuff away or give it away.** Forget the garage sale. Give your stuff away to someone who needs it more. It's good karma.
- **Bless those who traffic against you.** Remember at all times that you are not a perfect driver and that you sure hope someone is as alert

as you are when that SUV slips in front of you and you have to slow down to avoid a collision. Bless that driver and hope that someone will save you when you traffic against someone else.
- **Stop listening to the news.** Try it for a week and see if it doesn't make a difference.
- **Breathe out twice as long as you breathe in every now and then.** This will clear out the dead air at the bottom of your lungs.
- **Decide to do something you have always wanted to do.** Then later figure out how you will do it. This is how we manifest our dreams.
- **Nap.** Thomas Edison would take a nap when he got stuck. Nap for those who think they are too busy.
- **Get rid of anything remotely negative or hateful on your car, in your office, or in your home.** Much of what passes for humor makes joy more difficult.
- **Sing like you are in the shower.** Sing every chance you get, everywhere you can. I promise you no one will stroke out because you hit a sour note.

Your Turn

What do you believe? What do you take a stand for? What is your bottom line, even if people misunderstand you, judge you, laugh at you, leave you, dislike you? What word are you hesitant to apply to yourself: Musician? Artist? Worthwhile Human Being? Let yourself believe for a moment that you are something wonderful you would like to be. Pretend for a moment that you can join The Musicians' Club and no one can throw you out. You might feel as if lightning should strike you. That is a good sign. It means you are occupying more space.

I know the real writers do it the right way, not the way you do it. The real poets use more imagery. The real artists can draw like Leonardo when they are six. But maybe, just maybe, you are wrong about that. Let yourself entertain an outrageous idea and see what happens to your body and your spirit.

How happy are you willing to become? How much joy can you stand?

Chapter 3

Loving Ourselves First

What if we started loving ourselves right now, as is? What if we embraced all of our experiences, wounds, and talents and loved ourselves up big time? I have learned much about the power of loving myself even when I don't feel I deserve to be loved—especially when I don't feel I deserve to be loved. It is simply a fact that the more I know and love myself with all my imperfections, the more I am able to give to others. The more I wait to be "perfect" to love or be loved, the more I cripple my ability to embrace the power of love that is around me all the time.

Song: I Deserve to Be Loved
(from the CD *Alive, Alive*)

A therapist once asked me to write down a list of the rules I grew up with, spoken and unspoken. I came up with sixty-four. She then asked me to write new rules for myself. Voila! A song was born! People have sobbed singing this song. I once overheard a child, after hearing this song for the first time, mumble, "But I don't belong in this world." It broke my heart. These words are simple and the melody is nothing fancy, but somehow music can get through and set us free when spoken words only paste pretty stickers over our wounds.

I deserve to be loved.
I deserve to be loved.
I deserve to be loved.
Everybody doesn't have to approve.

You deserve to be loved.
You deserve to be loved.
You deserve to be loved.
Everybody doesn't have to approve.

We deserve to be loved.
We deserve to be loved.
We deserve to be loved.
Everybody doesn't have to approve.
I—I—I deserve to be loved.
I—I—I deserve to be loved.

I get to make mistakes.
I get to make mistakes.
I get to make mistakes.
That's one of the ways I learn.
You get to make mistakes . . .
We get to make mistakes . . .
I—I—I get to make mistakes.
I—I—I get to make mistakes.

I get to hope and dream.
I get to hope and dream.
I get to hope and dream.
I get to do things that don't work out.
You get to hope and dream . . .
We get to hope and dream . . .
I—I—I get to hope and dream.
I—I—I get to hope and dream.

I belong in this world.
I belong in this world.
I belong in this world.
I'm the only one of me.
You belong in this world . . .
We belong in this world . . .
I—I—I belong in this world.
I—I—I belong in this world.

Impeccable Self-Care

Since we deserve to be loved, we had better begin taking good care of ourselves, impeccably good care of ourselves. This sounds simple, but the Dinosaur Voice of "you're being unbelievably selfish!" can undermine our attempts at resting, setting limits, and telling the truth about who we are and what we really want.

I do not know very many people who have truly committed to impeccable self-care. Most people think they want to take good care of themselves, but they postpone it. "After I get this graduate school application finished, I will really start working on reducing my stress!" they say. Or after the children are all taken care of, or after that friend gets her depression under control, or after this project is done. Later, later, later, and it never gets done.

If our deep belief is that we aren't worthy of impeccable self-care, we will have difficulty giving ourselves permission to take a nap or stroll through the park. To overcome our resistance, it helps to entertain the idea that our beloved partner or children or friends actually get less if we don't give ourselves more. We can learn to give ourselves permission to nurture our bodies, our minds, and our spirits as they deserve to be nurtured.

Any "idiot" can work hard and get stressed. Only wise people realize that it is the effectiveness and not the quantity of our work that matters. Sometimes resting and receiving can be productive and generous, but we will never learn this if we accept the inevitability of living in frenzy.

Put Your Hand on my Shoulder and Walk with Me

Asking for and receiving help is essential if we are going to take good care of ourselves. Not asking for help out of stubbornness or pride is a fear-based reaction. We think we are being independent, but really we are isolating ourselves from others because of our need to control. Giving can be a power trip and receiving can be a great act of vulnerability and connection.

Dependency is not a lot of fun, but being too independent can be cruel, depriving those we love of a chance to know us and contribute to us. Instead of independence, we need to embrace our interdependence. When I depend upon the kindness of strangers, for example, I am asking for help but I am giving the gift of receiving help as well. I could never travel to Africa by myself if I were clinging to the illusion that I must be independent all of the time to be worthwhile. I depend upon the kindness of strangers, but so do we all.

Interdependence is wonderfully human. Life is an ensemble act, after all. But even if we understand the value of asking for help, sometimes we still hesitate to reach out because we are afraid people won't be able to say no. If we are gracious, though, and give others an easy way out, our asking for help is a request and not a form of bullying. If our request for help is granted, then we need to accept assistance with gratitude. To live healthy, cheerful lives, our giving and receiving need to be balanced and fluid. Remember that graveyards are full of indispensable people.

If we don't ask for help and instead do everything for ourselves, it is almost impossible not to build up resentments for how others are not pitching in. Saying, "No, no, I don't need any help," when we really do and then resenting our gift is a surefire recipe for disconnection and disharmony.

Some samples of how to ask for help:

- "I just realized I need to ask for more help. If I don't learn to take care of myself as I give to others, I might get sick or resentful. Therefore, I am going to start asking for help more often."
- "You have probably noticed that I have been crabby lately. I am tired and I have been taking it out on you. I realize now that instead of asking for help when I need it, I have been doing everything myself and then I resent my 'generosity.' From now on, I am going to ask for more help. This is not easy for me. But I want to be healthier and happier and I don't want to let my resentments leak out on the people I love."

- "You can say 'no' when I ask you for help. I want you to say 'no' if you feel you can't help. But my job is to ask for help more often."

Learning how to say "No" graciously.

Keep in mind that any "Yes" has a "No" embedded in it. When you say "yes" to something, you say "no" to something else and vice versa.

When you say "yes" while your belly tells you to say "no," you are more likely not to follow through or to sabotage your work in some other way.

Here are some sentences that will help your "yeses" be true "yeses" and your "no's" be true "no's:"

- "Thank you for asking! Let me think about it and get back to you."
- "Thank you for asking! I'm saying 'no' to everything right now. I am majorly over-extended, and it is affecting my health. I will let you know when I have the time and energy to take on something new."
- "What an interesting idea! I'm flattered that you would ask me. Let me talk to my cat about this, and I will get back to you."
- "NO!" (with a big smile), "but thank you for asking."
- "I would love to, but right now I am in over my head, and I'm saying no to all new commitments until I regain my sanity."
- "That sounds like fun, and I usually love doing things like that, but I have a bad habit of saying 'yes' too often, and it is starting to affect my health. Let me think about it and see if I can do it. Thank you for asking me."
- "No. "(a complete sentence)
- "No, but I could use some help with . . ."

Your Turn

What gets in the way of your taking care of yourself? What reasons for ignoring your body do you consistently trust? Here are some examples: "If I don't do it, it won't get done or it won't get done right." "Everyone else seems to be able to push through their weariness. I am a giant, selfish, wimp." "If I stop to rest, I will fall apart and I will never be able to get up again."

What are you going to do to start taking better care of yourself? How will you build self-care into every day? Write out a self-care plan; right now! (No, on second thought, you had better wait until you have finished cooking those brownies for school, and stamping those envelopes for the hospital fundraiser, and picking up the dry cleaning for your spouse, and . . .)

Chapter 4

Increasing Our Response Ability

"Life is not a problem to be solved. Life is a mystery to be lived."
Joseph Campbell

Jack Canfield, author of *Chicken Soup for the Soul*, developed the simple formula E + R = O. "E" stands for an event, that is, something outside of us that happens to us. Earthquakes are events; car crashes are events; our parents are events; our children are events. Other people's feelings and judgments are events outside of ourselves over which we have no control. We do have control, however, over the "R" in our lives or how we respond to events. That is where our power lies. The "O" stands for the outcome or how happy and fulfilled we are. This Big "O" depends entirely on the "R" of our response.

This equation is a basic recipe for happiness and decent living. It is simple, deceptively so. We ONLY have to learn to take responsibility for our responses. We ONLY have to learn to increase the continuum of possible responses, and our lives will be fuller, more enriched. This is like saying we ONLY have to learn to love our neighbors, and then we can enjoy world peace. The statement is true, but we must spend a lifetime learning how to apply it.

Being Imprisoned In Our Own Responses

The belief that we are responsible for our own happiness seems straightforward enough, and most of us agree with this idea to some extent. The problem is that we forget we are responsible for our responses all the time, especially at those times during our everyday lives when we need to remember it most. We get mad at a clerk in the store. We think his behavior, his rudeness perhaps, "made" us angry. Or when a car pulls out in front of us and we cannot help but get enraged at his stupidity. We forget we are choosing our responses and instead blame the event for our stress. We had a bad day because bad things happened to us and that is just how it is.

When we think someone has "made" us angry, we are not only inaccurate; we are giving away our power. All of us slip into the role of victim sometimes, but when our ability to respond gets so limited that we see affronts to our dignity everywhere, we become imprisoned in our responses.

Actually these responses, more precisely, are emotional reactions. We're not thinking about what we're doing. We do not have our happiness in mind, much less anyone else's. We are having a temper tantrum. We have been wronged. We are right. The other guy is the bad guy, and he should stop immediately and beg humbly for our forgiveness. Whenever we think, "How dare she!" we are thoroughly stuck in our own self-righteous, miserable muck. And it *feels so good!*—for the moment anyway. However, the damage we do to our bodies, our psyches and our relationships outweighs the short-term good feeling of giving in to this primal exasperation.

Being Addicted to Being Right

We may think it doesn't matter very much how we treat the store clerk because we don't have a relationship with her. We feel anonymous in our cars, so what does it matter if we yell and scream a little? Even if our behavior did not impact the stranger much, we have sent out bad vibes to the universe and we have raised the stress level in our bodies for no good reason. We may think if we treat the people in our lives well, then it is okay to blow off a little steam with strangers. The problem with this thinking is that we get good at whatever we practice, and if we practice leaking our venom out on anyone who happens to spark it, then we will treat our loved ones and co-workers the same way. We will be defining ourselves as victims all day long without realizing it.

Our problems increase when this behavior becomes habit. Our bodies get addicted to being "right," just as our bodies get addicted to the effects of nicotine and the euphoric effects of exercise. We "get a little high" every time we indulge ourselves in riding the white steed of our righteous superiority.

This may sound harsh, but addiction to "being right" is so widespread in our culture today that I think I need to state the problem as boldly as possible. I feel great compassion for myself and others when we are consumed by this wave of temporary madness.

It is very human, deeply human, to want to protect our turf, whether it be physical, mental, emotional, or spiritual. We have a survival instinct deeply embedded in our brains. I call this the "reptilian brain." It responds like a thug bodyguard. We need this bodyguard under certain circumstances. When we are in acute physical danger, we need to be able to react quickly to save our own skins and the lives of those we love.

I know I am perfectly capable of attacking a grizzly bear that attempts to eat one of my children. I wouldn't give it a second thought. I wouldn't give it a first thought. I would just do it. But the clerk in the grocery store who I perceive as being slow or rude or incompetent is not a grizzly bear. I am not in danger. I am just waiting longer than I wanted. This is not the end of the world. This is a small thing, and I don't want to sweat the small things. Most things, when I have some perspective, are small things.

Before we will be willing to give up these juicy reactions, we have to be clear that the short-term gratification of primal urges is diminishing our happiness and the happiness of those we love. We have to be clear about this, or we will be unwilling to do the work it takes to "kick the habit."

Relinquishing our addiction to "being right" is extremely difficult. The longer we've been addicted, the more difficult it is to sort out the subtle and not so subtle ways we overpower, control, bully and demean others.

This is heavy stuff. If this were easy, though, we would already have kicked the righteousness habit. If this were obvious, bullies of all sorts wouldn't be taken seriously. Their bullying would be seen for what it is: a way of masking their pain and insecurity.

Moving From Reaction to Response

The quality of our lives is directly and inextricably linked to our ability to respond. Increasing our ability to respond is directly and inextricably linked to our commitment to do the work it takes to move out of reaction and into a thoughtful response. We will only be willing to do this work if we look at the Outcome of our lives, the "O," and see that it is not what we want it to be. We must become conscious and committed to crafting our lives. We must give up making excuses for our unhappiness and lack of fulfillment. We must gaze steadily without blinking into our reflection in the mirror and say, "The buck stops here. Hallelujah, I am free because the buck stops here!"

If we do not make this commitment to craft the "O" in our lives, if we do not increase our "response ability," we will live a default outcome, letting life happen to us instead of choosing what we want in our lives.

Let me unpack this a bit more. Our responses—not events—determine our outcomes. If we are unhappy, we need to change our behavior or our thinking about an event, instead of wasting time trying to change the event. For example, complaining is an attempt to change an event. It may feel like a response, but it is only an emotional reaction. Complaining resembles taking action, but it doesn't change anything. It sure can feel good, though.

Complaint addicts, (and I've imbibed myself plenty of times,) demand company—some say they take prisoners. This is why one truly miserable person can create such a cloud of unhappiness around him or her. And that's also why our only empowering response to the misery others try to inflict upon us is to remember at all times that we are responsible for our responses. We can't control other people's choices. Get in a tug-of-war with a martyr, and I promise you will lose every time.

Levels of Response

To know how well our response is working, we need to check how our actions have affected our outcome. Are we happier? More serene? More abundant? Did we achieve the outcome we wanted? If the answer is no, then we need to get back to work on our response. It's as simple as that. I say simple with a grin, because it is not simple at all. It is challenging, courageous, soul-stretching work, and not too many are willing to take it on. But, again, accepting complete responsibility for our responses is the only path to a full, decent, soulful life.

In order to get intentional about what we want the outcome of our lives to be, we need to look at our responses and see how they are serving us. To provide a frame in which to examine our responses, I have invented a level system. The following chart gives a description of the levels. A more detailed explanation follows the chart.

Levels of Response

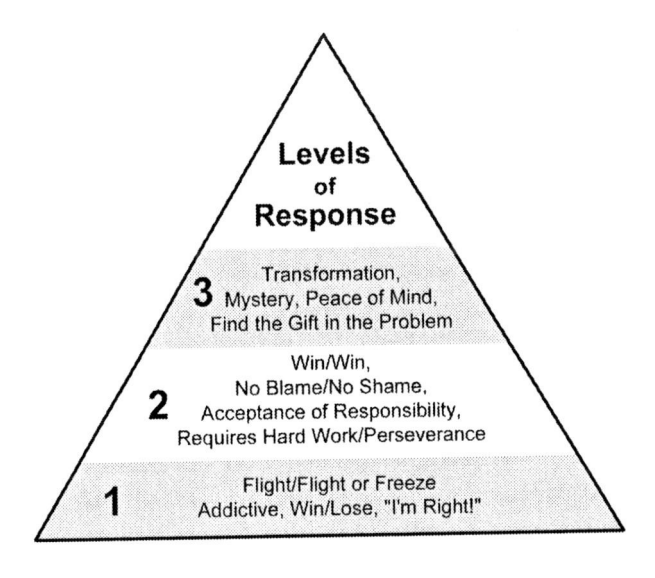

- **3** Transformation, Mystery, Peace of Mind, Find the Gift in the Problem
- **2** Win/Win, No Blame/No Shame, Acceptance of Responsibility, Requires Hard Work/Perseverance
- **1** Flight/Flight or Freeze, Addictive, Win/Lose, "I'm Right!"

Illustration by Bekki Levien

Level One

When we are in Level One, we don't take time to respond, we simply react. These are the "no-brainer" reactions, the ones that you could predict, the ones you could most easily imagine. If someone hurts us, it's only natural for us to want to hurt him back. This is fight/flight or freeze behavior and comes from the most primitive part of our brains. Some people practice Level One behaviors so often, their marriages, workplaces, and churches can get thoroughly mired in revenge, self-righteousness, and rage.

Unfortunately, Level One reactions sometimes cost lives. People get in fights at the grocery store waiting in line and end up biting off a finger. People shoot at others from their cars for making an improper lane change. These are extreme examples, but we all lose a little part of the quality and even the length of our lives when we overuse Level One responses.

I've already mentioned Level One behaviors on our roads, but with 40,000 acts of road rage a year, I think it is worth repeating. How many of us, for example, give away our serenity almost every day when we enter our cars? I've known people who are sweet-tempered most of the time who get righteously indignant if someone makes a driving error. They swear, bang the steering wheel with their fist, and insult the other driver's intelligence. All this over an improper turn or for driving too slowly.

Level One reactions are addictive. It is fun. Temper tantrums feel good at some level. So does pouting. We create our own adrenaline and give ourselves the illusion of power in Level One. For these reasons, none of us ever leaves Level One until we deeply understand that the outcome of our responses isn't what we want in our lives. The payoff for Level One—that surge of energy and life—is so great that we won't try to do something else until the cost of our impulsive behavior gets too high. We will binge eat to stuff our feelings until we understand that binge eating only creates more shame, which in turn adds to our bad feelings. We will yell at other drivers in our cars until we understand that we are creating our own stress and are shortening the length and reducing the quality of our lives.

Politics in America are stuck in Level One and sinking fast. People are assumed to be guilty if someone accuses them, even if no proof is offered. Name-calling and character assassination have replaced thoughtful discussion. We don't discuss issues to try to understand each other. We debate, bully, and demonize our opponents. We polarize and marginalize people we disagree with. Millions of dollars finance the Big Lie machine. Good, caring people get caught up in this fervor and I'm afraid it is going to get worse before it gets better because Level One responses feed on themselves and are insatiable.

When Level One reactions rule a family, all its members suffer. When Level One responses are the norm in politics, our whole country suffers. The United States is so powerful that when we are stuck in self-righteous actions, the whole world is affected. **Note:** I am not picking on one side or the other here, so if you are starting to get a little steamed, just notice that this is a Level One response. Politics seems to bring out the worst in everyone these days, and that is just my point.

Level Two

Level Two is not nearly as much "fun" as Level One because these responses require thought and effort. Sometimes they run counter to the prevailing conventional "wisdom." Level Two responses move into the problem-solving stage. Instead of riding high and mighty atop our righteous indignation, we look for solutions that benefit everyone. We know there is never really any win/lose; there is only lose/lose. Injustice is very expensive. If our continuing racial strife doesn't prove that point, nothing will.

When we are in Level Two, we commit to finding a solution that works for all. We use good listening techniques. We talk problems over. We give "I Messages." (I feel . . . when you . . .) We take timeouts. We gather a "tool chest" of techniques and strategies to help us. We get curious instead of getting even. This takes a lifetime of work and it is more difficult to sustain in an atmosphere of rampaging Level One reactions.

Level Three

Level Three is harder to define. In Level Three we find transformation—the magic in situations we didn't think could be transformed. We discover the gifts buried in our problems. In Level Three people say things such as: "Cancer is the best thing that ever happened to me," or "I wouldn't trade the eight years of captivity and torture I endured because of what I learned." (A paraphrase of Admiral Stockdale, who was a prisoner of war in Vietnam.)

It takes faith, courage, perseverance, and luck to find Level Three responses. They are not self-evident as Level One reactions are. Revenge seems so "logical." A violent "response" to injustice, we're told is "inevitable," so we all sadly nod our heads and go to war. But it is the people who are able to find the "illogical" solutions—forgiving our enemies "70 times 7," for example—who change the world at a cellular level.

Heroes such as Gandhi, Martin Luther King Jr., and Jane Goodall all show remarkable heart, wisdom, and courage in the face of great temptations to hate or become violent. They are inspiring, but sometimes their lives seem too big and grand, too far above our meager struggles to show us a way out of our problems. Knowing that people like this exist helps me, but I need many more examples of how to transform my daily challenges, and that is why I share these next stories.

Shift Happens

In some ways this entire book is an example of shifting from Level One to Levels Two and Three. When I am learning something, I need lots of examples, so I want to share some stories and poems about shifting out of Level One. These stories and poems sometimes make me look pretty good. But just for the record, if I had to watch a video of my worst partnering, parenting, and friendship moments, I don't think I could bear it.

The reason I have devoted so much of my time and energy to shifting is because I do not like who I am or how I feel when I am in Level One. There may be saints out there who have done all this hard work just to be "good," but I am not one of them. In fact, when I am trying to be "good," I am smack dab in the middle of Level One.

Katie and Sylvia

When my daughter Katie (Kathleen) was in sixth grade, my family invited a Spanish girl, Sylvia, also a sixth grader, to come live with us for six weeks. Everything went fine for a while, and then my daughter started acting cold and unfriendly toward our young guest. Kathleen would talk to her in a harsh voice, ignore Sylvia when she spoke, and in every subtle and not so subtle way let Sylvia know she wasn't welcome.

At first I confronted Kathleen about her behavior. "Kathleen, you are treating our guest badly. Stop it right now," I told her in my best parental demeanor. Amazingly, my ordering her to change didn't work.

So I took her aside and tried to get her to understand what was going on. "Kathleen, how would you want to be treated if you were thousands of miles away from home?" I asked her. "Would you want Sylvia's mother to do what I am doing now?"

"Yes," she said meekly, she would want that. "Yes," she said nodding, she understood. "Yes," she reluctantly agreed, she would start being nice to Sylvia because that was the right thing to do. And she meant it, she really did. The only problem was that her behavior didn't change.

After all this work and Kathleen's refusal to change, I was tempted to go back to a Level One response. I wanted to throttle her. I was so ashamed of her. It is important to me to have my home be a place of safety and warmth for all who enter. I was suffering for Sylvia and for myself. Kathleen's behavior was the big "E" I wanted to change.

When I'm stuck with a problem, I will often seek out a friend I think will help me change my perspective. Going to people who will just agree with me and reinforce my feelings of victimization feels good, but it doesn't lead to a shift. I wanted a shift; I just didn't know how to get one.

A friend helped me see Kathleen's perspective more clearly. I was caught in my shame, drowning, as it were, in the muck of Level One. After I really "got" my daughter's feelings, I sat quietly and listened for a solution. This strategy works well for me. About thirty seconds after I opened myself to the possibility of transformation, I could see in my mind the actual picture of what I needed to do.

The next time Kathleen did something mean to Sylvia, I didn't say a word. This is an important point. I have a deep belief in the power of words, and it isn't easy for me to just shut up. But I did. I kept my mouth closed and just walked across the room to my daughter and kissed her on the temple. That was all, just a kiss.

Katie's obnoxious behavior stopped. From my point of view, this felt like a little miracle. I had solved the problem by abandoning my efforts to solve the problem. That is one of the qualities of Level Three: Many of the solutions are "illogical."

It isn't necessarily logical to expect a change from just a kiss on the temple. And, in fact, I wasn't trying to change things exactly; I was just finally giving my daughter what she needed. She needed to know I loved her and that I loved her deep in her "ickiness." She knew how I felt about her behavior. Sylvia did, too. We had had many talks. Kathleen was lost behind the door marked "Kathleen is a piece of excrement." I was banging on the door, trying to force her to open it. That just pushed her further into her shame. By suddenly appearing on the other side of the door with her, we had the chance to emerge together.

This is subtle stuff. I couldn't just ignore her meanness and sympathize with her. We aren't doing anyone any favors when we do this. This is what has given empathy a bad name, I think. We must address the inappropriate, uncivilized behaviors, but we must also call for the best, seeing the gold, the precious uniqueness in all the people we love.

Leaving Level One and moving on to Levels Two and Three is a decision. We must first decide with our minds that it is worth the effort. Level Three responses are so much more work than Level One that we will never begin the task unless we are clear that it is in our own best interests as well as in the best interests of the world to do so.

Nice Girl Road Rage

Let's go back to the topic of road rage. A friend of mine once flipped off a motorcycle driver who drove too close to her car. Instead of driving off, saying to himself, "Wow! I need to be more careful from now on. I must have really frightened that woman," he circled back and buzzed around her car several times. He probably thought something more like, "Bitch!" instead of "Thank you, Transforming Angel!" This incident scared my friend deeply and taught her not to flip off motorcyclists ever again.

But if we only stop our behavior because we are afraid of the bigger guy whacking us, we are still in Level One. This is the law of the jungle. Deciding to move up to Level Two or Three rests on our deep understanding that Level One is bad for us and bad for the world.

Moving to Level Two takes effort. It is a skill that we will get better at when we practice. We can hone and improve these skills in a variety of workshops and by reading books. Many people have walked this way before us, and there are many signposts.

But when we attempt to move to Level Three we find we don't need skills as much as we need to be willing to be transformed. Victor Frankl, in his book *Man's Search For Meaning*, chronicles his experiences in a Nazi concentration camp. What he discovered was that it wasn't the most beautiful, the most courageous, or the strongest that survived. The people who overcame their suffering had something they wanted to live for; they had meaning in their lives. Frankl would visualize himself lecturing to a class about what he had learned in the camps. He would think these thoughts while Nazi doctors tortured him.

If Dr. Frankl could do this, in the midst of such suffering, then I can find a way to imagine there might be a Level Three response in any situation that comes my way. Even if I can't immediately find a Level Three response, Frankl's experience helps me to know that one exists.

We need to constantly challenge ourselves to seek the high road. The high road doesn't mean you tolerate abuse, sit on your hands and smile, so to speak. The high road is the road of justice and respect. It takes well-developed courage muscles to walk this road, and we will all fall short some of the time.

Our country was founded on such principles, and they still work. Most religions have at their heart something similar to "The Golden Rule." Loving your neighbor as yourself creates magic. If we commit to the habit of finding Level Three responses, we will get better and better at it. We will get faster. Our lives will gradually fill with more joy, love, appreciation, and humor. Our healthy relationships will thrive, and our unhealthy ones will transform or fall away as we become more and more unwilling to tolerate injustice to ourselves or others.

Story: Fake It Until You Make It

A few years ago I was at a meeting with six other people. We were discussing the interpersonal skills students need in order to graduate. Our group consisted of counselors, teachers, and administrators.

Almost immediately, I knew I was in trouble. One of the group members, a male high school teacher, irritated and intimidated me. He was just the type of person I have the most trouble with: a know-it-all who dominates the conversation. (I'm afraid I can be like this myself, so it is no surprise that I dropped into Level One around this man.)

I was sure the undertone of his words read something like: "If you don't agree with me, you are obviously inferior, which you are obviously anyway, since I am so obviously well-read and intelligent." I knew that if the conversation progressed the way I had experienced in the past, we would hate each other in about five minutes. Nothing overt would be said, of course; we are much too civilized for that. Still, I knew that he and I were destined to collide if I didn't shift quickly.

I just didn't want to go there. I could see it all coming; I knew I would be in the "right" because he was such a jerk, obviously—and anyone would agree, I was sure—but I still didn't want to go there.

I got quiet. I hadn't been talking much anyway, so there wasn't much difference in how I was behaving outwardly, but as I sat and shifted my response, he stopped talking and turned to me. This was the first time he had stopped and noticed anyone. I had a smile on my face because I had just discovered the solution. He asked me why I was smiling.

"Oh, nothing," I replied, "just a personal thought."

I had decided at that moment to treat everyone in the room as if I already liked them. What if these people were already my friends? How would I treat them?

The result of my shift to Level Three was that I listened to the Pontificating Man differently. He wasn't the Pontificating Man anymore. I started to appreciate the incredible breadth of his knowledge. He knew a lot about interpersonal communication; he just didn't know how to do it very well. But instead of feeling irritated, I felt compassion for him. He was just being human, right there in front of my eyes. He was just as fallible as I.

I enjoyed the two-hour meeting, and I learned a lot. As we closed, I let people know that I needed a ride home if anyone were going my way. Informed Man, formerly Pontificating Man, volunteered.

I get lots of rides from lots of people. This is one of the side benefits of losing my sight and not being able to drive. The powerlessness I have suffered has been outweighed by the humility I have learned in graciously accepting help.

We spent about ten minutes in the car together, and by the time he dropped me off at my front door, I wasn't pretending anymore; he *was* a friend of mine. I really liked him. No kidding.

I worked at his school as part of my job, and every time I was in the building, I ran into him. I think he was my little angel, reminding me of my arrogance and of the sweetness of climbing down off my high horse of self-righteousness.

Story: "Father, Forgive Them."

To learn how to find a Level Three response, we have to believe transformation is possible in any situation, no matter how challenging. We have to experience the magic and freedom of this type of choice for ourselves. We need to see it in action in other people's lives if we are going to be able to develop the creative muscles we will need to find the gift in any situation.

Several years ago a woman in my church told this story about her daughter. It remains one of the most powerful stories of transformation I have ever heard.

My friend's daughter had grown up in a small town in Texas, raised in a loving, Southern Baptist home. She was innocent and trusting, a credit to her family, church, and community. She went to Houston to go to college.

During her freshman year, she was gang raped. This beautiful, innocent girl had her first sexual experience with men who were hating and humiliating her. We can all guess the predicted outcome: years of therapy, a hatred or fear of men, repressed or overindulged sexuality. We see this response all the time.

But this is not what happened to this young woman raised in love and faith. While these hate-filled men were raping her, while they were on top of her snarling vile words into her terrified face, while they were trying to take away from her everything that was precious and whole—while they were doing this, she was praying for them: "Father, forgive them; they know not what they do."

As one would expect, friend's daughter was emotionally and physically wounded by the rape. Her body was damaged, and for a while, doctors told her she would never have children. Yet she was able to marry and have a healthy sexual life. She was able to have children, after all. The rapists had been unsuccessful in their attempt to take away her dignity, her worthiness. She had been clear that the rape was about them and their rage and pain, not about her. Raised in love and forgiveness, in the reality of those words, she was able to find in herself the greatest protection: forgiveness. She was able to surround herself and her attackers with love when she needed it most. What a miracle of healing and transformation!

I don't think even now I could do what that lovely eighteen-year-old did. But hearing her story teaches me that it is possible to find a Level Three response in even the most horrible situations. And I do know that the more I practice seeking Level Three, the easier it has been for me to find compassion and transformation when I need it most. This young girl transcended an ugly crime because she found Level Three forgiveness.

The Power of True Forgiveness

Level One is about fear and power. It has a sense of urgency about it. When we say we forgive someone in Level One, we try to be good or try to avoid deeply dealing with our grief or anger. I'm afraid many religious people think that forgiveness is "good" and anger is "bad;" therefore, they never let themselves deal honestly with the grief process. Or they may punish themselves for being so wicked and not being able to forgive their brother for molesting them when they were children.

Let's jump to Level Three now and look at the transformational power of true forgiveness. You will know you are in Level Three forgiveness about your father's abuse, for example, if you no longer feel you even need to forgive him. You see his essence, and you love him. You do not make excuses for him, you do not allow him to abuse you or anyone else, but you feel no anger. You are set free by releasing your rage and judgment. You feel lighter and more full of life's sweet juices than you could if you were spending your precious energy rehearsing your case against him to tell Peter at the Pearly Gates. (I write more about Level Three forgiveness in Chapter 29, *My Daddy is a Stranger*.)

A great example of Level Three forgiveness is the Dali Lama. Even though the Chinese invaded his country, raping and massacring nuns and monks, he lives his life in gratitude. His enemies give him a chance to practice compassion. If ever anyone had a right to live in bitterness, it is the Dali Lama, yet his being is so full of love that he literally transforms people just by stopping and shaking their hands. How about that?

Story: KKK Transformation

Let's take racism, which can be extremely difficult to forgive, through the Levels. Racism is born in Level One, as it is always about fear and power. Hate, especially when spoken in the name of a god, is still hate and flourishes in Level One. But even racism can be transcendent, as illustrated in this story.

Several years ago I saw a program on public television about a man who had belonged to the Ku Klux Klan. His father and grandfather were both KKK members. Of course he was in the KKK! What else could he have been in that situation? If he had been born in Ireland he would have been Catholic. If he had been born in India he would have been Hindu. Of course he was KKK.

He also thought he was a Christian, even though one of the basic tenants of Christianity is Jesus' admonition for us to "love thy neighbor as thyself." Christ did not add, "except for anyone you don't understand or anyone you are afraid of." This man felt no distress because of the discrepancy between his beliefs and his behavior. He did not know there was any discrepancy. It breaks my heart when people use God as an excuse to hate.

One day this life-long KKK member was sitting at home, maybe munching on some potato chips and drinking beer, as he watched a televangelist on TV. A miracle occurred. He got it. He felt the dissonance between his belief in Christ and his hatred. He understood that loving thy neighbor as thyself does not have an asterisk. Christ called him to love everyone: Jews, Catholics, homosexuals, and African-Americans. Epiphany! Transformation!

Our KKK friend (and there but for the grace of God go all of us) jumped from a lifetime of Level One into Level Three in an instant. That turned out to be the easy part. Now he had to go back to the practical, unemotional, hard-working Level Two and look at all of his behavior, all of his relationships, all of his beliefs one by one and see if they matched his newly found understanding of Christian love. If they didn't match, he needed to change them, one friend, one belief, one behavior, and one family member at a time.

This is what happens when people go in for treatment for addictions. Surrendering is a Level Three behavior, but it is only the beginning. Once people have surrendered and begun their recovery, they face a lifetime of daily choices to recover or relapse. Some people rebel and cry out that it isn't fair and that recovery is too hard. That is Level One. A Level Three response to recovery is gratitude: "Thank you for forcing me to stay awake every day and for not letting me slip into the mindlessness that invites my addiction to return. I don't want to get away with anything. I want to get caught!"

The fact that such instantaneous transformations are possible gives me hope for the world. Maybe one such epiphany will start a chain reaction that moves across the globe until all of our fears, prejudices, and hates fall from us and we see the divine essence of every human being and the sacredness of our planet for once and for all. Sweet dream, huh?

Key Points for Using the Levels of Response

1. **We need to remember that everyone operates from Level One sometimes.** We don't want to feel shame about this; we want to be smart about it. When we operate from Level One consciously or unconsciously, we create more pain for ourselves and others.

2. **The only reason any of us ever leaves Level One is because we realize we don't like the outcome of our response.** Level One is addictive and fun. Temper tantrums are fun. Pouting is fun. Being a victim and feeling self-righteous is fun. Complaining is fun. Panic may not be fun, but at least it's exciting. We only start doing the hard work on Levels Two and Three when we understand deeply that these "fun" responses are escalating rather than solving our problems.
3. **"You're in Level One!" can only be said to someone who has invited your feedback.** Otherwise, you are in Level One as well. Our job is to take responsibility for our own responses. We need to be on the lookout for our own Level One responses. We need to learn to recognize our own "red flags" that let us know we are on a slippery slope of reaction. We need to ask others to gently tell us when they see us in Level One. Our job is NOT to police and judge other people's responses. We do this out of our own fear and shame.
4. **Anything can be ruined in Level One.** If "love thy neighbor as thyself" can be used as an excuse to burn people at the stake, then we humans can ruin anything. Any behavior that comes out of fear or a need to dominate is Level One.
5. **Fear has many cousins:** a sense of urgency (this must be done now!), a need to control both our environment and other people, and an uptightness about being on time or others being on time. Fundamentalism of all sorts is also a disguise for fear. We want Answers because Mystery is too messy and too scary. We want to impose our fundamentalism on others because that is the only way we will feel safe. Learn to spot your fears and all their disguises.

Getting Hooked on Creating the Big "O" of Our Lives

Shifting out of Level One is easier if we are clear about what we want in and out of our lives. Remember, Level One is instinctive; it's a no-brainer. We will be suckered into the muck of Level One if we don't learn how to swim. We need the positive energy of our dreams to pull us out of our bad habits and out of seductive, destructive behaviors and thoughts.

We cannot control the events of our lives; we can only become clear about the essence of what we want our lives to be: joyful, loving, creative, faith-based. People die. People get scared and leave. We can get fired from a job, go blind, and lose our partner. No amount of money, no amount of worry, no amount of nagging can protect us from what life has to give and take from us.

I wrote a song once called "Compost Happens." Here are some of the words from the chorus: "What are you going to do when the compost happens? What are you going to do when the compost happens? What are you going to do when the compost happens? 'Cuz it's going to happen to you."

We do not get to choose when or where the compost happens or how much drops on us out of the sky. It does not matter how good we have been, how carefully we have planned. We still might get hit by a car as we walk along a lonely country road, as did Stephen King.

So, we need to get clear about what we want in and what we want out of our lives and then work on that every day. Easy, peasy!

Creating Our Reality

I dreamed my relationship with Murray. I had never known a marriage like ours, never known a man like him. But I knew the qualities I wanted in a relationship: honesty, humor, spiritual depth. Murray is the littlest guy I have ever gone with (only five foot eight). His legs are skinnier than mine were when I was fifteen. He is sillier than anyone I would have thought I would have in my life. He isn't the man I pictured, but he has the soul I craved.

Because of my commitment to respect and joy, to truth and creativity as the center of my life, I have only a few relatives that come to my home. But they are keepers! My home is a sacred space, as am I, and only those people who want to play, laugh, cry, and be real in that space need come.

I have dreamed my career. "I want to speak!" I said out loud and now I am a keynote speaker. "I want to travel professionally all over the world!" I said out loud, and now I have been to Europe and Africa. "I want to sing and perform!" I said out loud, and now I am in a singing group, The Free Range Chix. "I will have a book available in bookstores in 2005!" I said out loud, and, here it is.

I am my own boss. I only do work I love and on my own terms. If success is the quality of our journey, as Jennifer James says, then I am as successful as anyone I have ever known. I say this not to brag (though women probably ought to brag more anyway), but to offer my life as proof that someone coming from blue-collar, alcoholic beginnings can invent her own life. If I can do it, you can do it, too.

Crazymakers

If we have even one crazymaker in our lives, he or she will "wag the dog," suck up tons of energy and never change. Carolyn Myss calls these people "energy vampires."

When I teach, I tell people that I have eliminated crazymakers from my life and that these include some family members. I tell them this because our cultural pull to keep family members in our lives no matter how destructive they are runs contrary to everything I am saying in this book. Let me repeat: You are sacred space. You deserve to be treated as sacred space, and anyone who refuses to treat you respectfully, anyone who refuses to honor your boundaries, gets the heave ho, even if, or especially if, these people are family members.

Setting healthy boundaries is easier to do when we have children. Sometimes it is easier for us to protect our young than to protect ourselves. We can often muster amazing amounts of courage to do what is right when our children's happiness is at stake.

But when it comes to taking care of ourselves, we may have become habituated to disrespectful behavior. We may have gotten used to "walking on eggshells" around someone, but let me tell you loud and clear: You should not have to walk on eggshells around anyone for fear they are going to go off on you. If you let yourself be treated this way or let your children be treated this way, you are allowing them to be abused and teaching them that this is normal. This will increase their chances of becoming abuse victims in the future because this is what will feel natural to them, and they will seek out people who treat them this way.

Does this sound too harsh? Why do you think the cycles of abuse continue? We make excuses for the racists in our families (Oh, he is so old; it's too late for him to change now), or we say our mother loves us the best she can, which may be true, but her "love" might eat your liver.

When I worked in a drug and alcohol treatment center, I learned that sometimes the most loving act you can make is one of drawing the line. "No more!" you say, as you change the locks on your house and call the police on your son. "Tough Love" they call it, and it is tough to do. But it is love, not fear, that motivates these acts.

When I am forced to cut someone out of my life because they are a crazymaker, I do so with love. When I was first learning to protect myself, I had to be angry to give myself the energy to make the move. But when I love someone, I love them forever, and if they ever call me from an AA meeting and ask me to come and support them, I will be there in an instant. However, I will not waste my vital juices protecting myself and my loved ones from people who are committed to self-delusion, addiction, disrespect or cruelty.

The decision to eliminate crazymakers from my life is probably the single most important decision I have ever made. I have never regretted it for a moment. All the time I spent in endless conversations about problems that did not change, the constant eggshell walking—all this energy has been freed to bring love, creativity, and a deep service to humanity into my life.

As you weed the crazymakers from your life, find people to support you. Find people who understand—people who won't say, "But he's your father!" or "But how can you not talk to your brother?" Surround yourself with people who are loving and strong, people with healthy boundaries and a sense of humor. Be gentle with yourself, and get ready for the storm of complaints you might get when you pull someone's anchor off your lifeboat and toss it back into the ocean with your blessings. "Your problem isn't my problem!" you say. "But this is my life, I am sacred space, and I only have so much energy on any given day. I choose to spend my energy being creative and becoming all I was intended to be. Good luck to you!"

Story: Weeding Crazymakers out of Your Sacred Garden

I was in a women's group once with three other women. We gathered weekly for meditations in order to enhance our spiritual journey. For several weeks I had not enjoyed the company of one of the women. It seemed to me that every time we met, we ended up discussing how we had left her out, or in some other way had done her wrong. I was getting bored with the process and decided that if it happened again, I would just leave the group. I didn't need to fix her or the group, I decided. I needed to take care of myself.

We met at my house and were giving each person a turn to speak about what was in her mind and heart. The hot tub awaited us, so after some check-in time, I suggested we all go out and finish in the hot tub. The woman I was having trouble with, Belinda, got mad. We were leaving her out again. Everyone else had checked in except her, blah, blah, blah.

I listened for a while and then stated calmly that I felt the group wasn't working for me and that I was going to drop out.

Belinda didn't like this idea. She felt I had made a commitment to stay and work through the interpersonal stuff that came up. She accused me of not having what it takes to stick with it when things get tough.

Fortunately, I knew this wasn't true. I'm a great sticking-with-it person, but I didn't want to stick with it with her. I had never made that commitment to the group; we were supposed to be a spiritual growth group, not a therapy group.

I recognized that she was attacking me, which was good news for me. Earlier in my life, I would have taken her accusations to heart and felt guilty. She would have had me back in line.

Because I wasn't getting hooked into the accusations, I stayed clear enough to set a boundary. "You do not have my permission to build my character right now," I told her calmly. I felt elated. How clear, how free of enmeshment I was!!

Belinda, however, wasn't elated. She was, in fact, outraged. Her accusations continued, gaining momentum. The other two members of the group sat in silence. I didn't know if they understood what was happening between Belinda and me, but I didn't need them to understand. I knew I was being attacked, knew I was setting a boundary, and Belinda could like it or not like it. I knew I didn't want to hang around with a person who didn't respect my requests, and I didn't want to hang around with a person who kept dragging us all into discussions about how much we were victimizing her. Been there, done that.

"You do not have my permission to build my character right now" has been a sentence that remains in my repertoire. I can ask for feedback or reject it. I do not have to accept the "gift" of unsolicited character building.

I lost a "friend" that day but gained an inner strength that has never left me. Belinda has gone on to create problems for other people in the same kind of insidious way. But she isn't creating those problems for me.

Song: Crazymaker, Crazymaker

Fiddler on the Roof *fans, get ready!*

Crazymaker, Crazymaker, leave me alone!
You're sucking all the life from my bones!
Nothing I give you is ever enough.
I'm tired of your drama games.

Crazymaker, Crazymaker, I know it's true.
There's nothing about your misery I can do.
You are committed to your suffering and pain.
I'm letting go of you.

Your problem isn't my problem.
Everyone else cannot always be wrong!
You've been here before, oh so often.
I'm sure I can't cure you, not even in song!

Crazymaker, Crazymaker I set you free
To live out your life in delightful misery.
There's no hope of ever filling your hole,

So I'll be on my way,
To sing, dance, and play,
And leave you to find someone new!

Two Strategies for Shifting Your Responses

The intent of these strategies is to help you shift out of the responses you typically use and to find more creative and playful ways of dealing with daily, chronic challenges.

1. "Actually, this is a good thing!"

A teacher named Cindy and I invented this technique one day when we were setting up a presentation for her school. We were preparing for an all-school assembly as well as classroom lessons. My goal was to help students and staff learn how to have more fun and create a safer environment at the same time.

This was one of those days when Murphy was in charge. You know Murphy's law: What can go wrong does go wrong. The room we were planning to use wasn't available. Then the schedule was different than we had expected. Then the CD player was broken. After the first few disappointments, our troubles started getting funny. When we went to use the copier and it was broken, Cindy said, "Actually, this is a good thing!" Then we did our best to figure out why this was a good thing.

In the case of the copier, we decided it was good that it was broken. We were happy that we needed to walk to another building to use their copier because we could use the exercise. When that copier turned out to be broken as well, we decided we had needed the time for brainstorming. We were getting clear that Murphy was in charge of the day. We started laughing. When the third copier wasn't working, we started laughing again, a little hysterically. Then we started searching for things that had gone wrong so we could say, "Actually, this is a good thing" and laugh some more.

Surprisingly, our problems really were a good thing. We felt proud that we could turn any minor problem into an opportunity. Our mishaps became challenges, opportunities for us to stretch our creativity muscles. We also became great friends, even in our short time together.

2. "This is perfect!"

This strategy is a cousin of "Actually, this is a good thing!" but it takes it to a higher level. We imagine that whatever we are dealing with, whatever loss or disappointment we suffer is sent to us at this time and this moment by our Coaching Angels, and it is perfect.

When I am able to do this—to believe that there is perfection, even in this depression, I feel a great weight is lifted. I am not doing my life wrong; I have not been bad and brought this thing upon myself. It is perfect, and all of my feelings—despair, fury, lethargy—are all perfect. Even my doubt is perfect.

This does not automatically shift me out of those uncomfortable feelings, but it stops me from clinging to them, from wanting to make them or myself different. What is, is, and it is perfect.

You might want to write a letter to someone explaining how all of your problems are the perfect problems for you to have right now. You might get a few laughs, if nothing else.

Example:

> Dear Mom,
>
> Guess what! I got fired today! And you will never believe why! My boss thought I was anti-Semitic. She said one of my co-workers accused me of making an anti-Semitic remark. I don't remember making any such remark. Does that sound like me? So she fired me right there on the spot. Isn't that a scream!
>
> Getting fired was painful, but it is really perfect, in a way, because they fired me for such a ridiculous reason. I know there must be something deeply wrong with them, not me! Isn't that great! And I am so stubborn that I would never have quit this job even though I was miserable, so, actually, it is a good thing. No, Mom, getting fired is the perfect thing!
>
> Love,
> Vicki

(This is a true story, though I did not see the perfection so quickly. Years later, when I married my Jewish Murray, I thought, "Not so anti-Semitic, now, am I?")

Your Turn

What Level One habits do you have that you would like to change? Who might be able to coach you and help keep you accountable? How will you celebrate your progress? (Remember, progress, not perfection!)

What are those little irritations that steal your serenity and joy most often? Make a list of these. Some examples: waiting in line, people cutting in front of you, people who repeat themselves, people who repeat themselves (grin,) pontificating.

Now that you have listed these irritations, go back and find the positive aspect of the situations. Start every sentence with: "Actually, this is a good thing because . . ."

For the next 21 days (that's how many days it's supposed to take to create a new habit), find a way to use, "Actually, this is a good thing!" Put a sign up on your mirror to remind you of your goal. Celebrate in your journal about the times you were able to transform an irritation into something positive.

Do you have any Crazymakers in your life? If you can't separate yourself from them completely, see if you can find a way to limit your contact with them. Plan ahead. What will you say to end the phone call that can go on forever? Lie if you have to. Your sanity and well-being are at stake. Crazymakers will not be happy no matter what you do, so how will you have a good time even if they are complaining? Have practice conversations with a friend where you say, "Maybe so" or "Huh" to outrageous comments that will lead you back to Level One misery.

What do you want in your life and what do you want out of your life? Dream big. Let yourself imagine a life that is full of people, activities and surroundings that increase your ability to serve the world. For example, I love having lots of cozy spaces in my home and my yard, places where I can drink up the beauty of flowers and art. I want to work with people who want to work with me and I want to be paid well doing it. I want laughter and fun and truth around me, and I want to sing, sing, sing!

Chapter 5

Creating Powerful Stories for Ourselves

We all have tons of stories we have collected about ourselves over the years. The problem is that many of these stories are self-limiting. Many of the stories stem from one incident, one person's cruel comment, or from comparing ourselves to other people. We don't just tell these stories to ourselves; we chant them: "I'm no good at math. I can't sing. I can't deal with technology. I am not creative."

We don't realize these are stories, conclusions we have drawn based on scant evidence and then accepted as God's Truth. For example, in middle school my son Martin was told he was an underachiever. Talk about boxes! Now who got that bright idea and decided to tell my son this story? He tried to use it as an excuse with me once, and, luckily, I blew it off. "Who told you that?" I asked. "What a bunch of crap."

If Martin or his parents had bought into this label, then he would have had even more difficulty developing the habits and attitudes he needed to succeed in school. (By the way, his senior year of college he was one of the top 350 math students in the country. Put that in your pipe and smoke it, Mr. Underachiever Labeler Person!)

When children first enter school, they still seem more than willing to believe they are capable until someone tells them otherwise. If I ask a group of five year olds if they can sing, they all raise their hands. When I ask a group of adults this question, maybe twenty percent raise their hands. Were all those children wrong? Are there only so many spots for singers on the planet, and we have to weed out those who are unfit to sing? Why are we so vicious with people when they sing off key? What is this power trip anyway?

Fact: Everyone can learn to sing if given enough help. Not everyone is a match for the American Idol competition, but that is a good thing. Bob Dylan never would have made it past the judges and neither would Barbra Streisand. Their voices would not fit the narrow limits of what

American Idol is looking for. I think everyone has the right to sing, and I know that singing stimulates brain activity and reduces stress, so why not sing out!

Singing is a metaphor for embracing all of the creative melodies flowing through us that I am calling voice. We sing our lives when we plant our garden the way we want instead of the way we think gardens are supposed to grow. We sing our lives when we paint every wall in our entryway a different color because the combination of hues brings us joy. We sing our lives when we dare to not be workaholics in a culture that takes workaholics for granted. (If you want to stir up your life, experiment with being the happy one in an environment where people feel overworked and victimized.)

Why don't we all "sing" out? Why aren't more of us singing and humming our lives as we walk down the street, shop for groceries, and raise our children? Because we are stuck in the limited story we tell ourselves about our abilities and possibilities. Family members and friends, unfortunately, are often all too eager to help us define ourselves. We are the clumsy one, isn't that hilarious? Or we are the one who never follows through. Or we are the one who is stupid because we didn't learn to read as fast as our sister did.

In this environment we learn that mistakes are terrible and must be avoided at all costs. (This is why gifted children procrastinate. If they don't even try, then they won't have to risk being anything less than perfect. They won't have to risk making a mistake other people can see.) Embarrassment, then, becomes terminal. We practice playing it safe and not risking until we become very good at staying small. "This is just how I am," we tell ourselves—and our creativity and possibility wither.

In my workshops I have people give themselves a little pinch. "This is embarrassment," I say. "It hurts a little, but it goes away quickly, doesn't it?" Are you going to let a little pain like that steal your life?" I ask them to take that voice that wants them to stop risking because they might be embarrassed, grab it by the throat, shake it, and say, "You're not the boss of me!" They inevitably giggle and I rejoice at the sound of their limiting beliefs flying away.

Comparison: Little Murder

As the years go by, we collect these "true" stories people have told us about ourselves, and we start making up our own. We start practicing one of the most dangerous, soul-killing habits: comparing. We compare ourselves, secretly most of the time, to people who we perceive as successful. We compare ourselves to speakers and dancers, chefs and holiday decorators and we find ourselves lacking.

I think this is our Dinosaur Voice at work, whispering in our ear that we are not as good as that other person. We should just shut up and give up if we know what is good for us. We must accept "reality." We must bow to The Facts. We must live a diminished life because that is as good as it is going to get for us this time around. And besides, that other person is certainly full of herself, isn't she? Everyone loses in this game.

If you think I am exaggerating, I wish you could observe any writing seminar I teach for adults or children. Someone will be brave enough to read what they have written aloud, and I will ask, "Who just listened to this writing and thought to yourself 'Mine is not as good'?" Hands go up all over. Then I say, "This is extremely important. One of you who raised your hand must now read what you have written. This is how we unmask the Dinosaur and get your liver out of its mouth."

Someone always reads and we are always amazed because we learn a delicious, life-saving fact. We are not inferior or less than; we are different. There wasn't a "right" way to write your story; there were lots of ways.

The question shouldn't be whether your writing or your life is "good" or not because who knows what is good? The Catholic Church didn't think Galileo's ideas were any good and he was only suggesting what he was observing— perhaps the sun did not revolve around the earth. This idea was too scary for the church to entertain because they "knew" they would have to give up their faith if they changed their dogma. It took them three hundred years to apologize, which demonstrates how powerful this clinging to old stories can be.

The question we need to be asking ourselves when we are writing or living is: Is it true for me? Does it resonate? Did I communicate what I intended? How close did I get to my truth? How could I get closer?

Shifting from comparing to curiosity might well be the step each of us could take which would lead to world peace. I mean this. Can you entertain the idea right now that world peace could be just this close, just a matter of letting go of comparing—and embracing curiosity instead?

Catching Our Stories in the Act

In my workshops, I help people get in touch with the stories they are telling themselves by having them stand on an imaginary power line. "How do you feel about broccoli, cooked any way you like?" I will ask them. If they love it, they stand on the "1" end, and if they hate it, they go to the "10" end, and everywhere in between. This is a safe way to share. "Is there a correct place to be on this line?" I will ask. No. But we all have our broccoli stories to tell. On the "1" end we can assume people have had positive broccoli experiences, and on the "10" end we can assume that people's stories involved throwing up. These broccoli stories are based on experience and are true for each of us.

We believe our experience is an immutable fact. We didn't get asked to the junior prom, therefore we are unattractive. We were told by our beloved grandfather that we couldn't carry a tune in a bucket when we were four, so we have never sung another note. We were shamed by a math teacher when he handed back test papers in class ("This is the worst paper I've ever graded!"), so we never took another math class. Our experiences are real and so we believe the stories we tell ourselves about our experiences are real and written in stone. I beg to differ.

We made up the stories we tell ourselves and that means we can change them. But what continually amazes me is that even though we made up our self-limiting stories and they are, for the most part, bunk, we cling to them, sometimes desperately. I see this in every workshop or class I teach.

Practicing Entertaining New Ideas

Once at a workshop I was leading, I asked the staff to stand on the line according to how creative they saw themselves. Two people headed toward the "10" end of the line. "What makes you think you aren't creative?" I asked them. Here is where it gets interesting. "When I was in fourth grade..." began one woman. Fourth grade! She decided when she was ten years old that she was not creative. That should make us all sit down in awe. Ten years old and she wrote off a giant talent: creativity. She was not creative, period, and that would be True for her for the rest of her life.

I find it interesting that when people tell me their self-limiting stories, they speak with assurance, but their energy is flat. It's like the flat line on an oscilloscope: loud and defining, hopeless.

This teacher told us that when she was in fourth grade she was asked to do a metal hammering art project. She didn't want to do it. It was prescribed and left no room for her imagination. She did a bad job on it, got a bad grade and then decided forever that she was not creative. Is this amazing or what? It was the artist in her that rebelled against the stifling rules of expression. But instead of celebrating her inner artist, she tried to kill it.

She hadn't been very successful in annihilating her expressiveness, but the story lingered. When I asked her to try entertaining a new idea, she reluctantly agreed. "Try saying, 'Maybe I am creative,'" I suggested. She looked like the proverbial deer in the headlights. To say, "Maybe I am creative" would destroy years of illusion building, years of chanting, years of opting out whenever creativity was called for. In spite of all she had to "lose," she began saying, "Maybe I am creative," tremulously at first, but with building enthusiasm.

"Now," I said, "I know you are creative. Let's check the reality with your colleagues. Raise your hand if you know for a fact that Luanne here is creative." All the hands went up.

"How do you respond to this?" I asked her, knowing the answer.

"They are just being kind," she said.

"So they are all liars," I said. I can be brutal when I'm going after these stories.

"Well, yes, but nice liars," she said, grinning now.

"Do you have any evidence that maybe these nice liars are right? Have you ever done anything creative?"

"Well, I did make this necklace I am wearing," she said

Good grief!

The other woman on the "10" end of the line was the principal. She was sure she wasn't creative. I hammered at her until she admitted that she loved to cook new recipes. In fact, the loaf sandwiches she had supplied us at lunch were her creation.

"But this doesn't count," she said. "I am only following a recipe."

See, this is where our Dinosaur gets so tricky. It wants us to keep our limiting stories. To do this, he tells us that "real" writers, singers, artists, chefs, whatever it is that we think we aren't, do it differently. I'm not really an artist because I can't draw realistically. What about Van Gogh? I'm not really a singer because I can't sing a pleasant note. What about Joe Cocker? I'm not really smart because I didn't score well on an intelligence test. What about Thomas Edison? I'm not smart because I'm in third grade and can't read well. What about John Fitzgerald Kennedy?

When I start on one of these expeditions, I tell people: "When someone here starts clinging to their story, it will be absolutely clear to the rest of us what is going on. We will be amazed. But when it is our turn, we will be just as stubborn, just as convinced that people are just being nice to us."

And so it goes.

I might be really smug here if this didn't happen to me all the time. The difference, I hope, is that I am interested in discovering these stories and letting them go. Even so, it is still hard. Am I really a singer? A songwriter? A musician? When I let myself say, "Yes," I feel lightning is going to strike me dead on the spot.

A singer is someone who sings. I sing. My songs make people laugh and cry. Doesn't that count? Just because Whitney Houston exists doesn't mean my voice doesn't have a right to be heard. Yet I continue to struggle to allow myself to embrace my voice as it is now and as it could become. But I am struggling in the right direction, I think, and that is what I am encouraging you to do as well.

Know that you are packing around lots of stories that steal joy from you. Know that releasing these stories will not always be easy, but that the freedom and joy you recover when you do, will fuel you through life's hardships.

Know, too, that when you cling to self-limiting stories, you deprive your partner, your friends, your colleagues, your family, and the world of the best of you. This, I think, is a sin, a missing of the mark, a denial of the bliss in our bellies that wants to be. I think it corrupts our relationships, insidiously perhaps, but I think that many problems in relationships stem from our unwillingness to embrace our genius. This leads us to be jealous, which sends us into shaming and blaming.

Which stories about myself I choose to believe is up to me. If I choose to listen to the ninety-nine people who loved my performance instead of the one very crabby person who didn't, that is my choice, too. What about constructive criticism, you might be asking right now. What about it? Jennifer James, in her book *The Slug Manual: The Art of Criticism*, says there is no such thing as constructive criticism. It is all just a power trip. Brenda Ueland, in her book *If You Want to Write*, suggests that we concentrate on what is working and let the rest take care of itself. This is the model I use in working with myself and others when I'm teaching writing, and it is far more effective than anything else I have ever tried.

I am not suggesting we never listen to feedback. I am always listening for how I could improve. As I deepen my listening for the essence in myself and others, I become more and more effective.

But if I let one bad evaluation dominate my thinking, then I will be crushed, lose momentum, and shrink back into safety. When I receive such an evaluation now, I tell myself the story that maybe I scared someone or triggered someone's childhood issues. I believe love is personal but that most criticism is probably a projection of a person's own fears and doubts.

It is up to us, then, to discover our stories and invite them out to dance with us. Does this story fill me with the sweet juice of life? Yes? Then I'll keep it. Does this story make me feel flat and dusty? Yes? Then I'll chuck it! We can sing to those old, life-sucking stories, paraphrasing Ray Charles, "Hit the road, Lack!"

Story: Matthew Entertains a New Idea

One bright, sunny spring day in Vancouver, B.C., I met a young bellman. His boss had asked him to help me with the automatic teller machine across the street. Oh, Canada!

I was in the gorgeous city of Vancouver because I was presenting at an international conference of community educators. I had received a standing ovation in my workshop, something I had never seen or experienced before, and I was high, in love with Canada and life.

We had quite an adventure together in the short time we spent traipsing around looking for a machine that would work for me. It was one of those magical moments, moments that enrich my life. I like to believe that Matthew and I were forever different after our short encounter. I remember thinking, "Oh, if his mother knew what I was saying to him, she would love me now!"

"Do you know anything I can do about my blushing?" the bellman asked. He stood beside me, punching the buttons on the Visa machine, trying to help me get more Canadian money.

"What had I said or done to make him feel safe enough to ask this question," I wondered. Maybe it was my cane and my asking for help. Maybe it was my smile or my laugh or my wrinkles. Maybe it was the sticker that said 'joy' marking my debit card. Whatever it was that gave him the courage to ask his question, I was grateful and ready to listen for magic.

He said blushing was a problem that had plagued him all his life and it was a constant source of misery for him. He blushed easily and often, and he hated it. He sounded hopeless. I suppose I could have told him he was being silly and overreacting, but he must have known I never would have said any such thing, or he never would have shared his secret with this stranger.

"Well, first of all, you are telling yourself a story that whatever is happening to you is embarrassing. Then you tell yourself the story that blushing is terrible."

"It is!" he said vehemently. "I hate it."

"I tell myself a different story about your blushing," I said. "I find it endearing. I think some young woman is going to come around some day, see you blush, and think, 'Whoa! This is the guy for me!'"

"Really?" he said, hope flooding his voice. "I thought girls hated that."

"The girls who hate that are weeds in your garden. Better to throw them out fast. Leave room for the sweet-smelling flowers."

Our conversation ventured into other stories he was telling himself. He thought he was stupid because he had a hard time learning to read. He was sure his whole life was over because he was twenty and had not yet started college. He dreaded the years stretching out ahead of him. He felt his life was over and he had blown it.

"Your future feels like a huge anvil hanging over your head, doesn't it?" I said to him.

He turned and looked at me as if I were a magician. "How did you know? That is exactly what it feels like!"

We only had about fifteen minutes together, but it felt like one of those small miracles to me. I would not have met Matthew if it weren't for my vision loss. I would never have been able to invite Matthew to change his stories if he hadn't been brave enough to ask me if I could help him with his blushing problem. I think it rather marvelous that I could not see his blushing. Sometimes I can feel it, but I simply cannot see the subtleties of a blush.

I was living the mystery, surfing the mystery, and here was this sweet boy/man known as Matthew before me in all of his vulnerable glory. Did I help him change his life? Yes, I'm sure I did. Did he start taking those drama classes he said he would like to take? (After he told me with absolute despair in his voice that he couldn't think of anything that he wanted to do with his life, I asked, "Are you sure there isn't something in your belly that wants to become?" "Well," he said, in the tone I have come to recognize when people start listening to their genius, "I have always wanted to be an actor.")

Did he sign up for that class that his belly wanted him to take? I don't know. Will it be harder for him to resist the call of his bliss? I think it will.

Matthew, like all of us, has a battle raging in him between what he thinks his limitations are and what he is called to become on this planet. The voices in our culture that tell us what is possible and impossible for us are strong and sure. Those subtle calls to our destiny are like the voice that told Kevin Costner in the movie *Field of Dreams*, "If you build it, he will come." These inklings and nudges toward our greatness can sound crazy. We don't understand them and we are afraid no one else will either.

So which voice in our head are we going to listen to: the Muse or the Dinosaur? We decide every day, and the quality of our lives rests on these infinite decisions of trust vs. fear.

Story: Not a Happy Physics Party

A friend of mine once needed to take a physics class in order to graduate in her major. The class had more than 400 students. As she sat in the huge lecture hall, looking at all the faces around her, she felt overwhelmed. She believed science was her weak subject, and after the first week, she was completely discouraged. She went to every class, attended every lab. She read every assignment, and she still didn't understand.

Finally, the week before finals, she went to visit her professor. She hadn't gone to see him sooner because she felt that, with that class size, he wouldn't have the time or energy to deal with her little problem.

"I'm sorry to have waited so long," she said, standing in his office with her shoulders hunched. "I'm completely lost in your class, and I don't know what to do. I must pass this course for my major."

"When did you first get lost?" he asked. She stood quietly in front of him, trying to gather the courage to tell him the truth. "The first week?" he asked softly.

"Yes," she said. "But I've gone to every class, attended every lab, and read all the materials. Nothing makes sense."

"Well," he said, "do you have any time right now?"

They sat down together, and for the next four hours he taught her the entire course. "Oh, that's what you meant," she exclaimed over and over again. "I see how this fits together now." She must have been a dream come true for him, a student who was eager to learn and had done the work. She needed someone to help her put all the pieces together. It was like she had all the parts of a car lying around her, but she didn't have the first idea of how to put it all together. He helped her organize the chaos, the wheels, the motor and the interior until she finally had a fully functioning understanding of the physics debris that had filled her mind all semester.

She got an "A" on the final, missing only one question, one she had misread. She got a "B+" in the course. Her professor told her he would have liked to have given her the "A" she deserved, but since she had done so poorly all term, he couldn't justify it. "But you and I know you earned an A," he said.

If she had just given up that first week or in the middle of the term, if she had stopped attending class or going to the labs, she would have failed the course and would have had to delay graduation. If she had asked for help the first week, though, she would not have needed to suffer the entire semester.

She was afraid she was stupid and afraid she wasn't important enough to ask the professor for help. Her goal of graduating as an occupational therapist was so strong, however, that she overcame her fears and succeeded.

My friend had to change the story that she was not smart, not worthy. What I have learned to do during these battles is to say to that voice that tells me I am not good enough, "Maybe so." Then I go on anyway. Too bad for you, Dinosaur Voice!

Poem: My True Voice

As I mentioned in the introduction, on my fiftieth birthday I had a grand party. A friend loaned me a karaoke machine, and I invited all the musicians I knew to join me. We had an impromptu concert in my backyard, and I had so much fun I made myself a promise, a commitment to my voice.

Now I had been singing for a long time—I had even produced my own CD and sold hundreds around the world. But I sang only to get the words of my songs into the world. I didn't think I was "good enough" to be a "singer." I sang in public all the time, but I didn't tell myself the story that I was a singer because, to me, a singer was someone whose voice was good enough that people would come out just to hear her sing. I relied on the message, on my passion, and on my desire to bring out the genius in everyone, but I did this in spite of what I believed about my voice, not because of it.

Because of the joy I felt at my fiftieth birthday party, I decided it didn't matter if I had any vocal ability or not. I decided to trust my singing, to let it lead me wherever it might lead even if my voice was not good enough to deserve this attention. I took my first step on the journey of claiming my true voice.

One year later I had performed in a musical, helped form a singing group, The Free Range Chix; attended a week-long Natural Singer workshop, and had become part of a keynote/concert duo. I was writing songs like crazy, songs that made people laugh and cry, and I was creating wild characters: (The Cosmic Waitress, who, with a New Jersey accent, demands: "So what do you want already? Speak up? What are you waiting for?")

I'm not waiting for anything or anyone anymore. Where this path of claiming my voice will lead, I don't know for sure. Maybe Off Broadway, maybe "Oprah." It really doesn't matter. Simply claiming my voice, traveling this road less traveled, is making all the difference.

When I sing,
my true voice,
with its tendrils of curiosity and courage,
reaches deep inside me
and reveals a part of me I have never known.
The debris,
gathered over a lifetime,
that covers my true voice
falls away
like so much peeling paint.

When I sing,
I sand the rough edges from my true voice,
letting my glory emerge
like a sculpture called from marble.

When I sing,
my true voice defines me,
clarifies me
as I let it flow from me.

When I sing,
I craft my voice.
I experiment,
imitating Bette
or Bonnie
or Joni.

I let a song sing me,
trying to find my way in it,
letting it find me,
and together we create our unique union.
I seek the truth of the song
and of my voice.

I discover
what has always been
and what was meant to be
within me.
My job is to show up,
to be willing to let my emerging voice crack
and screech,
or to be flat,
unsightly,
and disharmonious.

My job is to let my voice be a loud wrong if need be
for others to hear and judge
if they must.

I commit to finding
the courage to continue to discover
what is really in me
instead of what I think should be in me.

I promise myself
I will let the jagged edges show
and even cut me as they are born
if that is what needs to happen.

I sing
every day
with my voice as it is,
perfect
or imperfect, or perfectly imperfect.

Song: I Feel Fifty
(from the CD *Daring to Sing*)

The year before I turned fifty I spent a lot of time contemplating what growing older meant to me. I had heard a parody of "I Feel Pretty" sung by a local musician, Neal Gladstone, and I decided to write my own version.

I feel fifty,
oh, so fifty.
It's quite nifty how fifty I feel.
I'm turning fifty, and I can't believe it's real.

It's not alarming;
in fact, it's charming.
For once I'm not harming the sky or the sea.
I'm just turning fifty, and I'm finally accepting me.

See the older woman in that mirror there?
Who can that wise woman be?
Such a lot of class, such a lot of sass, such a lot of ass, such a lot of me!

I don't wear pantyhose.
I got rid of those.
I found that pantyhose don't let me breathe.
Some man invented those in some dark, misogynistic dream.

I'm not crabby,
just a little flabby.
Feeling fabby and foolish and free.
I'm turning fifty, and I'm finally turning into ME.

Your Turn

What stories have people told you about yourself? What stories did you make up all on your own? Listen carefully for just a week and see if you can "catch" them. Even if you think they are absolutely and forever true, write them down anyway. Give yourself a chance to re-examine a decision you made about yourself when you were ten, or twenty-five, or forty.

What stories are you telling your partner or your children or your friends that are not serving them or you well? Write a letter to yourself or someone you love that tells the opposite story. Listen to yourself as you do this, and you will learn a lot about how your Predator operates in you.

Chapter 6

Falling in Love with Truth

Song: Truth Rap
(from the CD *Calling for the Best*)

I wrote this song, for children, when I was an elementary school counselor, but I have found it helpful many times since with adults.

Let's talk about truth.
It's when you don't need proof.
My word is enough. My word is enough.
Even when it gets tough,
my word,
It's ME!
My word is enough.

Let's talk about lies.
They're bad for your insides.
You can't hide from yourself.
You can't hide from yourself.

Falling in Love with Truth

> *"The truth shall set you free, but first it will make you miserable."*
>
> —*Message on a poster*

This saying found me twenty years ago and it has stuck with me. The picture on the poster was of a cute little kitty going through a wringer, and I have often felt just like that poor cat. I used to be afraid of the truth, terrified even. I was afraid that people would tell me something despicable about myself and I would never get over it. I would suffer forever, their words beating me in my sleep like some kind of self-esteem battering ram.

I was afraid for good reasons. I grew up in an atmosphere where not only were mistakes inevitable, but were pounced upon with vicious glee. In my family, people made cruel, uninvited comments about appearance, intelligence, and worthiness to be on the planet. "Why are your teeth so yellow? Don't you ever brush them?" "What a fool you are for asking that question. Don't you already know that? You idiot." Souls and self-esteem were in imminent danger in my home.

Every cruel comment, every "helpful" criticism, increased the size and weight of my battering ram of shame. I learned to protect myself by becoming a pathological pleaser. If no one ever got mad at me, if no one were ever disappointed, if I were perfect, maybe I could protect myself from hurtful remarks. I did not have the courage to be disliked. I did not have the courage to find out who I really was because I feared I would discover I was despicable and deserved the abuse I had endured.

When I began therapy in my early thirties, I started falling in love with truth. I found the truth did, in fact, set me free. I learned that I suffered more when I lacked the courage to look at what was true for me and, instead, clung to my illusions. My counselor helped me discover I was angrier at my abused mother than my brutalizing father. The story of my childhood got turned inside out. My sweet mother, whose love had saved me, my innocent, powerless, victimized mother—well, the truth was I was furious with her. My fury terrified my mother and me and it took us a couple of years to recover. From that point on, though, our relationship was based on mutual respect and, until the day she died, we were amazingly close.

Bargaining with the Truth

In my experience, very few people want to know the whole truth. We are afraid if we are honest with ourselves about who we really are and what we really want, we will have to get a divorce, move to Alaska to study whales, or quit our jobs. And maybe we will have to make big changes if we let ourselves know who we really are. But whatever is true for us *is true for us* and our truth isn't going anywhere. Avoiding what is true steals our energy and our joy because we use so much of our life force defending the castle we have built around our illusions.

Most of us want to know some of what is true, as long as we can control the truth we let ourselves know. We are afraid if we know the truth about our loved ones, we won't be able to love them anymore. I avoided therapy for years because I was afraid if I admitted to myself that my mother did not do her motherly job of protecting me, I would have to stop loving her. I would have to throw out all of my good memories. I was afraid to let myself and the people I loved be human.

When I shifted to embracing my humanity, all of it, a huge weight lifted. My chronic feelings of anxiety dissolved over time as if by magic. Instead, I felt a lightness of spirit and a return of joy. I discovered talents and strengths I had never suspected. Instead of being the sniveling coward I always thought I was, I found I could make courageous leaps forward in my life.

All of us can bargain for a long time before we are willing to surrender to what "living in truth and taking responsibility" means. This is a rigorous, daily path to follow that accepts no excuses. It is the road less traveled for good reasons, but the only road worth traveling, in my opinion. Even though I have lost friends, a job, and a marriage because I have committed to this path of truth and authenticity, I don't regret one moment of my adventure away from fear.

Story: My Illusion of Control Falls in the Lake

I used to think I could make myself safe if I were only careful enough. When bad things happened, as they inevitably did, I blamed myself for not being vigilant. If I had only been less exuberant, I wouldn't have frightened that friend away. If I had only been more considerate, I would have had more support when I felt alone and lost. It was all up to me.

I received a wonderful cosmic lesson in how much I could control the grief in my life one summer at Wallowa Lake. I was still married to my first husband and I was in the beginning stages of losing my vision. I could still read and I could drive in daylight, but my vision at night was severely limited.

Will and I were walking back with our friends, Dick and Martha, to their boat. We had attended a lecture at a writing conference, and it was starting to get dark. I stepped onto the dock where their boat was tied, confident that I could see well enough to get myself to the boat safely. Martha even asked me if I needed any help, and I said, "No, not if there are no surprises."

What I meant by that was that if docks did what they were supposed to do, that is, had all of their boards in good repair, and if no one had left any giant spiked traps for me en route, I would be fine. I walked along the dock slowly, being careful, responsible, safe. I saw the boat and walked a few steps beyond it, and, as it turned out, just one step too many.

In that long moment, poised over the unknown, before I fell into whatever it was I was going to fall into, I remember thinking, "I took only one step too many, just one step. That isn't so much. I've only made a tiny mistake and now I might have to pay a huge price for it. I've been so careful! I've been so good. This isn't fair." Then, suddenly, I was falling, out of control, and at the mercy of the trickster, Coyote. (He likes to smack us out of our illusions sometimes.)

Wallowa Lake is cold, even in the summer, but I didn't notice that. I didn't notice I couldn't breathe under water, and I didn't notice I was fully clothed. I did notice that I was sinking and sinking and sinking, and I wondered, with a sense of calm detachment, "How will I ever be able to come to the surface again?"

I don't remember turning around under water. I can't imagine how I could have turned around. I don't remember kicking to get myself to the surface. I am pretty sure I didn't kick or do anything to save myself.

Somehow, though, my body hurled itself out of the water, like a trained dolphin jumping for fish. My arms were raised in a large "V." Martha and Will caught one arm apiece and hauled me to the safety of the dock. At first I crumpled on the wooden planks and sobbed from my backbone, huge wrenching sobs of grief and frustration over my loss of vision. I felt horrible, and I felt great.

Then, with no transition time, I started laughing hysterically. It was very funny, after all. Here I was, capable Vicki, being so careful, being courteous, making room for those behind me to get in the boat first (Aren't I a good girl?). And then, whoosh! Vanished! Where did Vicki go?

So much for being careful. Being careful didn't save me. My best hadn't saved me. In the end, I was vulnerable to Coyote. Ha, ha, ha.

I felt Divine Intervention in that sudden soak in Wallowa Lake. Like my mother's death, it was one of those cosmic, terrifying, life-enhancing moments, which I do not regret. I am grateful for my plunge into the lake and for the circumstances that conspired to leave me sleeping with my dying mother, singing to her, and holding her hand when she was too weak to hold mine.

I don't think safety is all it's cracked up to be. Once I learned to practice giving up the illusion of safety and to instead surf the flow of the present—being mindful, of course; (I'm not an idiot)—once I learned to live in faith rather than in fear, well, that, my dear, has made all the difference.

Poem: I Am a Greedy Bitch

After all this talk of taking a stand for truth no matter what the consequences, I have to confess here that I wish I could love truth and not pay any price. For that reason, I am a greedy bitch.

Note: The word "bitch" has a lot of power and I do not use it lightly. My fear of being a bitch has kept me quiet many times when I should have spoken up. At some level I am afraid I am going to step over the line sometime and end up being burned at the stake. When I have shared this fear with other women, I have found I have a lot of company.

I am a greedy bitch.
I want it all.
I want to pursue my truth,
to live a life of authenticity and integrity
and,
at the same time,
know that I will have the church packed at my funeral.

I want to have my cake and eat it, too.
I want to pursue the road less traveled,
and yet I want it constantly lined with cheerleaders.
"Way to go, Vicki!" they will say,
"You keep speaking that unpleasant truth! We are with you all the way!
Where do you smell a rat, Vicki? We want to know! Set us free again
    and again!"

Do you smell a rat in my thinking?
I do. Yes, I'll jump off that cliff again and again,
but please, could I have a parachute,
or a glider,
or a jet plane to save me?

And a cheering section.
Always a cheering section.

Sheesh!

Poem: I'm the One Who Smells the Rat

While we are on the subject . . .

I'm the one who smells the rat.
I'm the one who might notice
what others would rather not see,
like the fact, Melody,
that your mother has an icebox where her heart should be.
She is full of social graces
but lacks the capacity to love anyone,
especially you.

Or like the fact, Robyn,
that it's your dad as well as your mom
who says "no" to your soulful wings.

Your dad as well as your mom
who looks to find what is wrong
instead of what is magnificent about you.

I will not tell you what I see unless you ask me,
But if you know me at all, you will know that I know.

I'm the disagreeable person who,
amid the glowing reviews of a Harry Potter celebration,
points out that the fat kid, once again, is the bad guy.
In this movie for children to be good is to be skinny.
Evil, then, must lurk in cellulite.
This magical tale that encircles the globe
unintentionally feeds human self-hate,
and helps increase obesity and diabetes astronomically.

What a bore I am!
Why can't I shut up and go along?
If I am the one who wants to focus on what works,
then why am I the one who constantly notices the dead rat?
Am I on some kind of a psycho-spiritual, cosmic, New Age power trip?

I hope not.
I don't like feeling I am the only one who smells the rat.
I love being with people who aren't at peace
with the cacophony of self-deception.

I have tried to go along to get along.
I've tried pretending I don't know what I know.
I've tried obliterating what I know.
I've tried to squeeze what I know to be true
into the little box labeled "People Will Like Me if I am Good Enough"
or the box that says: "People Will Leave You and Hate You
If You Know This or Speak This."
My body won't let me pretend anymore.

Maybe the world needs difficult people like me
to peel back the cover and expose group agreements by saying,
"We made this all up, you know,
and we can change our minds about what is possible at any moment."
Maybe I serve humanity best
when I say to a leader,
"I smell your power trip."
Maybe I serve our marriage best
when I say to my husband on our anniversary
as he speaks earnestly to me
about the difference between miracles and blessings,
"Ho, hum. Talk to me about something real
or pass the sesame chicken."

I am the one who smells the rat,
and, truth be told,
no matter how much I whine and complain about it,
I wouldn't have it any other way.

Your Turn

Is there any place in your life where you are hiding from truth? This may be hard to sort out. Look for places where you are defensive or stubborn. Pretend something is true and then see if you could live with it. Could you live with the fact that your mother never loved you? You could. Could you live with the fact that you have let someone down, betrayed someone? You can live with these truths as well.

Or how about asking yourself if you could live with the fact that you are indeed brilliant? Maybe you are a scientist! Maybe you are a writer! Maybe you are an artist! Maybe you are a dangerous woman! Let yourself play with all kinds of possibilities.

Chapter 7

Choosing Courage

Comfort Zones

Everyone needs a comfort zone. We need a place where we can relax, a place to regroup. We need a place that nurtures us and protects us until we are ready to step out into the world again. We can't learn if we never feel safe, but we can't learn if we never feel uncomfortable either. This is one of life's delicious paradoxes.

If we stay in our comfort zones, we can't add anything new to our lives. Our comfort zone becomes our prison zone. We become paralyzed in our fear. The longer we stay in our comfort zone, the more difficult it becomes to step out into the unknown. We've all known people who decide that they don't want to be beginners anymore; they only want to do things they are already good at, so they never learn anything new.

Moving out of our comfort zones takes courage. It takes muscle. We are all batters in our own Game of Life, whether we like it or not. We need to step up to the plate, to strike out, to pop up, to get some base hits, and to slam an occasional home run. All the best home run hitters in history were great at striking out as well. We can sit in the dugout of our lives, watching the balls go by, wondering why we are so stiff and unhappy, or we can get into the batter's box, no matter what shape we are in, and start swinging.

That's enough of the baseball metaphor. I don't even play baseball anymore.

Give Your Courage Muscle A Workout

However flabby your courage muscle is right now, you can tone it. As the muscles in our body get stronger with repeated use, so our courage muscle gets stronger each time we use it. Start wherever you are and just do things that scare you. Don't do the scariest thing you can think of. Pick something small, do-able. This will give you confidence.

I don't care what kind of a coward you have been to this point, you can start becoming more courageous right this minute. When I took on my fear, I set a goal: I decided to no longer let my life be dominated by fear. I would no longer make decisions based on dread. If the only reason I avoided something was because I was afraid, I vowed to go ahead and do it anyway.

I started small. I started speaking up for myself more. After some practice, I even told my dad to stop telling me racist jokes. He accused me of being "high and mighty" but I didn't care. Racism is wrong, and I wasn't going to be "gracious" and listen to a hateful "joke." (Story follows.)

Many people consider me courageous now, but I know I have a lot of work to do. I am not even aware of all of my cowardly habits, but I am interested in ferreting them out. That's the best any of us can ever do.

Story: "That's Not Funny, Dad!"

Stopping my dad from telling me a racist joke was one of the bravest things I have ever done. The irony is that my dad had taught me the evils of racism when I was a child, but on this day, when I was in my early thirties, he decided in a phone conversation that he could tell me such a joke.

As I realized what kind of a joke we were headed toward, I was terrified, my heartbeat was drowning my hearing, but Dad had crossed the line. Maybe I couldn't always stand up for myself, but I could stand up for my children. I would not bring them up in a racist environment. There was not a cell in my body that could hear a nigger joke and remain silent. (I can barely type the letters to make that word.)

When I saw where the joke was heading, I interrupted Dad and said, "Dad, I don't like those kinds of jokes." I was as brave as I had ever been, facing a scary enemy, a man who I had seen physically attack my mother and verbally assault anyone who got in his way.

"My, aren't we high and mighty," he said.

High and mighty—for not wanting to hear a racist joke? He was trying to shame me into submission, but I repeated, "I don't like those kinds of jokes."

He hung up, and that was the end of my relationship with my father. Oh, we have seen each other since then, had a short lunch even, where I gave him pictures of my children and copies of songs I had written. But this was the end of his calling me or coming to visit, the end of the thin semblance of a relationship we had.

My father does not know my full name, nor would he recognize his grandchildren if he met them on the street. I have not spoken to him for over ten years, not since I lost my vision, got divorced, remarried, and became an international speaker. Simply saying "no" to my father severed our relationship.

Was it worth it? Would I do it again? You betcha! The entry fee for a relationship with my father is too high. I will not sacrifice my deeply held beliefs so that he might love me. I will not allow anyone in my life to abuse me or those I love. I take a stand for justice, and I will not change that because I want someone to love and approve of me.

This was a huge act of courage for me, the first of many steps that have led me to the life I now lead. I do not know how people can be truly happy, truly authentic, if they sacrifice their honor in order to be loved.

The Courage to Be Disliked

The fear of disapproval has dominated my thinking and behavior most of my life. The story I told myself about disapproval had a musical soundtrack that continually ran through my head. The mood was dangerous. Violence threatened. Disapproval was bad, bad, bad, and I could avoid it if only I were good, good, good.

I sacrificed the best of myself on the altar of approval seeking because I told myself this story. I had plenty of cultural encouragement. "Everything nice" was what little girls were made of—everyone knew that. In my family, where approval wasn't possible except with my mother, I learned the safest way to avoid being shamed or hit was to be innocuous, inconspicuous, and, if possible, invisible.

If I could be perfect, however, I might earn some approval, at least at school. I would be a Hero Child. I would get straight A's and never turn in an assignment late. I would be polite. I would be a peacemaker and never get angry at anyone. I would not be disagreeable because that would be bitchy, and I never wanted to give anyone any cause to call me a bitch. Disapproval would simply and surely kill me, I thought, and I could avoid disapproval by avoiding doing anything that would cause anyone to dislike me. I was sure if I were only good enough, I could control other people's feelings and opinions of me.

I had role models to imitate. Rebecca, who would become our homecoming queen in high school, bathed in universal approval. She had a soft, sweet smile for everyone and her beauty appeared effortless. I could get that much approval, I was sure, if I could only shave off all those nasty opinions I had about almost everything. I believed I could trick people into loving me if I tried hard enough. I could conform. I could fit in. I could make myself look like someone worthy of love.

I copied Rebecca's clothes, but I didn't have a talent for copying. Also, my coloring and body size were different, so I looked like a cheap imitation of the real thing, which is what I was. I continued my habit of imitating people who had what I thought I wanted into my thirties. If my attempts at replicating the success of other people's lives had been more successful, I might still be doing it.

When did I decide I wanted to learn to have the courage to be disliked and be myself? Probably when I started therapy after I began raging at my daughter Katie when she was a preschooler. I was more terrified of a rage I did not understand and seemed unable to control, than I was of losing the image of myself as a good mother. I hit bottom, luckily, before I hit Katie.

I was terrified of therapy, I now think, because my journey into the truth of who I really was meant I would have to give up looking good, and being "nice." I wasn't sure of all that I might lose, but I was afraid it would be everything. And, as it turned out, it pretty much was everything.

When I let go of trying to be good, I let go of lying to myself and others. I couldn't rationalize my exaggerations or deceptions anymore. I could no longer nod my head and agree when people gave excuses for why they were staying in abusive or deadening situations. No longer was I willing to sacrifice my truth for my own or someone else's self-delusion.

Since I made a commitment to "no more nice girl," I have changed careers, been shamed, vilified in the press, condescended to, patronized, and laid off. But I've also been more creative and productive than I ever dreamed I could be. I've found a soulful mate who is as interested in truth as I am. I have helped more people find their courage and take steps toward their dreams than I ever imagined I could.

And I've only just begun. I feel a move into hyper-drive coming. I can feel what my life will be like when I quit waiting for others to catch up and understand and approve of who I am and what I do. I see great contributions and adventure directly in front of me.

I still have some bad habits of approval-seeking. I will weed them out one at a time as I find them. No big deal. The scales are falling from my eyes and off my rocket ship. The freer I am from my need for approval, the sleeker my vessel. Without the burden of my need to be liked, I am more aerodynamically efficient for my trip through life.

I have the courage to be disliked and misunderstood. I also have the courage to be liked and understood. Here I am. Here I am. Here I am. Truly.

Song: WarriorBabe
(from the CD *Alive, Alive*)

This is the song I wrote to celebrate my continuing recovery from being a nice girl. I am still committed to being kind, generous, gracious, and caring, but I am giving up ignoring the truth inside me to please others. I tried this for thirty years, and I didn't like the way it worked, or didn't work, rather. No matter how much of myself I gave away in order to be loved, I still didn't feel I had enough love. Of course I didn't. My mouth wasn't connected to my belly. I had no belly! I had no center where I knew how I felt and what I wanted. No matter how much I got fed, no matter how much attention, love, and inclusion I received, it was never enough. It could never be enough.

Now I am committed to acting like the Bitch of the North if that is what it takes to honor the radiant being that I am. I have the courage to be disliked!

No more nice girl, no more nice girl for me.
No more "yessing" when I do not agree.
I'm saying no. I am getting clear.
Get ready; WarriorBabe is here.

Chorus:
Cuz I'm a WarriorBabe, WarriorBabe!
I'm a WarriorBabe.
I am a WarriorBabe, WarriorBabe. I'm a WarriorBabe.

I'm through with taking care of everyone else.
From now on I take good care of myself.
I am alive in my creative flow.
Get ready; WarriorBabe's aglow!

Chorus

I no longer feed my face when I'm sad.
Instead sometimes I just get mad.
I take a stand for the way I feel.
Get ready; WarriorBabe is real!

Chorus

There's nothing wrong with being nice, if you don't mind the cost.
It's just that when I'm nice too much my real self gets lost.

No more nice girl, no more nice girl for me.
No more "yessing" when I do not agree.
I'm saying no. I am getting clear.
Get ready; WarriorBabe is here.

Chorus:
Cuz I'm a WarriorBabe, WarriorBabe.
I'm a WarriorBabe.
I am a WarriorBabe, WarriorBabe.
I'm a WarriorBabe.

Song: "Come to the Cliff," She Said
(from the CD *Alive, Alive*)

When I heard a man say these words in conversation, I felt their resonance, and I decided they would be the title of my next song. To me, this song describes the process of coming to the cliff and jumping that we need to do if we are going to have authentic relationships and an authentic life. We jump when we are afraid. We jump when we would rather roll into a ball, cover ourselves with our over-loved "blankies" and suck our thumbs. We jump because we know we must. We jump because to stay on the edge of the cliff, waiting for safety, means our spirits will atrophy and rot. Spiritual gangrene stinks.

Chorus:
"Come to the cliff," she said. "Come. Lift up your head.
Let go of your fear and trust what you hear. Come to the cliff," she said.
"You can fly. You can fly. You can spread your wings in the sky.
Feed your soul. Feel your wholeness. Come to the cliff," she said.

He knew he was living a lie.
His life force was starting to die.
"How long must I wait before I feel safe?"
"Come to the cliff," she said.

He stood watching the ground.
He worried, fretted, and frowned.
"What will people say? Will I find my way?"
"Come to the cliff," she said.
When you've come to the edge of all that you know and you still have faith to try,
You can trust that you'll land with both feet on the ground or else be taught to fly.

Chorus

He kept his joys in a cage,
then wondered at his grief and his rage.
"Who will I be if I set my joys free?"
"Come to the cliff," she said.
He heard a voice in his heart say, "Now! It is time to start."
He unfolded his wings and started to sing.
"You've come to the cliff," she said.
"When you've come to the edge of all that you know and you still have faith to try,
you can trust that you'll land with both feet on the ground or else be taught to fly."

Chorus:
"Come to the cliff," she said. "Come. Lift up your head.
Let go of your fear and trust what you hear. Come to the cliff," she said.
"You can fly. You can fly. You can spread your wings in the sky.
Feed your soul. Feel your wholeness. Come to the cliff," she said.

"You can fly. You can fly.
You can spread your wings in the sky.
Feed your soul. Feel your wholeness.
Come to the cliff," she said.
"Come to the cliff," she said.

Your Turn

Okay! What brave thing needs doing in your life? You know what it is; you heard it when I asked the question. Is it an apology you need to make? A difficult conversation you need to start? A boundary you need to set? When will you do it? How will you get support? What will you do to celebrate becoming braver?

Who will you be if you set your joy free? Who might you terrify if you spread your wings and fly?

Chapter 8

Listening for Possibility

When we make a commitment to listening to our deepest self and to the deepest part of others, our world cannot remain the same. Listening takes us into our DNA, inviting us to experience profound insights, and enables us to access our courage. That is why listening is so dangerous and why so few of us do it well.

Listening deeply to what is true for us is essential if we want to shift out of complaining about a problem and move toward transformation and freedom. The more we complain about how unfair life is and how right we are, the more we sink into self-righteous muck.

Poem: Listening is Dangerous

If courageous listening is nourishing and transformational, why don't we teach it in schools? Why, even when we have experienced its power, do we forget to listen to ourselves and others? I think I have an answer:

Listening is dangerous.

If you truly listen to me, you risk losing
everything you ever thought precious—
what you believe about your parents,
what you think about your limitations,
what you think is possible for you and for the world.

If you choose to listen,
you do so at your own risk.

Authentic listening is an act of great vulnerability.

Don't do it.

Pretend to listen instead.

While "The Other" speaks,
gather your arguments,
your defenses,
your stories,
nod your head,
look involved.

You don't need to listen anyway because you Already Know.
There is no need to waste your time and energy
trying first to understand who is sitting before you.

No—
much better to collect your judgments,
prepare your attack,
or rehearse the joke you will tell when it's your turn.

Much better to search for arguments
than to open a room with a view—
a room where others can come and sit and be themselves,
a room where you will not judge them or debate,
or even necessarily tell them your story,
which is so much like theirs.

No—
letting people into this room might begin an awakening,
which could destroy the illusions lining those inner walls.

You might have to rewrite stories you have chanted to yourself for years,
the stories that keep you safe
and keep you from your greatest joys and possibilities.

Your magnificence is buried under this debris,
hidden from others
and yourself.
Safe.

Listening is dangerous.

Don't do it.

And if you don't listen to me,
then it will make it easier for me to not listen to you either.

I won't have to take any risks.
I won't have to change my opinions.
I won't have to let go of any of my own cherished beliefs.
My illusions will be safe
and you will have no power over me.

If I truly listen to you, though,
and let you into my heart and my body for these few moments,
let my self experience life from your point of view,
I risk losing everything in that terrible vulnerability.

I don't want to let authentic listening
become a suicide bomber that blows up my icons,
crumples my prejudices,
or dismantles my resentments.

I don't want to let go of any wrong I have ever suffered.
Nursing my grudges feeds me,
deeply,
viscerally.

I don't want to topple my Humpty Dumpty spiritual egg
and shatter my precious myths on the cobblestones of Truth.

No—
listening is just too dangerous for either of us.
Let's give eye contact,
nod and smile,
paraphrase occasionally,
but let's not risk losing our whole world.
Let's just look like we are listening instead.

Good.
Very good.
Thank you.

Poem: Good Listening is Not Interrupting (Except When It Is)

So you've decided you want to be a good listener, even though it can be dangerous? What are the rules, you may ask? There are lots of rules about everything, you know, at least according to the Dinosaur Voice in our heads. One rule about listening that you might have heard is: Never Interrupt!

Giving space and time for listening, not rushing in with solutions and advice—these are good habits. But when we are paying more attention to the rules than to the message, we are not really listening at all. We are being "good" again. (See how tricky perfectionism can be?)

Good listening IS **NOT** interrupting
when your dear friend needs time,
space, and
silence
to let her thoughts unfold,
one petal at a time.

Good listening IS **NOT** interrupting
when "Me! Me! Me!"
gets louder than the sacred space I've reserved in my heart for
You, You, You.

Good listening **IS** interrupting
when the "Yes!" of my response
mingles with the "Yes!" of yours.

Good listening **IS** interrupting
when our thoughts and laughter tumble together
like happy rocks in a polisher.
When the synergy and mystery of our commingling
don't need the space and time of silence—
that delicious, love-filled waiting—
then my interruption can be a joining of hands to celebrate.

Good listening is not interrupting
except when it is.

But when my interrupting is not listening,
when my exuberance overrides my good intentions,
when my hungry, giant ME! barges in with your "important" ideas,
and I see the sweet, tender, not-quite-formed blossom of you
shrink back into its protective leaf,
hidden awhile longer from me and maybe you, too.
Well, then I am disappointed in me,
sorry I couldn't hold my horses.

It is at those moments of my poor listening
that I hope you will give me another chance to try again,
to listen well.
to hold the space of sacred discovery
by being silent or,
perhaps,
by a joyful, loving interruption.

Story: Courageous Listening With Martin

I learned about transformational listening from Stephen Covey's book Seven Habits of Highly Effective People. *Habit 5 is "Seek first to understand." The more I practice this habit, the better my life gets.*

When my son Martin was about ten he wanted to buy a portable CD player. He already had a portable tape player and a CD player for his room. I felt a portable CD player was extravagant. He didn't. I was being reasonable. He was crying.

Our interaction could have been videotaped, and I would have been comfortable having it played at any parent/teacher meeting. I was doing great. I was talking calmly. I was being reasonable. Tears were shooting out of Martin's eyes, however, and he was becoming more upset as we talked.

Something in me made me take a moment to look at our situation. Here was Mother on one side of the room talking kindly and reasonably with her son. Here was Son on the other side of the room crying and feeling unloved and unheard. What was wrong with this picture?

I wasn't listening; that's what was wrong. I looked like I was listening. I even thought I was listening. What I was really doing, though, was being right. I was looking good and being right. I was very right. Martin was wrong. He was ten, I was forty, and that was that.

Fortunately, I love my son more than I love being right. I took a moment to reflect and then remembered what real listening sounds like. "Martin, I don't feel that I am being a good listener," I said. "Let me tell you what I've heard you say so far and then you tell me if I have understood you, okay?" Martin, still crying, nodded his head.

"You like the quality of a CD player better than a walkman," I said. "You have saved your money, and you feel you have a right to spend it any way you want. Have I understood you?"

By this time, Martin had stopped crying. He was sitting quietly, listening carefully. "Yes," he said," that's it."

"Could you let me know what you heard me say?" I asked.

Martin paused for a moment and then said, "You are afraid I will care more about things than people."

I was struck dumb. That was exactly what I had been saying, only he said it more succinctly than I ever had. He *had* understood, and yet I had kept up my pounding, my lecturing. It was soft-spoken lecturing, but lecturing nonetheless.

"Yes," I said, "you have understood me. What do you suppose we can do now? How do we reach a solution that makes us both happy. I think you should be able to buy the CD player. But what can you do to help me know you don't care more about things than people?"

Again Martin paused and thought. What more beautiful sight can a parent see than watching her beloved son think about how he is going to show he cares more about people than things? I was grateful at that moment for whatever in me had reminded me to take the time to stop and listen, really listen.

Martin decided to donate part of his allowance to a charity. He picked Mothers Against Drunk Drivers after sorting through all the requests for donations my husband and I received for two weeks. I had shifted from being "right" to modeling for Martin what was most important—my relationship with him. I also modeled being a good listener. Instead of lecturing my son on how he should be, I demonstrated how I want him to be. We both experienced shifting from win/lose to win/win and it changed our relationship for the better. Courageous listening automatically shifts everyone into Level Three. It is magic, every time.

Your Turn

Are you thinking of any times when you could have been a better listener? You can always do a "Do-Over:" "Hey! I am realizing I did not do a good job listening to you the other day, last week, last year, when you were two. Let me give it another try."

What are your listening bad habits? Confess them to everyone you love. Whose listening do you admire? Share your appreciation and ask for coaching.

Chapter 9

Living in Integrity

Integrity means your behavior matches what you say you believe. If you claim to be a Christian, for example, and you want to follow the teachings of Christ, then you are out of integrity if you propagate hate. As I said before, when Jesus said, "Love thy neighbor as thyself," he did not wink his eye. This sentence does not contain an asterisk. Ministers who follow the teachings of Christ cannot carry signs that say, "God hates fags."

When we live in integrity, what we say matches what we do. If we make an agreement or a promise, we keep it. We don't make excuses if we break a promise; we take corrective action. This is easy to say, but takes enormous commitment to fulfill. Our relationships, though, are based on what Stephen Covey calls our emotional bank accounts. Everything we say and do either adds or withdraws from these accounts.

We need to be impeccable with our speech and our behavior. This is a Level Two habit that requires discipline. It is absolutely not sexy. It is a little boring, to tell the truth. But it is the foundation of all relationships. When parents make a promise to their children, which should never be done lightly, they should do their utmost to fulfill it. Capriciously voiding a negotiated agreement is bullying. Lovers need to be impeccable with one another. We are sacred space. Why would we speak sloppily, calling someone who is sacred a cruel name? This is a destructive habit. Sticks and stones do break bones, but names can hurt for a lifetime.

The Golden Rule, "Do unto others as you would have them do unto you," may be out of fashion, but it is still the basis of world peace, understanding diversity, and living authentically ever after.

Poem: Promises are Sacred

Keeping agreements is absolutely fundamental if you want to live your life in integrity. I advise my college students to start making their word their deed if they want an instant self-esteem fix. *Every time you make a promise you don't keep you destroy a piece of your self-esteem.* You can start immediately to rebuild your self worth just by keeping every single agreement you make. (I never said it was easy.)

A promise is sacred.

"Okay. I'll do it," you say.

You have just committed a sacred act:
You have made a promise.
You have given your word.

Even though you do this every day,
this promise making,
and even though we walk through our shattered promises
and the shattered promises of others regularly,
this promise making is a Grand Moment,
a building of relationship
one agreement at a time.

Promises sweep out of our mouths all day long:
"I will call you."
"I will pick up some milk on the way home."
"I will clean my room when I get home from school."

All these small promises
make up a life.
All these small promises, when kept,
build trust
and self-confidence.

But promises broken
break relationships.
Promises broken,
agreements made and forgotten,

promises ignored,
teach others who we are
and who we are not.

Promises kept
teach others how important they are to us.

When our word is our deed,
when what comes out of our mouths
is what actually happens,
we teach others to trust and respect us.

But even the best laid plans,
we know,
sometimes go astray.
Since we live under Murphy and His Law
and know that what can go wrong will go wrong,
we need to have a plan about what we will do
when our promises are not kept.

If I break a promise,
I will show you how important you are to me
by coming to you immediately
and confessing.
"I know I made a promise and didn't keep it.
I'm sorry.
Here is what I will do to rebuild your trust
and my self-worth."

Pretending you didn't break a promise is a trust-breaking, self-esteem
    rotting habit.
Saying, "You didn't remind me!" isn't a valid excuse.
Saying, "I got distracted!" doesn't get you off the hook.
Saying, "I said yes when I meant no!" isn't a step forward
unless it is an epiphany.

"Oh, my goodness," you say to yourself,
"What have I done! There I went and said yes when I meant no.
Bad habit. My bad habit.
I will take action to change my behavior immediately."

An apology is only good once.
"I'm sorry" only works
if the next sentence out of your mouth is your plan of action.
"I'm sorry" is only good if you change your behavior
so you don't break your promise again.

If you think "I'm sorry" wipes the slate clean,
then start imagining how you will feel when you have to say,
"I'm sorry I forgot to blow out the candles again and your house burned
    down,"
or,
"I'm sorry I was speeding again, Officer."
The insurance company doesn't care if you are sorry;
your rates will go up anyway.
The Department of Motor Vehicles doesn't care if you are sorry—
they will take your license anyway.

Promises are sacred
unless we make them meaningless
or profane.
Your promise is a profanity
when you say, "Oh, I am always late.
Don't believe me when I say I will be there at nine.
Isn't it funny how I am always late?
Isn't this just a darling little eccentricity of mine?
Isn't your time just not as important as mine?
Don't I have this great system for getting there late?
I suppose I am smart enough to devise a system that would get me there
    on time,
but why would I do that?
I'm so cute this way."

Promises are profanities if you say:
"I know I didn't follow through on a promise,
but why did you bully me into saying yes when I really meant no?
I am not responsible for what comes out of my mouth.
I just say things.
You know I don't mean them.
You know 'I'll vacuum Tuesday' doesn't mean that I will vacuum Tuesday.
It means that I imagine I will vacuum sometime,
but I don't really know when.
I am very busy, you know.
You should know not to count on me.
My word is not my deed.
My promises are a game we play,
and you know it.
Trust? What is that?
I don't steal from you, do I?
If I were stealing that would be bad,
but I am not stealing from you."

Yes, you are stealing from me.
You steal my trust every time you say you will do something that you
    don't do.

A promise is a sacred commitment.
Kept promises build trust bridges between us.
Kept promises build a trampoline of self-worth and confidence underneath
    us,
a trampoline that will support us when times get hard.

Here is my stand:
What I say I will do, I will do.
You can count on it.
You can count on me.
I walk my talk.

I prove my love
every time I open my mouth
and a promise escapes my lips and travels through your ears
into your heart.

A promise is sacred.

Song: "Sorry" Doesn't Work Here Anymore
(from the CD *Daring to Sing*)

When we break our agreements, we corrode our friendships. I wrote this song as a way of setting limits with a friend who consistently broke her promises but was always truly sorry. "I'm sorry" quit working, and our friendship disintegrated. Thinking that saying you are sorry is enough will get you into a heap of trouble. Letting someone get away with being sorry all the time but not confronting them to change their behavior will keep you in abusive relationships. Be a WarriorBabe or a WarriorDude! You are sacred space!

You tell me that you're sorry.
Now, that's all well and good.
You did something to me
that you didn't think you should.
But sorry's just the first step
on the road to recovery.
If you don't change what you're doing,
you
will be history.

Chorus:
Sorry doesn't work here,
sorry doesn't work here,
no, sorry doesn't work here anymore.

I don't think you're lying.
I know that you're sincere.

But your incessant "sorrys"
are burning holes in my ears.
You think saying sorry is all you ever have to do.
but if you don't change your behavior,
I will fire you.

Chorus

You tell me that you're struggling, and I can see that's true.
You're having trouble changing what you say and what you do.
But you've used up all my pity. You're just as strong as me.
If you keep making messes,
You'll live alone in your debris.

Sorry won't fix what's broken.
Sorrys irritate the sore.
You've used up all your sorrys;
I don't want to hear that anymore.

Cuz sorry doesn't work here.
Sorry doesn't work here.
Sorry doesn't work here.
Sorry doesn't work here.
Sorry.
I said sorry.
I said sorry, sorry, sorry, sorry, sorry.
Sorry doesn't work here anymore.

Murray Teaches Vicki to Make Requests

Living in integrity also means being clear about asking for what we want. As I've said, if we make an agreement, we must keep it. But if we want something from someone, integrity demands that we speak up. We need to make a specific, concrete request and then be ready to graciously accept "no" for an answer. Our communication is clear, our behavior is in alignment with our words and the resonance feels absolutely terrific.

"Is there a request hidden in there somewhere?"

This is what Murray said to me after I spent several minutes complaining about something he had done. I didn't know I was complaining, mind you. I thought I was displaying my knowledge of how right I was. Murray should change, based on my sharing. That was what I thought, anyway.

When Murray asked if I had a request, he immediately shifted me out of my complaining, problem-keeping mode and shifted me to a problem-solving mode.

"Oh," I said, rather meekly, "I do have a request."

Problem solved. Fight avoided. Murray is a genius again.

Requests are different from complaints. A complaint gives the illusion of power, but making a request is powerful. Complaints feel good like eating too much ice cream: it feels good at the time but then leads to an upset stomach. Complaining gives us a surge of sweet adrenaline but creates relationship hangovers and only helps us keep our problems.

Requests, on the other hand, are clean and clear. "Will you do this for me by this date?" is a question that can be answered with either a yes or no, or it can be renegotiated.

Example: Complaint: "Murray," (said with a slight whine), "this door sticks and has stuck for the six years we have lived here."

Murray, helping me to move out of complaining and into problem solving: "Quit your bitching."

Oops! That was Murray making the problem worse. Here is Murray problem solving: "Is there a request buried in there somewhere, darling, my most beloved?"

Me, returning to sanity: "Yes, dearest one. This door has been driving me nuts for years. I don't know why I never thought to ask you to fix it or to have you help me fix it myself. Would you fix it or help me fix it?"

"Sure, you gorgeous thing. When would you like to get together and fix this door?"

"How about right now, my knight in shining armor? You know how I love 'no waiting.'"

Instead of engaging in whining and name-calling, we have solved a problem, had a few laughs, and I have learned how to be more powerful in this world and how to use a new tool! Hooray!

Your Turn

Start paying attention to what comes out of your mouth. Be an observer of how often you make commitments with no plan of how you will follow through. If you catch yourself saying something you don't plan on doing, go ahead and say, "Wait a minute! I don't know for sure that I will call you. I might call you, but I'm not sure." Pay attention to how you feel when you start doing what you say you will do. I promise you, you will get hooked!

Any requests you need to make? Do you make statements instead of requests, hoping your beloved will guess at what you want? Are you open for feedback if you are doing this?

Chapter 10

Unpacking Our Personal Baggage

If we don't unpack our personal baggage, exposing it to the light, we will carry it with us our whole lives. And unexamined baggage tends to expand and rot, so we end up dragging our stinking pain into all of our relationships. Stuffing all of our unresolved grief takes up more and more of our energy and time and interferes with our ability to hear the subtleties of our Muse calling us to our greatness.

We never enter relationships with a clean slate. We are all packing old scars, grudges, losses, and humiliations. If we are clear about what we are dragging behind us into a relationship, we stand a better chance of forming an intimate bond. We can share who we really are and discover who we can become together because we aren't afraid to know what is true.

Story: It Will Never Happen to Me

Alcoholism thrives on both sides of my family. Because of this fact, I thought I already knew what I needed to know about addiction, knew more than any book could ever teach me because I had lived it.

When I was in my early thirties, my church offered a seminar on alcoholism, and because I was on familiar territory and I knew I would be surrounded by people I trusted, I gave myself permission to go to this seminar, thinking that a little more education couldn't do me any harm. I already knew everything they could tell me, but I might be of help to others in the class. So I thought.

This seminar was a life-changing event for me. The instructor began the discussion by asking us to describe an alcoholic. We listed traits: irresponsible, undependable, volatile. I spit out my comments with a long-simmering, rarely revealed anger. After we had made our list, the instructor told us that a university research study had done personality inventories on some college students. They followed these students over twenty years, and some of them became alcoholics. Here was the clincher for me: There were few similarities in the personalities of the students who became alcoholics. As alcoholics they resembled each other, which was why we could come up with a list so easily. But they didn't start out that way.

This was big news to me, the "expert" on alcoholism. Then the workshop leader told us about a book by Claudia Black titled *It Will Never Happen to Me*. That is when I knew I was in the middle of a miracle. I had been chanting this phrase to myself since I was ten years old: "This will never happen to me. My family is not going to be like this. I will be different."

My mother dropped out of high school. I had a college degree. My dad drank too much and got violent. I had married a man who hardly drank at all and was very gentle and loyal. I thought I had beaten the rap, escaped!

What I didn't know was that my excessive need to please, my knee-jerk accommodating, my deep feelings of unworthiness, and my fear of stepping out into the world in a big way—the shortcomings I desperately fought every day were all a part of the Adult Child of an Alcoholic (ACOA) syndrome. I was a part of a syndrome. It wasn't just my personal pathology after all! I didn't need to be ashamed of my feelings. I wasn't alone in the world anymore.

I felt as if I had won the lottery. I felt free and hopeful for the first time in my life. I thought I was doomed to feel an underlying anxiety—I thought I would be hiding out, pretending to feel comfortable, pretending to belong—for the rest of my life. "Hallelujah!!" I cheered to myself. "I'm a child of an alcoholic! Now I can get some help!"

I have been in recovery ever since, every day of my life, just like those who are addicted to substances. I was addicted to fear, and it has been a long, slow march toward courage and freedom for me.

I read books after this class and went to workshops, and I thought I was handling my recovery pretty well. I didn't need counseling. I could do it myself. This need to do it alone is part of growing up in a house where the unspoken rules are: Don't trust, Don't talk and Don't feel, but I hadn't understood that yet.

Then one day my headstrong four-year-old daughter, Katie, made me so mad I was headed across the room to "spank" her, at least, that is the story I was telling myself. My jaw was clenched, and I was full of a mysterious, hot rage. I was a pleaser. I never let myself feel anger, especially not this ugly, out-of-control madness that possessed me. I never showed this side of myself to any adult, but I was beginning to get into the habit of showing it to my beloved daughter.

As I stormed toward her bed, Katie was huddled up against her headboard, looking at me in terror, crying. The terror in her eyes brought me to my senses. "No!" I thought. "I will not pass this on to my children."

I left her room and called a counselor for the earliest appointment I could get. When I drove to his office a week or so later, I gripped the steering wheel so tightly my arms were numb to my shoulders. What was I so afraid of? I didn't know.

I'm not going to go into great detail about my therapy. What I do want to emphasize is that I was afraid to know the truth; I was afraid I might find out I was irredeemable, and that is why I had avoided counseling. This is shame, and it kills. What I found out pretty quickly in therapy was that I wasn't mad at my dad as much as I was mad at my sweet mother.

I had relied on her to protect me from him, and she hadn't. For many reasons, I had never given myself permission to feel angry with my poor, victimized mother. Anger, as I knew it, was physically and emotionally dangerous. Conflict should be avoided at all costs. If I got that mad at my mother, would she still love me? Would I still love her? I felt I would be risking too much to get mad at her. I would be risking too much to even let myself know how mad I was at her. So I felt anxious all the time instead.

But the truth was that I was mad, furious. Not facing the truth didn't make it go away; it made it leak out in all kinds of other ways—self-hate and fury at my daughter, just to name a few. I needed to face the truth in order to be free and joyful.

I've been on this road for twenty years now. I am a recovering coward, and I have to practice being brave every day. My world keeps getting bigger. I am more and more creative. I have worked with children all over the U.S. and in Europe about being brave, and I think that is an amazing miracle. The bartender's daughter who used to be too afraid to tell people what she wanted or to even know what she wanted, this girl now keynotes at conferences, makes CDs, and writes and performs musical comedy. I never would have guessed this life was waiting for me behind the truth curtain I was so afraid to pull back.

Everything has a cost: pleasing, pretending, absorbing abuse. Telling yourself the truth has a cost as well. You might lose friends, jobs, a marriage, or even a relationship with family members. But I am here to say the cost of unpacking our pain and fear is worth it.

Poem: My Killer Wail

This poem is almost twenty years old, and I think it illustrates why it is we avoid feeling our grief. We are afraid it might kill us or someone we love.

A wail waits in me.
Dormant,
so still, I often forget its gigantic mass.

But when I see a father tenderly caress a daughter,
or hear a kind word when I'm wounded,
the giant sorrow within me stirs.
I feel its immensity, and I am afraid.

How could so much sorrow live within me,
undetected by me,
and undetectable by those I love?
What will happen if I accidentally give it life?

If I let this growth within me,
this mass of murder, loose,
what will be left of me?
Will the wail swallow me?

This sleeping giant inside me feels too big to escape.
My eardrums are too weak,
my voice too frail
to scream this cosmic keen.

Hiding in Beige

I used to hide in beige. I wore beige shoes, beige print blouses, and polyester, beige pants. To wear a color, I felt, was to make too much of a statement, opening me to judgment and misinterpretation. I might stand out and collect unwanted attention. I might be obliterated. I knew I was much safer if I sought a beige invisibility.

I have learned, though, that none of us is invisible, as much as we might like to pretend that we are. My very "beigeness" gave me away to anyone with eyes to see. Just because we are unconscious about our motives and feelings doesn't mean they don't give us away every moment.

But in my thirties I mistakenly believed I could control the pain in my life. I hoped my clothes or my pleasing manners or my curtains that matched the pillows on my couch would help me blend in with people who seemed to know what they were doing. I thought I could fool people into thinking I belonged.

I am diligent, hardworking, and creative. When I put my mind to a goal, I accomplish it. So I looked around, imitated what I saw other women doing and finally succeeded in decorating my life with neat and tidy matching furniture and clothes. I felt that I had achieved the safest, most visible, most acceptable hiding place ever.

When I got completely neat and tidy—when my hair accessory matched my belt, which matched my shoes, which matched some color in my outfit, when the rugs and couches and table cloths and napkins and napkin rings and plates and linoleum all coordinated just right—when I got to this perfectly controlled spot, I hated the décor and the world my need for approval had created. I was hidden so completely in my neat and tidy surroundings that I had no room to breathe.

Other people weren't necessary in my perfectly decorated home. In fact, actual living bodies interfered with the perfection of my carefully chosen furnishings. Their clothes didn't match the decor or they messed up my prettily arranged domestic showcase.

Now, twenty years later, my goal isn't to hide who I am. It is to show up completely, unabashedly. My goal is to emerge into myself, to spread my wings, and to yodel my song into the mountains, to become so completely myself that when I die there is nothing left. As Bernard Shaw says, I will be all used up.

I have learned that being visible isn't nearly as dangerous as trying to stay invisible. I've learned I like the process of becoming visible much more than the illusionary safety of trying to control what I reveal. Being safe is really a way of being sorry. I show up anyway so I may as well show up in all my resplendent glory.

I am visible. And I can usually see you, no matter how hard you try to hide. I invite anyone who wants to play with me to show up, as is, and we will create our party together. I have found this to be more fun than hiding in beige.

Poem: Just an Electric Skillet

I had no idea I was a perfectionist until I was in my late thirties. To be a perfectionist, I thought a person had to actually achieve some perfection, and I knew that I never even came close. But that is exactly what a perfectionist is: someone who is obsessed with their flaws. Perfectionists aren't really perfectionists; the are "mistakeists;" They can see only what is wrong with the picture, never fully enjoying anything they have created because they are living inside its imperfections.

I've been told the Navahos deliberately include a flaw in their blankets because they know they are only human and don't want to offend Great Spirit by seeking perfection. I don't know if this is true, but the thought of intentionally keeping an error, holding an error as sacred, as a gift of humility—well, I like this idea a lot. It comforts me and helps me surrender a bit of my perfectionism whenever I am lucky enough to uncover it. (I can never surrender it all because if I tried to surrender all of my perfectionism, I would be stuck in perfectionism again.)

This poem captures a rather mundane moment in my life as I was standing at my kitchen sink cleaning the bottom of an electric skillet. I include it here as part of unpacking my personal baggage because I think my suffering over not being able to get the bottom of this skillet clean reveals how perfectionism weaves its way into our everyday lives, stealing our joy.

You are standing at the sink washing dishes,
gazing out the window into your postage-stamp-sized backyard.
You are thirty-one, married, with two small, healthy children.
You are a teacher; your husband is a teacher.
You have everything you ever dreamed of having.

But the bottom of the used electric skillet you bought at Goodwill
    haunts you.
If only you could get it to shine,
maybe your life would shine.
Maybe you would have at last done it right.
Maybe you would be able to see,
in the reflection of the scoured frying pan,
a validation for your life,
a validation for the choices you have made.

You feel bullied by the bottom of this electric skillet,
and you are ashamed of being so weak.
You are sure you will never tell anyone about this moment.

The bottoms of all your other pots must shine too,
every bit of baked-on food removed.
They must glow like new,
preferably hanging from a rack over the stove,
their copper bottoms shining,
reflecting to the world your right to breathe.

The view from the window above the sink also accuses you.
Where there were blackberry vines only a year ago,
flowers now grow.
You dug out those prickly vines
the summer before your son was born,
your body bloated by the nine-pound boy you were carrying.
Standing on swollen feet,
wearing silly little girl maternity clothes,
you chopped and piled and dug,
sweat dripped into your eyes.

The blackberry vines used to cover your fence.
Now, after all of your work,
you see that the fence sags.
You can see with clarity,
through your kitchen window that needs washing,
the flower beds your husband so painstakingly double dug.
But the flowers are all wrong, you think,
just rows of dahlias and zinnias.
There is no art in it,
just stupid color.

"How can anyone wreck a flower garden?" you wonder.
You aren't sure how this could be done,
but you are sure you have done it.
You can't even plant a flower garden correctly.

And besides that, the yard is still uneven, small.
The ground, rough and sloping.
The cement on the patio is cracked.

"You are a professional," you think, "married to a professional.
Why are you living like losers?"

Maybe if the bottom of the frying pan is shiny enough,
the past will crumble with the crud
as it swirls down the drain.

Then you see the scratches on your stainless steel sink,
The permanent scratches that you did not even make,
and you know it is hopeless.
You know for sure you are too scratched,
too covered in decades of grime.
You will never shine again.

Poem: If It's Not Personal . . .

Once we own our personal baggage, magic can happen. We can be free of the tyranny of taking everything personally: rejection, abandonment, criticism. When it is not personal, when our right to inhabit the planet is not at stake, then we can play with life as a metaphor, as a dream. We can let life be our teacher instead of our jailer.

If it's not personal,
these unreturned phone calls from friends,
these unreciprocated invitations,
this lack of feedback—
all this seeming rejection—
if it's not personal
then I don't have to make any final decisions
about my value as a human being
and the limits of what's possible for me.

If my pain is not personal,
then my lower-middle-class alcoholic upbringing
hasn't put me in a bubble that suffocates my dreams.
My future is mine to create,
and the best may still be yet to come.

If this doubt and fear isn't my personal pathology,
then I don't have to worry about any pattern repeating endlessly
for the rest of my life.
If it's not personal,
then this too shall pass.
The seven years of drought will be replaced by seven years of bounty.

If it's not personal,
then it's not personal.
It's not stuck to my personality.
I don't have to die to escape it.

If it's not personal,
then it isn't following me,
stalking me,
like some comet's tail
or my shadow,
Jungian or solar.

If it's not personal,
then I can stay alive
instead of drowning in the Slough of Despair.
I will be ready when the ship comes,
or the fishing boat,
or the yacht,
or when I find shore
and shelter
and coconuts to eat and drink.

If it's not personal,
then all I have to do is survive
with as much joy as I can muster,
or, rather,
as much joy as I can let curl around my feet
or purr into my ear.

If it's not personal,
then what am I supposed to learn from this ache in my belly?
Aye, there's the rub.
Once I start looking for "supposed to's"
I am trapped again in taking it personally.

So, if I don't take my pain and doubt personally,
what is my next step?

I will get back to basics.
I will live one day at a time.
I will ask myself how I feel and what I want.
I will take a breath and take the next step right in front of me.
I will pay attention to the inklings and nudges I am feeling.

I surrender now to this mysterious vortex of doubt.
I let the howling swirl take me where it will—
perhaps into a shaman's death,
again,
and yet again.

Amen.

Story: How Our Inner Baby Tyrannosaurus Wrecks Love

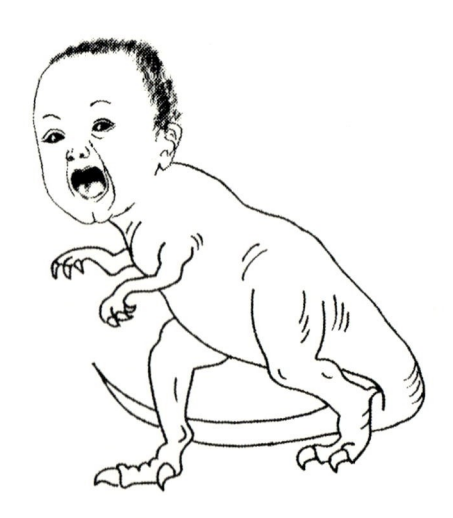

Illustration by Bekki Levien

When Murray and I first got together and fell madly in love, I felt connected and in partnership as I never had before. Consequently, I felt safe enough, loved enough, for all my demons to emerge. One of my most traumatic demons was my baby hunger.

When babies are hungry, they cry. If they don't get fed, they scream. If they scream long enough, they get hysterical, and then even food won't comfort them. We all have a baby inside us who gets hungry and needy. We may not be hungry for food; we may be hungry for love and comfort, for complete safety. What baby wants, that baby demands, one hundred percent. And if that baby can't crawl back into the safety of the womb, it wants to be comforted by what one of my therapists referred to as The Cosmic Teat.

When you are forty, society frowns on nursing, so I drink lattes instead. That's on my good days. On my bad days, the baby commandeers the driver's seat of my behavior. The Dinosaur part of my brain is making decisions and demands. Remember how small the brain of a dinosaur is? Remember how big their bodies are? Is it any wonder that when we let our voracious baby hunger run our giant adult body we get ourselves into big trouble?

When our baby-hunger takes over, and our body still looks like an adult, bad things happen: relationships get ruined, people get trashed. The tyrannosaurus/baby wrecks what it wants most: love.

Some people with character disorders live out their whole lives as tyrannosaurus wreckers. You probably know some. They are never happy. It's always someone else's fault and everyone else is selfish (especially you). They have a hole inside them that keeps them from becoming whole. The more they get fed, the hungrier they become.

I have a little hole inside me where love seeps out. It's patched most of the time, but sometimes it is open—and that which I need most, leaks out of me. It's my job at those times to recognize the leak and to do whatever I can to repair it.

My Baby Tyrannosaurus in Action

One morning, fairly early in our love-at-first-sight relationship, I walked Murray to work. I felt completely miserable, at war with myself. Murray had called me his old girlfriend's name three times, once at a, well, very inopportune moment.

Normally, I am not a jealous person. I have been blessed with men in my life who adore me. I am used to being "the one." (No brag, just fact.). I am very lucky, considering my childhood, that I drew good, caring men into my life. I just lucked out on this one, no doubt about it.

Even though Murray was smitten, he was holding back; I could feel it. Now he will tell you he was still stuck in "bigger, better deal" mentality. Why should he give himself completely to this woman who was four years older than he? Could he get someone prettier? A trophy wife, maybe?

I am absolutely sure that my being blind did not enter into Murray's hesitance to commit. If it had, I don't think I would have stayed with him. When we first started dating, he was a little daunted by my two teen-aged children, as he had no children of his own. But I don't think this was his psychic stumbling block either. I think he was held captive in the killer cultural spell of big breast, youthful beauty.

This alone wouldn't have been enough to rattle me so completely. But when he called me his old girlfriend's name while I was in the beginning stages of menopausal hormonal madness, I transformed into the baby tyrannosaurus wrecks.

When I confessed my anger and jealousy, feeling ugly and unforgivable, Murray was very understanding. He listened calmly as I ranted and then mentioned something about the gift for me in my struggle; I looked over at him and seriously considered biting him somewhere with lots of sensitive nerve endings. Gift? What gift? I felt hopeless, ugly, alone, and stuck.

We walked to the hospital where he worked as an occupational therapist on the psychiatric ward, got some coffee, and talked some more. I admitted I wanted him to change his behavior; that I thought if only he changed his behavior, all would be well for me. I would be happy. My happiness was up to him.

Now I knew that wasn't true. I knew I could change my response and take responsibility for my own happiness, but I just couldn't see how to get there. When Murray leaned over, tenderly took my hand, and said he had absolute faith in my ability to get through this, to come out the other side, I thought, "What, are you completely nuts?"

The night before this discussion I had the worst nightmare I can remember. I can't fully describe the horror I felt in the dream. Everything I thought I knew was in question. The dream ended with me pulling out a knife and eviscerating Murray, leaving his entrails dangling. The horror of his insides spilling out all over our white sheets woke me up hollering, moaning.

Murray woke up, turned over, and held me while I shook. I told him of my dream. My insecurities with him had been translated into my fear of what I perceived as his lack of desire for me. I desperately needed to be held, and Murray held me for a while, and then fell back to sleep while I was still shaking. (Note to men: Falling asleep when your lover is still crying is a bad idea.)

What kind of a man could fall asleep at such a moment? I wondered. How could he really love me, know that I was suffering, and fall asleep? I woke Murray up, and asked him to stay awake until I was calm, but I was deeply hurt that I had to ask. All women know this one: If I have to ask, it doesn't count. These thoughts tortured me when I woke up, which was why I felt so miserable that morning with Murray.

When my dear friend from graduate school, Sadie, called to tell me she would pick me up at three for our previously planned trip to the beach, I cried. "I won't be any fun!" I wailed. She assured me that it would be okay. I didn't have to be fun all of the time. "Sure," I thought, "I am this insane Bitch from the North, driving sweet Murray away from me, and now I will be this out-of-control raving lunatic and will ruin one of my closest friendships.

I had returned from walking Murray to work full of pain. In desperation, I spent the whole day on the couch listening to Marianne Williamson, praying for a miracle. Then Sadie came to pick me up for our trip to the beach.

After about fifteen minutes in the car, I was laughing. Sadie helped me see I was smack dab in the middle of a Core Issue: baby belly hunger, or what I have been calling our inner baby tyrannosaurus wrecks. I had known this neediness in my life plenty of times, but I had always felt ashamed. I tried to put a sack over this screaming, needy baby. I wanted to tie her up and drown her. I had never learned to sit with her, much less to love her.

That was my work for the next two days: I sat with my voracious, needy girl baby. Everything in me wanted to run. I felt as if I were detoxing. I told Sadie if there had been a pill in front of me that would have taken away the pain, I would have taken it first and asked questions later—questions such as: would this cause me to eat my children's livers right out of their bodies? Since I had no such pill, the closest thing I could think of was to eat chocolate.

We went to a movie, and I bought a box of Raisinettes and ate the whole thing. The first third of the box tasted great. The second third tasted okay. The last third didn't taste good, and when I finished the box, I felt horrible. But I felt great. I had been completely clear about what I had been doing. My observer self was back. I was no longer drowning in this violent sea of need.

Murray joined Sadie and me for our second night at the beach, and it was one of the sweetest times of my life. The three of us frolicked on the beach, Murray teaching us Aikido, becoming this magnificent being in the sand. We ate mangoes, laughed, and thoroughly enjoyed being alive.

Not long after that dance with madness, I got on hormones. My doctor was wise enough to listen to me and to not need to look at some hormonal number. Within two days my affable, sane disposition returned. I love hormone replacement therapy!

I don't regret my journey into temporary insanity. For one thing, I got a great song out of it: "Menopause". (Murray was right after all; there was a gift in this for me.) Also, I realized it is good for me to let go of control and ask for help. Even more important, I realized that I could be ugly and still be surrounded by people who could tolerate my messiness and love me anyway. I was able to experience yet another lesson in humility, lessons I don't ask for consciously, but lessons I am especially grateful for—once they are over, that is.

Song: Menopause!

Lyrics by Vicki Hannah Lein
Melody by Vicki Hannah Lein & Suzannah Doyle
(from the CD *Daring to Sing*)

I have had women come up to me after hearing this song with tears in their eyes. "I was crazy for two years!" one woman told me. "No one took me seriously, and it was the worst period of my life."
Go, WarriorBabe!

Do you feel little bugs crawling on your body?
Do you want to disembowel your mate?
Then you'd better deal with being perimenopausal
before it's way too late.
Your symptoms may start in your early forties
from mild to completely insane.
It's not just your personal pathology;
this beast you really must tame.

Chorus:
Wrap your claws around menopause
because it's gonna happen to you.
Wrap your claws around menopause,
or it will wrap its claws around you!

Estrogen, progesterone, too,
in a pill, patch, or a cream—
Anything to balance your mood
to keep you from wanting to scream!
You can call a hot flash a power surge,
but you still get wet.
No matter how many layers you peel off your back,
you're going to sweat, and sweat, and sweat!

Chorus

The doctor says your mood might alter a bit,
but what the hell does he know?
You swing from wanting to cry until your guts stream out
to tearing the meat from his bones!
Your husband might be very understanding.

He might even think you're still cute.
But before he thinks about giving advice,
he'd better just stay mute.

Chorus

Oh, calm down now.
You're becoming histrionic!
It can't be all that bad.
So sometimes you feel a little bit crabby,
and sometimes you feel a little sad.
It's just as simple as mind over matter.
Think of something pleasant, like dessert!
You women make such a big deal out of nothing.
You cry when you're not even hurt!

Wrap your claws around men—then pause.
His life's not worth a plug nickel now.
Wrap your claws around men, then pause.
His liver will look good on my wall.

We're at the mercy of our hormones.
This is just a scientific fact.
No matter how many encounter groups we go to,
when our hormones are low,
all our neurosis will show!
So . . .

Wrap your claws around menopause.
It's biology, a matter of fate.
Wrap your claws around menopause.
Don't linger! Start now! Don't wait!

Poem: Little Girl in Gray

When I am least expecting it, a piece of my personal baggage, a piece I am sure I have completely unpacked, mysteriously reappears. Sometimes I fall over my unhealed wounds before I am aware I'm feeling that old pain again. When this happens, I try to be like Dr. John Nash in the movie A Beautiful Mind; I try to have a "diet of the mind." My demons still lurk and beckon, and I see and hear them, but more often than not I turn and say, "Ptooie! I spit on you!" or "Maybe so, but I am going on even if you are right."

"Little Girl in Gray" is my personal declaration of independence from a shame buried deep in my bones. I came by my story of being deeply alone and unlovable honestly enough, as I have shared in this chapter, but it has been a self-fulfilling prophesy for me. My feelings of disconnection created more disconnection in my life. By telling myself the truth at last, the whole truth of my secret neediness, I have set myself free.

I am a little girl
dressed in gray
standing by a wall.

I am available to anyone who might love me,
available to all the families and parties I see swirling in front of me.

I am a beckoning green light for everyone,
whether that person is good for me or not.
I stand desperate to be loved.
I will fix myself anyway you want
if you will only love me.

Because I am so easily won,
you don't want me.
You smell a rat.
If I were worthwhile,
precious,
you would have to overcome some obstacles,
some resistance,
to have me.

Like the princess trapped in a tower,
you,
my prince,
would have to battle dragons to have me.

Or,
like gold,
I would be buried under rock,
hidden and rare.

But I am as rare as sunlight in southern California.
I am ubiquitous.
You may enjoy me,
but you don't need to pay any special attention to me,
because if I go away,
I will be back before you have missed me.

WOMAN WITH A VOICE

Even my good friends wander off from my table at the summer festival
with that searching look in their eyes,
moving away from me
toward the real party,
which is obviously not me.

I believe that all the parties are outside of me.
I believe that,
like the Velveteen Rabbit,
I am not quite real until somebody loves me,
touches me,
includes me.

I will be this little girl for more than fifty years.
For more than fifty years,
I will fool some people into thinking that I am the party.
I will get myself included,
pretending that I am not the little girl in gray,
standing by the wall waiting, available.
But everyone will know,
through some invisible, secret, needy smell,
obvious to everyone except me,
that I am really an Outsider,
too Available,
too Easy.

Then one miraculous day
the little girl in gray inside me
left her place at the wall.
She took off her gray dress
and danced naked in the grass.
She grew into a woman,
ripe and mature,

and she found that she was,
in fact,
her own party;
that she had been her own party all along.

She finally understood the Cosmic Joke,
that everything she had been searching for,
longing for,
aching for,
was inside her all the time.

She learned
there really is no place like home
and that she is Home.

Now she delights in her solitude,
enjoys bringing a selected few into her joyful sanctuary.
She feels complete,
content,
grateful,
and fully, deeply alive.

She cuddles the little girl dressed in gray on her lap,
while sitting in her wicker armchair
on her Mexican-tiled deck,
listening to the fountain she helped build.
She watches her beloved spouse and partner
tend to the watering of his hummingbird garden,
which so far has drawn no hummingbirds.

She does this as she types this poem
and is no longer always easily available,
no longer a never-ending green light to all who might love her.

She is still accessible,
but now she is also happy,
and,
not incidentally,
free,
truly free,
for the first time in her life.

Your Turn

What baggage are you bringing into your relationships, both personal and professional? What were the rules of your family of origin, spoken and unspoken? Who can you talk to? What books will you read to help you get clearer about what your issues are? What problems do you not want to repeat? Are you being stubborn about getting help for some biochemical or emotional issue? Who can you talk to about all this right now?

Chapter 11

Taking on Shame and Jealousy

In the next two chapters I hope to shed some light on those emotions that can most easily interfere with our happiness and our connection to our genius and hope: shame, jealousy, and grief.

These emotions are part of our human landscape. We don't need to be afraid of them, for without sadness and loss, we would be unable to appreciate our joys. That is just how we are built. The deeper we are able to go into the shadows, the higher we can fly in our brilliance. Avoiding our problems only feeds them, allowing them to outgrow our avoidance and become septic.

Shame: The Mistake that Defines Us

I start with the most potentially destructive, pervasive emotion on our palette: shame. Most of our defensiveness and much of our aggression toward ourselves and others is caused by our shame. Shame wants to obliterate us because we have no right to occupy space on the planet. You might be feeling shame's insidious, stinging tentacles starting to curl around you as you read about its power. Never underestimate the power of shame to steal your happiness!

John Bradshaw, in his book *Healing the Shame That Binds You*, turns the spotlight on shame, describing it as the feeling that you haven't made a mistake, but that you are a mistake. Shame is the feeling that we ought to be obliterated. We have fooled people into loving us, but, the truth is, we are unlovable and despicable at our core.

When we feel shame it's like we are sitting in a box and we fart. We think the whole world smells our stink. In order to release ourselves from our shame, we need to lift off the lid of our box and let people see us. When we do this we realize that our imperfections may smell, but they aren't stinking up the whole world. Everyone farts, after all. It's not such a big deal.

Shame feels so horrible we don't even want to admit we are feeling it. We feel ashamed of our shame, and that is the problem. When we are ashamed of our shame, we will not even let ourselves know we are feeling it. We will act it out by shaming others or by continuing a constant stream of inner invective that numbs our possibilities. We will all feel shame, and if we are not ashamed of our shame, we will be able to pull back the curtain, admit it, get curious about it, and heal.

It is shame that won't let you consider a new idea, the thought that you might be able to sing, for example. Shame tells you it is just not possible. Do not even think about it. Shame claims to be a big "T" Truth. It is contemptuous and arrogant, never doubting the absolute finality of its opinion.

Shame is the Dinosaur Voice in us that squelches an idea before it has had time to breathe. Our inner Dinosaur Voice collects evidence from other people, compares us unfavorably with everyone, and is always pointing directly at our fear that no one who really knew us would be able to stand the stench.

We pass our shame on to others when we say things such as:

"You mean you don't know how to spell . . . ?"

"You've never been to Disneyland?"

"After all your years as a . . . , you don't know how to . . . ?"

"You can't carry a tune in a bucket!"

"Keep your day job!"

We can pass on our shame with a dismissive tone of voice or gesture. We can pass on our shame by "shushing" others; this happens to little girls all the time. They are taught they are "too much" and should "settle down." Boys are shamed out of their feelings, their dancing, their sweet vulnerabilities.

If you object when you notice shaming behavior, the chances are you will be shamed even more. You might have someone respond to you by saying: "Can't you take a joke?" or "My, aren't you high and mighty?" You will know you have been shamed when you feel shame. It doesn't mean the other person necessarily meant to shame you, but it is important to know when you feel shame and to know what you might do when you feel it.

Here are some ideas that might help you deal with your shame:

- Say, "I'm feeling ashamed right now."
- Give yourself some time to think. Don't do anything for a few minutes, hours, or days.
- Remember that everyone feels shame; there is no shame in feeling shame.
- Trust your gut. Your shame will want you to believe you are making it up, blowing everything out of proportion. Maybe so, but don't shame yourself for whatever you feel.
- Pat yourself on the back when you catch your shame. "Aha! Got you!" will give you courage, even as you are suffering under shame's dominion.
- Remember that the person who is shaming you has been shamed himself. Toddlers don't shame others unless they have been taught to shame.
- Remember that you will get better at exposing your shame. Your Dinosaur Voice wants you to feel overwhelmed and to give up. "Well, you noticed me this time," it might say, "but you have just touched the tip of the iceberg! If you take this on you will be crushed, obliterated."
- Remember that the Dinosaur Voice can assume an infinite number of disguises. One of my shame voices tells me that I shouldn't "bother" anyone. That sounds reasonable, but my Dinosaur Voice would have me not bothering people by not breathing any of "their" oxygen. It would have me shrink and shrink until I am so small no one will notice me. This Voice wants me to believe that there is a limited amount of happiness in the world and that I am stealing from someone else if I am happy, energetic, brilliant, or creative. Shame tells me I should just stop already!

Shame makes losers of us all. No one benefits when we let our shame dominate our lives. With faith and practice we can learn to discriminate between the voices that call us to our glory ("That would be a brave thing to do!") and the voices that obliterate our joy.

If we don't take the challenge of facing our shame head-on, we will pass our shame on to our friends, lovers, and children. We will do this by baking guilt-filled cookies and by criticizing people when we are jealous of them instead of owning our jealousy. We will let our children's exuberance trigger our fears and we will stick pins in their joy balloons.

We will have trouble encouraging anyone to get out of a box that is bigger than ours; we will be the crabs pulling the escaping crabs back into the bucket. We will add to the world's misery and our own, one crummy thought at a time.

But if we take shame head on, great joy and freedom await us! It is a never-ending choice, every day, all day. Uncovering our shame means being alive, being present, and it is the only road to true intimacy.

Poem: The Massacre of Magic

To set ourselves free from the suffocating force of shame, we must learn to lean into it. We must be willing to let our shame speak its most hateful accusations. We must run to face the monster that wants to massacre our magic.

Surrender to the shame that wrenches your muscles
and threatens to choke your bowels.
Surrender to your black stomach,
full of bile and acid.
Surrender to the horror
and your most nauseating dread.
Let yourself flow into slimy darkness,
into a claustrophobic, airless tunnel.

Maybe you will finally have to know
that you don't belong here
in the family of man.
Maybe you will finally know
for sure
that you are a mistake—
only now being discovered
and needing to be wiped out.

But you surrender
because your memory is alive with other disasters
transformed,
transmuted,
transported.

You remember you have fallen in love with truth,
a mild ecstasy.
You remember you trust truth
even more than you believe criticism.
You have broken into pieces and have been made whole again.
You remember your magic has been massacred before
only to be reborn—
resilient,
fresh,
and alive.

You trust this gnawing in the pit of your stomach now,
trust the pain,
the dreaded dread.
You know that,
like Alice,
you can let yourself flow down the hole into nothingness.
You are ready to change your attitudes and beliefs at depth
every moment.

This kick in the stomach is an invitation to be free.
You know you will laugh sometime,
maybe soon,
but probably not as soon as you would like.
You know you may be finished with this wrestling
before this wrestling is finished with you.

"Oh, well," you say,
as you pitch backward into the blackness,
into your only hope of redemption.

Poem: Anguish on Stage

As I mentioned in the introduction, on my fiftieth birthday I made a commitment to myself as a singer. Six months later I tried out for an outrageous musical, Six Women with Brain Death or Expiring Minds Want to Know. *I took a stand for myself as a singer even though I had plenty of Dinosaur talk inside my head about how I didn't have a strong voice. I "knew" I couldn't sing harmony. I "knew" my voice was not worthy of being taken seriously. I decided I didn't care how "good" or "bad" my voice was. I decided I would honor the singing beauty in me and let go of the outcome.*

The musical pushed me to my limits. We often sang six-part harmony, and I had to learn everything by ear. I worked hard because I did not want to hold the cast back. I was, I hope, touchingly earnest. I might have been obnoxious as well.

One night at rehearsal a cast member said something to me that triggered my shame. She did not do anything wrong. This poem is not about her; it is about me. Our shame will get stimulated. The question is: what can we do when our shame is triggered? This is what I did.

"We all know you can't see."

We were on stage rehearsing for a musical
just last night.
She told me that I was blocking her from the view of the audience.
"I can't see," I said, with my tongue partially in my cheek,
trying to explain why I might have been crowding her.
"We all know you can't see," she responded.

Was she displaying her terrific, ironic sense of humor?
Or was she letting me know of her smoldering resentment?
Have I been a "blind princess,"
wanting special favors and attention?
Have I been driving her crazy since we started rehearsing six weeks
 ago?

Her words entered my body and opened a hole in me.
Or, rather,
they were able to enter an ancient, suffocating emptiness in me,
so familiar.
I used to live in that emptiness.

Before she spoke those words to me,
I was happy, exhilarated, even,
so grateful to be back on stage for the first time in fifteen years,
the first time since I lost my central vision.

Then those words were spoken.
Suddenly
a cavern opened up and devoured my joy,
my hope,
and my courage.

Shame consumed me,
stole all my oxygen,
shut down my brain,
and sent my heart racing,
trying to keep my frail existence ahead of the slathering beast chasing me.

So now the work of transforming my pain into strength begins.
Now I start searching for the magic in this adversity.
Now I must remember what I have learned on this journey.
I must remember to get interested, not defensive.
I must remember to walk straight into a difficult conversation.
And I must remember to do this as soon as possible.

I will ask her at tonight's rehearsal:
"Were you irritated with me last night?"
I will remember to listen to whatever she says.
I will remember to keep my heart open.

Maybe her irritation is just the story my shame wants me to believe.
Maybe she likes me and feels so comfortable
that she feels safe to enter the territory of "blind jokes."
If so, she stumbled into a deep wound,
a breath-sucking fear:
I worry
that in my quest to survive and thrive,
I will step on someone's toes.
I worry
that I have asked too much.
I worry that I have paid too little attention to other people's needs.

Maybe I have been selfish.
Even worse,
maybe I have been inviting pity all along,
secretly,
while trying to appear to be a valiant warrior.

Maybe her vision for that sort of corruption is acute.
Maybe she has caught me,
and if that is true, fine,
for I want to get "caught."
I have fallen in love with truth,
and I know that truth will eventually set me free.
Or maybe this is all her stuff.

Maybe my bravery
or my weakness
or my need for help
or my asking for help
or my cheerfulness
or my memory
(I had all my lines for the play memorized first)
—maybe all or some of these things drive her nuts.

Maybe my striving to pull my weight,
to learn the songs early because I knew I would miss a week of rehearsals—
maybe this was misunderstood as my wanting to shame others.
Maybe she was shamed.

And if it is her stuff,
her agony leaking out,
that doesn't matter either.
I am not responsible for her pain,
and I'm sure she came by her pain honestly,
as we all have.

I know how to meet her rage with compassion,
and I can do what I need to do to protect myself from any further
"acid spills."

This is what my head says.
My body, though, is still entangled in the anguish.

What a word! Anguish.
It's like wringing out your soul
with hands lacerated by third degree burns,
the crispy skin feeling like daggers
in my most vulnerable flesh.

Could I possibly share my anguish with her?
Could she know what it is like for me
to not be able to read or drive
or see my children's faces?
Could I ever communicate to her,
or to anyone,
what the loss of color means to me?
If I let myself feel the losses I suffer in just one day,
I would collapse.

Is it her wonderful imagination,
her ability to empathize with my experience,
that irritates her?
Is she angry because I make her feel emotions she has long denied?
Is she harboring some ancient, giant, sleeping grief
that my loss brings to life in her,
something ugly,
terrifying even,
like a semi-decayed corpse?

I don't know, and it doesn't matter.
My job today is to have mercy
for myself,
for her,
for all of us "lost souls crying out in the darkness."

I will recover.
I will stand in my commitment to love, compassion, and truth.
I will learn more about myself,
be less vulnerable to this kidney punch to my spirit.

This transformation will take time,
and I will give myself time,
time to gently heal,
time to gently refill the coffers
of my faith
and my belief in my goodness.

I will kindly give myself time to restore my sparkle.

Epilogue: The next day I fulfilled my promise to myself. I waited for a quiet moment when we were alone backstage and asked, "Did I do something to irritate you yesterday?" She looked at me with shock.
"When?" she asked.

I didn't want to make it a big deal, more tangled and difficult to get out of, so I said, "Oh, I don't know. I just had the feeling I had irritated you yesterday and I wanted to make sure I didn't owe you an apology for something."

"No, we are fine," she said and walked quickly away.

For the rest of rehearsals and during the entire run of the show, she couldn't have been sweeter to me. Did I "catch" her being "bad" and that shaped her up? Was it all in my head from beginning to end? It really doesn't matter. What mattered to me was that I had the courage to do something to take away the unhappy feeling in my belly without making anyone wrong.

Jealousy: Shame's Green-Eyed Partner

I lost a dear friend once, one of those daily friends who is up-to-date on every issue in your life. She made the decision to move away, and then she started acting strangely: She started bossing me around, telling me to do things I already knew how to do, telling me, unbidden, that my roof color did not match my house color. (It does.)

I could not figure out what was going on. She had just started painting again after years of neglect, and her genius was pouring out. She was a fabulous painter and is one of the most talented people I have ever known.

But she was ambivalent about her art streaming out of her. What I did not know then that I know now, is: "Our deepest fear is not that we are inadequate. Our deepest fear is that we are powerful beyond measure" (Marianne Williamson, *A Return to Love*). My friend was terrified of her genius and started backing away from it.

I, on the other hand, was stepping fully into my creativity, traveling nationally, giving workshops, and making my dreams come true. Her help had been essential for my success. And although I had expressed my gratitude many times, something between us wasn't quite right. Even so, her new, critical behavior baffled me.

Could it be, that with all of her talent and success, she was jealous of me? Couldn't be. Here I was—legally blind, recently divorced and remarried, losing my job—what was there to be jealous about? I knew my insecurities inside out, but she knew them, too! She had seen my struggle, known all of my doubts—how could she look at the end product and deny me all my courageous acts of perseverance?

When I offered the suggestion that perhaps she was jealous of me and that's why she had gotten so critical and controlling, she blew up. "I am NOT JEALOUS OF YOU!" she almost screamed in my face. She is a therapist, and she knows darn well that protesting too much is a sure sign that you fear something is true. But she just could not see this. She could not entertain the idea, even for a moment, that perhaps she was jealous of my successes. Thus ended our friendship. Where could we have gone from here? She moved away, and, after a few phone calls and e-mails, our friendship dropped off the planet.

It was not her jealousy that destroyed our friendship, but rather her shame about the possibility that she was jealous. This is why we need to shine the light on shame and then on jealousy. They are corrosive emotions that can destroy even the strongest relationships, but only if we are afraid of them.

Your Turn

Do you remember any moments in which you felt shame, moments when you wanted to put a paper bag over your head or to just dissolve into nothingness? Confess them to someone, shine the light on these "terrible" things you have done, and I guarantee you that the person listening will not be as horrified as you are. This is practicing revealing shame instead of being ashamed of it. Go ahead; let it all hang out.

Fess up! Of whom are you jealous? Who do you think "has it made" or has an easier job than you do and gets the credit you think you deserve. (Oh, these are nasty feelings! No wonder we don't want to admit them to ourselves.) Whom do you think might be jealous of you, but is afraid to admit it?

Chapter 12

Loving Our Bodies "As Is"

When women look in the mirror at our bodies, we are invited to tell ourselves nasty stories about how unattractive we are. This makes us great consumers of beauty products, but steals the joy from our lives. Our corporate culture invites women, especially, to feel enormous body shame. It is only in industrialized countries, those with advertising, that eating disorders even exist. I have seen girls as young as seven on "diets," and sororities are often epidemic with women who are literally dying to be thin. Very few women, even those touted to be among the most beautiful in the world, truly love their bodies.

Men don't fare much better. They are encouraged to believe they don't have the right "male stuff," be it hair or penis girth. (Americans, with 4% of the world's population consume 40% of the Viagra produced.) While I have great compassion for men, since I am a woman, this chapter will focus on what it is like to be a woman trying to love herself in this culture.

In her book *Dance of Intimacy*, Harriet Learner tells of a woman who avoided making love with her husband when she was on her back. She believed her breasts were too big and drooped when she was in this position. She was sure her husband found her disgusting. When she was finally persuaded to share her fears, her husband told her he loved her breasts exactly as they were. He found them beautiful in the position that embarrassed her most. Her fear of being authentic with her husband was a huge barrier between them.

Accepting our bodies "as is" is an important step toward being able to love anyone else. Don't kid yourself into thinking your hypercritical obsession with the imperfection of your body does not leak out onto other people, including your children. When we hate anything, especially ourselves and our precious bodies, we invite self-doubt into our world and the world of those we love. Loving our bodies "as is" helps us love others as they are. So let's start now, shall we?

Poem: Body Confessions

I once led a workshop at a wellness conference titled "Dare to Love Your Body As Is." We had a great time singing, dancing, twirling boas and just generally being outrageous.

One woman shared that she had weighed more than her first husband, and, even though this bothered her, her husband assured her it was no problem for him—no problem until he divorced her, after 31 years of marriage, for a thirty-year-old. Then he informed her that her weight had always been a problem for him.

Now she was remarried and had lost 31 pounds for her wedding, but then had gained it all back. She was worried her new husband might be lying to her as her first husband did.

"I wrote a poem about a similar situation," I said. "Did I include it in the packet?" Yes, by golly, (by Muse) it was there. "Would you read it for us?" I asked.

The woman began to read and we all began to cry. This was the first time I had heard this poem in public, I almost had not included it in the handouts (Who puts a poem that revealing in a handout, for crying out loud?!) Our tears united us and when several women made guttural noises of agreement as the woman read the poem, I felt I had made sisters for life.

I'm afraid.
I'm afraid to wear sleeveless vests anymore,
afraid that my arms are too round now,
afraid that my skin is too blotchy.

I'm afraid people will look at my bare arms and think,
"She should have stopped wearing sleeveless vests long ago.
Doesn't she know how ridiculous she looks?
How embarrassing for her."

I'm afraid that the bulginess on my legs
will repel my husband,
that when he runs his hand down my thigh, he is being kind.
He loves me, and he knows I love being touched,

but I am afraid there is a revulsion growing in him
that he won't be able to hide.
Someday,
my body,
my being,
will revolt him.
Of this, I am very afraid.

I'm afraid my breasts,
no longer perky but full of a heaviness from hormonal weight gain,
will become flaccid,
and sag,
and that the sagging will disgust
my husband
and me.

I'm afraid these wrinkles and dark circles on my face,
the soft translucent skin below my eyes,
will become a hideous mask,
and that no one will be able to see the essence of me,
the vibrant, three-year-old Vicki that still lives in me.

I'm afraid to let my gray hair grow out.
I'm afraid my striking silver hair
will propel me into a decade I'm not ready to inhabit yet.
I'm afraid my gray hair will end my desirability.
I'm afraid I will be an old woman and therefore discounted,
an embarrassing, smelly leftover.

I'm afraid that as I age
and as my belly sags from one side of the bed to the other as I turn
that I will secretly hate myself,
no matter what I say out loud
to myself or to others.

I'm afraid that as I age I will become invisible,
that I will wait at counters and no one will ask me what I want.
I'm afraid my voice will become stardust,
audible,
maybe even magical,
but not taken seriously.

I'm afraid this culture hates women so completely,
so deeply,
especially old women,
that I will be unable to resist a tidal wave of obliteration.

Yet, as I write these words,
I feel a steeliness growing in me.
"Hell no!"
I hear my soul shouting,
my eyes shining like comets,
"My beauty is a spell
that I cast over myself.
No one else has anything to do with it."

It's all a cosmic joke anyway, isn't it?
Pretty funny, all that cellulite.
Sagging breasts are just moving toward their lover, after all,
kissing gravity,
moving inexorably toward that great trickster,
that great leveler,
that great meaning-maker,
Death.

Well, pucker up!
Pucker up, Aging!
Pucker up, Death!
Pucker up, World!

Here I've been.
Here I am.
And here I come!

Beautiful woman
Photo by Jan Bateman

Song: Tiny Boobies
(from the CD *Daring to Sing*)

When I was in middle school, my breasts stubbornly refused to grow. All my other friends, it seemed, had breasts, big ones, and I was forced to wear pretend bras so I wouldn't look ridiculous dressing down in PE. But maybe my attempt not to look ridiculous only made me look more pathetic.

The story I told myself, the story the eighth grade boys told me as well, was that having small breasts meant that I wasn't sexy, alluring, attractive, or a real woman. I despaired at ever being able to attract a man.

I am happy to report that there has been no shortage of men in my life; in fact, I have been blessed with men who think I am pretty wonderful!

So here is a little song I wrote that celebrates my little breasts.

Tiny boobies
set me free.
I can go jogging;
no jiggling you'll see.

Tiny boobies:
I look good all over.
Cuz my femininity doesn't live in my mammaries.

Poem: Body Freedom

Sometimes we need to fake it until we make it; we need to practice imagining what it would be like if we were suddenly in love with our bodies, every pore, right now.

What if I were body-free?
What if I trusted my body to lead me into the mysteries of my soul?
What if I trusted the truth of the flow of my body so completely
that no one's response mattered?

Could I learn to dance like there's nobody watching?
Could I learn to be soul-naked with my husband?
Could I learn to be soul-naked when I am alone,
and when I walk, run, and dance down the street?

What if I fell in love with the truth that my body always knows more
    than I do?
What if I trusted my body to tell me where to go, move, speak, and
    cry?
What if I fell in love with the feeling my body gives me when I walk,
    run, climb, and
roll around on the floor?

What if I loved my body,
every cell,
every toe and elbow?

What if I got interested in my new weight
and talked to it,
letting it tell me the truth about what I need to know?

What if the flow of juices through my body felt so yummy
I couldn't wait to move every day?
What if moving my body felt
like eating a sun-warmed, red-all-the-way-through strawberry?
What if I enjoyed moving as much as I enjoy lying down and taking a nap?
What if, instead of feeling like I've got to overcome a hump to get
    myself moving,
I felt an excitement,
a Yes!,
a You-can't-stop-me energy?

What if the first thing I thought about every morning was the joy of
    anticipating
how I would get to move and dance all day?
What if I did move and dance all day,
not counting the calories I'm working off,
but feeling the deep satisfaction of extending my joints
and compressing my organs,
letting the blood squish out and rush back in again?

What if I appreciated agility
and felt gratitude for standing and turning and jumping up and down?

What if I called all my moving "sacred" throughout my day?
What if I say "yes" to my body the way I've said "yes" to my creativity?

What if I accept myself as I am,
love myself right now?

Yes, I can do that.
Yes, I will do that.

Story: The Love Diet

Her doctor's scales topped out at 370, so she wasn't sure how much she weighed at her peak. She wore a size thirty, and she was a teacher. She had been told during her teacher training that she would never get a job because she was too fat. This, naturally, discouraged her, and she only ate more and got fatter.

She is a size eight now, has been for two years, and she never went on a diet.

Amy told me this story after an in-service lesson I presented to the staff at the elementary school where I had started a part-time job as a counselor. The in-service had been about how we only have power in our lives when we take full responsibility for our responses to the events that life throws at us. I talked about how fear-based decisions never led to anything good and about dieting specifically.

"How can you become wonderful if you are telling yourself how fat and ugly you are?" I had asked. "Hating yourself only sets you up to comfort yourself by eating, which puts on more weight, which creates more self-hate, which creates more dieting to get rid of the self-hate.

"We need to start by loving ourselves and our bodies as they are. We need to move our bodies because we like how we feel when we move. We need to pay attention to what we eat, eat only what makes us feel good, and only eat when we are hungry and until we are full."

I knew this was true because a good friend of mine had lost a lot of weight just by putting a picture of a yummy body in her bathroom. Everyday she looked at the picture and it helped pull her toward the yumminess in her own body. The weight fell off of her, effortlessly.

After Amy told me her story I had to ask her: "How did you do it? You must be an expert at getting a vision, setting a goal, and sticking with it."

"Oh, I learned not to set too big of a goal," she said with a laugh. "I had done that many times and just got discouraged. I started by walking five minutes a day. That was all I could do. Little by little I built up until I could walk ten minutes a day, and then a half an hour.

"What I'm saving for now is an operation to get rid of all the extra skin that still hangs on me. I have a second job in the summer, and all that money is saved for my operation. I have five thousand dollars so far, but I need to get to about twenty thousand."

I had no doubt she would do it.

Song: All Women Are Beautiful
by Vicki Hannah Lein & Suzannah Doyle
(from the CDs *Daring to Sing* and *The Free Range Chix: Unclogged*)

Imagine women dancing around, waving scarves in the air, wearing tiaras and just generally frolicking as they sing these words.

Chorus:
All women, all women, all women are beautiful.
All women, all women, all women are fine.
All women, all women, all women are beautiful
'Cause all women are drenched in the Divine!

No matter what anyone's ever told you,
you're a part of the sacred fire.
You were born to make your magic,
Live your deepest desire.

Chorus

Listen to the music flowing through you.
Dance your wildest melody.
Trust the wisdom of your bravest song.
Celebrate life's harmony.

Chorus

Everyone's telling you who you ought to be,
how you're too fat or too thin.
But if you listen to your own true voice,
You'll find the goddess within.

Chorus

Your Turn

What are you afraid to tell your lover about your body? What do you wish you felt about your body? Would you like to write a thank you note to your body for all it has done for you? Can you entertain the idea that you are beautiful just as you are?

Try observing yourself moving and eating for a week. Don't judge anything you do, just notice how you feel when you eat and when you move. Do you eat after you are full? Do you eat when you are sad or bored? Answer these questions without judgment. "Hmm," you say to yourself, "that's interesting. I'm eating when I am not really hungry. One bite of chocolate is more satisfying that a whole piece of cake. How about that?"

Mothers talk to your daughters. Pull back the curtain and tell your stories and reveal your struggles. If you suspect your child has an eating disorder, **get help immediately from someone with experience dealing with recovery.** Waiting may be fatal. (This advice comes from a dear friend who knows.)

Chapter 13

Grieving as We Go

Grieving is hard work. Each person's grief is unique, taking us into our past to revisit losses and rocketing us into the future, terrifying us with losses we are sure we would never survive. Dealing with loss is difficult enough in a culture that understands and respects how grief can deepen our spirits and enrich our lives. In a culture such as ours, one that avoids loss and teaches its children that any disappointment is a disaster, grieving can be lonely and alienating. Death, divorce, cancer, or career doubt can stake us to the ground with few resources to give us a helping hand.

A friend of mine spent the first forty years of her life staying out of her emotions. She is an engineer and likes to deal with the facts, ma'am, just the facts. She was one of those people who said they hated "touchy-feely" activities. Well, that is one plan of action. In my experience, though, this is not a life-enhancing plan for human beings. Trying to stay blissfully unaware of what we are feeling only seems to leave us vulnerable to raging emotions that run through us and leak out of us, wreaking havoc.

The piper must be paid and my friend's dues came in the form of depression. As a lifelong introspection avoider, my friend was struck down with her depression without any tools or friends who knew this terrain who could help her find a way out. Knowledge is power, and knowing how we feel, even if we don't know why we feel a certain way, is essential if we are to live an authentic, creative life.

Depression is an inherent part of the grieving process. But if we fight our grief, if we don't embrace the gifts we can receive from any loss, then depression can burrow deep into our bones and deny us the simple joy of waking up, eager to live another day. My mother, whose father and husband were violent alcoholics, was depressed until her late forties. Her chronic depression entwined itself with her feelings of unworthiness so completely, she had no hope of ever living without struggle. Only after she divorced my father and got on antidepressants did I learn that my mother had a sense of humor. Until then she had been too heavily burdened with hopelessness to let her impishness come out to play.

Scott Peck, in his book *The Road Less Traveled*, asserts that depression can be a gift. Depression can let us know when we are not living the life our belly is calling us to live. That is why just taking an antidepressant may mask the true cause of the depression and will retard our growth. That said, I am a believer in antidepressants and believe they are one tool or strategy to deal with biological depression. How could I not feel this way after witnessing my mother's resurrection?

My sweet Murray suffered for years from low-grade depression that sucked the joy out of his life. He was reluctant, as many people are, to entertain the idea that he might have a biochemical disorder that would benefit from antidepressants. For years I urged Murray to seek a medical opinion, but my entreaties were met with an implacable "no."

When Murray finally agreed to try an antidepressant, it made a huge difference in his life and our relationship. But after only two months of relief, he was ready to give it up because he felt shame at having to take something to feel better. He didn't say he felt shame, of course. He made statements such as: "I don't want to be dependent on this for the rest of my life."

I was flabbergasted, stunned that he would even consider stopping his medication after such a short time. "You are going to quit after only two months, two great months?" I asked incredulously. "Can't you just keep using it through the summer, so you can enjoy life a little before you experiment?" He agreed to wait, and then, without discussing it with me again, went off his meds.

This breaking of an agreement, this sneaking off to do what he wants without letting me know, is a sure shame indicator. It is his body and his choice. He did not need to hide what he was doing from me. His shame made him feel he needed to keep it a secret.

After only a few weeks, he came home from work hunched over, shouting, "I surrender! I surrender!" Already his depression had reemerged to destroy his joy. (I have since learned it is a very bad idea to go on and off antidepressants because they may well lose their effectiveness.)

Murray has done a lot of emotional work as well as taking his medication. Some people need both. I have never been on antidepressants, but I would take them in a minute if a non-situational depression set in, one that just won't lift. Depression runs in my family, as it does in Murray's, and I believe once things get to a certain point, some people must take an antidepressant in order to shift. No shame, just biochemistry.

Our inner Predator would have us think that it is somehow cowardly to use medication to lift our spirits. This voice would have us "do it ourselves." This voice defines being strong as never showing emotion, never needing help.

Actually, it takes tremendous courage to face your problems instead of avoid them. Avoidance is cowardly, and I am speaking, as I mentioned before, as a recovering coward. All the excuses in the world are just that: excuses. They don't change the facts or reduce the losses that must be grieved. Grieving makes us better human beings, more compassionate, wiser. Failing to grieve sets us up for addictions, rigidity, and illness.

I'm not saying we should all sit in a puddle and wail, although that might be just the thing to do sometimes. Grief is tricky and needs to be respected. It will do what it is going to do with us, and we just have to trust and let it work itself out. Maybe going right back to work after a loss would be exactly the right thing for some people to do. Others may need time to talk and cry. Thinking that we are not human beings when we are at work or in school is nonsense. Research shows that we need to honor our emotions; otherwise, we get sick. People are more productive when they are treated respectfully, allowed to be human, to laugh and cry and celebrate.

Grieving well is an art. "Grieve as you go" is my motto, because I know that when we save up our grief, we can become clinically depressed or sick. Grief does not go away; it waits and then flows through us however it wants. We need to surrender just at the moment when we most want to cling or throw a tantrum. Tough stuff. Ask any recovering alcoholic.

Grieving is the least fun part of authentically living our lives, but the more we are able to acknowledge and grieve our losses as we go, the more we can love and be joyful. Even though I have taught workshops about the grieving process, when I am in the dark places where my Predator Voice wants me to give up and despair, I lose faith and fear I will drown in despondency. I've been through it enough now to know that I will come through these dreary feelings, and it still takes all my courage and wisdom to get through my grief.

Before I descend into the depths, I want to share what the journey can look like after some time to grieve and find some humor in the situation.

Song: Ode to Blindness
(from the CD *Daring to Sing*)

This song came to me after dealing with blindness for nine years. It is not the first step of the grieving process, but, if you keep putting one foot in front of the other, you will get to the humor eventually.

Introduction (spoken)

I want to tell you some true stories
about things that have happened to me,
so you'll have some idea about all the adventures you might have
if, God forbid, you are ever unable to see.

Don't brush your teeth with Preparation H.
It foams but it does not clean.
And listen for the little birdie to chirp
to make sure that the light is green.
And keep your ears wide open
in case someone says: "You're going the wrong way!"
That's my advice I have for you
if you go blind today.

If you go blind today,
life can still be fun
if you don't go insane
when people say (arms crossed) "It's over there"
when you ask for directions.

Don't walk into an airport bathroom
without closely checking the sign,
cuz if you're in the wrong bathroom,
the men won't fuss or whine.
They'll simply raise their faces to you
like so many cows chewing their hay!
That's the advice I have for you
if you go blind today.

If you go blind today,
life can still be fun
if you don't go insane when people say,
"Can you hear?" after a ten-minute conversation!

Don't touch the butt of the man standing next to you
unless you're sure that he's your mate.
For if he's not your husband, Oy! The problems you'll create!
Just wave your cane and smile sweetly
and say, "Are you talking to me!" Hey!
That's the advice I have for you
if you go blind today.

If you go blind today,
life can still be fun
if you don't go insane
when people say, "Your seat is 38B!" (Loud and slow)
Exasperation!

Going blind is really a bummer,
but it's not a tragedy.
Don't let your joy die on your retina,
and you can be just as happy as me!

If you go blind today,
life can still be fun
if you don't go insane

when you stick your fingers in a socket
when you're trying to screw in a light bulb.
or when you accidentally wash your face with hair conditioner
or when you lose your sense of humor.

Don't lose your sense of humor!
If you go blind today.

Story: No More Stars

I mentioned earlier that I inherited my eye disease from my mother. We didn't know her disease was genetic until I started having problems in 1983. This is the story of my first round with vision loss. You may notice that I am not as cheerful about my struggle in this story as I am in Ode to Blindness.

"I can't see the stars!" I exclaimed to my friends, trying to control my panic.

We were on a backpacking trip, camped in the intersection of Indigo Creek and the wild Illinois River. We'd just finished a gourmet dinner made on our camp stoves and were gazing at the night sky. This was a ritual we all enjoyed before we climbed into our sleeping bags to read with flashlights until we fell asleep to the sounds of the rushing water.

As I stood among the grasses of Indigo Flat with my dear friends, I noticed I couldn't see the stars. I couldn't believe it at first. Where had the stars gone? I knew I had been able to see them easily the last time I had tried. When was that? I couldn't remember.

That summer evening I could not see Orion, whose belt I always picked out of the sky with a joy I couldn't explain. I couldn't even see the Big Dipper. All the stars I loved disappeared as soon as I looked straight at them. I could only see stars with my peripheral vision, which seemed a cheap substitute for the real thing at the time. At that moment I realized how much stars meant to me. (*Note: It is no accident that Orion is on the cover of this book.*)

I successfully buried the panic I felt as I stood in the open under the stars I could no longer see. And I successfully fooled myself into believing that whatever was keeping me from seeing those stars had nothing to do with my mother—it couldn't.

Still, I was concerned enough, even though I had been assured Mom's condition wasn't genetic, to see an opthamologist as soon as I returned from the backpacking trip. Just a precaution, a sensible precaution, I told myself. No need to worry. I'll go by myself to his office. Of course I will. I'm being responsible and mature. I don't need any help.

The doctor, after hearing of my mother's eye problem and looking at my eyes through several different instruments, sat down in his chair by the sink, and told me I had macular degeneration of the retina. I was 32. He asked if I wanted to see a specialist. Would I like a second opinion? Would I like someone else to confirm the fact that I was going blind? Yes, I did, as a matter of fact, want a second opinion. I would like to see a specialist; I would like at least one other person to confirm (confirm!) the fact that I was going blind, thank you very much. I wanted one more step between me and not being able to read, at least one more step.

He looked sympathetic when he told me I was probably going to go blind, and I hated him for his pity. He didn't move closer to me, he didn't touch me; he just sat a little longer in his chair, paused a beat longer between words. I think he was waiting for me to react. Maybe he was waiting to see if I understood the importance of his words.

I knew what the news meant. Since I was fifteen, hadn't I been driving Mom to the mall to shop because she couldn't drive herself? Didn't I wipe the edges of the sink where she couldn't see the scum building up? Didn't I pick her up when she fell face-first onto the pavement in a parking garage after she tripped over a curb? Didn't I carry her tote bag with her bulky Braille books—books she read so slowly she forgot the beginnings of the sentences before she got to the end?

Didn't I censor my letters because her husband would read them to her aloud? Didn't I see her frustration as she tried to see what her grandchildren looked like, my children—pouring over pictures, trying to get them in just the right light at just the right angle so she could make out their features—then giving up in frustration? I knew what the news meant.

As I sat in the patient's chair with the eye machine swung to the left, I thought these thoughts—not one at a time but in one big glob. I could hardly breathe. My doctor, a man I'd just met, sat in discomfort across the room, waiting. I didn't want him to look at me. I didn't know what I was showing on the outside. Inside I was no longer living one day at a time. I was living the rest of my life, suffering all the losses ahead of me in one blurry mass.

But I wouldn't cry. I promised myself that. This man who knew nothing about me except my mother's history and the appearance of my retinas was not going to share this moment with me. He was outside of me, separate from me—he had nothing to do with me. I wouldn't cry in front of him and his white-uniformed nurse and his sympathetic receptionist. I wouldn't let them comfort me, even if they'd offered. I didn't want them to shake their heads after I'd left, pitying the young woman with the old person's disease. They hadn't earned the right to comfort me. My pain, deep and raw, was too big for public display.

I held myself together until I got to my car, hand shaking as I tried to get my key in the lock. I yanked the door open, crawled inside, and slammed the door shut. I started gasping, and then I couldn't stop shaking and crying, couldn't stop feeling. I knew, even in my panic, that I wasn't invisible, that someone might see me through the windshield and might offer to help.

I didn't want help. I didn't need help. I needed to escape these black, hot waves. Bam! Bam! Then a rest and—bam! I needed to drive some place, get away from the man who knew and his nurse who knew and the receptionist who had given me the map to the eye clinic in Salem, the place I would visit in ten days for a second opinion. Even the parking lot was contaminated with blindness, even the street. His office felt radioactive, and the farther away I got, the safer I'd be.

On the way home, I considered not telling my husband, Will. Maybe I wouldn't have to tell anyone. Maybe no one would know. I could get through this by myself.

But my body was shaking too much, and when I walked in the door, I collapsed in Will's arms. I couldn't look at his face, at his eyes, and not respond. His look held a question I didn't have to answer. He held me and rocked me, and I sobbed.

My daughter, Katie, only five, stood by the side of the rocking chair with her two crying, shaking parents, and wondered at their intensity. She must have asked, "What's wrong, Mommy? Daddy, what's wrong with Mommy?" Will must have told her something. What did he say? "Your mom has the same thing wrong with her eyes that Grandma Shirley has." I don't remember his words; I do remember the small comfort of Will crying with me, for me, for us and for our children. For our future.

I couldn't shield my daughter from the bright light of my pain, so she ran into her room and hid under her covers, wrapping herself securely in her ragged baby blanket, sobbing until one of us could go to her. I know the feel of that time under the covers—the world seems tilted, the colors altered. And I couldn't go to her, couldn't make my legs move or my chest quit heaving.

Even in Will's arms I couldn't escape the white hot fact of being alone. This wasn't happening to anyone else; this was happening to me. No one else could get between me and my fading vision. I would be alone in not being able to read, alone in not being able to drive to Safeway, alone in not being able to see my children's faces. Alone in my blurry, distorted world.

Ten days later I saw a specialist in Salem. After dilating my eyes and looking through several instruments, he told me I didn't have macular degeneration. Instead, I had drusen, little spots on my retina, which can precede macular degeneration but didn't necessarily mean I would get it.

"I don't have macular degeneration?" I kept asking.

"No, you have drusen," the doctor explained patiently. After about four repetitions, he suggested I take some tests if I wanted to be sure I was not going blind. I wanted to be sure I was not going blind.

I went to Portland and had four hours of eye tests, four hours of torturous, scientific bombardment. In one test, I put my face up against a machine that flashed a bright light and then a dimmer red light in order to see how quickly my eyes adapted. Flash. Wait. Wait. "Can you see the little red lights yet?" "No." More waiting. "Can you see the little red lights now?"

"No."

The technician's fingers drummed on the machine. "Can you see the little red lights now?"

"No, not yet." Christ! You think I don't want to see the stupid little red lights? You think I wouldn't see them if I could? I can't see them! I can't see them! Why can't these "helpers" wait quietly or change the way they ask questions? I'm failing. I know I'm failing.

The technicians discuss the results of my test, whisper on the other side of the room. They can't tell me anything, naturally; the doctor is supposed to do that. I only catch bits of what they're saying: "Isn't there supposed to be more difference here?" "Yes, there should be." "I don't understand." "She can't see the little red lights," said in an even lower whisper. "But what do we put down on the report?"

In another test, after electrodes were hooked to both eyes, I shifted my eyes from right to left as a light blinked on and off. Back and forth, shift, shift, focus on the right, then focus on the left—for forty minutes. I felt myself getting hysterical. I started imagining myself screaming, ripping wires off my eyes, breaking glass. If these people were KGB, I thought, I'd tell them anything they wanted to know. But I didn't want them to know how close I was to the edge of something—something snarling, something bigger than I was.

The tests were inconclusive, my new doctor said, the doctor I loved because he had taken away the finality of my first doctor's diagnosis, blotted out macular degeneration—the "M.D." words. Yes, my eyes didn't adjust well to light changes, but that didn't mean I had Macular Degeneration. He didn't know what I had, he just knew what I didn't have, and that was all right with me. I still couldn't see stars, except for Jupiter and Venus, but I wasn't going blind.

And then, four years later, a blood vessel burst in my left eye.

I'd gotten used to not being able to see well at night, had made adjustments, had asked for help when I couldn't make something out. Will had given me the key with the little light to find the lock to the door of our new Subaru. I'd learned not to fill my coffee cups unless I was in the light; otherwise, I had to spend too much time wiping up the spill, feeling stupid, mad at myself for not realizing I couldn't see something. I hitched rides with friends after dark if I could and, if I couldn't find a ride, I only drove on roads I knew well, piggybacking on other drivers, following safely, I hoped, in their wake.

When people asked about my vision, I told them I had "low-light vision problems" because if I said I had night blindness, they thought I only had trouble seeing at night. They were confused when I couldn't see if my eye makeup was on right because the shadow in the mirror blocked the light a little bit.

When I walked after dark with my son Martin, four years old at the time, I'd ask him to tell me when there was a curb coming up. He'd take my arm and never forgot to remind me of a pothole or bump, even though he couldn't remember to brush his teeth most mornings without being told.

I feared that if I thought I was going blind I might make it come true, so I quit checking my eyes every morning for distortion. I tried to forget about the possibility of distortion.

But low-light vision adaptations crept into my life. I bought a headlamp to take on camping trips so I could see to read a book or walk out in the woods. I didn't mind looking foolish and didn't mind people making fun of the lamp: "Hey, what are you? A coal miner?" I'd accepted, adjusted, adapted, evolved—perfectly, or if not perfectly, slightly imperfectly, which was really more perfect anyway.

I told friends the story of my misdiagnosis of macular degeneration with a laugh and a "knock on wood." I felt lucky, resigned to the fact that my low-light vision wasn't as good as other people's. I had resolved my vision loss, I thought, maturely accepted my limitations and gone on growing and changing, becoming a better person every day in every way.

A few years later, on July 9, 1988, on yet another camping trip, my world changed forever. When I looked at my round metal drinking cup, it wasn't round anymore. (Maybe I should stop camping. Maybe the spirit gods are angry when I camp. Maybe if I wore only red socks or only blue socks, I could trick this thing into looking the other way.)

I'd been checking for wavy lines ever since I'd lost seeing the stars. I knew that was the "bad sign," the serious sign of macular degeneration. But this flat cup wasn't my imagination; this wasn't me being a hypochondriac, begging for attention and acceptance. This was a cup that should have been round and wasn't. This was a cup I couldn't make round because I wanted it to be round.

I finished eating lunch without saying anything to anyone.

"Hmm," I thought to myself, "a cup that should be round is flat on one side. Hmm. That's strange. Hmm. Interesting. Hmm."

Several hours later, when the distortion hadn't gone away, I realized I probably ought to tell someone about what I was seeing. "I'm having some distortion problems," I said to two friends as we stood at the edge of the trees, watching our children play soccer on the grassy field in the center of the campground.

"Oh?" they said. (They didn't know that distorted vision might mean I was going blind.) "Is the distortion in both eyes?"

"Well, I don't know," I said, surprised I hadn't thought to check. "No, it is just my left eye."

To myself I thought, "Hmm. Hmm."

A few hours later, I told someone else, a dear friend of mine who knew of my eye problems. "I'm having some distortion problems," I said.

"You are? What's it like?" he asked.

"When I look at this cup it is flat on one side," I explained.

"Hmm. Hmm," we thought together.

At dinner, I decided to tell everyone at the picnic table, incidentally including my husband, who was sitting next to me, making a sandwich. When I said, "I'm having some distorted vision problems." He stood upright, his face white."

You're going to the eye doctor Monday," he said rather officiously, and for once I didn't mind getting bossed around.

"Oh, you think I need to go to all that trouble?" I said. Will knew what warped vision meant; he'd been there when I'd come home from the doctor's that first time; he'd gone with me to Salem for the second diagnosis of drusen. He knew my mother. He knew I was in trouble.

"Oh, you think I need to go see the eye doctor about these wavy lines?" I asked, almost casually. Of course I needed to see a doctor. My vision was deteriorating by the hour. Of course I needed to see the doctor, but I didn't want to need to see a doctor. If I didn't see the doctor, maybe I'd just be able to see straight lines, go on reading, and go on driving.

My vision went haywire on Saturday; on Sunday I drove my children 130 miles south to leave them with their grandparents, waved goodbye to Will, who was leaving for a chemistry institute in Seattle for four weeks and decided: yes, I probably ought to call the doctor about my eyes first thing Monday morning.

Sleep eluded me that Sunday night. I walked with friends early Monday morning—yup, yup, I'm going to call the doctor today; I am a little worried. I saw my optometrist, who took one look in my left eye and started making phone calls to Portland and Corvallis. Could they see me now? Friday? Friday isn't soon enough. Thursday? No, right now. Get her in right now.

"Is this related to my vision problem, or is this something different?"

"Yes," my optometrist, a friend of mine, said, "this is related to the problems you had before."

"But I have drusen, don't I?" I asked with a quiver in my voice. I must have drusen. I have drusen. Drusen don't necessarily mean that I have—but I didn't say the "M.D." words out loud. Didn't even let them wander through my mind as a possibility.

The optometrist said he saw red leakage, which indicated bleeding. The ophthalmologist in Portland might be able to use a laser to stop the leakage and repair the damage. Could a doctor make lines straight again? I want my vision back. I believe that everything in my life would be perfect, even wonderfully messy, if I could just see straight lines again.

Later, sitting at the kitchen table, filling the time before my appointment the next day, I read a story in the newspaper article about Cambodian refugees in Thai camps, waiting, waiting, despairing, and I think, "Vicki, you are upset about a little blurred vision? How can you be upset over something so trivial?" But I AM upset. I am more than upset; I am terrified.

I'm ashamed of my raw greed, my obsessive desire to be healthy, to make my eyes work right. I don't care what God wants. I don't care what His will is for me today. Fix my eyes! I scream inside my head. Fix my eyes! I need them. I use them. I use them more than most people. Haven't I suffered enough?

I'll turn this into a metaphor—I know I will, and that makes me angry. I don't want to transform my pain; I don't want to learn what I can learn from this challenge. I don't want to be blind, and I don't want to be a terrific blind person, though I would probably be a terrific blind person, one of those who gives inspiring speeches at graduation and has articles in the paper that make people shake their heads and say, "Isn't she amazing?"

I don't want to be amazing: I want to be able to read and drive and see my children, to watch their faces as they grow up. To hell with personal growth.

"Dear God," I silently pray, "the doctors can cut my eye open, both eyes, anything—just let them fix it. I'll wear a black patch over my left eye the rest of my life—I'll pretend I am a pirate—and never complain—if I just get to have one good eye."

The next morning I wake up and tell God I'm willing to be healed, opening my chest and my body in a way that makes me feel vulnerable, almost sexual. I realize to my dismay I'm making another bargain, and bargaining does not work. If I want to be healed I need to be willing to be healed, to accept healing. I accept in that moment, alone in my bed, before I get up and get ready to go have eye surgery—I accept the truth in that moment that healing costs. I'm not sure I'm able to pay, but at that moment I'm willing to be willing to pay.

Two friends drive me to Portland. An intern examines me at the University Hospital. Another woman dilates my eyes, three sets of drops. Another technician takes pictures of my eyes. He's just returned from his twenty-year class reunion, so he is one year older than I am. I joke with him about how something he says reveals his personality, then apologize, telling him those are the perils of having a counseling graduate student as a patient.

The intern brings in a picture that Mark, the technician, had taken and hung on the wall in one of the examining rooms, a picture of an old woman (silver, white hair) holding a baby (blond, white hair). She is holding the baby up and smiling; the sun is shining through their hair, making it glow. Some unfeeling lout has marked across it with a pen, just as someone or something has slashed through my retina.

Is the picture ruined forever? I wondered. Does he have the negative tucked away safely somewhere, somewhere without people with pens? Is there someplace safe like that where I can find the negative of my retina? My "real" retina, the one that hasn't been ruined?

Mark gets the camera set up and I scoot up to the machine, letting my chin rest. The intern comes in and injects the dye. The camera clicks. More clicks. Then my stomach is hit with a wave of contractions. We're ready, though, my friends and I, because I'd had this test before and had thrown up every time. Only two percent throw up. Again I'm in the special minority, a place I'd coveted all my life (didn't I secretly enjoy getting the extra attention of having a blind mother?). But now I didn't want to be special, didn't want to be one of the few who throw up or have their retinas degenerate.

More waiting in the hall lined with chairs. I try not to overhear some gray-haired ladies talking. I think, "This is too much like being in a book." One lady complains loudly of the inconveniences of losing her sight.

"The worst is not being able to drive, being so dependent," she says. "I used to be able to get around in my house, but I'm starting to have more trouble."

Another three women gather around the speaker. I'm aware of what they cannot see—that I can still see for now. They nod, and cluck their agreement. They could be talking of the difficulty of getting ripe tomatoes for all the emotion in their words.

"I'm not like them," I think. Not now, not ever. How can they talk about it as if it were normal. How can they sound so damn accepting? I'll never accept this. You won't find me clucking over the tragedy of my lost eyesight, sharing my despair with strangers in a waiting room. They are not here, and I'm not hearing them, and my friends aren't watching me hear them, and this isn't happening.

"Are you Smally?" I say to the man in the white coat standing by the door of an examination room. Not Dr. S. Not Mike Smally— just Smally, as in "Are you here to see Robertson or Smally?"

He looks startled, amused. "Yes, I'm Smally." He's my doctor, the one who told me I didn't have macular degeneration four years ago. I recognize him now. He moves like some animal. I ask one of my friends later, what kind of animal he resembles. She thinks he reminds her a three-toed sloth. Yes, a sloth.

That sounds mean or disparaging but I trust this sloth, this man who moves slowly through the haste of patients and panic. He's a friendly sloth, approachable. He enters a room, reads, looks, directs his answers to the person who's asked the questions. He is a man of power, power we've all given him, power he's earned—the power to fix this bleeding in my eye, my impending blindness. He is the Man Who Knows and Can Do Something. We don't hold our breath when he is in the room, but we breath shallowly so as not to disturb his Thought. Think hard, Doctor Man, I pray. Find The Answer. Do Something.

He tells me, after seeing the results of the fluorescein angiogram that he recommends the laser. The laser surgery might make my vision worse. A beam might bounce off one of the little mirrors on the special contact he'll put on my eye to direct the laser. I might lose my central vision in that eye. Probably not, but he needs to tell me the risks.

"Do it," I tell him. Do it. Stop the leak, the red leak. (Is it my imagination, or can I feel the danger building in my eye— leaking and bleeding, bleeding and leaking.)

Dr. Smally leaves the room, and my friend wants to see the pictures of the angiogram. We fumble with the light switch on the viewer. Then there it is: my blind spot. My retina is a sea of red, the blood vessel a volcano. My blind spot is the crater. I recognize its shape; I've been seeing it from the inside. "It's beautiful," I say. I feel a tug to have this picture on my wall somewhere. It's artwork. My eye. My scar. My volcano.

After the laser treatment, the jagged edges of the rupture will be smooth, the blind spot almost a perfect circle. And I realize I miss the rough edges. The smooth edges are safer, sealed, less likely to stay active and interfere on that half of millimeter of central vision that makes the difference between being able to read and having to listen to books on tape for the rest of my life. So I'm glad it's smooth. But I miss its asymmetry—it felt more like me then.

They prepare me for the laser surgery. I've been telling jokes, laughing until the third shot to numb my eye feels like it will go through my head. The needle touched parts of me I didn't know, had never had occasion to know. I laughed after I flopped on the table like a fish, surprised by the needle, its length, its invasiveness. "That's one way to shut me up, I guess," I say after the first shock is over.

Then, as I sit up and look across the room, "I can't see!" I say in alarm. Dr. Smally turns to me, "Your eyelid is closed," he says gently. "Oh." I say sheepishly.

My friends laugh at how funny I look: "It's amazing how much one numbed eye affects someone's appearance," one of my friends says with a giggle. The nurse whispers, "With friends like this, who needs enemies?" and they quiet down. I knew they loved me; I knew their laughter was mixed with fear, and that they hadn't separated from me, that they'd be on the table taking the shot if they could. I felt loved in their laughter even though I could understand how they might seem insensitive to an outsider. This doctor and nurse couldn't know of the hours they had spent holding me, would spend holding me, comforting me, letting me cry and curse God.

In the room with the laser, I still have the giggles. "Now this really would be rude," I think, "to giggle through laser surgery." But the giggles still come and my friends are summarily dismissed from the room, leaving like two guilty little girls. The nurse holds my head against the machine, and I am thankful my eye is numb and I have no responsibility. I don't want to have to look up right or down center or hold my eye still. I don't want to know that if I do anything wrong my eyesight might be blasted away. "Do it for me, Doc," I pray. "Just do it very carefully."

He turns on the laser gun, and I pray, asking God to steady Dr. Smally's hand and help him shoot straight. The nurse adjusts her hand on my head, and I think: "I moved! I moved! The light beam is so small, so narrow, will my small movement make a difference? I can't hold my head steady myself, that's your job, Dr. Sloth! These are my eyes! I must not move!"

The surgery is over. Mark takes more pictures, more interns look into my eyes. A patch. I ask the nurse if they come in any colors. But I'm happy with the white gauze patch; I want people to know I've been wounded. I'm disappointed I don't need to wear it longer than just the rest of the day. How will people know how much I've suffered and how terrified I am without the patch?

In two weeks or so, they say, my eye will have calmed down and I'll know how much I will be able to see. Two weeks. I have hope for two weeks. For two weeks, every day my eye might get better. For two weeks, I have nothing to do except recover and look for signs of improvement. For two weeks, I postpone feeling hopeless.

A month later I return to see if the laser surgery has worked. It has a 50/50 chance of working, and I'm confident it has. That is my job, after all, to have faith, believe, visualize, transform. I've done all that. I'm finding meaning in my injury; I'm making changes in my life. Someone asks me how my eye is, and I tell them of all the changes I'm making in my life. The stuff spiritual growth freaks would be proud to hear. And I am proud. Aren't I amazing? Yup, yup, amazing.

Nothing magic happened after two weeks or a month, but my eye did not get worse either. I knew I still might need more laser surgery, still might go blind.

My Philosophy of Life Reveals Itself

I have a system established to deal with life, a philosophy to deal with pain, confusion, grief. It works pretty well, even when I end up choking on my own bile, sunk in the pit of my despair. But when I'm hit with something hard, like the potential loss of my vision, my system scraps itself. I don't want to ask for help; I don't want to need help. I don't want to accept, accommodate, and transform my pain. I just want my retina to quit bleeding, quit leaking. I want to be fixed, and I want someone or something else to do it.

At these moments, I think of God of the Trip Wire, God the Capricious. He lounges on some celestial chaise, eating peeled grapes. He leans over, when the fancy strikes him, and tugs on a cruel string that sends me into blackness, away from seeing stars and my children's faces.

Then I feel blamed. This is my fault, somehow, my failure to recognize a "blindness" in my life. My injury becomes a metaphor, and my job is to integrate the metaphor of my pain into my life and thereby overcome it—and be richer and stronger besides. "All pain is a metaphor," a friend, a former therapist, told me in a note. Maybe that's why I quit going to her; maybe asking me to be responsible for the disintegration of my retinas is too much. What kind of a god would ask this of me? What kind of friends would expect me to accept this loss willingly?

I remember reading about a little girl who was severely burned in a fire. She was one of those extraordinary people, one of those we read about, then shake our heads and say "Isn't she amazing?" Her mother talked of the struggles the family had overcome. In the picture the little girl leans against a door jam, scars disfiguring her face. (I'm not supposed to think the scars are beautiful, am I? Those transformed scars?) This damaged girl looks shy, self-effacing. What a trooper she is.

I don't want to be a trooper. I don't want a world that makes me have to be a trooper, that makes little girls have to be troopers. I don't want a world that forces friends of mine to struggle to cope with sexual abuse when they were children. And this is the only world I have, and I used to like it, in spite of the burns and the sexual abuse. I used to think there was a way for me to find beauty and peace amid all this. I used to think death was a part of life and gave meaning to life. Now I feel God is a thief. He steals and then demands love. I don't love God now. I don't like Him. I think he set up a crummy system.

I don't care about building my character anymore. I want to see.

Poem: Despair? Again Today?

If only we could schedule our grieving! If only we could control or predict the process! Alas, grief has its own timetable and we must surrender to it, again and again.

I wrote this poem from the bottom, from the place of no hope. When I wrote it I had been waking up depressed day after day. I knew it was part of grieving for my mother's death, and that helped some. But after eight months of grieving, I started telling myself I was a big wimp. Everyone loses their mother at some point, my friendly Dinosaur reminded me. I should buck up and quit being such a baby. Shame attacking again! Even knowing that shame was my true enemy, knowing and trusting the process, I was still slogging around at the bottom, inching through each day as best I could, picking up one foot and then the other. I could not imagine ever feeling better. To me, this is the definition of despair.

I wake up.
How do I feel today?
I scan my emotional landscape,
searching for energy pockets,
for hope.

Do I feel like doing anything today?
No.
I don't even feel like getting out of bed.
I'm in a psychological Alaska,
where the nights are infinite.
Time creeps by,
and I feel death is the biggest truth,
the only truth today.
I wish I felt like doing anything:
laundry,
cleaning the garage.
Oh, wouldn't it be lovely to feel excited about organizing the garage
or even to feel like I have the energy to force myself to organize the garage?
Alas, today I have none of it,
none of me.

I am not relentlessly uplifting today.
Is hope a fraud?
I'm not sure.
This too shall pass,
right?
I will again wake up feeling delightfully expectant,
right?
I will have that feeling of eager anticipation again—
when I can't wait to get to my computer and start working on this book again,
when I look up and see that three hours have passed effortlessly.

Really? It's one o'clock?
Already? I missed lunch, and I am not even hungry!

Will I ever again feel lost in the flow,
trusting that this day, this hour, this moment has meaning?

"God loves artists," Julia Cameron says in her book *The Artist's Way*.
And on those days of creative flow, I know that God loves this artist.
But today I feel like life is a giant hoax.
We are all just going to die anyway; why not get it over with?
What difference can my life make to anyone in any way that matters?

This is depression talking—
grief having its way with me.
I know this,
but my hope still dissolves.

So I trudge through the long hours of the day,
hoping I might stumble into a pocket of joy.
I do the things I can force myself to do that usually help:
sit by the fire,
take a bath, walk in the weather, talk deeply with my beloved Murray.
His touch always helps, and
my nightly foot rub might be the only event throughout the long day
    that lifts me up.

I will get through today the best I can
and be ready to start again fresh tomorrow,
asking myself the question:
"How do I feel today?"
I will be ready to do whatever I can do,
one second at a time,
one foot set hesitantly in front of the other.

Sadness, Where Are You Hiding?

This essay was written right after my son, Martin, graduated from high school in 1999. His graduation, a celebration and a loss, triggered the memory of other losses, which is how grief works.

I feel its heaviness, waiting. I want to schedule a good cry for three o'clock when I'm at home and have time. Or I will even take it when it happens of its own accord.

But my sadness doesn't come.

My daughter, on the lookout for tears, can spot them before they erupt. "No crying!" she will admonish, as she did last night at my son's graduation from high school.

I fear I am losing or have lost him. I don't know that boys come back. Right now I can't remember any boys who did come back.

I'm afraid Martin won't come back, will find me irrelevant and irritating. He will fill his life full and only give me time begrudgingly. He will move to Japan and not want me to come and visit, as did one man I know.

"I'm afraid I will lose Martin," I tell my mother this morning.

"You won't lose Martin," she says.

"Will I not lose him the way you haven't lost your son, David," I say, somewhat cruelly.

"That's different," she says.

So where do the tears hide? I stumble over them at odd places and times—coffee shops, walking in the woods, listening to e-mails. I don't plan them, and usually they are inconvenient. I have learned to appreciate those moments when my tears come upon me because I have learned they cannot be scheduled and that they weigh heavily on me if I don't let them escape.

My friend Lisa says I am no good at sadness. I'm a little surprised at this. I'm so much better than anyone else in my family. But she is right. I am no good at sadness.

I don't know how to make sadness happen, and I don't know how to let it happen. It's a Catch-22 for me, that elusive place where I cannot take action. I need to allow the flow of feeling to come, but I can't take action to allow it because that blocks the allowing. This smells like healthy surrender, letting go, trusting that sadness won't kill me or make me too vulnerable.

I cry more than most people I know, at least that's how it looks to me. But I don't cry enough. My tears get blocked, and I get irritable and judgmental, no fun to be or to be around. I feel trapped in a web of blackberry vines. They hurt me and hurt anyone around me.

I know Lisa is right. I am no good at sadness. When I was a little girl, sadness was not a safe emotion. I can easily imagine what would have happened to me if I had allowed myself to feel or show sadness. Someone might have ridiculed my tears. But even if they hadn't seen them, even if I had cried myself to sleep at night, I would have felt I was just creating a pool of tears I would drown in. And I had too much work to do; I was too busy surviving to spend my time crying.

A little over two months ago my daughter Katie almost died of a cardiac arrest. Last night on an "NYPD Blue" rerun a man collapsed playing basketball and died of a cardiac arrest on the spot. The paramedics didn't get there in time as they did with Katie.

I didn't cry as I watched the scene, even with the CPR, and the excruciating wait for the ambulance. I thought I probably "should" be crying. I wondered why I wasn't crying. I could feel this huge sadness boulder back there in me, but if felt too heavy, too dense. It would not dissolve because of a television show.

This grief boulder I carry around makes me tired. Maybe I'm afraid of the boulder, afraid it will crush me. Maybe I could change my images of sadness from drowning pools and crushing boulders ala Indiana Jones into something I could handle. Maybe I could start thinking of my sadness as a cleansing brook flowing from my heart through my eyes.

Giving myself something to imagine will at least give me something to do.

I like it better when I have something to do, instead of something I need to feel, yet can't make myself feel.

Yes, I will imagine this cleansing brook flowing from my heart through my eyes. I will imagine I am flowing into a meadow. The sun is shining. I am safe. The animals come to drink from the brook of my tears. This sadness is a vital part of the wheel of life.

Yes, that helps. Now I have something to do.

Martin and His Mom in Europe

I wrote this piece while sitting in a garden in Heidelberg with my twenty-one-year-old son. My mother had died in April, and it was the end of May. Martin, recently graduated from college, and I were on a two-week trip, which included Paris, Frankfurt, and a NATO school in The Netherlands. We would sit outside in the unseasonable warmth, drinking beer, and talk about math, physics, and his girlfriend. Not since he sat on my lap and I read him The Cat in the Hat *had Martin and I enjoyed so much mom/son time together.*

Ever since I almost lost Katie when she was twenty, I have treasured every moment I have with my children. Sometimes my exquisite joy threatens to burst through my seams, embarrassing them, but I usually manage to let my love glow with restraint. At least that is the story I tell myself.

I knew, though, that the opportunity to travel in Europe with Martin might well never come again. I enjoyed every single moment, even when the bar below our hotel room was blaring Danke Schön at three o'clock in the morning.

Grief heals in tiny pieces.
A flake of memory breaks off from the loss,
floats up
into your heart and your eyes,
and whispers,
"Please, never again."

Oh, this is grief again, creeping into my consciousness and my hope. Grief, the spoiler, corrupts my joy, robs me of the richness of now and casts me into the pit of jagged doubt. This grief wants guarantees, wants to know what is on the next page of my life and in the next ten chapters, so I can relax and feel safe again, knowing all my big losses lay in the past and none in the future. "Knowing" isn't the same as trusting. Trust is letting go of knowing, relaxing into what is and dancing to create what might become.

If I let myself be a living, walking, breathing Gratitude—for just this moment, I risk the exquisite vulnerability of receiving. I risk letting myself be filled, crowding out my resentments and regrets. I risk being flooded with beauty for small miracles—the sound of water splashing in a fountain, the sound of small children speaking in German, the feeling of the day's gentle warmth caressing me.

Our coffee is strong in bright orange cups and saucers on a mint green tablecloth.

My son sits writing in his journal across the table from me.

Pictures try to capture the moment, but they fail.

"Kiss the joy as it flies," William Blake wrote.

"Kiss the joy as it flies," I say.

"Laugh deeply and speak from your heart.

The Yellowstone caldera is thirty thousand years overdue, you know. We have no time to waste on trivialities."

Poem: The Call of the Grave

Another insidious aspect of grieving is the pull toward death. I feel it now as I write, those swirling energies that would take me down with my mother. This is another part of pulling back the curtain.

I feel my dead mother calling me to join her.
"We are all going to die anyway," she whispers in my ear.
"Why delay things? What is the point?"

I wonder if this ache in my heart is caffeine
or Death tickling me.
Or is this palpitation just the bug I've been fighting for two months.
Will it suddenly get virulent and travel to my heart and kill me,
dropping me dead on my office rug,
the way a virus killed my friend Christy recently.
Christy, in better shape than anyone her age, my age, that I know,
Christy, dropping dead on the floor at the hairdresser
while getting her nails done.

Then forty-eight-year-old Jeremy dies in his sleep.
They don't know why yet.
Murray used to work with him.

Then Charlie next door, only forty-two, also dies in his sleep.
Cause uncertain.

And the call to the grave gets louder with each death.

Trina's husband falls off a fishing boat and drowns.
Feisty Jane dies in her sleep, stroked out.

All this, since April when Mom died.

And I feel her grave calling me.

My body feels old and achy.
Why exercise? It's too late anyway.
What difference would it make?
We're all going to die anyway.
Why not speed it up, get it over with?

Well, there's my friend Harriet, who sped it up
and left her husband and two teenage daughters to pick up the pieces.
I could not do that to those I love.

So I am stuck living, waking up each morning with this heavy cloak
   over my joy.

What is the point?

I start exercising five days a week in response to a friend's challenge.
My body likes yoga.

I'm writing even though my Predator Voice tells me
I am boring and self-indulgent, narcissistic.
No one will ever want to read this crap.

And I write on.

A woman who says she can talk with the dead
asked Jeremy's departed spirit if he had anything he wanted to say to
   those left behind.

"Just keep swimming," he said,
Like Dory said in *Finding Nemo*,
Just keep swimming until you find home or are found.

I guess I will just keep swimming.

Poem: She's the One Who Didn't Die

This poem was inspired by a group of teenagers trained by my good friend Lola Broomberg. They are truly courageous kids, teens who have suffered the loss of someone close to them, usually a parent. They are willing to tell their story in a series of dramatic skits in order to help themselves grieve their losses and also to help create an environment where talking about loss is okay.

During their performance, one girl wrote of her call to death. I combined her words with the words of the other performers to create this poem.

She is the one
whose glance lingers on the kitchen knives,
whose attention fixes on the plastic dry cleaner bags,
as she hangs her favorite shirt in the closet.

She is the one
who daydreams about her car
idling in her garage,
the door tightly closed,
carbon monoxide gently lulling her into a dreamless sleep.

She is the one
who can only hear empty echoes
in her friends' tentative expressions of sympathy and support,
who doubts if anyone would really miss her if she suddenly vanished as
   her mother did.

She is the one whose mom vanished for a month before her body was discovered,
or the one whose dad died of AIDS,
or the one whose dad died when a car fell off of a jack.

She is the one who imagines
that her death might give her life meaning.
She imagines if she kills herself,
she will be remembered,
never forgotten,
her funeral crammed with teenagers and tears.

But she is the one who didn't die
and resolves,
with a shaky, small voice,
to live.

She is the one who has the courage
to rebuild her life,
moment by excruciating moment.

She is the one whose life muscles are bulging
as she creates meaning
one small act at a time.

She is the one the fire has not destroyed,
but rather made stronger.

She is the one who lives,
despite the dread that sometimes smothers her,
despite that aching loneliness
she can feel in the middle of the "busyness" around her,
despite that huge, gaping, black hole
she fears might be lurking underneath her very next step.

She is the one who,
because of her great grief,
learns to face the dragons,
becoming the hero in her own "little" life.

She is the one who lives.

Guided Writing: Meeting a Bear

In many of my writing classes I do an exercise I adapted from Tristan Rainer's book A New Diary. *Deceptively simple, this exercise is one of the most powerful writing experiences I have ever facilitated. It is always perfect, always giving me just what I need, and inevitably my students amaze themselves with the beauty and profundity of what they write.*
If you would like to try it, here is what you do:

1. *Turn on some sweet music.*
2. *Imagine a place in nature. Accept the first thought that comes into your mind.*
3. *Write as if you were in a waking dream (I am walking along a lake.)*
4. *Describe what you see, hear, smell, feel, and think.*
5. *After awhile you find a small object and take it with you.*
6. *You meet an animal and it travels with you.*
7. *You encounter some problem that at first you don't think you will be able to overcome. You overcome it.*
8. *What did you learn? (Optional)*

You are the boss of this writing. Let it take you where it will. This is where it took me one time. Every guided writing experience is destined to be different.

I am walking along an ice cliff. My path is white, and the rock wall next to me is white. The sky is a deep, clear blue, and off to my right is a white nothingness. I am warm and feel safe, even though this kind of environment would usually scare me. I am wrapped in fur, and it is cold, but the cold air invigorates my skin. I am safe.

My path is still and calm, serene. I wonder if I have ever been anywhere that felt so clean and clear. My path is solid, though a little crunchy, and I enjoy hearing the sound as I tramp along. I am singing, and my voice echoes out into the cavern and back to me. I know I am not alone. I feel absolutely lovely. As I walk along, I feel a hard crunch under my boot. I step back and look down and see something small and dark that I have smashed into the snow.

I dig it out with my gloved hands and find that it is a little carving, a bird, much like the one I made when I was in blind school. I take off my gloves and feel the texture of the wood, the smooth curves. Just feeling the wood, stroking the wood, gives me pleasure. It is exactly like the bird I carved.

I remember now that it took a long time for the bird to take form out of the wood. I had to feel and feel and sand and sand, much longer than I thought necessary. Gradually, though, the bird emerged and has kept me company ever since. I wipe off the bird, surprised that it is undamaged from the snow. I put it in my pocket where it is safe and warm.

I continue walking on the path, yodeling now, just like the record I got in the Netherlands. I am one with the world, right with the world.

Now a real bird flies down by my head, swooping so close that its wing tip almost touches my face, or maybe it does touch my face. The bird lands on a branch. Where did the branch come from? It's sticking up, naked, out of the snow. And the bird sings. And sings. Ah, I love the singing. The bird is blue and bright yellow, so bright I can see the colors and I start to cry. I miss these vivid colors in my life. I sit and listen to the bird singing, caressing the carved bird in my pocket, grateful to be alive.

I hear the growl of a bear, big and black, coming down the path toward me. This bear should be asleep, I think. What is he doing out now, all hungry and coming toward me?

I just sit and wait, watching the bear, fingering my bird, yodeling. I stand up and face the bear. The bear stops his growling, stands up on his hind legs, and looks at me.

I get a deep sense of bear, of the strength of bear, of his hunger and his ferocity. He is of the seasons. Bears go into a cave, sleep, and then wake up hungry and crabby. He needs to eat, but somehow I know I am not his dinner. I move to the side of the path, pressing myself up against the cliff to make room for the bear. He ambles down the path, and I am left with his strong bear odor to keep me company.

What did I learn? Strength is not always pretty. But, like the bear coming out in the winter, it can surprise me and be there when I thought I was surrounded only by frozen nothingness.

Poem: A Fallow Field

A fallow field
isn't a dead field.

A fallow field
buries secrets
in dark, rich soul soil.
The secrets decay,
rot.
Sometimes they smell,
and the stench hurts.

A fallow field only looks dormant or dead,
just as lying in a recliner
for seven hours in one day
watching old movies
might look unproductive or dead.

All those months—
when I feared my work had deserted me,
when the phone calls and e-mails
died.

All those months—
of wondering how I could possibly fill up another fifty years.

All those months—
of waking up at the bottom of the pond,
in the muck,
eyes clogged with algae and doubt,
lungs unable to gather the oxygen I needed
to jump-start the dead battery of hope in my chest.

All those months I felt dead,
useless.

But all those months were fallow months,
I know now,
months where invisible microbes of brilliance were at work in me,
combining and recombining green ideas,
with bold red strategies,
into a rocket ship of creativity.

I thought my battery was leaking all of its power
when really I was plugged in,
recharging my solar soul,
getting ready . . .

Your Turn

Are you avoiding your grief? How did you feel when you read this last question? If it made you mad, then you are avoiding your grief. It is okay to avoid it, just make a conscious decision to do so. Live in the Land of Denial as long as you like. I am not being sarcastic here. Denial can be a perfect response to give us time to recoup. Know, though, that you cannot live there forever. Your grief denied will rise and haunt you until you embrace your loss.

Make a timeline of your life and list all of the losses, great and small, that you can remember. Did you have any accompanying physical symptoms? Who supported you? How did you support yourself? You might want to write a Do-Over, reliving the experience as you wish it had happened. It is never too late to heal.

Grief will last as long as it lasts. In many ways you will never "get over" any significant loss. Be merciful with yourself and take whatever actions or create whatever rituals you would like to honor your love and your loss. Write letters to people who have died. They may still have great wisdom and support to offer.

Chapter 14

Speaking Our Appreciation and Gratitude

"The world is full of suffering and the overcoming of it."
Helen Keller

One of the best habits you can possibly cultivate to overcome your suffering every day is the habit of gratitude. Feeling grateful is so simple that we tend to dismiss the attitude of gratitude as childish or trite. I can tell you that gratitude is the ultimate story shifter. In a heartbeat you can move from self-pity to an overwhelming sense of abundance and joy.

For some reason (probably a Level One power trip), we are often stingy with our appreciation. I know one woman who thinks people shouldn't be thanked for what they "should be doing anyway." She is married to a sweet, generous man and rarely thanks him for anything. She never says she is sorry either. These are relationship-destroying habits, bad for our health and bad for the planet.

No matter how much appreciation you already give, you can always give more. Do you want to wait until the funeral to tell someone how much you love them? People do drop dead, you know, without warning. Much better to voice your appreciation as you go along, so you don't have to experience that horrible feeling of regret. We are all sacred space all of the time, and our inner light can shine brighter when we give and receive honest appreciation.

As with anything, appreciation can be corrupted in Level One when it is used to manipulate. Don't do that.

Accepting Leads to Appreciation

It is hard to feel gratitude and to appreciate what we have if we can't accept the truth about our past and the people we love.

Accepting means letting it be. It means you quit fighting. "This is just how it is," you say to yourself. "My father can't love me the way I want him to. It doesn't matter how good I am, how well I communicate, what a great job I have, or how terrific my children have turned out. He loves the best he can, but it just isn't the way I want to be loved."

Okay. There it is. You have accepted it, and you can live with it. It's not your preference, it's not even what you deserve, but that is how it is.

Accepting sets us free. When we turn our eyes away from what we want to change, when we let go of all that mental pulling and pushing, we have energy to use elsewhere. Your dad may not be able to love you the way you want to be loved, but YOU can learn to love you the way you want to be loved. This sounds simple, but letting go can be very difficult. It will take time and energy to learn to love yourself well.

But if you choose to accept, let go, and go on with your life, you will find something magical begins to happen: the more you love yourself, the more lovable you become. You will find all that you ever wanted from your father will come to you from the most unexpected places. I promise! This is how life works. Ask anyone who has let go.

Once you have stopped trying to beat love out of a turnip, you may have the energy to look around at the abundance surrounding you. Instead of concentrating on what is missing, you might start deeply appreciating the people in your life. What if you got hit by a truck today? Would you have anyone you needed to call from the hospital to tell them how much you love them? You might even have to postpone dying just to make all your phone calls.

What would your life be like if you spent some time every day letting people know you notice who they are, what they do, and how they contribute to your life? This doesn't and shouldn't be some smarmy, fake, "Oh, you're so wonderful!" garbage. Your appreciation needs to resemble the way you express your delight when you smell an exquisite lilac in those first days of spring. (If you haven't experienced spring lilacs, put it on your "100 things to do in my life" list.)

Express your appreciation lightly, with sincerity and warmth, to strangers and loved ones alike. Let your appreciations be tiny, wondrous discoveries, delightful truths that flow out of you like spring water. Do this and every day will be sprinkled with laughter and sweet tears. Simple acknowledgements can and do save lives.

Song: Well Done
(from the CD *Alive, Alive*)

I wrote this song as I was listening to keynote speaker Margarita Suarez at an Oregon Counseling Association conference. She encouraged all of us to jump off that cliff of safety and live our lives more fully. As a therapist for over thirty years, she told us that, in her opinion, the single most limiting factor in people's lives is having never heard "well done." She said men especially need to hear "well done, son."

As soon as I heard these words, my inner Muse said, "That is a song!" I started writing, and at the end of the conference, as I had the group in a circle for the closing song ("It Takes a Whole Village" from my CD Alive, Alive) I heard my Muse again say, "Sing the song!"

"But I have not even sung it out loud to myself yet!" I protested.

"Sing the song!" my Muse insisted, and so I did.

After the conference, two women came up and asked me for the words to the first verse, which was all I had completed at the time. I got a note from one of the women later, telling me she had calligraphied the words, framed them, and given them to her son for his birthday.

I have sung this song at baccalaureates and at almost every presentation I have made for the last several years. A friend played it at her mother's funeral. One high school class calligraphied the song for Mother's Day. It is a simple song with a simple message, and it often makes people cry. I can hear Willie Nelson singing it, and I'm hoping he will want to record it. If you know him, will you ask him?

Well done, son, well done.
I love who you've become.
You're just the way I hoped you'd be.
I love the man in you I see.
Well done, son, well done.

Well done, Dad, well done.
You've helped me to become
The best I could be; you set me free.
I love the you in me I see.
Well done, Dad, well done.

My daughter, my love, well done.
I love who you've become.
You're just the way I hoped you'd be.
A woman strong, courageous and free.
My daughter, my love, well done.

Well done, Mom, well done.
You've helped me to become
The best I could be; you set me free.
I love the you in me I see.
Well done, Mom, well done.

Well done, friends, well done.
You've helped me to become
the best I could be; you set me free.
I love the truth in you I see.
Well done, my friends, well done.

Poem: Murray is My Hero

Murray
Photo by Jan Bateman

In my writing workshops I often have people write about a hero in their lives. Many people cry as they write and read their work aloud. I believe the tears are stored up appreciation. We think these thoughts, but we don't always remember to say them.

Murray isn't a big man; in fact, he weighs less than I do,
which I think is against the rules somehow.
He isn't your aggressive, take-charge kind of guy.
Sometimes he lets himself blend too much into the background,
at least from my point of view.

He doesn't run a big company,
doesn't have a Ph.D.
By the world's standards,
he might be considered pretty average.

But I know my Murray is a giant.
He is the most courageous man I know.
Murray is the one who remembers my best when I'm at my worst.

When I listened to the rough cut of my new CD,
torturing myself with thoughts of: "How awful I sound!
So many flat notes!
Everything sounds the same!
I am just kidding myself.
I suck,"
Murray is the one to remind me that I am a better singer now,
that my listening has improved, and that my standards are now higher.
This is a good thing, he tells me,
nothing to get discouraged about.
Ah, Murray.

Murray is the one who will find the magic when I have lost it.
He is the one who will turn a situation inside out
and show me the sparkling beauty I couldn't see,
so attached to the outside roughage was I.

Murray fools people because his grandeur isn't always obvious.
You have to know what you are looking at and what you are looking for
if you want to see the hero in my beloved.

But if you take the time and have the imagination
to let yourself experience the wonder that my sweet Murray is,
your life will be forever enriched.

And I get to live with him.

Story: Bus Stop Epiphany
(also published in *Wise Women Speak: Changes Along the Path*)

In *"No More Stars,"* I wrote about when a blood vessel burst in my left eye and I knew I had inherited my mother's eye disease. At that time we thought she had macular degeneration, but as it turned out we both inherited Sorsby's Macular Dystrophy, a rare genetic disorder. In November of 1994 I lost my central vision completely. My children have a 50/50 chance of inheriting this disease.

For two years after I lost my central vision and my ability to drive, I managed to avoid using the public buses. This was an act of stubbornness born of pride. I viewed riding the bus as a loss of dignity. People who ride the bus in small towns are generally those who have less power: students, people who can't afford a car or who have lost their licenses, and the disabled. Even though I was legally blind, I did not want to think of myself as handicapped.

So at 43, I was disabled because I couldn't see, but I had stubbornly refused to accept this fact. I wanted my old life back, the life of driving my own car anywhere I wanted to go. If I couldn't have my own car, at least I could continue to ride in private cars driven by my new husband or friends. Riding the public bus, as I saw it then, was a loss of status.

But circumstances forced me to "lower" myself to public transportation. My job with the school district changed mid-year, and I suddenly had to work in five different locations. I could no longer find solutions to my transportation problems without including the bus.

It was a cold, wet January morning when I finally stood, for the first time, at the bus shelter. I was in a crabby mood. I didn't like advertising the fact that I couldn't see by holding my white cane, but I wasn't so obstinate that I would put myself at risk by not letting people know I couldn't see well.

Also, when I am using my cane, people help me without lecturing me. "The sign is right there," they will say if I ask for information without my cane. If I am carrying my magic white stick with a red tip, people's hearts open and they may even walk me where I am going to make sure I get to the right place. I need my cane, and I use it when I have to, but I hated the fact that I needed to use it at all.

As I stood under the shelter, a woman with shoulder-length gray hair approached me. She was very short, and I could see, even with my limited vision, that something was wrong with her teeth. They were sticking out, which affected her speech.

"I missed my ride," she said in a loud voice. Her tone was full of a whining complaint, an unusual tone for most adults.

"I missed my ride," she said again. "They were going to take me to the Opportunity Center, but I missed my ride." She paused for a moment. "Is there a bus coming?"

Why would I be standing under the shelter on this dark rainy day if there weren't a bus coming? I thought to myself. I was obviously still consumed with my crabby self-pity. But I answered her civilly enough, "Yes, bus two, headed downtown, will be here in about five minutes."

"I missed my ride," she said again.

"Yes," I said, "I know."

"I missed my ride. Is there a bus coming?"

I knew now for sure that this woman was developmentally disabled. She was exactly the kind of person I didn't want to have to hang out with. And here she was.

Her need for assistance, though, dragged me out of feeling sorry for myself. I started to feel more gracious and generous toward her.

"A bus will be here in a few minutes to take you downtown," I said in a soft voice. "Just wait here, and you will get your ride."

"What's that you're holding?" she asked, pointing to my cane.

"This is a cane for blind people. I am legally blind. I can't see what I look at straight on, but I can see all around what I'm looking at," I said, holding up my hand in front of my face to show what I couldn't see and then sweeping around in a circle to show what I could see.

Explaining my vision to people is difficult. The word *blind* usually connotes no vision at all to most people. They are confused when I say I am legally blind when I seem to get around easily. I tried to use simple words to explain my disability to this woman because I thought she would have more trouble understanding than most people.

"Can you see the road?" she asked.

"Yes," I said, looking down.

"Can you see that sign over there?" she asked pointing across the street to the sign on a pole beside the bank.

"Yes, I can see there is a sign there, but I can't read it."

"I can," she said proudly, and then read the sign. "Citizen's Valley Bank."

"How do you get around?" she asked. I thought it was a funny question, as I was standing with her at a bus stop, and by that time I was thoroughly enjoying the whole interchange. I loved her frankness, her curiosity. She asked me questions the way young children do. If she wanted to know something, she just asked.

I told her I rode the bus, got rides from friends and my husband, and walked.

"Does your husband still love you?" she asked. "Do your friends still love you?"

I let a few heartbeats pass and then said, "Yes, they do."

She thought about that for a few moments. "How did you get this blindness? Can I get it? Am I going to go blind?"

"I got this from my mother. It is inherited. You won't get what I have. It is very rare."

"I won't go blind then. I won't be like you?"

"You won't get what I have. You might get something else, but you won't get what I have."

That seemed to satisfy her. We were quiet for the next few minutes, and then the bus came.

We climbed on the bus with the three other people who were waiting in the bus shelter. I sat near the bus driver, and she sat directly across from me.

In the same outside voice, slightly too loud for close conversation, she said, "I'm going to pray for a miracle for you. It's not right that you inherited blindness from your mom. You should be able to see. I'm going to pray for you."

"Thank you," I said. "I appreciate your prayer."

I was aware of all the other people on the bus, aware that they all knew I couldn't see, that they all knew she had some kind of developmental disability. I imagined they thought us a poignant pair. And I didn't care what they thought.

I was filled with my own thoughts and feelings. I felt loved and seen and part of the fragile human race. This woman with the steel gray hair and odd teeth had spoken what many people with better social skills only think. "Does your husband still love you? Do your friends still love you?" In other words, are you diminished by your blindness? Are you still worthy?

She had spoken of her fears that she might get what I had. The thought of not being able to read the sign scared her.

She isn't the only person who is afraid of my blindness. Once I had a friend walk by me without speaking. I hadn't recognized him as he walked by, but when my daughter told me who it was, I hollered a hello. I hadn't spoken to him since my vision loss, but he was aware of it. He stayed fifteen feet away from me, and when I told him I hadn't spoken sooner because I couldn't see him, he said, "I know," staying firmly planted at a distance.

My blindness isn't contagious. My powerlessness and helplessness aren't contagious either. But I have been wounded by people acting as if my struggle could somehow bushwhack them.

This woman and I had stood in the rain together, waiting for the bus for very different, yet extremely similar reasons. We both needed help. The fact that we needed help was obvious to everyone. We couldn't hide.

I didn't mind having a visible disability so much anymore. I had enjoyed a very human moment with this woman, and she had been compassionate and generous with me. She had been honest. I would rather hang out with her than be in a meeting with people pretending competence and vying for a place on the power ladder.

For the first time since my vision loss, I was thankful for my blindness, for being forced to deal with my limitations. I was finally forced to ask for and receive help graciously.

I felt grateful for the many daily lessons in humility I received—not being able to plug in my stereo, not being able to proofread documents, having to ask for rides. I am a tough nut, and it has taken big problems to bring me to my knees and force me to admit that I am merely, only, and remarkably, human.

When I first began having vision problems, I felt a capricious god was punishing me. I was drowning in "new age guilt," feeling that I had brought my blindness on myself by having negative thoughts. Was there something in my life I did not want to look at? Could this be how the universe works?

After trying all kinds of therapies, including antioxidants and psychic healings, I finally found some peace.

During a deep relaxation session with a dear friend, I dreamed I was flying through the cosmos, far beyond the Milky Way. I heard a call and came before a bodiless council. They asked if I were willing to take on this life, which would include blindness. I was told my purpose in this life was to be a vortex of healing into the past and into the future.

This experience changed my view of what was happening to me and my role in it. I no longer felt like a victim. My disease was not an accident; I had done nothing wrong. I wasn't being punished. I had willingly taken on my disease, and my job was to figure out what being "a vortex of healing into the past and into the future" meant.

Fifteen years have passed since I started losing my vision. Ten years have gone by since I lost my central vision and became legally blind. I have traveled through the land of despair and self-pity, of hopelessness and terror. I have felt overwhelmed by not being able to find something I dropped on the floor or by making a long distance phone call. I have known the strange loneliness of the afflicted, the disappearance of support from people who "know better." I have had to build muscles I didn't know I had, muscles that help me pick myself up again and again, muscles that give me peace when I find myself alone.

The mundane troubles I face—not being able to find the sponge by the sink because it is partially hidden and too camouflaged for me to see, not being able to locate the sweet pickle relish in the refrigerator—these common irritants, while occasionally getting the better of me, give me a chance to practice a daily meditation. What is important? What isn't important? How do I need help? How can I give help? How am I alone, and how am I connected? How do I need to slow down, and how do I need to take action?

Being a vortex of healing into the future is easy for me to understand. All of my work is about healing, about helping people cast away the gargoyles of their personalities which guard the gate to the garden where Buddha, Christ, and the Goddess wait for all of us.

When a Petal Falls, It's Still a Rose

What I have learned on this journey?

1. **We are not alone in our suffering.**

When I first lost my vision, I felt all alone. Now I know that everyone has some kind of disability. Maybe they have no sense of humor or maybe they can never admit when they are wrong. My disability isn't a particularly bad one, as it turns out. I am in no physical pain. Blindness hasn't changed my appearance (except that I now look a lot better in pictures, at least to me!). My blindness tends to bring out the best in people. My experience at the bus stop is just one example of hundreds of interactions I have had with strangers. My need for help, their giving of help, and my gracious receiving makes for some magical everyday moments.

2. **We need to look for the blessing in whatever challenge comes our way without feeling guilty that we have brought our affliction upon ourselves.**

Feeling that we brought our cancer or our blindness upon ourselves by worrying just creates more worrying. I think it is much more helpful to say to ourselves: "Okay. I've got this thing. I need to deal with it. What blessings can I find in this experience?" Personally, I have gained so much from my adventure with blindness that if I were offered perfect vision in exchange for losing what I have learned, I would remain blind. Gladly. I am more patient, more serene, kinder and generally a better person because I have been forced to ask for help. I see the world in soft focus, much like an impressionistic painting. Who is to say my vision or my life is diminished?

3. **It is not what happens to us that counts. The story we tell ourselves about what happens to us defines our experience.**

Am I a cripple? Am I a victim? Or am I a woman with a challenge to overcome? Am I diminished? Damaged goods? Or am I a hero in my own life? Whatever story I choose to tell myself will determine what my day or life is like. The choice is up to me.

4. **Whatever we practice we get good at and we are always practicing something.**

If we practice courage, we will get braver. If we practice being timid, our lives will shrink. If we practice asking for help, we will get better at it. If we practice self-pity, we will get good at that, too. (Make no mistake here. I have practiced self-pity plenty. I don't like how I feel or who I am when I do this, so I have decided to practice gratitude instead.)

5. **Our troubles do not need to separate us from others. They can be a bridge to a deepening of character and relationships.**

If we practice taking responsibility for our lives, reaching out, being braver, and letting people know who we really are, our lives will be transformed and transforming.

Song: Still a Rose
(from the CD *Alive, Alive*)

A young woman with a disability played a song with this title at a Very Special Arts performance at a national occupational therapy conference I attended with Murray in Baltimore. I was so touched by her saxophone playing that I took the title, made up a new melody, and wrote this song.

I am a person with a disability.
When you look at me, what do you see?
Do you see only what is wrong
or do you see the ways that I am strong?
Am I a cripple, or do you suppose
that when a petal falls it's still a rose?

Chorus:
**Do you suppose, do you suppose
that when a petal falls it's still a rose?
Do you suppose, do you suppose
that when a petal falls it's still a rose?
When a petal falls, when a petal falls,
when a petal falls it's still a rose.
When a petal falls, when a petal falls,
when a petal falls it's still a rose.**

Finding magic in adversity
means learning a whole new way to see.
You've got to treasure what you've got
instead of yearning after what you've lost.
Are you a victim, or could you suppose
that when a petal falls it's still a rose.

Chorus

So when sad things happen to you,
here are a few things you can do:
You can search for the gift inside
and always work on your state of mind.
You'll find the blessing if you will suppose
that when your petal falls you're still a rose.

Chorus

Song: Gratitude
(from the CD *Alive, Alive*)

>*I'm ending this section with a song I wrote when I was in blind school after I first lost my vision. I was devastated when one day I could read and drive and the next day I couldn't. I felt like I had been hit by a truck; I was single, my job was going away, and I was feeling quite sorry for myself. Then I went to blind school and met a man who really had been hit by a truck, a drunk driver actually, and had lost a leg and total vision in both eyes. As I watched him struggle to just get from our classroom to the sidewalk outside the building, I thought, "I am so lucky!" And that was nothing but the truth.*

Gratitude, gratitude.
It's an attitude.
Gratitude, gratitude.
It's an attitude.
You can be grateful for what you've got
or complain about what's not.
It's up to you.

Your Turn

>*Here are some activities you can do to help you learn to accept and appreciate more often.*

1. Make a list of everyone who has been kind to you today. Then try making a list of everyone who has been kind to you for the last week. Stretch your mind after that and make a list of everyone in the last year. Are you counting the clerks who went out of their way to help you? The postal worker who takes extra care with your packages? Now make a list for your whole life. I dare you to have a day of self-pity after this exercise.
2. Pick ten people from your list to appreciate. You can send them a card, call them, see them in person, or just send them an anonymous thank

you card. Do something. Take action. I guarantee you will feel better about yourself, other people, and your place in the world, and it won't have cost you anything except time.

3. See beauty everywhere. Would you be a more joyful person if every morning as you awoke, you looked around your room and noticed the beauty hanging on your walls? Or what about the beauty lying next to you, if you are lucky enough to have someone to snuggle with before you arise and greet the day. Have you really looked at people in your life lately, and I mean REALLY looked?

4. What would happen if you wrote a poem about how your partner, friend, or teacher is a hero to you? If you have children you could write them a new poem every year to store with their school photos. You will never regret words of love you have spoken, but you can easily regret words you have saved, like good china, for some special occasion that never arrives.

Part II

Loving in Harmony

Vicki and Murray
Jan Bateman photo

When we love someone deeply, we invite every neurosis we have harbored in secret to come out and play. And, just to make our lives really interesting, built-in cultural problems, such as gender communication style differences, can collide with a lack of clear agreements to create one big relationship mess. This happens with good friends as well as with lovers.

In this section I attempt to map out this tricky territory. What I offer here, Murray and I have learned the hard way. If I show the safety lines we've built and reveal the rocks we've fallen over, our struggles will have been put to good use.

Chapter 15

The Heart of the Matter: Men and Women are Different

Duh.

Man School

When Murray and I have a difficult interaction, I sometimes accuse him of having just returned from Man School. I never need to explain what I mean. Once when a bank clerk overheard me make this comment, he knew exactly what I was talking about. "You mean where men go to learn how to forget important things and to not pay attention to how their wives feel?"

"Yup," I said.

"All men are graduates," he said with a grin.

Murray learns how to be defensive in Man School. If I am unhappy, he thinks he is responsible. He should never have done whatever it was that he did to make me unhappy. He feels enormous pressure to fix me—and is ashamed that he can't. He wants me to just shut up. My problem isn't my problem anymore; it is his problem and his problem is that I have brought up a problem. (Around and around we go and where we stop, nobody knows!)

We had such a tangled, frustrating discussion the other day. I had been listening to a fascinating book, *A Mind at a Time* by Mel Levine. He articulates eight ways the mind is wired. His theory is that we all have a unique brain profile. When we accept and appreciate this, we can take steps toward using our strengths more and finding strategies to help us deal with our weaknesses.

The chapter on memory was especially fascinating to me, as Murray and I have memories that work very differently. Briefly, there are three types of memory: short-term, active working memory, and long-term.

Short-term lasts just a few seconds when we receive information. We decide quickly what we will do with it. Active working memory acts like RAM on a computer; we use this to keep track of our schedule, i.e. where we are going when we start driving down the road. Long-term memory is the most durable. Once something is there, it sticks, even if we can't always find what we want to remember, hence the "ah-ha in the shower" phenomenon.

My daughter, Katie, has a phenomenal memory. She can recognize people she hasn't seen since second grade, can remember their names and how they knew each other. Her active working memory is excellent, as is mine. Murray's long-term memory is better than mine, but his active working memory leaks. For example, he will start driving down the street in any direction that takes his fancy, drive for a while, and only then think about where he is going. This makes me crazy. I am incapable of this kind of behavior. I don't understand it. The story I told myself about this for a while was that Murray was, well, stupid.

Murray has a Master's degree from USC; he is not stupid. When I chant the "Murray is stupid" story, though, I damage Murray, myself and our future together.

My conversation with Murray that morning began something like this. "Now that we realize we are differently wired, it becomes a matter of strategies. I have a good active working memory, but I also have tons of strategies to help me. If I make a promise and I don't have anything to write myself a note, I move my watch to my other arm. When I want to remember to return something to someone, I put it out on the floor where I can't miss it. I am very clever!"

Murray, though, forgets things all the time, but has few strategies to help him to remember. He forgot the date of Katie's birthday recently. He forgot where I was when I spent the night in Portland. He forgets the names of people I work with every week. He forgets a lot, and it gets in the way of our relationship. Every time he has to ask me something that he has already been told, I feel disconnected from him.

Adding to my confusion, Murray remembers all of **his** important appointments, such as the time and place of his work conferences and what time his karate class starts. I don't have anything to do with these scheduled events, and he seems to manage just fine by himself. Why is it, then, he needs me to remind him over and over about activities and people in our daily lives?

"Is it a memory weakness, then, or a refusal to seek strategies to deal with the memory weakness that is the real problem?" I asked. Because of my visual challenges, I need to have lots of strategies to deal with daily living. Maybe finding solutions instead of repeating the same error isn't about how our brains are wired as much as the fact that I hate, I mean hate, making the same mistake twice. Murray doesn't seem to mind. Is this the difference between us? If so, I wanted to hang out in this place and explore it for a while.

Murray didn't want to explore. He got mad. "You have no invitation to fix me," he said. "To whom is he speaking?" I wondered. Since when do we need an invitation, an explicit invitation, to be curious and explore with each other? We are a green light for each other all the time. No subjects are taboo.

He accused me of being insensitive and continuing to speak when it was hurting him. I said I was not going to tiptoe around any subject with him. I felt like the Bitch of the North again, but that only convinced me that we were dealing with Murray's shame and my fear of being a bad girl.

"Well, I hear a clear message to shut up," I said, "and I will do that if that is what you want me to do, but is that really what you want? If I shut up, this will still all be here to be dealt with later."

Some silent moments passed. Both of us calmed down. Murray felt safe again and we were able to talk about this strategy thing without a lot of emotion.

"Have you been sneaking off to Man School again?" I asked.

"Yup," he said. "I'm an A student!" my sweet husband finally admitted. We grinned at each other. It's amazing how much a grin can heal.

I know Murray has been to Man School when:

- He starts making up facts to support an argument.
- He tries to get me to shut up by accusing me of being insensitive, a bully, or an addict.
- He gives me complete responsibility for remembering the names and connections among the people in our lives.

Story: What It's Like To Be Murray
By Murray Lein

Murray wrote this to help me understand his world and appreciate his contributions. This piece reminded me to look at all the things he does well that I don't even notice. He is like the Energizer bunny as he flits around the house and yard tending the plants that grow and the machines that break. He doesn't always tell me what he has accomplished, just as I do not tell him all of the housework tasks I have taken care of. (Other people's work can be invisible if we aren't careful.)

Even though Murray does a lot to help maintain and beautify our home, he doesn't always do what he says he will do. One example occurred when our hot tub was on the fritz. Murray had talked with the spa store and they had suggested jiggling the thermostat to see if that would get it working again. Murray had agreed to do this and went outside specifically to work on the hot tub. When he came back in the house, I assumed he had done what he set out to do, and he let me believe he had done just that. Later, when the truth emerged, (he had not jiggled the thermostat after all,) Murray wrote this letter to help me understand how his brain works.

How my brain works:

> Beloved Vicki,
>
> I know I told you that I would reset the thermostat on the hot tub as the serviceman suggested, and I know that the task seemed pretty straightforward to you, but here is how my brain approached keeping my promise to you:
>
> As I went to turn the thermostat on and off, I saw something that made me switch tracks mid-stride. Our little pond in the backyard, which, as you know, I have to walk by to get to the hot tub, was full of muck. The water was cloudy. Leaf particles were floating around, and the plants looked like they were dissolving. Inner shriek!
>
> "Murray to the rescue!" I said to myself as I rolled up my sleeves. First get the screen and strain some of the crud. Drain some

water by tilting the pump over the side of the pond with the fountain still running. Pull the filter off of the pump and hose off the sludge. Brrr, that water is cold. Get the hose and add water. Meanwhile, Vicki, you are upstairs waiting for me to jiggle the thermostat.

Now, with the pond task taken care of, I needed to bring circulation back to my arms. The spa water could help do that. It wasn't too cold. If only the heater hadn't pooped out. So many things had seemed to go on the fritz the last couple of days. Well, at least the garage door opener was working again. I only had to schedule an appointment with the repair guy. Oh, that reminds me to replace the bulb in the garage. Well, I think to myself, Vicki's still waiting, assuming I have done what I said I would do. Better get going on switching the thermostat on and off.

Later, as we are driving down the street, you, my beloved, said, "Maybe that will get the hot tub working again."

I can't recall what I said, but I know that I did not say, "Oh, darn, I forgot to jiggle the thermostat. I had to do some emergency pond rescue. I'll do the hot tub later." No, I drove on, pretending that I had jiggled the thermostat as I said I would. Now I really was in hot water!

The next day I confessed my lack of integrity as we discussed attention control. The sin, as I see it, was not forgetting to do the hot tub, but rather in pretending that I hadn't forgotten. I had practiced not admitting my mistakes, which is always a bad idea if you want to be honest with your beloved.

Your comment: "This is a trivial event in our lives, one that could easily be overlooked, but our lives are made up of such 'trivia'" woke me up. Thank you.

Love,
Murray

Note from Vicki: The habit of lying is bad for everyone. Why should Murray need to lie? If he is afraid of me, we need to talk about that. If he has a problem with his memory, then we should work together to find strategies to help him. One thing I know for sure: if we do not admit there is a problem, then we are doomed to repeat it.

This little interaction is a sample of our relationship and of Murray's relationship with himself. We are different, thank God! Let's make those differences interesting and not the source of conflict and shame.

Tips for Men

I think it is important that I include in this chapter some strong advice for men about how to deal with the women in their lives. Women can be overpowering, nagging, and downright bitchy, and it is best if you stop them before they get good at it. If Murray didn't know how to set some limits with me, well, it could get pretty ugly. I do not want to be a micromanaging, fault-finding, negative know-it-all, but sometimes my worst parts take over, and if Murray weren't strong enough to help me snap back into my best self, we would have parted ways long ago.

Micromanaging

"Honey, why don't you put your asparagus on the top of your plate? Then you will have room for the bread at the end of the buffet."

I have never heard this exact sentence, but I've heard women ask "questions" that aren't really questions, and I've heard women sticking their noses into their men's business to such a degree that it is embarrassing for those who witness this inappropriate mothering. How does he manage to tie his shoes if you aren't around to tell him?

Sometimes old married couples can get into this kind of disrespectful micromanaging, but I have heard couples in their twenties act this way as well. What is wrong with a woman who thinks her man is so incompetent, and what is wrong with a man who lets himself be bossed around?

This behavior is ugly and insidious. Stop it, gently, as soon as you see it. Here are some suggestions about how to set a limit with your sweetie:

- "Honey, thanks, but I don't need any help figuring out how to fill my plate."
- "Darling, I have noticed a pattern that I think is unhealthy for both of us. Are you in a mood where you can talk about it? I've noticed that you sometimes tell me to do things that I can decide how to do by myself. Each little comment isn't so important, maybe, but when you tell me how to do things I can do perfectly well on my own, I feel disrespected. I think this is a dangerous habit for both of us."

Complaining

It is easy to fall into the habit of complaining. I am one of the most positive people you could meet and still I have been known to fall into the habit of concentrating on what is going wrong instead of on what is going right. One complaint isn't too bad ("Murray, I don't like it when you leave your cups all over the house"), but when one comment becomes six and then twenty, it can be a little much.

Brave, wise Murray has told me, when I am on a roll, "No more complaining! I just don't want to hear anymore complaining for the next few minutes. No, the next few hours. No, the rest of the day!"

When he says something like this, I am grateful that he has called my attention to my negativity. "Thank you," I say, "you are right. I have been complaining a lot lately, and I will stop completely right this second. In fact, I will switch to appreciation. Murray, I really appreciate the way you take care of the hot tub. It is a lot of work, and I never even have to think about it."

Murray has stopped my destructive behavior, and I have switched from feeling crummy to feeling great just by switching my focus. Yay, Murray!

Being Right

Murray helps me let go of the reigns of my high horse. "I am tired of being wrong. I want to be right for a while," he will tell me. This works like a charm.

Important note to women: You have to cooperate here. If you keep arguing or micromanaging or complaining when you have been given this feedback, you will pour acid on your relationship. Even if you feel you are really, really right, stop anyway. Give your man a chance to breathe. You can always come back to a problem later. I warn you: If you run over your man, you will emasculate him. If he decides not to take it, he will leave you. If he does take it, his masculinity will leave, and you will be all alone anyway.

Let's not let any shame creep in here! We have all picked up lots of bad habits along the way. The trick is to recognize them and then change. No one is perfect. We will probably have to be told to stop more than once. Oh, well. Stick with it, be open to feedback, keep loving yourself and your lover, friend, child, or parent, and you will build the courage you need to live authentically ever after.

Poem: How to Spot a Real Man

Here is my advice to my daughter and all daughters about what is really important in a man or a woman: essence, not appearance. Neither looks or a good résumé, but character and proven integrity are the essential ingredients of a healthy relationship.

How to Spot a Real Man:
It isn't easy—
our world values the image of a man much more than his essence.
But I can tell you with certainty,
my beloved daughter,
where manhood lies
and where it will never be found.

What you will see in a real man,
day after day,
may seem as "boring" as it is essential.
He will be dependable.
What he says he will do, he does.

His dependability will become exciting to you
because he will be dependably interesting,
dependably funny,
and dependably unexpected.

When you are afraid,
You can count on a real man to hold you, stroke your hair
and murmur into your ear that everything will be all right.
You will believe him.

A real man will probably want to fix things.
Maybe he will repair broken machines around the house,
or maybe he will tinker with the car,
or maybe he will pay the bills.
Maybe he will paint a river on your ceiling.
A man has to make an impact on his world.

But a wise man also will know when not to fix things,
when to just listen,
and listen,
offering no solutions,
no platitudes.
He will know how to be completely present with you in your pain
and grief
and fear.
His listening and his presence will give you the strength to find your
    own solutions.

A real man won't let you abuse him.
He will kindly, but firmly, stop you when you get crabby and pick at him
or when you micromanage which route he takes to the movies.
A real man won't let you become a shrew.
He won't be afraid of you;
he will love you in the middle of your worst bitchiness,
but he will not allow you to hurt him as you flail about,
trying to feel better.

A real man will touch your body with reverence no matter what your
    body looks like.
He will love you as a Twiggy
or as a model for Rubens,
with your luscious thighs and round belly.
He will lightly trace your "imperfections"—
your nose that is too big
or the stretch marks on your breasts
and on your abdomen,
the stretch marks you won as you grew your babies,
whether they were his babies or not.

A real man will know how to laugh,
and he will make you laugh.
He will see the humor in a situation sometimes before you do,
and he will help you find your way out of your self-created morasses
with his lighthearted touch.

A real man won't know everything or pretend to know what he doesn't
    know.
A real man will be an eager learner.
He will be curious about this wild life around us.
He will know that his mistakes are opportunities to set himself free.

He will need to learn from you to be complete,
and he will know this.
He will know what wisdom you possess within your golden female dust,
which he must gather tenderly with his mouth and ears and heart.

A real man may be charming,
but extremely charming men are often not real men at all.
Their charm hides a lack of character, so be suspicious.
Dessert is fun, but you can't survive on a diet of chocolate and meringue.
It rots your teeth,
your confidence,
and your soul.

Beware of a man who pulls you away from people who love you,
people whom you have always trusted.
Beware of a man who wants you to keep secrets,
a man who makes you feel as if he possesses the key to a strange,
 exciting existence.
Listen to your belly,
listen to your heart,
and run, run, as fast as you can
as soon as you know you have met a soul-killing man,
because, believe me, my daughter,
they exist.
And you are no match for them.

Don't be their next meal.

Trust your women friends
when they tell you they smell a rat.
They will see the shreds of your self-confidence stuck in his teeth
when you see only the glamour of his smile.
Listen well and deeply to these warnings
because your life is at stake.

My darling,
the real men are often the ones who are not in the foreground of the picture.
They don't always pop out easily.
They are the ones who didn't get their pictures in the yearbook much;
they instead took the pictures or put the yearbook together.
Often they are not flashy or handsome.
Men who are too gorgeous or too athletically talented can get spoiled.
They only see themselves and their beauty.
The world acclaims them,
teaches them to look in the mirror and marvel at their perfection.
Not many can resist the lure of this power.
It's like the Ring of All Power
that corrupts any who stay under its influence too long,
even the humble, sweet Bilbos among us.

No, sweet daughter,
look for a man who knows his passion,
a man who uses his talents to improve the world,
a man who doesn't need the adoration of fans
or the outward trappings of McMansions or Jaguars
to know his worth.

Look for a man who knows he is a man already,
one who doesn't need to prove it to himself and to the world and to you
    every day.
A man who needs to prove he is a man
can never prove he is a man
because his needing to prove he is a man
proves he isn't.

Look for a man who gazes at you with such love in his eyes
you think you will burst or melt.
Look for a man who can't believe in his good luck in finding you.
Look for a man who will let you comfort him when he is troubled,
a man who will let you contribute to him.
This is essential.
A man who needs to solve all of his problems alone
is a man who doesn't need a wife;
he needs a girl child to father and dominate.
This is not intimacy.
This is a form of infancy,
a pattern that may prevent either member of the duet from ever
    growing up.

Look for a man who knows how to stay connected,
even when he needs to take his space,
a man who knows he needs to go shoot at targets
or to kick people in a martial arts class.

But a man who needs to kick you away to get his privacy is not a man;
he is a boy pretending to be a man.
Boys pretending to be men can be very dangerous.
They pull you in and then shove you away
because they fear being seen.
If you ever discover they are boys pretending to be men,
they might start to nibble away at you,
weakening your power to see them,
weakening your confidence in yourself and what you know.

My beloved daughter
and all beloved daughters,
you must be strong in yourself to find a man worthy of you.
Before you seek a real man to share your life,
find your own passions,
your own way to serve the world.
Try all the colors of the palette
until you discover those which most truly reveal your soul.
Once you are whole and beautiful within yourself,
you will be ready to find a partner who can reflect your beauty back to you.
You will be able to appreciate his delicious male strength,
while knowing you do not need him for your survival.

May you have the faith,
the courage,
and the wisdom to spot a real man when you see him.
May your precious life, then, be blessed with deep intimacy,
the most dangerous,
fabulous,
and rare adventure any two people can co-create.

Love,
Mom

Poem: How to Spot a Good Woman
For my son and all sons.

Don't look for a woman who needs you—
look for a woman who wants you.

A woman who needs you to feel secure
or complete
may look whole on the outside,
but inside she leaks.
She needs to patch her own holes,
but she doesn't know that.
She thinks someone,
YOU,
from the outside,
will bring harmony and peace to her inner cacophony.
She may make you feel big and strong,
powerful, and competent.
She may look good on your arm,
but she will be drinking from the marrow of your soul,
and,
eventually,
she will learn you cannot save her.
She will hate you for this
and her subtle and not so subtle nibbles at your self-confidence
will destroy you
if you give her enough time.

Instead,
look for a woman who wants you,
wants you for your sense of humor and your quick wit,
for the way life seems brighter when you are around.
A woman who wants you
will focus her loving light on what is good and brilliant about you,
but she will not be blind to your shortcomings.

She will make you feel safe enough to admit you don't know,
or that you are wrong.
She will never take advantage of you when you show your vulnerability.
She will love you more for having the strength to reveal
how tender you can be.

Beware of women who are too beautiful.
Their beauty can be a spell
which lures you into the sweet promise of Perpetually Fulfilled Desire.
You won't be able to see the flesh and blood woman behind the spell.
The Beautiful Woman knows this.
She is afraid she is nothing without the spell of her Beauty,
and she will be your Love Goddess perhaps for years.
But one day one of you will tire of the dance.
One day she will notice her Beauty is beginning to fade,
or you will,
and she will not know who she is without It.

Instead,
look for a woman who feels attractive
and radiates a juicy optimism.
Her spirit should be lively,
even if her personality is quiet.
Life should be an adventure to her,
a heroic journey with you as a valiant partner.

You want a woman who can make her own way on the Road
but doesn't have to.
You want a woman who isn't afraid of her strength
or your weakness.

You want a woman who shines her Beauty into the world
from her art,
whatever shape it takes,
from her children,

be they of her flesh or her compassion.
You deserve a woman
who isn't intimidated by your brilliance
or troubled by your pain.

Do not look for a woman who has not suffered,
for such women can be easily drowned by trivialities.
Instead,
look for a woman who has transformed her pain into compassion and
    wisdom,
a woman whose connection with Spirit and Soul
keep her humble and hopeful.

Stay away from a woman who needs rescuing
for she will take you down with her Ship of Wounds.
Instead,
look for a woman who can ask for and receive help graciously,
one to whom you can turn for consolation or inspiration.

A good woman may or may not be a good cook.
But that is not a problem for you because you can cook if it's important
    to you.
A good woman may or may not keep a clean house,
But you know how to pick up your own socks and mop your own floors.
The two of you will figure all this out.

My son and all sons,
be a good man, first,
then invite a good woman to find you.
Walk in the world letting your light shine.
Be ready to recognize her light when she turns her gaze your way.

And learn how to tango.

Song: Song for Men
(from the CD *Daring to Sing*)

> Since I write so many songs for women—"Menopause," "All Women Are Beautiful," "WarriorBabe"—I thought it would be a good idea to write a song for men. Here it is:

This is a song for the men out in the audience.
We want you to know we understand.
Sometimes when you're living with a woman,
(Spoken) it really doesn't matter what you do.
If you do or if you don't,
you're damned.

It starts sounding like a simple question.
But you know there is more than that at stake.
Cuz if you get the wrong answer to this question,
the sofa will be your only mate.

(Spoken) And it goes something like this:
"Honey, do I look fat in this dress?"
Now tell me, what are you gonna say?
"No, honey. You don't look fat in that dress!"
"You mean I look fat some other way?"

The problem lies in the question
and that it has passed from her lips.
She thinks your love's connected
to what is on her hips.

So . . . when you hear,
"Honey, do I look fat in this dress?"
Say, "I want you! I want you now!"
"Honey, you mean I look good in this dress?"
"So good, let me show you how."

You need to answer the deeper question:
Is your love for me still deep and true?
You say, "Honey, I love you more now
than when I said 'I do.'"

Your Turn

What qualities do you appreciate about the opposite sex? How is that person sleeping next to you your hero?

Did any of the "Tips for Men" strike home? Do you have any micromanaging bad habits? If in doubt, ask the person you think "benefits" from your unsought advice.

Chapter 16

Agreeing to Couple Well

Write Your Love Down While It's Hot

There will be times in your relationship when you will not be able to remember why you ever got together with your partner in the first place. Those qualities you thought you loved about your knight in shining armor—his commitment to his family and his land, for example—will be the very things that drive you crazy.

Write down, with glowing descriptions, why you love each other and keep it in a place where you can easily find it. When you find yourselves disgusted with each other, pull out that document and it will map your way back to the heart of your relationship. Your brain will clear, and you won't care nearly as much about being right as about being connected and compassionate.

Poem: Why I Love Murray

Once when I was particularly angry with Murray, I forced myself to write a list of why I loved him. Writing the list shifted me out of my anger and the list has helped me ever since.

- He rubs my feet almost every day.
- He initiates tough conversations.
- When he is speaking with his Habib from India accent, I think I might just explode in delight.
- He has seen me at my worst and loves me anyway.
- He lets me know when I'm wrong, usually in a loving way.
- He admits it when he's defensive and then looks at his behavior and changes.
- He often shifts before I do.

- He makes painting look like it is no big deal. He makes all the work he does look light and easy.
- He reminds me of what I do know when I forget.
- When he speaks from his magical self, he is full of profound, luscious wisdom.
- He is one of the funniest people I know.
- When I am suffering, full of doubt and despair, he will just say, out of the blue, "I'm cuckoo bullets for you, 24/7."
- He will throw me a rope to help me climb out of an emotional pit before I even know I need one. And again, out of the blue, he will say, "Who is responsible for my happiness?"—before I even form the worry that my lack of cheerfulness will surely drown him.
- He is the most tenderhearted, bravest man I know, and when he is doing karate, he is HOT!

Getting Clear About Our Agreements

Once you are clear about why you love someone, get clear about what guide ropes you want to put in place to help you when the sea of life gets stormy. Agreements can be wonderful guide ropes. Speak your agreements clearly and be on the lookout for unspoken agreements. While some invisible agreements are helpful "given's" in a relationship, others are insidious and damaging. These unhelpful rules we follow almost instinctively can be a slow-acting acid on our love.

For example, "Do not tell me the truth about how I did, even when I ask, because my ego is too fragile" is a rule which will lead to emotional bankruptcy. The rule: "You must guess at what makes me happy, but you will always guess wrong. My happiness is your responsibility and you are failing" is a rule which breeds martyrs and resentment.

At our wedding festival, (Murray called it our "Hallow wedding" because it was the Saturday before Halloween), we pledged the following vows to each other. Both of us had been married before, and we were familiar with some obstacles to avoid. These are agreements we use on a daily basis to keep our behavior smack dab in the center of our love.

When we are in trouble, we go back and look at how well we are keeping these five simple agreements.

Murray and Vicki's Holy Agreements:

1. Don't Say "Yes" When You Mean "No" and then Blame Me
2. Love Yourself Well
3. Love Each Other Well
4. Own Your Own Farts
5. Take Turns

These agreements serve as our marriage life raft. Once, when Murray was most deeply lost in his stuff, he actually wanted to renegotiate Agreement #4: Own Your Own Farts. I told him we could talk about this, since no subject is taboo, but there was no way in hell I would stay married to a man who didn't take a stand for admitting his mistakes. His wanting to renegotiate this agreement only helped confirm my belief in how lost he was. (The poem "A Fight to the Death" chronicles this time in our marriage.)

These agreements have worked well for us, and you are welcome to borrow or amend them or to make up your own. It is very important, though, to have an agreement about your core commitments if you want to get through those inevitable dark times. Do you believe that no topic is taboo? Do you want to have a transparent relationship, where you continually share what is going on within you?

Note: While we are on the subject of sharing feelings and thoughts, let me say upfront that I do not believe every thought and feeling needs to be shared in order to have a truly authentic relationship. "I was just being honest" can be an excuse for offering unasked for advice or hurtful criticism. Save me from such truth telling! Irresponsible sharing leads to such comments as, "I never liked the name Kathleen. Did I ever tell you that?" My daughter's name is Kathleen, and I cannot think of one good reason why this friend felt she needed to share this opinion with me. I think she was angry with me, and this was her anger leaking out, but that is another story.

Your Turn

Write out a list of why you love your partner. Do it right now! If you put it off, it will go and live with all those other things you tell yourself you are going to do and then never do. Make lists about why you love your friends, your children, and your parents. Write about people who have encouraged you. Get it all down now, and then share it. Life is short!

Chapter 17

Agreement #1: Don't Say "Yes" When You Mean "No" and then Blame Me

Avoiding Martyr Hell

This is the anti-martyr agreement. You will know you have broken this agreement when:

- You feel resentment (This is because you said "yes" when you meant "no").
- You are angry for even being asked something, as if someone violated you just by making a request.

Most of us don't think we are martyrs; we just think other people are ungrateful. We don't introduce ourselves with: "Hi, I'm Vicki Hannah Lein, and I am a martyr. You cannot trust what comes out of my mouth because I will always be trying to guess what you want. My 'yeses' don't necessarily mean 'yes.' I have a hard time saying 'no,' so I go ahead and do what I don't really want to do and then secretly blame you. I feel like a victim. You made me a victim. I will hate you or myself soon."

No, I have never heard anyone introduce themselves this way, but I sure have known a lot of people who act as if this is the song they wake up humming each morning. If you do what you don't want to do, you will build up resentment. You might become passive-aggressive by chronically arriving ten minutes late or starting arguments over nothing. You might make hostile comments and then say, "I was just kidding!" when people protest. Regardless of how you act out your resentment, it will interfere with your sacred intimacy.

This martyr behavior might sneak up on you. We are all capable of it. If you take on Agreement #1, though, at least you are saying you want to be caught when you are practicing being a martyr. "Did you say yes when you meant no?" will be a question you welcome instead of fear, because you know that a subtext of martyrdom is acid on a loving connection, whether it be between a parent and child, lovers, or friends.

Blinded by Being Right

Justine, a woman my mother met when she was in blind school, came to visit me with her guide dog. She often did presentations and assured me she would love to present to classes in the two elementary schools where I worked. "You can stop anytime you want," I told her. "There is absolutely no need to do any more presentations than you want to. When this stops being fun, we will stop."

I had been clear. I had done my job, I thought. I cannot force her to say "no" when she means "no," but I can be as clear as possible.

Well, you know what happened. Even though I could see Justine was getting tired, even though I kept saying we didn't need to present to all the classes, that is what we ended up doing.

Justine felt she had done me a big favor and that I owed her. Now, I was grateful for the gift she had given to my students; they had loved her and her dog. But I never wanted her to do more than she wanted to do and then become resentful. She wanted to be a victim and I didn't feel I had perpetrated any wrong on her. This disagreement ended our friendship.

I told this story because I want you to know what a sneaky devil this martyr thing is. If you don't put it right up front in your relationship, it will insidiously destroy trust, honesty, and love. If you don't have this agreement, you will always have to be guessing about whether or not your lover, parents, or friends really mean what they say. It does not have to be this way unless you let it be this way.

Getting in between a dedicated martyr and her "gift" is like putting yourself between an addict and her drug of choice. You can do it, but you will end up a bloody heap. You cannot control someone else. You can only control what you do and what comes out of your mouth.

Poem: What I Can and Can't Control

This is a good a place to take on the seductive notion of our being able to control what happens to us.

What I Can't Control:

I can't control my desire to control.
I can't control other people's addictions.
I can't control the number of difficulties that come into my life.
I can't control how I feel.
I can't always control whether or not I judge how I feel.
I can't always prevent my illusions from inviting me to despair.
I can't control who lives and who dies.

What I Can Control:

I can control what I do about how I feel.
I can control what I do about my judgments.
I can control how much exercise I get in my life.
I can control the food I put in my body.

What I Can Do:

I can surrender.
I can surrender to help.
I can surrender to sadness.
I can sit quietly and let myself be whatever I am.
I can reach out to people.
I can ask for peace.

I can live through disappointment.
I can live through despair.
I can live through heartache.
I can live through other people's pain.
I can live through not getting what I want when I want it.

I can make an agreement with myself that it is okay to be angry, sad, listless,
even though feeling listless makes me think of a boat without a keel, easily toppled.
I can make an agreement with myself that I can topple sometimes.
I will right myself eventually.

I can embrace malaise and look for the gift inside it.
I can remember a therapist telling me: "Vicki, if pain were a distant memory, you would be no damn good."

I can love people and live through the loss of them.
I can live through the untidiness of grief.
I can feel grief and gratitude simultaneously.
I can be furious at my friend for deserting me, and I can miss her.
I can feel compassion for a friend
and still feel bored about hearing her same ol,' same ol' story.

I can have discipline in my life,
the discipline to move my body,
to speak my appreciations,
to honor my word,
and to meditate for serenity.

I can chant daily:
Divine Spirit,
grant me the serenity to accept the things I cannot change,
the courage to change the things I can,
and the wisdom to know the difference.

Story: Doggie Do's and Don't's

We can also get into trouble when we guess at what other people want or when we ignore what they say, assuming they are lying about what they want.

Here is a small example: in January 2004, my two children and I flew down to California to visit my nephew, his wife, and their new baby. They also have two yellow labs. They are big dogs, and they were excited we were there. Daniel chose to keep the dogs in their kennels most of the time we were there because he was nervous about our comfort when they were out. That is what he said he did, and that is what I think he did. This is one of those situations, though, where it would be easy for Daniel or his wife to build up resentment at us for stifling their dogs, even though we assured Daniel we could handle a little bit of dog wildness.

If Daniel felt resentment, he would not want us to visit as much next time because he would feel bad about locking up his dogs. Do you see how these little decisions can be so destructive? Daniel is a fellow who means what he says and does not hold grudges, so I am confident he isn't resenting me, but I did wonder about it.

Martyrdom Antidote

We are all martyrs sometimes, and the best we can do is to "own our own farts" and fess up. We might say something like: "Oops! I feel resentment, and I want to blame you. I must have said yes when I meant no. I need to renegotiate that yes. Sorry if any of my resentment has leaked onto you."

People who are committed to unconscious martyrdom are no fun for me, and I stay away from them as much as possible. I can only control the promises I make. I cannot control other people lying to themselves and to me. This is a toughie!

"Don't say 'yes' when you mean 'no' and then blame me" may be the most important of the five agreements. Sand blowing on a rock may not seem very powerful, but we all know what sand can do over time. Martyrdom kills relationships and needs to be nipped in the bud before it bites you in the butt.

Your Turn

Have you been saying "yes" when the truth inside you says "no"? Are you feeling any resentment? What decisions do you need to renegotiate so that you are in integrity with what is true for you?

Is there anyone in your life who says "yes" when they mean "no" and then blames you? If so, remember you cannot control what other people think or do. All you can do is give feedback to people about how their behavior affects you. Here are two examples: "Even though you said you wanted to do this, I'm getting the feeling you'd rather not. Is that right?" or "I know you love to say 'yes,' but I want you to really think through this before you give me an answer."

Martyrdom is addictive. Be vigilant and compassionate with your own and other's acts of martyrdom, but don't be a victim either. Beat that martyrdom out of the bushes with questions such as: "Are you resentful? You seem resentful." You may have to cut dedicated martyrs out of your life all together. Any nominations?

Chapter 18

Agreement #2: Love Yourself Well

"Love your neighbor as yourself" is one of the deepest tenants of Christianity. It is a great idea, a great mission statement, if you will. Following that bit of wisdom can keep us all busy for a lifetime. But to love our neighbor, our friend, our partner, and our children well, we need to love ourselves first. "Appreciating me starts here," a friend said to me recently, after spending a little time resenting someone for not appreciating her as much as she thought she deserved. Then she realized, "Hey! I could have had a V8! I could appreciate myself first, and then it won't be necessary for anyone else to appreciate me. I just may decide I prefer to hang out with people who do rather than people who don't."

In order to love yourself well, you have to be willing to know yourself well, to give yourself unconditional love and acceptance. When you practice on yourself, you will get really good at loving other people well, too.

Those of us who are nice girls and boys will have a difficult time remembering to love ourselves well first. Chronic pleasers and givers always want to take care of the other person first. We give and give until there is nothing left in our bellies, and then we spin into resentment, depression, or self-righteousness, and we don't know how it all happened. Feeling "used" happens when we decide to give ourselves away first, before filling the coffers of our self-esteem, before we taste the sweetness of our own richness.

So, making a commitment to love yourself well first in order to love your partner, child, or friend is a huge act of courage. It goes against our culture, especially for women.

Maybe this analogy will help: When you are on a plane, the flight attendant always explains what you should do "in the unlikely event that the cabin should lose pressure." He tells you to first put the oxygen mask over your own face and then help others. If you fail to do this, he will not tell you, you will be unconscious in a matter of seconds and will be unable to help anyone else. You will have become a burden to those around you because you failed to take care of your own needs first.

"Oh, that is so selfish!" you might be saying to yourself. You bet it is. Mindful selfishness creates a great bounty of love from which you can give to others more than you ever dreamed. Being afraid of being selfish or looking selfish to others is an act of cowardice. If you practice looking good to yourself and others by knee-jerk giving, you will pay in the end. Unconscious, fear-based giving by parents creates children who crumble at the least little disappointment. Ungrateful family members will never learn to tap into their own generosity if you are hogging all the giving.

Whew! Big stuff! If I have convinced you even a little, try some of these activities and habits. They will help you in your quest of loving yourself well:

- Make a commitment to getting your needs met in a straightforward manner.
- Ask for what you need.
- Accept help.
- Be proactive in planning for your self-care by scheduling massages, counseling appointments, retreats, workshops, coffee dates—whatever it takes to love yourself well.

Seeing the Gift in Asking for Help

We are so afraid of being needy that we don't ask for help when we require it. We pretend we don't need when we do. When we don't ask for help when we need it, we deny our humanity and miss opportunities for connections that can enrich our lives and others' lives as well.

When I first lost my central vision, I did not want to need help, but I didn't learn to loathe asking for help out of nowhere. I met a woman once who bragged to me about her brother, who was completely blind. "He doesn't use a cane or a dog," she said.

"How does he get around?" I asked, mystified as to why this man would be so stubborn about using any kind of help.

"Oh, he falls down a lot and has broken some bones," she said.

"I'll bet he has," I thought to myself. Would she be so proud of him if he had been hit by a car? "He's dead, but he never asked for help," could be the epitaph on his tombstone.

This story taught me a lesson. In what ways was I being stubborn like this man? I understood his impulse; I still have it. I catch myself all the time not asking for help when I need it. I don't even think to ask for help. It never occurs to me that there is help for me. If I am not mindful, I just slog on alone, falling down a lot and breaking my spiritual bones unnecessarily.

I have had to learn to ask for help since I lost my vision, and this has been a good thing. I can no longer drive, so I always ride with someone else or ride public transportation. When I hitch a ride, the journey is more fun for both of us. I make connections when I would have spent a lot of time by myself in my car. I miss driving, but I feel enriched by my increased connections with people.

I can't read, so now people read to me, or I listen to books on tape. I have come to love falling asleep to a book on tape. It reminds me of when I was a child and my dad read to me at night. When people read to me, as my friends did when they read *The Artist's Way* by Julia Cameron, we all laughed together and talked as we went. It is communal and lovely, much more interesting than reading the book or even listening to it alone.

My inability to read and drive has forced me to ask for more help than I like. In that way, my blindness is a daily gift, a constant reminder of my limitations, my imperfections, and my need for other people. My blindness is a healing meditation, and it keeps me grounded. I have been blessed with the gift of having to ask for help, and, in asking for help I have been forced to learn how to receive graciously. Now I know the beauty of both giving and receiving.

Song: Crazy
(from the CD *Daring to Sing*)

When we don't take good care of ourselves and love ourselves well, we get, well, crazy.

Crazy, I'm crazy for feeling so crazy.
I'm crazy, crazy 'cuz I have **WAY** too much to do.
I do the work of at least four people.
No wonder I'm starting to pick on you.

Flurry. I live my life in such flurry,
Wondering who in the world I could sue.

I'm crazy for thinking that my life will just change.
I'm crazy for frenetic trying
And for why-why-whying.
I need to change what I think and do.

Worry. I'll stop practicing worry.
And start loving myself so I can love you.
Massages, walking, long soaks in the bathtub . . .
I'm through with frenetic trying,
And useless why-why-whying.
Since life is precious,
I'll practice gratitude.

Your Turn

Okay! What are you going to do to take care of yourself? Pedicures? Massages? Walks at night with the dogs all by yourself? Or maybe you can write yourself a love letter. (Here's one I wrote to myself.) "Vicki, I love you so much I am going to make sure you get enough fruits and vegetables every day. Not only that, but I will give you exercise and walk out in the fresh air. I will buy you nurturing CDs such as Jennifer Berezan's "ReTURNING." I will love you so well you will be able to love the world from a deep place. You will amaze yourself and others because you began by trusting my love of you. Go, girl!"

Chapter 19

Agreement #3: Love Each Other Well

Everything in this book supports this agreement, but here are some habits that will help you to always be the kind of generous, gracious lover you want to be:

- Have "Golden Eyes" for your lover, reflecting back their best when times are rough. When we are anchored in our beloved's magnificence, we can reduce the amount of seasickness our love suffers during stormy turmoil.
- Seek first to understand. This means you are willing to be the grown up, and listen first. Listen until you get what it is like to be your lover. Then and only then do you ask to be listened to. (This is Habit Five from the book *Seven Habits of Highly Effective People* by Stephen Covey. I highly recommend it.)
- Be willing to change the story you are telling yourself about your beloved's behavior, especially if that story creates conflict or ugliness. If you can find some humor in the situation, you might want to kiss him instead of smack him one.

Story: Murray and the Ketchup

Because of my vision problems, Murray and I decided to organize the refrigerator in a way that would help me find things. The leftovers would go on the top shelf, milk and other large items on the second shelf, and so on.

Murray readily agreed to this plan. He is an occupational therapist, after all, and he knows about making accommodations to help people perform necessary tasks, such as feeding yourself from the refrigerator.

So why did the ketchup, among other things, keep getting moved?

"How thoughtless he is," I said to myself. "How incredible, especially since he is a professional!" I fumed. "Does he hate me?" I wondered.

"Does he have any idea how difficult it is to live with low vision? This is such a simple thing for him to do, and it makes a big difference to me. If he really loved me, the ketchup would stay put."

We reviewed our plan. Murray again agreed that keeping things in the same place in the refrigerator was a reasonable request, and he should honor it. Yet the ketchup moved again, and I thought, "I hate him!" Well, I did not exactly hate him, but I was confused and hurt, and no matter how many times I confronted him, the ketchup still wandered the shelves of the refrigerator.

And then I thought of a new story: "Murray doesn't hate me. I know he doesn't hate me. He has attention deficit, is easily bored, and I'll bet he is just projecting his boredom onto the ketchup. He thinks the ketchup bottle gets restless, so he moves it."

Now this version is probably more true than the "He hates me" story I told myself, but that isn't important. What is important is that changing my story changed how I felt about this continual problem. Instead of being angry and hurt, I laughed. It became a joke, and (here is the interesting part) the ketchup has stayed put ever since I shared my new story about why the ketchup was roving the refrigerator with the "culprit." Maybe Murray's memory works better when it is bathed in love rather than irritation.

Your Turn

What little things could you do to love your sweetie better: bring her coffee in the morning? Hang up his clothes? Thank him for taking out the garbage? Tell him you are committed to being a better listener, to not interrupting with solutions? Just come up and start rubbing her neck? Rub her feet every single day? (I promise you will never hear, "Not tonight, honey. I have a headache.")

Chapter 20

Agreement #4: Own Your Own Farts

"Owning our own farts" means we are willing to admit when we make a mistake. We don't have to hunker down and protect our "ugliness;" rather, we offer admitting our mistakes as a gift of trust to each other. When we are truly committed, we accept the gift graciously. We love our partner more for having the courage to show us who they are without pretense, and our partner loves us more because of our unconditional acceptance of their very real, human self.

Being committed to admitting our mistakes means we want to know right away when we have blown it. We want the people in our lives to feel safe to tell us when we are jumping into problem solving instead of listening. We want to know when we have not kept an agreement. We want to be in integrity more than we want to stay out of trouble. Because we want to keep our relationship current and clean we admit our mistakes promptly and completely.

When a mistake is being pointed out to us with kindness, we must always be willing to entertain the idea we are "guilty." "Maybe so," we will say. "I will think about what you have said." It never hurts to consider the possibility we have messed up. Actually, we might have a chance to learn something that will increase our enjoyment of life forever. Bring it on!

As time goes on and admitting our mistakes becomes a habit, we are less likely to become relationally constipated. As my sweet mother always said, "It's better to fart and bear the shame than hold it in and bear the pain." If we learn to cheerfully own up to even our most obnoxious behavior, we will keep our relational digestive system regular. People get irritable when their bellies bloat and they're full of unexpended gas. The same thing happens when people try to hide and repress their stinky side.

The more we practice owning our misbehavior with graciousness and humor, the sooner we can move from one problem to the next. Getting stuck, getting mired in shame and self-righteousness, puts an end to growth. Our problems, because we refuse to deal with them, become septic. Small transgressions turn into the Alps and we are frozen in an unhelpful dynamic.

Story: "You Ate My Mint!"

Murray and I were sitting at dinner with a dear friend and her new guy. I had met him once, briefly, at a conference, but we had never spent any time together.

My friend had met this man at a Jean Houston Mystery Weekend, a rather expensive, yearlong spiritual growth commitment. I say this only because I want to show how both of these people were committed to learning about and acting on a higher truth in their lives.

Retreat weekends and workshops can be extremely helpful, but I believe that God and spiritual growth are in the details. In the mundane interactions of our everyday lives, we reveal ourselves, whether we like it or not and whether we want to admit it or not.

"You ate my mint!" Lena said. Ben did not respond.

"You ate my mint. I can't believe you ate my mint!" she said with some exasperation.

Lena is an extremely generous and gracious person. I knew she didn't care about the mint per se, but she had already shared a story about how Ben had eaten her doughnuts when he already had several of his own.

He didn't turn and say, "Oh, good grief! Look what I did! We have already had conversations about this, about my taking your things without asking. It is a violation of your sacred space and an example of my being out of integrity. I can't believe I lost consciousness again with you. I am deeply sorry. I know it is only a mint, but it is not only a mint. My taking the mint without asking is an example of my bullying behavior in other ways. I need to listen more and grab less. What can I do to make peace with you?"

He didn't say anything resembling this. Energetically, he turned away. Lena was laughing as she spoke, but she was also a little outraged. He had violated her space again. She was being lighthearted about it, but she was deadly serious.

"I want you to get me another mint," she said.

"I ate it because you don't like sweets," he said.

"What a bunch of bull!" Lena exclaimed. "I like sweets just fine. I was going to offer this one to you, But now that you have eaten it without my permission, I want you to get me a mint to replace the one you ate."

Ben called over the waitress and made a long speech about how he had eaten his sweetie's mint and that he was now in the doghouse and would the waitress please do what she could to get him back into Lena's good graces.

He charmed the waitress and got the mint, plus several others, but he never owned his own fart. In fact, he ended up getting more charm points instead.

This is dangerous relationship behavior. Ben, in effect, was demeaning Lena's concern over her purloined mint, making her look a little petty, a little silly, while he glossed over his own brutish behavior. Brutish? Is that too strong? Not if you want to stay in a healthy, respectful relationship it's not.

Story: The Ginger Pig

Lena and I go out to lunch fairly often and had just enjoyed miso soup and California rolls at a local Japanese restaurant.

When the waitress came to take away the wooden platter, I asked if there were any ginger left. I couldn't see it, but I thought there might be some left. I love pickled ginger.

"I ate it all!" Lena gasped.

"No problem," I said, thinking, "How much do I want more pickled ginger? I could always order some more. Nope! I had enough; I'm fine."

I was fine, but Lena wasn't.

She apologized again for eating the rest of the ginger without checking with me. Let me make this clear: I had had some of the ginger, just not very much, not as much as I would have liked, but enough.

A day or so later Lena called and told me she needed to talk to me about something. My stomach took that flip it does when I think I'm in trouble. I don't avoid conflict anymore; I value conflict, I'm up to it, and still my stomach flips. Oh, well.

I wasn't in trouble at all; Lena was ashamed of herself.

"I feel so bad about eating all the ginger," she said.

"What are you talking about?" I asked. I had forgotten about it.

"The other day at the restaurant when I finished all the ginger without checking with you. Are you mad at me? Was that just too awful?"

Oh, I know this one. I have very strict Dinosaur Rules myself about how I'm supposed to check with everyone else's needs first, to make sure everyone else is cared for before I dare take care of myself. "You didn't offer him another cup of coffee," I will chastise myself. Then I have to go through a little letting go, forgiveness, aren't-we-humans-funny ritual, as I marvel at the depths of my perfectionism.

So I knew very well this soup Lena was stewing in.

"Oh, Lena," I assured her, "I forgot all about it. It held no emotional energy for me. So you forgot for a second about just how much ginger I might have wanted and you let yourself gloriously scarf it up. So what? We could have ordered more. There is plenty of pickled ginger in the world, and, you know, you get to be a ginger pig with me if you want. I celebrate your ginger pigness!"

We laughed as we often do, giggling with a delicious naughtiness. In fact, some of my favorite times with Lena are when either one of us is mired in this over-serious worry and the other rips it open and turns it inside out to our mutual delight.

I believe we laughed until we cried about "the ginger pig," and it became one of our friendship phrases that helps remind us of our belief in deep democracy, in valuing all our emotions and not trying to banish the "bad" ones and instead getting curious about them.

Lena, who is too careful sometimes about violating other people's boundaries, is met with Vietnam vet Ben, who is not careful enough and who doesn't seem as interested as he needs to be right now in getting more careful. The universe has put these two people together for a reason. But I believe that unless Ben gets more interested in listening better and violating less, their relationship is in danger. I think all relationships that don't have mutual respect and listening at their center may continue to exist on the physical plane, but emotionally, mentally, and spiritually there will be a withdrawal.

How long will Lena be willing to stand guard over all the mints in her life? The energy she expends standing guard will be taken away from the energy she could be using to generate more creativity and brilliance. And maybe now, more than ever, this is exactly the skill she needs to be learning. I think it probably is.

But once she learns how to stand her ground, if Ben doesn't respond with more openness and less charm when he is given feedback, I believe she will have to move on. And this is okay. They are perfect teachers for each other.

We humans are so funny! We will search all over the world for spiritual growth in workshop after workshop, and it is there, right before us, in the mint we stole after dinner. No need to be urgent about finding our stuff. It is all around us all of the time, waiting for us to get curious instead of defensive.

Poem: In My Stuff

Owning my own stuff helps clear the way so that I can own my own stuff with my beloved friends or my partner.

Well, here comes my stuff again.

I can go for weeks,
months,
with my head above water,
skipping over the waves,
enjoying the wind and the spray,
alive and vital.

Then,
quite without warning,
I can find myself
soul-deep in my "stuff."
My face is in the sand,
saltwater is up my nose,
and I am wondering,
"How did this happen to me again?"

Yet I know this "stuff" so well.
An old friend.
My stuff is where my insecurities live,
where I worry about what other people think.
It's where I am terrified of making mistakes,
And where I know I am not able to fool people.

When I'm in my stuff
I want to be invisible.
I don't want anyone to see through my carefully constructed screen.
I don't want anyone to see the ropes and pulleys,
the rust and rot.

When I'm in my stuff
I whine: "Why doesn't everyone love me all the time?"
Even my thoughts have a high-pitched, yodeling spin to them.
I want to cram myself in people's faces
and explain myself.
Boss man, won't you please understand?
Director woman, you need to know all of my reasons!
I want to roll on my back and beg for a quick belly rub,
but I don't want that at all.
Yuck!

When I am in my stuff
I want to not want everyone's slathering approval,
and I do want it,
and I want my wanting
not to show.

When I am in my stuff
I want to be out of it immediately.
I have no patience for my whining and whimpering.
I want to crawl under the house and lick my wounds and heal
alone.

My stuff is embarrassing,
disgusting,
like psychic vomit drooling down my chin.
Who puked up this smelly ugliness?
Who is that who is so needy and insecure all of a sudden?
Who is this sniveling mess
here with all of us grownups?

Oh, no! It's me!

I hear the silent whispers of invisible critics surrounding me:
"She is defensive, isn't she?"
"Needs to be the best, doesn't she?"
"Doesn't take correction well, does she?"
"Her neediness stinks, doesn't it?"
"It is she who smells so bad, isn't it?"

Can I have a do-over?
Can I do last night again?
Only this time I won't bat the helpful comment back at the vocal director.
This time I will say, "Okay," and give it a try.
This time I won't make excuses.
This time I will keep my fears to myself,
keep my perfectionist tendencies hidden.

This time I won't feel crazy and separate.
This time I will breathe deeply
and smile with compassion.
This time I will make friends with my stuff,
my stuff, that is always there waiting,
ready to support me,
to delight me with new adventures into consciousness.

"Venture out to an edge,
and you can bet you will fall into your stuff,"
the Voice of Wisdom within me whispers.

"Your stuff is familiar and seems terrible to you,
but it is nothing special.
You are not so awful.

"Your stuff will give you a chance to learn to love yourself even more
　　completely.
You will get another chance to resolve and release your unforgiveness.
You won't get to do it invisibly
or neatly,
but that is a good thing.

Some people might not like you.
They might prefer to not be around you.
Oh, well.
You're working on having the courage to be disliked anyway.
This just gives you more chance to practice."

Story: Finger-Holding Confessions

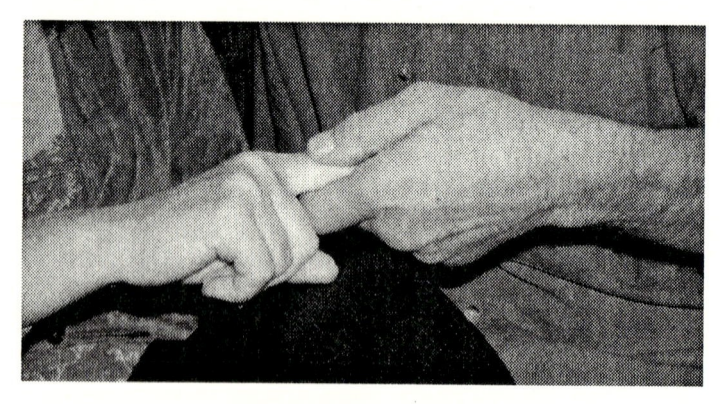

Finger-Holding Confession
Jan Bateman photo

Admitting our mistakes quickly is easier if we have a technique to expose them that does not shame anyone, invites listening, and often ends with raucous laughter. Murray and I call one of our favorite relationship-nourishing activities "Finger-Holding Confessions."

A confession, by nature, is a cleansing of sins. We know we have been "bad," but we don't always know how to extricate ourselves from our "badness" without making it worse. "Confessing" might very well save your relationship.

I discovered finger-holding confessions accidentally. Early in our relationship, I found myself tracking all of Murray's faults. I was not proud of this. In fact, I was ashamed of my behavior and afraid my despicableness would destroy our love. The more I hated myself, the more I tallied Murray's every mistake. I had his faults organized chronologically, by categories, and ranked according to my level of outrage. Yuck!

I did not know how to extricate myself from my acrimony. I thought I was keeping my constant judgments a secret, but, as I have come to know all too well, Murray knew. All men know when they are being seen as a giant fault walking the planet, looking for ways to disappoint their women. Double yuck!

I took some space, went to visit a friend, and asked for help from the forces of the cosmos that are smarter than I am. A vision came to me, and I knew what I would do the very first time the opportunity presented itself.

Coyote, the Trickster, who loves to mess with us, chose the moment for me. Murray and I were in the drive-through espresso line, and I heard the call: "Now!"

"Now?" I thought, "Right here in this drive-through line?"

"Yup," my Muse said. "Now." I have learned not to argue with my Muse's promptings. If she tells me, "If you build it, he will come," I build it.

"Murray," I said, "I need to talk to you. I have been extremely aware of your mistakes lately. Have you noticed?" Murray gave me a look even I could see. It said, "Duh."

I grabbed my sweater from the back seat and put it over my head. "I'm going to confess some thoughts and feelings I am having, and I don't want you to say anything except 'I love you.'"

I paused and thought for a moment. "And hold my finger so I don't feel so lonely, will you?" I held out my finger. Murray, the man I had been not-so-secretly criticizing for weeks, showed a generosity of spirit beyond what I deserved, grabbed my finger and said, "Fire away, baby."

"I've been keeping track of all of your mistakes and you have been making a ton of them!" I said.

"I love you," Murray answered. I could hear the smile in his voice.

"I'm mad at you for being so stupid, and I'm mad at me for feeling so judgmental, and I'm mad at you for making me feel so bad about myself for being so judgmental!"

"I love you," Murray said again, and I believed him.

I confessed more of my "horrible" thoughts, and as I spoke, I felt the snakes curled in my stomach untangle and flow out my mouth into the warmth of Murray's love for me. This allowed me to get to the bottom of what I was afraid of.

"Murray, I'm afraid I married someone who is not smart enough for me," I said to My Beloved, squeezing the words out of the darkest crevice in my secret, shadow self.

When I have shared this story during presentations, the men in the audience will inevitably groan. What a horrible thing to say, and what a horrible thing to have said to you, they tell me.

I agree. These were harsh words I had spoken to my sweetie. But knowing how horrible these thoughts and feelings were was why I had been carrying them around for so long. Hating those thoughts and feelings, though, did not make them go away. They were destroying me and our relationship.

Even after confessing this most vile fear, Murray simply said, "I love you."

What a guy!

This confession cracked our problem wide open, allowing us to shed some light and love on our struggle. If we were to move forward in our love, we needed some creative way to deal with our differences and the sludge it drags up from our unresolved pain.

Finger-holding confessions are one of the cornerstones of our relationship. Just as with any other tool, though, they can become corrupted if they are used as a way of being right or beating our partner into submission. But when they are used as a bridge to get back to the bedrock of our love, they are miraculous. When you stop thinking of your own argument and can only *listen*, "I love you" becomes more true than "I'm RIGHT!"

And, just in case you are wondering, Murray has confessed ugly thoughts and feelings to me as well. And, yes, I do stupid things too. We take turns.

Tips for Finger-Holding Confessions:

- **Confessions must be confessions and not a sneaky way to leak your anger.**
  You are not proud of these feelings or attitudes.
- **The only acceptable response by the listener is, "I love you."**
  If you feel unable to muster up these words, even if you don't particularly mean them, do not accept a request for a confession.
- **Practice having a confession before you need one in the heat of a misunderstanding.**
  The process sounds simple, but it isn't always easy to keep your mouth shut and just say, "I love you." It is one person's turn until they are done. If the other person wants to take a turn immediately, that is okay. Surprisingly, this rarely happens with Murray and me. We usually laugh. Confessions force deep listening, and that is a good thing!

How to Start a Confession:

- "I need to make a confession. I want you to hold my finger and just listen. When I pause, I want you to tell me you love me. That's all. You will have a chance to talk when I am finished, but for this part, you can only say you love me."
- (Putting a blanket over your head) "This is a very difficult conversation for me. I'm really going to need your support. I'm not saying I'm right—I don't even want to be right—but I have to talk about this, and this is the only way I know how to begin."

Your Turn

Any mistakes you need to own up to? It is never too late! Confess your sins! Receive absolution! Admit you were wrong, petty, jealous, terrified, needy—let all of your glorious faults spill into the Sea of Love.

Chapter 21

Agreement #5: Take Turns

Most couples tend to delegate tasks by gender (men drive, women make social arrangements) or by perceived talent (men drive, women make social arrangements.) And therein lies the rub. We get put in roles and have chores foisted on us, often without much thought. This unmindful division of labor is common, and it can work out just fine, but we need to be careful.

When we give up responsibility in an area—paying bills, making sure the car gets serviced—we accidentally lose competence. Many times after the death of a spouse, the survivor is forced to deal with a huge loss but also must climb a steep learning curve because she has to take on all those tasks she left to her partner.

Our world shrinks when we give up building competence in our weak areas. Our brains don't get stimulated, and we are not allowed to discover new areas of competence. We are stuck with our old stories.

Murray and I take turns doing almost everything: taking out the garbage, arranging social outings, being depressed, being magical. If Murray or I were always the strong one, our courage muscles would get flaccid.

Be careful not to freeze yourself or your loved one into a story of incompetence. We often do this in a teasing fashion, but it still re-enforces a limiting story.

Murray will often remind me, usually in a friendly way, when I have had my turn being right for too long. "I want to be right for awhile!" he will say.

"You are so right!" I will say, and we are off to the races.

Looking for each other's brilliance, taking turns being the one with the good ideas, the one with the wisdom, changes the way we listen for each other, and it affects every moment of our relationships. If I need to be the brilliant one all the time, for example, I will miss out on the brilliance of everyone I encounter. What a boring life, and what an inaccurate one.

If you don't take turns starting conversations about important issues in your relationship, you are asking for BIG trouble. Too often the woman becomes the only one initiating these difficult conversations. I think this happens because men feel shame when their women are unhappy, and they would rather just avoid unpleasantness. If I had to explain in one sentence why my first marriage failed, this would be it: I was in charge of relationship maintenance, and a relationship needs both people totally involved, totally committed to cleaning out the debris.

Both people need to look for dust and rust, undertones, the unspoken. I remember once, when I was holding back a conversation instead of initiating it, my brilliant Murray said, "Are we having a fight that I don't know about?"

We were! We were having a fight in my head that I was having by my little lonesome self. I was winning in my head, by the way, but I was also pounding a wedge between us. If Murray and I did not take turns bringing up our troubles, this little fight might have gone on for days before I was sick enough of my self-righteousness to start the conversation. All the time I spent avoiding would have cost us in connection and appreciation.

Taking turns is a huge agreement, but it is one that might save your relationship. If you realize while reading this book that your relationship is woefully imbalanced in this area, I advise you to take it on now. Take on just this one bad habit and commit to changing it. You might be delightfully surprised at how much fun you both have been missing because you have been hoeing in your designated ruts for so long.

Poem: Wordlessness

This poem celebrates some of the ways Murray takes his turn being brilliant with me.

Murray,
soulful explorer,
finds me in my deepest, wordless pits.
He knows to hold me, speaking softly,
calming a frightened animal,
which is what I am when I can't find my words.

He stays
and strokes my arm
and waits
with confidence,
knowing I will return.
He knows more than I do at those moments.

He waits
and loves me,
beams his love for me,
surrounds me in soul
until the melting happens and I return.

How much is that worth?
How many other people would know to stay?
How many people would know what I need
when I am incapable of saying what I need?

How much is it worth
that he stays outside my cave and speaks to me
until I find my way out?
How much is that gentle voice worth?
How much could you pay for that understanding of mystery?

How would I advertise for such a gift?
"Wanted: Man fluent in two languages: English and Mystery."
"Wanted: Sailor of soul seas."
"Wanted: A man who knows,
in the biblical sense,
how to listen."

What a gift I have
in this imperfect man of mine.
He knows enough to just stay there,
hanging out with me in my wild despair.
He never stops beaming faith.

Your Turn

Any roles you want to swap for a day or for a week? Let her do the driving. Let him initiate a conversation about how the relationship is going. Where are you not taking turns when it would be better if you were? Watch other couples and see how they trade responsibilities. Are you having any conflict because someone has been doing a task, say gardening for example, that they used to love but now find burdensome? Resentments are not always easy to ferret out, but they can cause a lot of heartache.

Your Turn, Again

Whatever agreements you choose for your relationship, make sure to schedule regular maintenance, just as you would on your car. In fact, you might even want to have a relationship checkup every time you change the oil in your car. (I am so practical!)

If you are interested in living authentically ever after, then it doesn't necessarily matter how you are doing with your agreements. What does matter is that whatever is really going on between you is what you are interested in. You don't want any taboo subjects between you. You need to confess those thoughts and feelings that are interfering with your serenity.

Once you have your agreements, write them down and sign them. Or have a ceremony and invite your friends. This will invigorate other couples and might help you honor your commitments. In any case, do something to help you remember what you have promised each other. You should know your agreements as well as you know your social security number.

Chapter 22

Fighting the Good Fight

"If you haven't stepped on anyone's toes, you haven't been for much of a walk."
                                    Barbara Kingsolver's grandfather

Can't we all just get along?
No.
I used to think a successful relationship was defined by its lack of conflict. No more. The story I used to tell was that fighting was horrible and destructive. I thought that people who loved each other could find a way to solve their problems without discomfort.

I know where I got this mistaken notion. When I was growing up, I never saw an argument that made anything better. Never. Conflict always made things worse—sometimes violently worse. It is no wonder that the first time I married I found myself a man who disliked conflict as much as I did. If we had been able to fight the good fight, as I am proposing in this book, we might have been able to save our marriage.

Murray and I know how to have a good, cleansing fight. That I can be as ugly and as fierce as I have been with him is a measure of our trust and love and allows us an intimacy that is a treasure.

I am not advocating a constant diet of conflict, nor am I suggesting a naive and destructive notion that "honesty is always the best policy." Sometimes it is better to keep things to ourselves. Sometimes it is better to let sleeping dogs lie, to allow time for a conflict to shift and find its own way out. If you decide to wait to deal with a problem, make sure you are making a Level Two decision instead of a fear-based one. Avoiding conflict as a habit, though, only gives us time to build our defenses, create our stories, and practice being a victim.

Learning to fight the good fight and to solve problems as they come can literally save you years of heartache and loneliness. This section offers poetry and some specific fights Murray and I have had along the way. I have never seen anything quite like this in any book, and that is one reason I offer it to you. If you can see specifically how Murray and I extricate ourselves from those inevitable conflicts that arise, then maybe you can find your way out of your own disagreements with more humor and grace.

Poem: When Confrontation Is Hard and Easy

Just to be clear—confrontation is still a challenge for me. Don't feel bad if your stomach flips at the thought of starting a conversation you feel will stimulate conflict.

When confrontation is hard for me,
it feels like I am facing a big man with hairy arms.
He is so big I can't see his face,
but I know he is snarling.
His hands are in big fists,
as big as footballs.
If I speak at all, he will turn his football fists on me,
and through his snarl he will hurl words at me
that will crack through my chest and break my possibility.

When confrontation is easy for me
it doesn't feel like confrontation.
I am sharing information
or asking for help understanding.
I feel like I am standing firmly on the earth
and have access to my brain and my heart.
I trust that ideas will surround me like butterflies
and that we will both feel that juicy aliveness
that comes when we romp in our genius.

Conflict Prevention

Having said all of that, we can avoid many conflicts if we do a little work up front. Fights caused by personality style differences will only get worse as understanding decreases and rancor skyrockets. Here are some strategies I recommend to minimize the damage of dealing with people who, guess what, are not like you!

Please Understand Me by David Keirsey and Marilyn Bates is an excellent book to introduce you to personality style differences. Being different is not wrong or bad, but our ignorance of honest differences might lead to self-doubt or to hostility. We can blame our partner with: "You never initiate social activities! Why am I the one who always has to do it?" Well, it's because you are the one who gets fed by contact with people, while your lover is someone who gets drained by the same experience.

Let's Not Repeat the Same Fight, Shall We?

Murray and I always used to get into a little jangle when we were going somewhere. After noticing this pattern, we took a closer look at what was happening. The problem was that when I say, "I'm ready," it means that I am heading for the car with my purse, coat, and anything else I need. I thought this is what everyone meant when they said, "I'm ready." When Murray would say he was ready, I would head for the car and then sit there for five minutes while he did heaven knows what. By the time he got to the car I felt disrespected, irritated, and I did not like him very much.

We solved this issue when we learned we were speaking a different language. "Oh," he said, "so when you say 'I'm ready,' that means you are completely ready! When I say, 'I'm ready,' I can imagine that I will probably be ready sometime soon. We learned to have Murray say he was "pre-ready." This let both of us know that I should not head to the car, and it helped Murray focus on getting straight from pre-ready to "ready."

This sounds simple, but I know many, many couples fight about the same stuff over and over. We solved this problem with humor, and now when Murray says "I'm pre-ready!" I love him just a little more. We are in this together; we are a team, and we figured out a great solution to a nagging problem.

Preference Inventory

Pay attention to when and where you get irritated with each other. Does one of you need time in the morning before making conversation? After work? Figure out what you want, and make a request: "I do not need help driving. When I am driving, I want you to just enjoy the ride. If you want to drive, ask. But do not drive for me." This is a request, but it is also an example of finding a pattern in your relationship that is not working for you.

Getting irritated, then, is an invitation to get interested: We can ask ourselves: "What is it about this situation that makes me mad?" Trying not to be irritated when we really are only builds resentment. All of our emotions, even the most unpleasant ones, are brimming with important information for us if we learn not to get lost in them.

Don't Get Defensive! Get Curious!

Another time to get interested is when you feel defensive. Everyone feels defensive sometimes, and that is nothing to be ashamed of. But we can get stuck to our defensiveness and committed to it. When we do this our momentary flush of rebellion can become a problem-provoking way of life.

I wrote the following poem in response to a friend's question: How can we disagree without getting defensive?" I know a lot about being defensive, and I have made a commitment to not be defensive about my defensiveness, but to just note it and go on. This has freed me from the shame that would bind me to a position, not allowing me to listen and change. We are defensive for good reasons. We come by this feeling honestly. Sometimes we need to be defensive to save ourselves from shaming onslaughts, or we think we do.

Once you realize that defensiveness only locks you in your problem, you can move straight to why you feel defensive and bypass proving how right you are. This will serve you well in all relationships, as we all know what it is like to have a boss or co-worker who cannot hear about any "problem" without getting defensive. It stops all communication completely, erodes trust, and perpetuates problems. So pull back the curtain!

Poem: How Can I Disagree with You Without Getting Defensive?

Good question.
How about staying put in yourself
and not telling me about me?
Instead of being defensive,
you could say, "I was confused when you said . . ." or
"That word felt harsh to me,
and I feel like I want to defend myself and the people I love."

You might try exploring what feeling defensive feels like in you.
Where does it live in your body?
What thoughts does it excite?
You can catalog the thoughts
without agreeing to really think them
or believe them.
Like storm clouds, you can notice them and their intensity
without going to live in them.

You might try just sitting still
and feeling the urgency in your reaction.
"Hmm," you might say to yourself, "I am churning with feeling.
This is interesting.
I wonder what this is all about."
Resist the urge to blame anyone—
your parents, your ex-lovers, yourself, or
me.

Pay attention to your desire to poke someone,
to push at something to make your jagged, hot feelings go away.

Notice when you feel yourself mounting your white horse
 of self-righteousness.
Oh, it feels so good, your being up there!
Those others deserve to be trampled a bit by your wisdom,
your absolute rightness.
It's intoxicating
being up this high.
The air is clear,
the issues are simple,
and you are right!
Sit with this feeling,
and don't judge it, either.

Of course you feel self-righteous sometimes.
It is a great distraction from the pain,
the fear,
the terrible, soul-shaking fear
that you will have to throw your love or your safety out
when you let a new truth in.

Instead of being defensive,
get curious.
What truth wants to be let in?
What truth might make you have to rewrite your history,
redraw your inner map of the world?

Pay attention to your belief
that the rewriting and redrawing will be painful and arduous.
Maybe,
just maybe,
if you decide to fall in love with truth,
with all truth,
all the time,
you will welcome the rewrites,
the revisions of cherished stories.

Maybe you will find the crashing cacophony of your illusions
will begin to sound like the French national anthem.
You will be like the woman in Rick's bar in *Casablanca*,
who stood up proudly amid the Nazis
and sang her freedom.
Maybe all the thunderous noise inside you
is your true song calling you.

What can you do when you disagree with me besides becoming defensive?
Celebrate!

Right behind defensiveness lies freedom,
a fresh look,
new, sweet air to breathe.
And maybe, if you face your fear, you might find what you are afraid of
isn't true at all,
Ha!
You might find that your discomfort is just me being me,
being human,
having my own stuff.
Then you will be nested inside your compassion,
and from that deep place of soul-listening,
you will truly love me,
will gently remove the rotting vines from in front of my eyes.
We will laugh together,
holding hands,
letting our hearts dance.

So go ahead and disagree with me.
Let the adventure begin!

Starting Difficult Conversations

Difficult conversations are the ones you would rather not have. You would rather just get along. You feel a little hopeless about it all anyway, and you are not proud of how you feel and of the thoughts that are pumping through your head. You would rather just avoid it all.

The reason you aren't avoiding the problem this time is that you have learned the hard way that avoiding doesn't make problems go away. Sometimes waiting until you are calm to start a conversation is a great idea, but avoiding a conversation means you are scared. Giving in to our fears only makes them stronger and makes the next step more difficult. Whatever we practice we get good at, and if we practice avoiding, we will get good at that. If we practice starting difficult conversations, we will get better at that as well.

Important Note #1: Do not start these difficult conversations in the middle of a discussion/fight that is already underway. These conversations need to happen quite separately from any specific content. You don't want to fall in the same hole again.

Important Note #2: Do not start or continue a difficult conversation on e-mail unless you want to make your problem worse. I have sent angry e-mail messages when I felt afraid to face the person I needed to talk to. My wanting to sidestep conflict created a wildfire of emotional responses that caused everyone more discomfort. So save e-mail for relaying information or giving appreciations. No one minds having their good deeds in print. And no one likes getting poked when they are sorting through their daily mail.

You've decided you need to start a difficult conversation, but you don't know what to say. Here are some **starters for difficult conversations:**

1. "I don't know how to start this conversation . . ."
2. "I'm really ashamed of myself for feeling the way I do, for thinking what I'm thinking. I need to begin somewhere, though, so I'm just going to start."
3. "This is really important to me, and I don't know how to talk about it. I want to try to carve out a place to talk about this so we don't go into our usual reactions. Are you willing to try to help me do this?"
4. "I've discovered a pattern we are in. I've written out the scenario and the dialogue we usually have. Look it over and tell me if you

agree that I've described our interaction accurately." (After agreement is reached on accuracy of description) "I, for one, do not want to continue this pattern. This is what I am willing to do to break myself out of my own bad habits. Are you satisfied with your response? Would you like to commit to another response? We can check back in a week and see how we are doing. I will report how I think I've done, and I'll ask you how you think I've done with my goal. You can tell me how you've done if you want, and if you are interested in how I think you've done on your goal, I'll tell you."

5. "I've discovered something about myself that I would like to share with you. I need you to just listen and not ask me to justify my feelings and ideas. I need some space to explore my thoughts and feelings. You are very important to me, and I don't want to keep this part of myself hidden from you. You can ask questions to help you understand—I would like this—but please don't give me solutions or criticize me right now. I might be ready or even eager for that sometime in the future, but not right now."
6. "What do you need to hear me say to help you stop being angry at me?"

What You Can Say If Things Go Wrong In a Conversation:

1. "Oops! We're falling back into the pattern I want to break. If we can't shift back to building new responses, then I want to put this conversation on hold for awhile."
2. "I want you to like me in the morning, and if we continue talking, I think you are just going to get madder and madder at me. Let's stop talking now and come back to this later."
3. "I'm feeling attacked, and I am not going to continue this conversation right now. I will bring this subject up later today."

The Art of Getting Angry

Skillful "angering" is difficult for most people. We either get it "too hot" and burn our victims, or we are "too cold" and withdraw, neglecting to speak about what angers us. The question is: How do we learn to get it "just right," to engender just the right amount of anger for the circumstances?

First, we need to get a clear picture of what we are like when our anger is either too hot or too cold. That will help us get the impetus to deal with our anger differently.

Poem: Too Hot

When my anger is too hot,
when my emotions have flooded my brain,
I say things that are true,
but I say them without compassion.
I speak my truth as a defense
or for revenge.
I want the person to hurt,
to know they have hurt me.
I want them to join me in my suffering.

When my anger is too hot,
my body fills with broken glass.
Sometimes I clench my jaw so tight
I'm afraid I might break my teeth.

When my anger is too hot,
I melt what I value:
my serenity,
my tender children,
my beloved husband.

My hot anger is very expensive
and a cheap thrill,
an emotional binge
that leaves me hung-over,
ripe fodder for my shame.

Story: Hot Anger with Martin and Dave Barry

The following story is an example of how one blistering moment of temper can be very expensive for a relationship.

I've already written about how my hot rage at my four-year-old Katie sent me into therapy. Unfortunately, Martin did not escape some of my lava, either. He was about twelve at the time. I had just lost my central vision. I was living alone, and my children visited me every other week. I asked Martin if he would read me the Dave Barry column in the Sunday paper. He said he didn't want to. Katie, ever interested at that time, in finding a way to one-up her brother, said she would read it to me.

My children's stinginess and sibling rivalry ruined my taste for Dave Barry. I told them I wasn't really in the mood for comedy anymore. Martin told me, in what I perceived as a slightly scolding tone, that he would have read it to me "if I had asked nicely."

I could feel a spiky, hot emotion rise in me, flooding my grieving brain. At first, my rage confused me. How dare he be so callous, picking on me in my most vulnerable spot? Then my anger turned vindictive, and I wanted to obliterate my son for being so cruel.

I thought of what I wanted to say to him. I realized a mother should never say to her son what I wanted to say to Martin at that moment. I let a few beats of time pass before I said, "You selfish little shit." You'll have to imagine what I chose not to say.

That one instant of self-indulgence broke trust with my son, just as my stalking rage with my daughter cost me her trust. It took me many months to repair and rebuild my relationship with Martin. He was a twelve-year-old watching his family break apart in front of him. His pillar-of-strength mother had just gone blind before his disbelieving eyes. He needed my help. How could I ask him for help?

I understood all this soon after my temper tantrum, but the acid of my vengeful comment burned the face of my sweet son for a long time.

Anger that is Too Cold

When my anger is too cold, I cannot muster words. I say nothing when someone hurts my feelings—and then I resent them. When I am too cold, I keep track of someone else's mistakes secretly, which destroys intimacy.

A few years ago I was having lunch with some friends. One woman was showing us pictures from her trip. Another friend was describing to me what was in the pictures. The friend showing the pictures said, trying to be helpful I'm sure, "Vicki doesn't need to see the pictures."

"Vicki doesn't need to see the pictures," I thought to myself. As if I were not there. As if my needs were all known. As if I could not speak for myself. I was dumbstruck. I felt small and stupid.

I promised myself I would make a date to talk to her, and tell her how I felt when she spoke for me as if I weren't there. I knew I had to have this difficult conversation or our friendship would be ruined. If I didn't speak to her about my hurt, I would stop trusting her, would start avoiding her, and would collect all the reasons she was bad and wrong.

I didn't get around to initiating this conversation because another incident occurred shortly thereafter which ended our friendship. "Vicki doesn't need to see the pictures" was her anger leaking out, a little venting of the volcano of anger boiling in her below the surface. Why was she so angry with me? I don't think she actually was angry with me at all. An adult child of an alcoholic herself, but one who had not worked on her recovery, everything about me set her off. Maybe some time down the road something will crack open in her, allowing us to rekindle our relationship. I hope so.

Getting Anger "Just Right"

When I have "just right" anger, I say what needs to be said right when I need to say it. I am not emotional. I am clear. I can think. I realize I have choices. I am not timid or frightened. I feel like a grownup.

Doing anger "just right" means telling your truth. It is not about blaming or making someone wrong, although people might feel that way because of their own shame.

Doing anger "just right" is boundary setting. It is a "get off my foot" message. We never know how someone else is going to react to our boundary message. They might be happy to know they have accidentally stepped on our territory. They might be ashamed and withdraw. They might be angry and attack. We have to be willing to accept whatever people do in response to our attempts to protect our sacred space.

We need to start noticing the details of a fight well fought, building a large file of examples. When we try to learn something new, one or two examples aren't enough. We need lots and lots of models so we can start imagining how we might weave this new skill into our daily lives. Finding the language we need when we need it is no easy task. If this were easy, we would have figured it out long ago.

The following story is an illustration of doing anger "just right." It is also probably the major turning point of my life. Very few people, I have learned, have an honest relationship with their parents. It is just too risky.

Story: "Mom, I'm Not a Kid Anymore."

After I entered therapy because of my rage toward my young daughter, my mother called me and started doing something she did often: telling me what to do. She wasn't rude about it; she was just trying to be helpful. But, suddenly, my body just couldn't take it anymore. I couldn't respond with the, "Okay, Mom," I knew I was supposed to say. Instead, I said, "Mom, I am thirty-two years old, and I don't want you to call me and tell me what to do."

You would have thought I had started an earthquake, and, in a sense, I had. I had broken the rules of our relationship. She was already worried about what was happening with me in therapy. She was feeling guilty about her part in the pain of my childhood, and now, I was not acting like the Vicki she had always known.

Mom disintegrated. She couldn't sleep at night, her hair started falling out, and still, I did not become the "good girl" I had always been.

My brother called and told me I should be nice to Mom. I told him I was being nice to Mom; I just didn't want her to treat me as if I were a little girl. He was furious with me and did not forgive me until Mom lay dying twenty years later.

I had been calm and clear when I set this limit with Mom. Her response to this firm request was huge, but I held to my belief that our relationship would be stronger in the end if we broke out of the cycle we had established when I was a child.

It took us many months to reach a new equilibrium in our relationship, but I am happy to say that after that we shared one of the best mother-daughter relationships I know of until she died in April of 2003. We could say anything to each other, and we respected each other. Doing my anger "just right" started a truth-telling conversation that continued until her death.

Confronting my sweet, victimized mother was one of the hardest, bravest things I have ever done. Very few people understood or supported me, but I knew I was doing what I had to do. It has made, in many ways, all the difference.

I had to be willing to lose my relationship with my mom in order to live an authentic life. My truth became more important than the pretend dance we had always done with each other. I did not decide to confront my mother. My body simply would not let me play the game anymore.

Because my mother and I disentangled ourselves, because I learned we were two separate people, I was finally able to discover my body is smarter than I am. I have trusted its wisdom in many difficult situations when my brain was wandering around, trying to "understand." I have learned to trust this biochemical reaction, this knowing. My body never lies to me.

Helpful Hints for Doing Anger "Just Right"

These are sentences I have discovered help me in those moments when it is hard to think. I find that by practicing these sentences beforehand, I am more likely to have them when I need them.

1. "Are you mad at me?"

This question can lead to a good discussion. Of course, the person you ask might lie about being angry, but if they do, you can usually tell. This is good information. If a person gets angry, but won't admit it when asked, they aren't good intimacy material. You know now that you need to protect yourself with them.

Usually, though, if you ask the question in an "I'd really like to know the answer and it's okay with me if you are mad" manner, they will tell you. Often it is just some miscommunication that angers the other person. Asking this question can help clear the air.

2. "Did I do something wrong?"

This question allows people to talk about an upset without using the word "angry." You are saying you are ready to admit you have been wrong. You don't want a fight. You will not be defensive. It is safe to let it all hang out with you.

This question might unveil judgment that is flying around, sucking the joy out of a friendship. The person might be judging you and is unaware of it and will stop when it is pointed out to them. They may be relieved to have the burden of judgment released. Or you may have completely misunderstood. Either way, the judgment is out in the open.

If you are hanging out with people who feel they have the right to judge you, consider picking new friends. If these people are relatives, I would just keep letting them know you feel judged and don't like it.

Many people want to make their secret judgments and just get away with it. When you continue to shine the light on their behavior, though, it makes it more difficult for them to be angry passively. You are doing what you can to invite a shift.

3. "Ow!"

This is for when you feel put down and are otherwise speechless. I could have said this when my friend said, "Vicki doesn't need to see the pictures." This would have let her know I was hurt and would have given me some time to get my wits back.

Saying "Ow!" is deceptively simple. We say it, though, because it gives instantaneous feedback. You can smile when you say it if you feel your feedback needs softening, but don't let people get away with "jokes" that you have to pay for. A joke is only funny if no one has to pay for it.

4. **"I care about you, and if I have hurt you in some way, I would really like to know about it."**

This sentence can open some hearts and start some good conversations.

Dealing with Temper Tantrums

Important note: No one has the right to abuse us physically or verbally. Just because someone is mad doesn't mean they get to say or do anything they like. We do not have to suffer other people's temper tantrums. (And they do not need to suffer ours!)

If someone is throwing a temper tantrum, here are some things you might say:

- "I feel abused."
- "You need to calm down and start talking to me without calling me names, or I will leave."
- "What you have said feels mean."
- "This is only making the problem worse. Let's take a time-out and cool off."
- "I can see that this has made you very angry. Let's not hurt each other, though. Let's take a break and cool off."
- "We are in that hurting place with each other again. Let's take a break and talk later."

If you want these statements to work, you need to say them without a "holier than thou" attitude. You know what it is like to be "too hot." Do not take abuse, but don't give any back either.

Your Turn

What fights do you keep repeating? How do you feel about conflict? Do you need to schedule some "pre-fight" time—time where you do some conflict prevention work? This can be especially helpful if you have "that time of the month" problems. Talk about it ahead of time and make a plan that includes some laughter.

How do you feel about conflict? Write out your best conflict experience and your worst. Share these writings with someone you trust. How can you start to practice dealing with conflict, even if it scares the breath right out of you? Can you admit when you feel defensive, so you can get curious about it?

When is your anger too hot? When is it too cold? How do you deal with other people's anger? How would you like to deal with it?

Now, tell some of your "just right "anger stories and collect some from your friends. Start having conversations about this with people you trust. Almost everyone has problems with anger, so welcome to the human race.

Chapter 23

Gracious Extrications from Difficult Situations

If you follow every suggestion in this book impeccably, you will still find yourself in hot, sticky water occasionally. This is as it should be. I encourage you to develop the habit of extricating yourself quickly from those difficult moments in your relationship. We want to shift what is happening, not make it worse by being sloppy with our mouths or by pouting. I love to pout, but it is not an effective strategy for getting to the bottom of what is going on between two people who love each other.

Story: Murray, the Thermostat, and Do-Overs

Once, when I was in my stuff and didn't know it, I said to Murray, as I stared at our new thermostat, "I don't know what you did to this thermostat, Murray, but it's not working."

Aren't I just the cutest thing?

I didn't even notice the bitchiness in my voice. Somewhere underneath this crabby complaint, I thought I was making a reasonable request to get the house warmer. I really was clueless and innocent in a viperous sort of way.

Murray waited a few moments and then came to me, saying, "You know, I really have a hard time listening to a sentence that begins with 'Murray I don't know what you did to this thermostat, but...'"

Caught. Hoist by my own petard. To my credit, I like getting caught. In fact, I want to get caught. I don't want to talk to my husband this way ever.

"Can I have a do-over?" I asked.

"You betcha," he replied.

"Honey, I'm cold. Could you look at this thermostat again? I don't think it is working right."

We laughed.

Now, "I don't know what you did to this thermostat . . ." is part of our partnering language. It has become part of our code that helps us to return to the loving, respectful relationship that is the best of both of us.

Authentic Apologies

Apologies get a bum rap. We misuse or abuse them all the time: "Shelly! Tell your brother you are sorry!" we admonish. "I'm sorry," Shelly says meekly, all the while plotting her revenge.

When we say we are sorry when we are not, we lie and further damage our relationships with others and with ourselves. An honest apology, however, can make a difference. It can open our hearts and allow for great shifts of understanding and compassion **if** it is followed by a change of behavior. To think that an apology, by itself, is enough is irresponsible and damaging. "But I said I'm sorry!" does not erase the behavior. True apologies build trust and strengthen relationships. We are all going to blow it. What do we do when we blow it? That is the question!

Five Steps of an Apology: (Adapted from Jennifer James.)

1. Do it now.
2. Say it all.
3. Share how you felt.
4. Affirm yourself.
5. Commit to and plan a change in behavior.

Step One: Do it now. This sounds easy, but how many of us have put off an apology we knew we needed to make because we were afraid to bring it up? The sooner we apologize, the sooner we can get back on the right track with ourselves. This is an important part of the process.

I used to live with chronic anxiety. I know that practicing avoiding difficult conversations contributed to my paralysis. Which comes first, the anxiety or the avoiding? It doesn't matter to me. If I get an anxious feeling, I immediately try to find the thought that created it. If there is any action that needs to be taken, a "do it now" that needs doing, I have learned to roll up my sleeves and plunge in. Nothing is worse for me than letting my anxiety have a chance to build a head of steam.

Step Two: Say it all. This means we need to say every part of what we did and not hold anything back. This step is about "the whole truth and nothing but the truth." If we keep something back in order to make ourselves look better at the moment, then we won't really be apologizing. Our apology will be a lie, and our self worth will deteriorate. It will be like having a wound that we don't fully clean. The behavior we have not admitted will get septic and our relationship with ourselves and others will suffer.

Step Three: Share how you felt. After you have completely owned up to your behavior without making any excuses or blaming the other person, you get to share your side of it. But you only get to share how you felt, not how the other person made you mad. This may seem like a subtle distinction, but it is crucial. Other people don't "make" us mad. We respond to the actions of others. We choose our responses. But we also feel. And when we share how we feel, we reveal who we are. The person you have injured will be more likely to listen to you after you have completely accepted responsibility for your actions. This step allows the other person to look inside of you and maybe feel some compassion.

Step Four: Affirm yourself. Apologizing is an act of courage. You apologize because you made a mistake, but that doesn't mean you are a mistake. You're apologizing because you broke your own inner rules. Step four allows you to state the kind of person you are committed to being. It can be as simple as, "I want to be a person who can be trusted. I let myself down by lying to you, and I won't do that again. Your friendship is important to me."

Step Five: Commit to and plan a change in behavior. An apology is only as good as the change in behavior that follows it. Talk is cheap, and this step shows that the person apologizing is serious and willing to change. Step five might sound something like: "I can't promise I won't ever be irritable again, but I don't want you to tolerate any of my crabby behavior. If I speak one word in an irritable tone, give me a time-out sign, and I will shut my mouth and take myself off somewhere until I am fit to talk to you respectfully. My intention is be to respectful at all times."

Sincere apologies work. They are noble moments. When we are young, we seem to be able to let go easily and go on with grace. I have seen "gnarly" teenagers show amazing character, either by admitting and apologizing or by forgiving and forgetting. Authentic apologies are simple and powerful.

Note: "I'm sorry" said every fifteen seconds is not an apology, unless it is an apology for existing. It is a self-defeating habit that serves no one. If you are a practitioner of knee-jerk apologies, stop right now, cold turkey—with no apologies!

Story: "Vicki, I Need to Talk to You"

It can take me a long time to overcome the shame I feel when I make a mistake. I can feel a pull to get defensive when someone is unhappy with me. I hate finding out I have been inconsiderate or unkind in some way. Even after all of the practice I have had apologizing instead of making excuses, even though I know how important it is to cheerfully admit my mistakes, I still have to buck up when someone starts talking and I hear that telltale tone in their voice.

"I have something I need to talk to you about," Rose said as she sat down at her kitchen table, pulling the chair around so that it faced me.

I gulped. My heart started beating faster, and I opened my ears and my heart.

"I hope I haven't been really bad," I thought to myself. "I hope I'm not going to get nailed, because I am feeling pretty fragile right now, (my mother had died only a few weeks earlier) and I'm not sure I have the strength to deal with an onslaught.

"Okay," I thought as I mustered my courage. "Bring it on."

"I've got something I need to talk to you about. It has just been nagging at me, and I need to talk to you and get it out," she said.

I sat quietly.

"Remember last year at the Seaside Wellness Conference we were going to do a workshop on Body Shame, and then this year, when you sent me your individual proposal, 'Loving Your Body As Is' which is so similar to our joint proposal last year, well, I felt as though I had been punched. You hadn't said anything to me about it, and I just felt bad when I read the description."

"Oh, good," I thought. "I blew it!" I meant it. This was a clear case, and I was guilty. This would not be one of those murky discussions that might be difficult for such a new friendship. I had made a mistake, and I knew what to do about it.

"You are right," I said. "That was incredibly sloppy of me. It didn't even occur to me to run it by you, but I should have. That was very sloppy of me, and I am very sorry. What can I do to make it right with you?"

We hugged.

I confessed more of my bad habit of getting excited about something and then just marching toward my goal, not always watching whom I might accidentally bump along the way. I was truly sorry and also grateful that she had called me on my behavior. What a gift!

"Would you like to do the workshop with me?" I asked.

She thought for a moment. "No, I don't think I'm really excited about that topic right now, but I did feel bad when I saw your proposal and we hadn't even talked about it."

"It just never even occurred to me to talk to you. I completely forgot that we had proposed a joint workshop last year. I guess I didn't forget exactly, but it just did not pop into my mind. Are you at peace with this, with me?" I asked.

We hugged again, and our friendship was stronger because she had the courage to pull back the curtain and speak her troubled feelings, and I had the courage to admit my mistake and to offer reparation.

Your Turn

Any do-overs you want to initiate? It is never too late. You can even act out horrible events in your past and make them turn out the way you wish they had. Get people you love and trust to help you physically recreate the scene. I believe a do-over such as this can change our body chemistry.

Any apologies you need to make? It is never too late to make reparations. If an apology would harm the person you need to make reparations with, write them a letter and then burn it. A heartfelt apology is an enemy of shame. You will feel much lighter when you fess up and offer to do whatever you can to make it better.

Chapter 24

Pulling Back the Curtain on Some Great Fights

In this chapter I let you see into some of the fights Murray and I have experienced, both the significant and the mundane. These stories were written shortly after the fight, and I'm glad I listened to the voice inside me that said, "You should get this down on paper while it's fresh."

While brewing this book for Bethany and Shaen, I realized these stories should be included. How often do we get to see this deeply inside any relationship? I believe that modeling is powerful and that most of us have not seen enough healthy fighting. I do not offer these as perfect fights or even fights you might like to copy. (I'd like to see you try!) No, these are just what they are: two humans who love each other coming together with all of their stuff, getting lost and getting found again. Bless us, one and all!

Story: Murray and the River Panic

I was sitting on a bench looking over a small set of rapids, thinking about my talk with a parent group in Iowa four days hence. Murray was calling the police, sure that I had been kidnapped, murdered, mugged, knowing I must be dead, or else I wouldn't have been "missing" along the banks of the Tumalo River for forty-five minutes. How had this miscommunication come to pass?

The answer was simple: a native Oregonian woman, more at home walking along a river than just about anywhere else, meets a native of dangerous Los Angeles, the son of Holocaust survivors. This was culture shock at its most basic.

Murray and I had endured a few bumpy relationship days before that walk on the river. We were out of synch, just missing the beat with each other. This didn't happen often, but it was wearing. We were on a week's vacation at Eagle Crest in a wonderful, two-bedroom townhouse overlooking the Deschutes River in central Oregon. The weather had been good, even to the point of the sun pouring in our bedroom window on the first morning. I had been premenstrual, but that had disappeared when the rays of the sun hit my face that first morning. We had days of leisure, horseback riding, walks, massages, but we were just a bit out of our usual relationship groove.

We drove into the day-use area of Tumalo State Park and into an empty parking lot. I jumped out of the car, as usual, and Murray took some time doing whatever mysterious things he does that gets him out of the car consistently after me. I waited, as I had waited for him to get ready to go on the walk. I wait for people a lot, I always have, but I have had to wait much more since I lost my central vision and my ability to drive. I get sick of waiting, and I was sick of waiting for Murray already, before we even started our walk.

We found our way down to a path along the river. "Hey, that looks like a good place to look for antlers!" Murray yelled as he took several steps off the path toward a tree. "I'm going to look for antlers."

I didn't want to wait, and I didn't wait. I also didn't let Murray know that I wasn't waiting. I kept walking along the path by the river.

I knew I was breaking a rule by not telling Murray that I was continuing on. But I felt rebellious. I was just walking along the path, after all. I felt hemmed in by the rules of a relationship that demanded I let Murray know exactly where I was. So I kept walking, and I didn't walk slowly. I was tired of waiting, and I needed some exercise.

When I got to the end of a meadow, where the path disappeared but where there was still an easy way to walk along the river, I turned and looked for Murray, sure that he would come running out of the woods from the path. He didn't. I waited exactly two heartbeats and then turned and kept walking. He can just catch up with me, I thought.

I walked along the river, sure that Murray would catch up at any moment. Then I came to a road. It headed in the right direction, so I followed it for a short distance until I came to a bridge over the river. The bridge led to a private house, but as soon as I got to the bridge, I could see that the path continued along the river. Cool! I thought, and kept walking. I figured if the blind woman could find this path, then the sighted man could as well.

I walked past one YCC bench, the letters carved large. I kept trying to read them as a word, and it wasn't until I saw them on the second bench that I realized they were the initials for Youth Conservation Corps. Kids had built these benches. Cool.

The second bench overlooked a set of rapids. The cliff on the other side of the river reflected the setting sun. I bathed in exquisite beauty of the moment. I sat and listened, and watched, and let myself think through my presentation for parents in Iowa. I had never done a presentation for parents just like this, and I was a little worried about it. I expected that Murray would show up any moment, especially now that I had stopped to wait for him. So I relaxed and thought my way through my talk.

I had a great time, got inspired, knew just what I would do, and then I listened to my watch. I had been sitting on the bench for twenty-five minutes.

Where was Murray, anyway? I got up to walk back to him, feeling fully recalibrated.

Murray must have known we needed this time apart, I thought. We are usually so in tune. He has probably been spending this time getting recalibrated himself. We will probably meet each other and be freshly in love all over again.

"Cool," I thought again.

Then I met an older couple walking toward me on the path. "Is your husband missing?" the woman asked me.

"I guess so," I said, realizing only now that something was wrong with the story I had been telling myself.

"Your husband drove off to look for a ranger," she said. "He says you have been missing for over forty-five minutes."

"Uh, oh," I thought and started to jog toward the car. Then I slowed down. I can't see well enough to jog along a path. I walked as fast as I could safely walk, and when I got close to the parking lot, I started calling Murray's name. I heard a shout, but I couldn't tell what had been said. I shouted back.

We hollered: "Murray! I'm over here!" and "Vicki! Where are you?" back and forth a few times, and then Murray emerged from the trees and started yelling at me.

"Where have you been? I was worried sick! I thought you had been captured; I knew you had been captured. I even called the police. Where have you been? How could you walk off and leave me?"

When I heard Murray mention the police, I got worried. "Murray, we have to call the police and tell them I am all right. You can finish lecturing me later."

But Murray needed to yell more right then.

"What were you thinking? How could you keep walking without me? I stopped for a moment to look for antlers under that tree, and when I looked up, you were gone."

Then he took my hand and in a softer voice said, "I am so glad you are safe. I have spent the last twenty minutes imagining that you were dead." And then he started to cry. I tried to put my arms around him to comfort him, but he remained stiff. I told him I had just walked along the river, that I had expected him to catch up at any minute, that it never occurred to me that he would be worried, that I would never intentionally trigger his fears, that I was sorry, and that this would never happen again.

Murray would have found me, if he had not given up so soon. I was just walking along the river. When he got to the road and saw the bridge, he assumed I couldn't possibly have walked that far, so he gave up, especially since he assumed I was in grave danger. If he had kept walking, he would have found me.

"We have to call the police, Murray," I said again. He agreed, and we walked to the car and drove to the phone.

Murray had recalibrated, all right, but not the way I had thought.

It took us a long time to unpack the miscommunication. I had wanted to be free, to break trail, to not wait, to do something I didn't get to do often. I felt alive and safe and beautiful in the woods. Murray said he felt broken, and that it wasn't necessarily bad that he was broken, but he was broken nonetheless.

I learned something about myself that I didn't know. When Murray had been crying about me, I froze. Outwardly I remained kind and conciliatory, but inside I became cold and still. I realized later that I am afraid of having someone love me so much they can hurt that much for me. I would much rather risk my own pain by loving others than cause other people pain because they love me. I'm still processing what this means in my day-to-day interactions—how I might be discouraging people from loving me, even though I long for more intimacy and feel that I am ready for depths of love and commitment when others aren't. Maybe this is a completely misleading story I chant to myself.

Murray and I got clearer about how deep our cultural differences are, not so much Jew and gentile as much as urban and rural. I need to feel free to walk at my own pace along the river sometimes. I crave it as if it were pure oxygen and I had been living in smog. Murray has trouble feeling secure when I walk along any river in my life, even when he knows where I am going and when I am coming back.

This incident contains metaphors that are rich for us. In later experiences, I have asked myself: how is this situation like when I felt I needed to break through the invisible container of our relationship by walking free along the river? How is this situation another cultural difference?

Who was wrong in this story? Who was right? Does it matter? I apologized to Murray; does he owe me an apology for overreacting and getting himself into such a stir? No. Blame and shame thrive in Level One and only perpetuate problems. The only important question is: What can we learn from this adventure that will help us love each other better in the future?

Story: Puerto Vallarta Fight

Murray and I were sitting beside each other on a bus in Puerto Vallarta on the last leg of a trip to visit friends in a nearby village. We were hot and tired, and I was listening to my book on tape, both earplugs in my ears. Murray turned to me and started talking. I couldn't make out his words because of the conflict with the book on tape so I snapped off my cassette and said, "What were you saying? I was listening to my book."

Even though I hadn't been able to make out his words, I knew he was irritated about something, both from the tone of his voice, which I had managed to hear above the story and the road noise, and the stiffness in his body.

"I don't think it is safe for you to be walking around with those plugs in your ears. When we were crossing the highway earlier today and you had those plugs in your ears, I couldn't tell if you could hear the traffic or not, and I didn't know if you were safe."

"Okay," I said, "I won't wear the earphones out in traffic anymore. I'm sorry."

"I felt responsible for your safety, and I couldn't tell if you were listening to the tape or to the traffic," he continued.

"Okay," I said again, "I won't do that anymore."

But Murray wasn't finished with me. "I really don't like it when you interrupt me when I'm trying to tell you something," he said a bit peevishly.

"Wait a minute," I said, "You seem to have two requests for me. One is that I not wear my earphones when I am walking around with you in traffic, and the second request is that I listen to the lecture you want to give me about doing that. Yes to one, no to two," I said, smiling.

Murray stopped talking then and turned to look out the window. A few moments passed and then he turned back to me. "I guess I was enjoying being right," he said.

"Yeah, you were having a good time there for awhile, but I wasn't. Would you like some 'right' time? I can listen to you be right for a while if you would like."

We laughed.

He thought for a moment. "I think I feel left out when you are listening to your tapes," he said.

"I think so, too," I said, warming to him.

"I could probably just let you know I was feeling left out instead of lecturing you, couldn't I?"

"Yes, you could probably do that," I replied, taking his hand.

"We got through that one pretty quickly, didn't we?" he said, kissing my bare shoulder. "We could have spent days working that one out."

"Years," I said. "I could have gotten mad and gotten stuck in my own rightness, or you could have denied feeling left out, and we could have had a whole tangle of other fights that branched out from this one."

"We could have," he said, slipping his arm around me. "Glad we didn't."

We sat in comfortable silence until another problem emerged. "It's too hot for your arm to be around me," I said smiling.

He took his arm away, laughing as I put my earphones back in my ears and restarted my cassette.

We rode back to our air-conditioned hotel in companionable silence.

Story: Suitcase Fight

Near the end of one of my seminar trips Murray joined me for a few days. He helped me pack my books and tapes and presentation materials, and then we went to Disneyland to play for the evening.

We checked at the desk about a room change we had requested. The road outside of the hotel was under construction, which I had learned, to my dismay, during the night before. "Have you ever seen 'My Cousin Vinny'?" I had asked the desk clerk. She didn't think that was as funny as I did. But she had promised to find us a quieter room and told us to check back when we returned from Disneyland.

We were exhausted as we boarded the shuttle back to the hotel. My lower back, legs, and feet ached so much I could hardly walk upright.

We checked at the desk, got our new room keys, and made our way to our old room to pack up our belongings and move.

I am pretty fast at that sort of thing, as Murray will tell you, and I packed quickly. Murray and I made our first trip to our new room, taking as much as we could carry. Murray gallantly offered to bring my two bulky presentation suitcases up to the room while I took a bath.

These two suitcases contained toys, puppets, and overheads I had collected for my presentations. They represented many, many hours of labor and a considerable sum of money.

I got into the bathtub while Murray went back to the old room to finish packing his stuff and to bring up the two presentation suitcases. He returned as I came out of the bathroom, and we collapsed into bed.

The next morning, the bell clerk called to ask if we were missing any luggage. The night security guard had found two suitcases right outside our door in the middle of the night. Murray told them that, yes, they were our bags, thanked him for finding them, and then hung up.

"I guess I must have left them outside the door," he said.

Murray has a history, in my opinion, of not paying attention to things that are important to me. He will move something of mine, and when I ask him about it, he will say, "Yeah, I moved that."

"Where is it?" I will ask with a certain amount of exasperation.

"I don't remember where I put it," he will say and then go on doing what he had been doing when I asked. This behavior confuses and distresses me. How can he not pay attention to the last part of a process?

So when I discovered that Murray had left my presentation materials, the materials I use to make a living, outside of our room for anyone to ransack or steal, I got mad.

Here is where Murray's fighting genius comes into play. "Go ahead and be mad," he said. "I deserve to have you mad at me."

This comment worked well. I don't like being mad at Murray. I love him. I know he always has my best interests at heart. He had been trying to help me. It was a stupid mistake; but he had been careless, not malevolent. I didn't want to be mad at him, but I was.

I said a few things to him in a loud voice, things such as, "How could you just leave the suitcases out in the hall? Do you realize how much work I would have had to do to undo your mistake?" I didn't call him any names because I never do that, but I was truly disgusted with him.

He didn't argue with me about what a stupid thing he had done. He agreed, which took some of the wind out of my sail. "How could I have been so stupid?" he kept saying.

"I know what happened," he finally said. "When I came into the room, you were getting out of the tub, and you were standing there naked. The curtains were open, and I shut the door to come in and close them so that no one could see you, and then I just forgot to go back out and bring in the luggage."

"Let me get this straight," I said. "You were so concerned about someone seeing me, though no one was near our room, that you didn't finish the task of bringing in the suitcases because you felt compelled to protect my privacy. Is that right?"

Murray sheepishly agreed that an imagined threat had displaced the real threat of losing my suitcases. I didn't much care if someone walking by got a glimpse of me naked. I hadn't even realized the curtains were open. Usually, I am careful about closing them, especially when I travel alone. But I was so tired that night, and Murray was with me, I had curbed my vigilance a bit.

We had been lucky that no one had stolen my suitcases, but we still had a problem to solve. I could add this event to the growing file I was creating on Murray's lack of mindfulness. I could become The Bitch of the North and start always looking for him to screw up. Murray, on the other hand, could start second-guessing himself and start making even more mistakes in an attempt to be more attentive.

We didn't like either one of these scenarios. Murray had given me permission to voice my anger, and I did. We used our finger-holding confession technique: Murray held my finger, and all he could say to me was, "I love you," no matter what vile things I said to him.

He took my finger, and I said everything that was in my belly. "I hate it when you do stuff like this. It makes me afraid to trust you," I told him.

"I love you," he replied softly.

"These materials took me hours and hours to collect. I'm not sure I could even recreate what is in the suitcases if someone had stolen them. I would have been left to deal with the consequences of your lack of mindfulness," I said, losing some of my irritation.

"I love you," Murray said again.

"I'm afraid you are a mindless dweeb and that I will become the bitch of the century as I look over your shoulder to keep you from messing up my life."

"I love you."

"I feel vulnerable and unprotected when you are careless with things that are important to me. I am afraid to trust you when you let me down like this, and I am afraid of what our relationship will become if I don't trust you."

Pay dirt. As soon as "I'm afraid" and "I feel vulnerable" start flowing, then shift happens.

"I love you," Murray said yet again and I think I finally heard him.

"I'm mad, mad, mad at you. You were really bad."

"I love you," he said with a smile.

Once I had cleared this out of my belly, we were ready to start problem solving. How could we avoid the pitfalls of my becoming a judgmental nag and Murray becoming an anxious goof up?

"Help me understand your thinking," I said. "My anxiety over the safety of the suitcases would have made it impossible for me to leave them in the hall. Your nakedness would not have worried me nearly as much as the possibility of losing my materials. No one would be hurt if I had been seen, it was late, and there was no one in the hall anyway. Help me understand."

Murray grew up in L.A. He explained to me that his deeply learned fears about personal safety in a big city had taken over, and he temporarily forgot his mission.

"But you forget your mission often," I said, "and that is a problem for me. I really don't understand how you can pick something up and move it and not remember where you put it. When you tell me you don't remember where you put something, I want to choke you. It is irritating on a practical level, but it is also no fun to be with someone who isn't present in his own life. I feel lonely when you say you don't remember where you put something."

Murray decided he would go to work at being mindful in his own life, not because I wanted him to, but because he knows his life is richer when he pays attention to what he does. He also decided to let me know when he is being careful (This was the word he came up with that best described what he wanted to work on). He would let me know when he was being careful because he was pretty sure I didn't notice how often he was careful; I only noticed when he wasn't.

I agreed. We also thought that I should confess my own lapses in carefulness so that I wouldn't be building a case of my own "perfection" while noticing only Murray's lapses in concentration.

We are still working on this as I write this story. I have found, to my chagrin, that I make a lot more mistakes regarding mindfulness than I had realized. Murray will say, "Did you make a *mistake?*" in a teasing, friendly way that helps me look at myself. He also lets me know when he is being careful, and that helps me not feel so anxious.

We aren't yet finished with this one. We both have much to learn. But we have created a living structure, which allows us both to grow without shame. We love and appreciate each other more now because of our struggle with the nearly lost suitcases.

As with most relationships, it is the mundane that threatens to mar the sacred. When compared to how much I love Murray and value our relationship, the suitcases are nothing. But it doesn't take too many poorly resolved suitcase events before the deeper structure of the relationship is threatened and then damaged, sometimes beyond repair.

My first marriage broke upon the rocks of daily living and our inability to find a way to solve problems such as this without creating shame, anger, and hopelessness. The frustration of my first marriage is what compels me to find new ways to solve these "mundane" challenges within an otherwise loving, encouraging relationship.

Murray Off and On
Written by Someone Who Knows Him and Loves Him Well

I wrote this when Murray and I were at the low point of our marriage. As I saw it, Murray's shame had him in its teeth, and Murray was scurrying around, pretending that this was not so. I was frustrated but determined. "I do not want to divorce your ass" I told him, "but I will not be married to a man who does not own his own farts." He was so lost in his stuff that he even asked if we could renegotiate this rule. He was nuts. This writing was one of my efforts to pull him (and us) out of the pit.

Before I share "Murray Off and On," which may sound like I'm being too tough on my sweetie, I will begin with "Vicki Off." (I suggested Murray write his own "Vicki Off and On," but since he didn't, I'm including my version of "Vicki Off.")

Vicki Off

When Vicki is off she:

- Keeps track of things: how many mistakes you've made, how many times you've exaggerated, how many times you have disappointed her.
- Withholds affection and approval.
- Is stingy and wants to get away with it.
- Can't keep herself from asking, before Murray has time to take a breath, "How much does that cost?"
- Nags, reminds, and in other disrespectful ways, micromanages.
- Focuses on what is not working and is sure that whatever is broken will always be broken.
- Interrupts instead of listens.
- Tries to fix your problem without your invitation.
- Is impatient if you don't think as fast as she does.
- Hurries, does too much, goes over the top.

Murray Off

- Is more concerned with being right than with anything else: loving himself, loving me, truth, trust, or kindness.
- Has amnesia about his patterns of behavior.
- Is argumentative, and when confronted about his argumentativeness, gets defensive and more argumentative.
- Uses, "It's a mystery," to avoid dealing with what I have said.
- Uses humor to hide. His humor becomes anger-tinged or obnoxious or too silly.
- Has a stiff energy running through, or rather, stuck in him. The undercurrent is "There is a lot at stake here. I have to win, and you

have to be wrong, or at least I can't be all wrong here. Everything is at stake. Everything is at stake."
- Hides instead of sharing what is going on.
- Listens poorly, doesn't remember, doesn't hear.
- Says, "That's just the way I am!" or "That's what I meant to do!" instead of being interested in how a behavior change might set him free.
- Thinks I am trying to make him wrong instead of trying to set him free.
- Thinks he is all alone in the world and can't trust anyone.
- Forgets that I have never given him self-serving feedback. I have never tried to distract him from looking at a flaw in me by pointing to a flaw in him.
- Talks without paying attention to how his words are received.
- Is stubborn about trying something new, such as investigating the possibility of acupuncture rather than surgery.
- Can't tell the difference between stubbornness and firmness.
- Stops bringing up reflections and insights.

Murray On

- Is handsome. His cheeks are like soft pillows I can lean into and be nurtured on. His eyes are deep pools that flow into the depths of the Great Mystery.
- Is very funny. Can be any number of characters who delight his listeners.
- Is a genius at developing activities to help children—activities that are fun, engaging, and teach skills without the children knowing it.
- Writes poetry and reads books that inspire and enrich him.
- Does projects out of joy and feels satisfied and complete when he finishes a task.
- Is open to all topics of discussion. There are no taboo subjects; in fact, he takes a stand for not having any taboo subjects.
- Doesn't worry about being "fixed" because he is always interested in new ways to be free.
- Trusts me.

- Trusts himself.
- Seeks contact with others.
- Spends time developing his unique interests.
- Seeks help when he needs it from me, friends, or his therapist.
- Follows through on agreements and promises.
- "Pulls back the curtain" and lets me see what his internal processes are.
- Is not afraid of his shame or of his shadow. He is interested in finding out how his Predator affects his life.
- Helps me understand how my Predator affects my life.
- Takes on the burden of his self-esteem and leaves me out of it.
- Looks for patterns in his behavior because he knows he will be set free when he can understand and change a destructive pattern.
- Believes that he is worthwhile. Deciding whether or not he is worthwhile or a piece of excrement is not on the agenda.
- Has a memory of the past and sees connections.
- Helps me see when I am off and tells me in a firm, loving manner.
- Is in touch with mystery. He can see a bigger, more soulful perspective about what is happening.
- Is open to and thoughtful about feedback, any feedback. He is willing to consider and trust what I think.
- Is concerned more about his integrity than about pleasing me.
- Is playful for the sake of playfulness, never as a means of hiding, distracting, or being angry.
- Is full of free-flowing, sparkling energy. He delights in small wonders.
- Stands solid on the ground. Breathes his own air without apologizing.
- Can be leaned upon.
- Can tolerate my feelings without having them be about him and his worth.
- Investigates things he is interested in and shares what he learns with me.
- Is generous, thoughtful, and sweet-tempered.
- Gets angry in a firm, clean way. He holds his ground without needing to be angry. He uses his anger to enforce his dignity.
- Loves truth more than being right.
- Loves me more than his shame.

- Gives to me from strength rather than from dependence on my approval.
- Listens to his own needs and takes care of them in flow.
- Is an emotional athlete: hearty, rugged, and fierce when he needs to be.
- Sees me completely and loves me deeply.
- Lets me love him as an equal.
- Says things that surprise and delight me.
- Is considerate without being obsequious, sweet without being smarmy, interested in the world without being pedantic.
- Ponders and shifts to a deep level, then shares his journey with me.

Poem: A Fight to the Death

This poem tells the story of the most significant fight Murray and I have had. Our marriage was teetering on a precipice. In this fight, I got as fierce and as ugly as I am capable of getting. Murray looked as if he were backed into a corner and his life were at stake. And, in a way, it was. He had to choose between hiding in his shame or loving himself and me. Murray hesitated, and there were long moments of silence. Would we stay married or not? I held my breath as Murray decided.

Shame,
that old wily dragon,
embraces my lover,
corrupting his belief in himself
and his faith in truth.

All problems and concerns,
instead of being objects of curiosity,
invitations for creativity,
worm their way into the bowels of my lover's soul.
Any unhappiness I have about his behavior
becomes a life and death struggle
between
the Dragon of Shame
and Truth.

The dragon,
smiling with gleeful, evil confidence,
bites into my lover's self-worth,
as the Truth, which will set him free,
quietly urges him to discover the courage to let himself know
what is really behind curtain number three,
the curtain behind which his essence waits to be lived.

"I have you now," the dragon says to my sweet lover.
"I know the Truth about you. You know this Truth as well.
It is disgusting.
You are disgusting.
Your only hope is to hide,
to burrow deep.
Don't let anyone find out what you are really like,
especially her."

The dragon is winning because my lover doesn't know he is in its clutches.
He doesn't know he is in a fight to the death
with the dragon that wants to devour his hope and his sweetness,
his vulnerability and magnificence.

No, my lover thinks he is in a struggle between life and death with,
you won't believe this,
but he thinks his enemy is
me.

He thinks I want to chew on his vital organs.
He thinks,
or rather the dragon has him think,
that if I see what is really inside him,
I will vomit my disgust all over his vulnerability.

He believes his only chance to save himself
is to divert my attention from his inner ugliness.
He becomes dragon-clever.

He tries to distract me from his liver by being extra considerate,
extra polite,
obsequious,
treating me like a sleeping Gorgon he must placate,
stepping carefully among all those eggshell land mines which surround me.

He thinks if he isn't careful he might wake Evil Vicki,
and then she will focus her gaze on his most vulnerable,
most secret,
most dragon-guarded
self.
And then,
he is certain,
Dangerous Vicki will rip his carotid artery from his neck.

When his ingratiating kindness makes me snarl,
when I become a little like the monster he thinks I am,
he tries a different tactic.
He gets angry.
He accuses me of bullying
or lying.
He tries to convince me that it is my stuff, not his,
that needs a good airing.
When I say,
"Nice try, buddy, but this time it isn't me.
I want to deal with the problem.
It is you who is turning all problems into a measure of your worth
and your right to even be on the planet and breathe."

When my gaze remains steady,
when I lower my defensive sail
and allow his accusations to fly by like puffs of wind,
this is when he gets the most devious;
this is when he gets
"logical."
"You are simply wrong," he tells me.

He is not even passionate about it.
Instead, he is "understanding."
He points out to me, or to whomever will listen,
how this problem we are having fits nicely into my stuff.

This is the diversion that almost gets me.
I do have stuff,
Lord knows,
and I need to be open and ready to hear about it.
But his logical demeanor tips me off.
He is a little *too* logical.
He acts a little too much like he has put on his dad's suit coat
and is trying to pass himself off as the reasonable man
who must placate the hysterical wife.

I say to him:
"With your head resting on the dragon's chest,
you can mount quite an argument indeed.
But your arguments are nothing more than your fear wearing a tie."
My words help me slip out of the "logical" shame-hold my lover tries
to put on me.

I decide this is a battle of life and death,
The life or death of our relationship.
"We will get to the bottom of this,"
I tell him.
"Or,
much as I don't want to,
I will divorce your ass."

I will not be married to a man who breaks agreements,
a man who will not admit his mistakes,
a man held prisoner by the beast of shame.
For to stay married to that man
means I will be married,
really,
to no one.

I will be married to the man who is always guessing about what he needs to do
to avoid the truth he fears will expose his worthlessness.
As he gives his soul to the shame dragon for snack food,
he is not present in his own body.
There is no one there for me to love,
no one there to love me.

As I scream in his face,
trying to break the dragon's spell,
as I shake him,
grabbing him by the shoulders
with the fierceness of Durga—
Hindu Goddess—
Protector of Innocence,
riding her lion
waving her six arms,
brandishing her swords—
as I let myself be this fierce,
this ugly,
this reprehensible,
this easily misunderstood Medusa of madness,
I tell him,
"The time to choose, my love, is now.
Will you consider for thirty seconds
the idea that you might be fighting with your shame and not me?
I just want thirty seconds.
Can you give me thirty seconds—
if not giving me thirty seconds means you lose me?"

We wait.

We wait inside one of those moments
where the world turns
and angels hold their breath.

We wait longer than I think I can bear,
and my hope starts to quiver.

Do I have the courage to risk it all for my lover,
for me,
for us?

Suddenly,
I see a crack appear in the dragon's scales covering my precious one.
Light bursts forth,
a beam of light of love and energy and vitality.
Just one beam of light,
and it is enough.

My lover is saved.
I am saved.
We are saved.

The dragon still flies by our home now and then.
I smell his fiery ash breath,
his despair and disgust.
But now when the dragon comes unbidden,
my lover and I reach out for each other.

Together,
we can face any monster,
and the facing of this monster,
this death breath,
makes us stronger,
more valiant,
more loving,
more loved,
more in love than ever.

Your Turn

Any fights you would like to revisit? It is never too late for a Do-Over, remember. Did you notice any places in Vicki-Murray fights where you might have gotten stuck? How about initiating a conversation with your fighting buddy and see if you can't concoct some plan to help you not get mired down in the same old places. For example, you might want to put clown noses around the house. It is hard to maintain your anger with a clown nose on. Be careful, though, that you don't go into Level One and use a clown nose to trivialize what someone is trying to tell you.

Part III

Loving Family and Friends

Chapter 25

Family: A Divinely Human Yearning

A dear friend once asked me, "What does family mean to you?" Good question.

Strong images of families haunt me: multiple generations gathered around the fire and the Christmas tree, snow drifting on the windowsills. Thanksgiving dinner with a browned turkey, heaps of food, a long table crowded with family, lively conversation and lots of laughter. I long for *My Big, Fat Greek Wedding* family all making noise and bossing everyone around.

My favorite family reunion fantasy is the ending scene in the movie *Anton Fischer*. He is an orphan, and at the end of the movie, he has the love of his life, a mentor, and a reclaimed family that sweeps him into their loving arms, ready to hold him to their collective bosom forever.

As I write this, I am essentially an orphan. My mother is dead, and though my father and sister live ninety minutes away from me, I haven't seen them in fifteen years. My brother lives in California and we have rare phone conversations, but we do not celebrate holidays together. So I am an orphan in the ways that count to me.

I am blessed with a fabulous husband, two incredible children, two nephews who have been through the family fires with me, a niece-in-law, and, as of December 2, 2003, eight months to the day after my mother died, a marvelous goddaughter. I am rich in family.

And yet I still yearn. I long for the large, loving family of my imagination. I want to be sure I am not left alone again when a loved one dies, as I was the night my mother died. I want to have people around me to honor life's significant events: marriages, deaths, births and graduations. I have an abundance of love and support now, and people are around me, but I still do not have all the family I hunger for. (I am reminded now of the story of Moses leading the Jews to the Promised Land. Even though God kept His promise to provide manna every day, even though their needs were met without effort, people still hungered after a useless Golden Calf. We humans are amazingly greedy.)

When my ex-mother-in-law died, I had an incredible opportunity to step back into the family I first married into, the family of my children. Seven siblings in my ex-father-in-law's family led to a zillion cousins. My ex-husband has three siblings, and whenever there is some family event or a biannual reunion, hoards of people come. But I don't belong to this family anymore, and, as much as I wanted to for sixteen years, I never belonged in the way I wanted to.

Since I grew up in chaos, I have had a "family wound" aching in my chest. I have tried to pretend it is not there or that I have healed it. I have wanted it to be smaller than it is, feeling ashamed that I could have such an unsightly psychological disfigurement.

As I write this, for the first time in my life, I am allowing the wound to be what it is and allowing whatever healing can come, as it will. I must learn to live in peace with this wound if it is ever to heal. So when I write about creating an authentic family, I do so with much history and emotion. I simply cannot pay the entrance fee into a family that demands its members to pretend. I cannot support family myths. I have tried, and I cannot do it.

My current family speaks truth and humor when we gather. There aren't many of us, it's true, but what we have is fabulous.

The next four chapters are a collection of stories and poems I have written to and about my children and my parents. Some details of history and family are missing, but it has not been my intention to write biographies. Instead, I am pulling back the curtain to share my journey with my family as authentically as I can, trusting that this sharing will be of benefit to someone, even if it is only me.

Before I share more about my children, I want to explain my philosophy of mothering.

The Art of Invisible Mothering

My best mothering moments have been the invisible ones, even though the visible moments—standing on the sidelines watching my children play soccer, for example—are more easily acknowledged in the eyes of the world.

When my daughter, Katie, was two, she started dressing herself. She was very clear about what she wanted to wear, and what she wanted was usually not what I wanted for her. I preferred the cute little dress or those Oshkosh B'Gosh outfits I had received as shower gifts. Katie preferred red tights and green skirts and sweat shirts with pink bunnies on them. She thought she looked great.

I let her have her way most days—the days I wanted peace, at least. My biggest test, though, came on Sundays when she dressed herself for church.

One day when she was about four she had on a green plaid skirt with her purple and white sweatshirt and red crew socks. She'd taken my lipstick and smeared it in the general vicinity of her lips and her hair was full of multi-colored clips. She thought she looked especially grand. Her innocence and joy made me catch my breath.

I could have forced her to clean up and change her clothes. I was bigger than she was. But we were going to church, and that made me pause and ponder some big questions: "Now what is the purpose of going to church?" I asked myself. "To celebrate God," I answered. "Are appearances important when it comes to this? Would making Katie change, and look more like the cute little girl I had fantasized, be for me or for her? Does God want the scrubbed little perfect-looking child or this indomitable spirit of joy here in front of me with red lipstick and a big grin on her face?" I chose the big grin and took my daughter to church "as is."

Katie sat in the front pew that morning, alone. (This was a Presbyterian church after all. No one ever sits in the first two rows unless there is no room anywhere else.) I was sitting in the choir loft, facing the congregation, so I could see all of her antics. She took all of her hair clips out and combed her hair with the look of a teenager getting ready for a date. She was quiet and poised, no small accomplishment for a young child in church.

No one else could see her very well except the choir members. The ones nearest me started chuckling, and I loved them at that moment. I had decided that Katie going to church happy and full of joy was more important than whether I looked good as a mother. I feared there would be judgments, silent or spoken, accusing me of letting Katie dishonor the church. Those voices might say I was an over-indulgent mother and irresponsible.

After church, a few women came up to me and complimented me on letting Katie come to church after obviously dressing herself. "I never could have let my children come to church that way," one grandmother said, "but I think I should have. Katie is absolutely delightful."

Martin required a different kind of invisible mothering. Easy-going from birth, Martin was cuddly, unlike his aloof, older sister. At eighteen months, with his blonde hair and hazel eyes, his quick wit and intelligence, he was one of the yummiest children I had ever known. I couldn't believe he was mine.

Even more significant, at least to me, Martin was male, a male I had nourished in my own body, and was therefore a safe male. Since the most important male in my childhood had been unsafe, I wanted to cuddle Martin's sweet maleness next to me. But cuddling felt better to me than it did to Martin. I squeezed him too hard, I'm sure, because Martin decided he didn't want hugs from me anymore. I was a lot stronger than he was, and I'm sure I could have overridden his objection, but I didn't. I knew he was right.

I am a powerful woman. My children have had to find their way through my strength as they grew up. They have had to find and preserve their own space. I have enough energy for two or three children easily and I could have overrun my two babies if I hadn't been careful. I have respected my children's need for their own psychic space, but I have never enjoyed their taking it.

So when Martin let me know I had squeezed him too tightly by not letting me hug him for about a year, I knew I had it coming. He would sit on my lap, but if I tried to pull him to me, he would wiggle out and away. If I were patient and let him sit where he wanted, he would let me read him a book, sucking his two fingers in imitation of his older sister. But it was clearly his way or the highway.

All those months of longing for my son, and not getting him, were painful, though good for me. I didn't want to steal something from my son that he didn't owe me. It was not his job in this world to heal the wounds caused by the men in my life. I am very grateful he had the will to stiff-arm me away from him when I invaded his space. I have known too many men who didn't separate from their mothers, and I didn't want Martin to be one of them. I was committed to raising a strong, kind man, a real man, and I knew I couldn't nourish manhood by sucking up all the oxygen around him or by getting my own needs met through him.

I only know of one mother who thought she was perfect, and she used to beat her children with shoes. The rest of us worry all the time about whether or not we are as good as our children deserve, and none of us is.

Those perfect little babies who come into the world with all of their sacredness intact deserve to be raised by adults who are all grown up themselves and healed from the injuries they suffered as children. But I don't know anyone like that. We are all wounded in some way, and as parents, we accidentally impose our wounds upon our children.

When we are at our best, we recognize our wounds and take ourselves to friends or therapists for healing. At our worst, we inflict our wounds on our children and perpetuate our pain. We either repeat what was done to us or we overreact, overcorrect as it were. We lose our good sense and abuse our children in a different way than we were abused.

For example, if our parents were too lax, we are over-controlling. If our parents used anger abusively, we pathologically avoid all conflict. If we suffered under authoritarian parents, we might react by being so permissive that we don't know how to set decent boundaries with our children. If we had no support for higher education, we might insist our children go to the schools we didn't get a chance to go to.

As good parents we want to give our children everything we didn't get, we want them not to suffer what we suffered. If we get our way, though, we will raise people who are crippled in spirit. Abuse turned inside out is still abuse.

Luckily, children are feisty if their spirits aren't broken by shame or violence. They will test limits. They will drive us mad. They will throw our own foibles back in our faces just when we want to see them least.

Letting children have their own psychic space is a task that is invisible. No one gets awards for this. No one says, "Oh, you have a PhD, and you are thrilled with your son becoming a carpenter. How wise and loving you are." Our children are supposed to surpass us if we are good parents, right? And the only way to measure success is in terms of education and money, right?

I've worked in schools with a 95 percent poverty rate. The parents can be addicts in jail or hardworking and loving.

I've also worked with achieving, highly educated parents. Some of these parents overrun their children, pressuring them to perform and succeed on the world's terms. They are intimately involved in every aspect of their children's lives: all their sporting events, their music lessons, and homework assignments. They give their children no room to find their own rhythms, make their own rules, or solve their own problems.

Unfortunately, this type of parenting accidentally cripples children. This is Level One parenting. It is fear-based and attempts to protect children from disappointment and failure. But children need lots of practice dealing with frustration and parents need to provide loving support not a hermetically sealed life of pure achievement.

Our children deserve more than any of us imperfect human beings can give them. All we can do is "pull back the curtain" and be ready to change our attitudes, beliefs, and behavior at depth when the welfare of our children requires it.

Your Turn

Here's how you might create your own invisible parenting moments:

- *Stop over-scheduling; allow children to have free time to invent their own games and make up their own rules.*

- *Let your children make farting noises at the table and then join them in giggling hysterically.*
- *Raise children for themselves, for their future, instead of raising them to repair your past. (This is not easy.)*

Thinking of any parenting "do-over's" you would like to write about? Any apologies you would like to make?

Chapter 26

Kathleen Rebecca

Kathleen Rebecca, high school graduation
Photo by Barb Barker

Poem: To My Daughter, Katie

This is the first poem I wrote to the sweet spirit born to me on November 19, 1978: Kathleen Rebecca. She has grown into a loving, beautiful, capable woman, partially because of and partially in spite of my parenting. A powerful force to reckon with, she has been and remains my greatest teacher.

This is a poem to my daughter, Katie,
who has taught me who I am,
whose dance to independence
has left me quite breathless.

Huge splashing tears
answer my ungentle words.
Delicate, beautiful, long-fingered hands
feebly cover those oh-so-true eyes,
which don't let me escape my wrongs.

My poor darling,
convenient dumping spot
for my psychic garbage.
Your tender spirit is too fragile to trample.

You frolicking dancer in the ocean's waves,
you tart, dancing in your underwear,
breathy singer of Silent Night.
You gentle, loving soul.

I celebrate the force,
so positive, challenging, loving and rich,
we call Katie, age 5 going on 6.

An Unsent Letter: Did I Break You?

In Chapter 4, I told the story of Katie's jealousy of our foreign exchange student, Sylvia, when they were in sixth grade. I wrote the following letter at the time but did not give it to Katie, as it was part of my process to work myself out of my rage and back into my heart and creativity. Katie did not need to read it, but I needed to write it.

> Dear Katie,
> Watching you be jealous of Sylvia hurts me. I wonder what I might have done to give you the idea that you weren't enough, that you need to worry about how much love you get or that you don't get enough. I'm afraid that something lacking in me has made you feel there is something lacking in you. There isn't. You are perfect as you are.

When you were a baby and a toddler, I was still working on becoming a whole person. As you know, my childhood had some difficult times. I grew up believing there was something wrong with me because my parents didn't get along. My dad drank and got violent. I made a vow to make a family that wasn't like the family I grew up in.

When I met your dad, he seemed the perfect husband for me. He came from a stable family and was kind, smart, and gentle. I knew he would never fly into violent rages as my dad had done. I knew he was safe. I knew he would be safe for my children.

You had been knocking at me for a long time before you were born, before you were even conceived. You wanted to be born. All during my pregnancy with you, I felt like a beautiful woman, a goddess. I felt like the first woman who ever gave birth. I thought of you with every bite of food I ate, every hike I took. I was growing a baby, a beautiful baby. I was growing you.

When I took you home from the hospital, this beautiful, perfect child, I was scared. Was I good enough to raise you and give you all the things I hadn't been given? Could I love you enough so you would never worry about your lovability?

I had imagined this little baby who would snuggle into me, a little bundle I could comfort and feel warm and self-confident about. You, from the moment you were born, had your own ideas about how you wanted to be. From the very beginning of our relationship, you let me know that you didn't come into this world to meet my expectations. You were and are your own person with your own destiny to fulfill. You aren't in this world to make me feel or look good.

We struggled when you were little, our wills clashing against one another. I often felt like a failure because I couldn't comfort you. It took me a long time to do the personal work I needed to do, to fill myself, instead of needing you or anyone else to do it. The more whole I become, the more beautiful and special you are to me. I think I become a better mom/coach every year. I hope you feel that way, too.

But I'm afraid those early years have left their mark. When Martin came along, you seemed to think there was less love for you. Now we see that happening again with Sylvia here. There's plenty of love for you always. If you ever feel low on love, all you have to do is let me know.

Someday you will feel completely full. When you feel jealous occasionally, you will say to yourself, "Oh, this is just information about myself. I'm feeling a little low on love. How can I love myself now or get what I need to fill myself?" You will learn that you always have to fill yourself, that no one and nothing can do that for you. This will make you feel very secure because you will always have yourself with you, and you will always feel that you are enough.

I love you very much. You have been one of my greatest teachers in life because you held so fast to yourself and wouldn't let me mold you into what I thought you should be. I always want to be a part of your life, cheering you on, celebrating with you and comforting you when things look bad. The life force in you is strong, and your natural graciousness and joy of living will bring you great success and satisfaction in life.

You have your own battles to fight—all of us do. I'm sorry for my part in creating more struggles for you, and I want you to know I'm willing to help you pass through them as best I can.

I'm proud to know you. You are a delight to watch growing up. I think we will be great friends forever.

Love,
Mom

Note in Katie's High School Yearbook

Katie asked me to write something to include in her senior yearbook.

My darling girl,
You have been one of the greatest blessings and one of the greatest challenges of my life. Your sense of humor, amazing abilities

of observation, and determination will carry you far in this world. No matter what you do or where you go, I will always be a solid, loving listener for your greatness.

Mom

P.S. My daughter, my love, well done.
I love who you've become.
You're just the way I hoped you'd be,
A woman strong, courageous and free.
My daughter, my love, well done.

Story: Katie's Heart

The next several selections concern one incident in Katie's life. On April 5, 1999, Katie collapsed in the Linn Benton Community College library. Her heart had gone into v-fib (ventricular fibrillation.). The paramedics were there in five minutes to shock her back into life. The crisis was over in some ways, but my adventure had yet to begin.

Monday, April 5, 1999

My hand was still on the doorknob of my office. I was returning from a walk with a friend, when I heard the phone ringing. I hurried to answer it. Josh, my twenty-year-old daughter's boyfriend, was on the other end. He offered no preambles, no "making nice" chatter, just, "Is there anyone there with you?" and then "I have bad news about Katie." What bad news could he have for me about Katie, I wondered. If it were really bad news, her father, my ex-husband, Will, would be calling.

"No one is here with me," I said, not yet curious about this unusual question.

"I have some bad news," he said again. Now he had my attention. The last time I had heard those words someone was dead. My grandmother told me when I returned home from work the summer after I graduated from high school, "I have some bad news." And then, without missing a beat, "Kelly Devlin is dead." Kelly was a school chum and my boyfriend's brother. He had died in a one-car accident.

Josh didn't pause after he told me he had bad news, but I still had time to flash through that thirty-year-old memory before he continued.

"Katie collapsed in the library at the college. She said she didn't feel well and was headed for the bathroom when she fainted."

Fainting. I could handle fainting. Katie did talk about being lightheaded sometimes, but I always told her to go eat something and then see if she was still lightheaded. She never was, as far as I knew.

"She's at the hospital now," he continued. I could handle that, too. The hospital was probably a good place to be if she had been unconscious. They would find out what was going on.

Josh continued, "The paramedics couldn't find a heartbeat and had to resuscitate her with paddles."

My mind raced: What? Couldn't find a heartbeat? Couldn't find a heartbeat? What do you mean they couldn't find a heartbeat? This didn't make sense. How could my healthy daughter have collapsed and lost her heartbeat?

My voice stayed calm, which surprised me. How can I be talking calmly, I wondered, when my daughter has just lost her heartbeat and has been taken to the hospital?

Katie is tall and blonde with beautiful teeth that only cost three thousand dollars to straighten. When she smiles, a very sweet smile for this day and age, her whole body lights up. She is simply warm, golden light with just a touch of imp thrown in. I had to get to my golden girl.

"How am I going to get to the hospital?" I asked Josh stupidly.

"I could have my parents pick you up, but I haven't been able to get hold of them," he said.

"No, I'll find someone who can take me," I told him, as if I knew I could do this. "I'll be right there."

I hung up the phone and started calling everyone I could think of. I remembered phone numbers for a few calls, but no one was home, and I then started on my phone book.

I started to shake, and I could feel myself losing control. I had to get a ride. I had to. Murray should be home by now, but he wasn't, and who knew when he would show up. I had to get to the hospital, fifteen miles away.

I got to the "B" section of my phone book and called Susan, a good friend of good friends of mine.

She answered the phone, and I said, "It's Vicki Lein," and then I couldn't speak.

"Are you okay?" she asked. "What's wrong?"

We suffered more excruciating silence as I struggled to get a word out. I was afraid I was frightening Susan. Finally, I choked out the words: "Katie collapsed and her heart stopped beating and she is in the hospital"—all the words rushing out like a string being pulled out of my mouth. "Can you give me a ride?" I asked, hoping I wasn't begging, even though I was not willing to take "no" for an answer.

She, of course, said, "Yes. I'll be right there."

Then I started to fall apart. I wrote a note for Murray and fed the dog, amazed that I could think about feeding our dog at a time when my daughter lay in the emergency room.

Waiting was torture. I paced and fretted, looking out the window every thirty seconds, until Susan came. I saw her car pull into my driveway and ran out and jumped in just as it rolled to a stop.

I don't remember what I said as I fastened my seat belt, except that Susan didn't know that Katie was in the Albany hospital instead of the much nearer Corvallis hospital. I had forgotten to tell her. Even though I was crazy with fear for my daughter, I still had energy to worry about whether I was inconveniencing Susan. Had I imposed on her because I had not made it clear that we were driving to Albany? Nice girl habits die hard.

I told her what I knew and then asked her how she was.

She laughed. "I will only be making small talk," she said.

"Small talk is fine with me now. I'm not one to let my worries take me away. I'll find out what I find out when I get to the hospital. Telling me how you are would be a welcome distraction."

So we chatted all the way to the hospital. Not chatted, really. We both knew and felt the underlying energy. I didn't know its color or shape yet. I just knew I was riding on something enormous that would probably impact my life forever.

We arrived at the emergency room entrance, and I jumped out of the car before it came to a complete stop. "You don't have to go in with me," I said, polite, not wanting to bother anyone, even when my daughter had almost died.

"I'm going to park the car, and then I am coming in, no arguments," she said.

"I don't have the strength to say no twice," I replied, grateful to her. I didn't want to be alone.

I walked in the wrong door, the door for doctors and was politely shown to the emergency room desk.

The woman behind the counter said Katie was getting a CAT scan and that I couldn't be with her. I stood numbly at the desk. Susan came in and told them I was Katie's mother. She could see I needed someone to advocate for me and stepped up to the counter to do so.

"Katie's mother?" the desk clerk said with surprise. "We thought the other woman was her mother. No one told us differently. I'll see if I can get a nurse who was working with Katie to come and give you some information."

I turned to Susan. "I don't throw temper tantrums," I said, "but if I did throw temper tantrums, now is when I would throw one." Susan agreed that a temper tantrum at this time wouldn't be very helpful.

Susan calmly but firmly explained to the desk clerk that I didn't have much information at all about what had happened. The clerk directed me over to a wall phone and said the head nurse would call me. The phone started to ring. As I picked up the receiver, I sat down in the chair and listened in disbelief as the nurse talked about Katie having seizures in the ambulance and of the paramedics having to restart her heart.

"Seizures?" I thought to myself. Seizures. Katie and "seizures" shouldn't be in the same sentence.

Then Josh appeared. "She is up in ICU. I'll take you there." He grabbed and held my hand as he talked to me, and I was aware that I needed to feel the strength of his hand and that our relationship would be forever different from this moment on.

I don't remember whether I said goodbye to Susan as Josh led me away or whether I thanked her. All I knew was that I had to get to my girl.

He took me up to the ICU and led me to Katie's room. Around her bed were two busy nurses, as well as Will and his second wife Debbie who was a former nurse. Katie was struggling to get the tube out of her throat and the IV lines out of her arms. She wanted to get out of bed and go home.

I told the nurses that I was Katie's mother and knelt down by the side of her bed next to her head. I stroked her head and talked calmly to her, something I would be doing for the next several hours.

People who have been without oxygen, I learned from my daughter, act weird. When I came into the intensive care unit of Albany General Hospital, I expected to find my daughter lying peacefully unconscious. I would go to her side and hold her hand and wait for her to wake up.

Instead, I found my daughter with a look on her face I hadn't seen since she was a toddler. She continued to thrash, attempting to pull out her intubation tube and her IV lines. She looked terrified and confused. When she could finally talk two days later, one of the first things she said was, "I want to go home!" Everything in her panicked body communicated her wish to go home.

My job, I discovered, wasn't just to sit and hold her hand; my job was to help her calm down and let the hospital staff help her. I wanted my soothing voice to penetrate her terror and pain, to lodge somewhere in her scrambled brain. I wanted to go home myself, home to a place of safety where my daughter left her towels on the bathroom floor, no matter how often I nagged her about it. But I had work to do, lots of work.

As I sat by her bedside, watching her finally let herself drift into a light sleep, I studied her face. Although I knew by that time her combativeness was expected because she had had a "cardiac event," and I knew this meant that the oxygen supply to her brain had been disrupted, I also knew she would be okay. I was sure she would recover fully because I could see her two future babies in my mind. But even though my mind was sure she was fine, my body was seized by a gripping fear of losing my baby.

The nurses kept giving her more drugs: Atavan, morphine, and something else. Two more milligrams and then two more again. She would just start to calm down and they would move a blanket or want to draw blood and she would startle again, and the battle would begin anew.

Sometimes when she startled she would open her eyes wide, as if she wanted to know what criminal had abducted her, and from which planet.

"Your job is to relax now, Katie," I said over and over. "Surrender to the help. It's okay to be afraid and sad. Just let your feelings flow through your body and out your feet. Don't hold on to anything. Just let everything flow through you."

She relaxed slightly, responding to my words, though she was not conscious. Something deeper in her absorbed the tone of what I was saying more than the content. I believe I was the Earth to her: solid, safe, and nurturing.

That night, one of my old friends from Albany reminded me I needed to be strong for Katie. I didn't need the reminder. I felt strong enough to do whatever it took. I have never felt like such a pillar of strength; in fact, the phrase "pillar of strength" had never made much sense to me. It does now. I felt energy flowing in me and through me, down into the earth and up into the stars. I was more than Katie's mother as I sat there with my hand on her head, cooing to her brain and heart to just relax, calm down.

I was more than Katie's mother—I was Primal Mother, Every Mother. I was the mother who lifts trucks off of her children, the mother who jumps in front of trains to push her children to safety. If I could have exchanged places with Katie in that hospital bed, I would have done it in a heartbeat. I would gladly have been the one who dropped and *didn't* get rescued. In this, I was no different than most mothers.

Grizzly Bear Mom in me had awakened, and she still growled within me weeks later. I was not entirely safe to be around for several weeks. I was still primal, on the alert for danger, ready to charge, ready to defend. I hoped I wouldn't lose any friends or ruin my marriage.

As I sat by Katie's side that first night, it was as though we were the only two people who existed. My lovely daughter with her sunshine smile was caught in some dulling force field. She was there, yet not there.

Lying here on this hospital bed before me was a young woman, who looked like my daughter, and I knew her to be my daughter, but she was so stripped of personality that I might not have recognized her if I hadn't given birth to her and loved her through all the years of her life. She wasn't twenty-year-old Katie; she was Katie at eighteen months, panicky and terrified. This writhing, palpable terror was stuck in her adult body. Her infant's brain wanted only to get off of the bed and go home, but it was her adult arms that grasped at the tubes and needles, her adult face that pleaded for release. It was terribly painful to watch.

Brain damage, of course, was the fear now that she was on lidocaine and was close to paddles that could shock her heart back to beating if it stopped again. The EMT's had given her CPR, at least I thought so at that time. Later Josh wasn't so sure. The paramedics arrived in five minutes, within the safety limits. I couldn't let myself imagine what it would be like to have Katie live but not be Katie anymore.

Katie's regular doctor took us aside and told us the basics. He spoke of good outcomes, but said the words "brain damage." I started to shake underneath my shock. We sat in the room where I was to sleep for the next two nights as he told Will, Debbie, and me what he knew. He was kind and wonderful, and he scared me. As we left the room, I grabbed Will and clutched him tight, as I hadn't done for many years. What I was thinking was, "This is our baby. We made her. Only you and I know her as we know her." We didn't say anything, but I felt Will quiver as he held me.

Martin, a high school senior, came that night after Youth Symphony practice. When I saw him walk in I fell apart. I walked into his arms and clung to him for support, leaning into the son and the man he had become, knowing that our roles had changed now forever in some way. I knew he didn't know what to do, felt overwhelmed by it all, but I needed his strength and to feel my son's body at that moment.

He went in to see her, scared and tentative. He leaned over to her and told her who he was. She didn't respond.

Tuesday, April 6, 1999

I slept a few hours on Monday night on the chair that turns into a single bed. I had no desire to go home and sleep in my own bed with Murray, to cuddle or snuggle. I had no excess energy for such things.

I sat next to Katie's bed when she woke up Tuesday morning, as had been my plan. I wanted to be with her when she needed me most. I was worried that she would wake up afraid, and I wanted to be there to help calm her if I could.

She awoke disoriented. I told her she was in the hospital and that she had collapsed in the library at LBCC. Josh had called 9-1-1 and she had been taken to the emergency room. Now she was in intensive care. Her arms had been placed in soft restraints, nonetheless, I had to help keep her from pulling out her tube.

Will and Debbie came later and then Glenn, the nurse on duty when Katie was admitted, came in. "I bet you don't remember me," he said, and she shook her head. Hallelujah! A response!

Katie seemed to be struggling to communicate, and Debbie asked her if she wanted the tube taken out. We had told her she had a tube down her throat to breathe for her since the drugs she had been given took away her ability to breathe on her own.

She shook her head no. She didn't want the tube out. "Do you want Josh?" I asked. She nodded.

He had been by her side almost constantly. I think he was out eating at that time. We told her he would be back soon.

We thought she might be able to get her tube out that day and be taken to a cardiac unit in Portland. I wanted that tube out for her. I concentrated on that small goal until it happened the next morning about ten. I didn't want to think about anything else, about the next steps. This first step had to happen before anything else could. I knew Katie was incredibly uncomfortable, and I just wanted that tube out and more of my daughter back.

Martin came in that day and leaned over to tell her who he was. I could tell how frightened he was, stiff and ready to bolt. He's here, I thought, because she is his sister, and he has to be here because he loves her, but it is taking so much out of him. Too real. Too mortal. Too much of this and he would fall to pieces.

When he leaned over and said loudly, "It's Martin," I loved him as much as I ever had. What mother ever wants to see one of her children bending over a hospital bed comforting her other child as she struggles to swim up from a thick, murky confusion? Not me. I had never practiced this scene in my head, never dreamed that "cardiac arrest" were words I would ever hear used to describe what had happened to any child of mine under sixty.

Katie lifted her hand and waved to him, a very sisterly gesture, which let me know my daughter was still there.

Katie got a bath that day, a long warm towel with rinse-less soap rubbed on her body. I did the right side, the nurse the left. I washed her face with a washcloth, as I hadn't done in many years. Her sweet, young, confused face.

As soon as the nurse changed her gown and the sheets under her (not a comfortable task for Katie, but encouraging for me because she could turn herself from side to side) as soon as she was clean and smelling good, she threw up.

I had never thought much about respirators before this. I had seen enough episodes of ER to know what they were and what they were for. I knew the terms "intubated" and "extubated." I had a notion that being intubated was the worst part of a hospital experience, and that most people didn't remember being intubated.

It didn't help me to know that Katie would probably not remember these days. She was in pain NOW, afraid NOW. Her feelings were real, even if she wouldn't remember. I treated every minute as if she would remember everything. I knew I would.

Watching Katie throw up with a tube down her throat almost pushed me over the edge. She soaked her gown and bedding with vomit, remains of the soup she had eaten the day before. She had eaten after all, we knew now. Soup from the Wine Depot.

How do you comfort a child throwing up around a respirator? The best you can.

The nurse cleaned her up again. I left and let others take over.

We all got lots of support. Monday night, old friends from Albany and their daughter came back from a birthday dinner. I hadn't seen the daughter in eight or nine years, and I couldn't believe she was twenty-three. Grown up. An adult with an adult job in Portland. She offered her apartment for our use while Katie was at the hospital in Portland. Will, Debbie, and Josh took her up on it. Murray, Mom and I would stay with Gale and Patrick, my dear friend and her husband.

A doctor friend of mine, Gunter, helped us interpret all the medical language. He read charts, talked to doctors, and helped calm us with his efficient authority. He had made a special trip to the hospital, I knew, and I was full of appreciation.

Sandra, a friend from the school where I had worked as a counselor, came on Tuesday on the way to work with lattes, and returned at noon with soup and salads. This thoughtfulness and steadiness taught me how I might help someone else in the future.

Mary, another old Albany friend, brought us a box of snacks and toothbrushes.

Wednesday, April 7, 1999

I was with Katie Wednesday morning when she woke up, just as I was on Tuesday morning. She was extubated that morning, but before that she asked for Josh. This was the morning she wrote on paper. First word: gum. Her throat felt like it was full of gum.

Wednesday's highlights included taking Katie to Portland in the ambulance. She must have asked if Josh could go with her at least twenty times. No one could go with her, the hospital staff told us over and over. Will would have wanted Debbie to go with her. My choice would have been Josh.

I rode with Josh to Portland, and we had a great talk. He is deep in my heart. I guess I'm sentimental about anyone who saves the life of one of my children.

When they took Katie out of the ambulance, she was crabby. "I don't need to be here!" she kept saying. "Why am I here?"

"You collapsed on Monday in the LBCC library," I told her for about the one-hundredth time.

"I did not collapse on Monday!" she said indignantly. "I went to the doctor on Monday!"

"Okay, Dear, whatever you say," I said to her angry face as they wheeled her into the hospital. Anger was a good sign, the nurses explained. It meant she was getting well.

That night, Katie terrified me as she pleaded for air. She kept saying, "I can't breathe, I can't breathe." Will and the doctor stood in the corner of the room unconcerned, talking about Katie's condition. They could read the oxygen numbers, which were fine, but I couldn't. I was angry that they were ignoring Katie's pleas and not giving either one of us the information that would have alleviated our fears. This was one of many times that my inability to see made me furious with life. My daughter needed me, and I needed to be able to see to help her.

After Katie was breathing easily again, she wailed, "I want to go home," with such desperation it broke my heart.

Later that night, Will hugged me before we left the hospital and said, "It's another world." This happened after we had all listened to the doctor tell us what was in store for us. He told us the worst-case scenario was Katie dying of complications. At best, she would need weeks or months to recover. School was out for this term. We had been hoping she would be able to get up off of her bed, laugh all the way back to Corvallis, and go back to school on Monday.

Thursday—Saturday, April 8-11, 1999

Katie asked for "Titanic" and "Tomorrow Never Dies" as the first two movies she wanted to see in the hospital. Go figure.

Josh whispered to Katie, as he wheeled her around the nurse's station, "Everyone here is looking at you and saying, 'What a babe!'" Josh was great medicine for Katie and for me.

Sunday—Monday, April 12-13, 1999

Martin spent the night with Katie and me on Sunday night, that last night in the hospital. He had missed too much of the experience, I felt, and I was glad to have him there. His timing was perfect. We watched the movie "Parenthood," and both Katie and I were renewed by Martin's unrestrained belly laughter. Watching comedies with Martin is one of our greatest joys.

Katie turned on the news Monday morning and we all heard about the fourteen-year-old girl who died at track practice when her heart stopped. The newscasters were discussing the middle school girl's funeral. I said a silent prayer for her family. Katie did not seem to notice the irony.

Love the One You're With

We spent a total of eight days in the hospital, long enough to run lots of tests, which didn't find anything wrong with Katie's heart. We were there long enough to have a computer implanted in a surgically-created pocket over her heart. This computer, the size of a pager, will shock her heart into beating if it should ever stop again. The nurse practitioner said it was like Katie having her own personal paramedics. I think of her defibrillator more as angel hands covering and protecting her sacred heartbeat.

Katie came home to live with Murray and me and recovered well. She missed spring term, but enrolled for summer and didn't miss a beat until she graduated from Oregon State University with a B.A. in business/marketing. The scar over her heart healed well, and she does not hesitate to wear skimpy tops in the summer, even though she often has to answer questions from strangers about the round lump on her chest.

I hear my daughter's laughter differently now. One of my biggest fears looking at her those first few days was that I would never see her sunshine smile again.

I watch television differently now, too. Recently in a drama, I saw someone who had been without oxygen for twenty minutes sitting up and chatting with the doctor after he finally got the lydocaine and the paddles to start his heart again. "That's not true! People don't recover that easily!" I shouted at the TV set. "They shouldn't do that! They shouldn't lie to people like that!" I felt just a little foolish yelling at the screen, but I felt angry because I had been so unprepared for the reality of what happens when the brain doesn't get a steady supply of oxygen.

I hear sirens differently now. I used to feel many things when I heard a siren: curiosity, anxiety, annoyance. Sometimes when vehicles would speed in front of my house I would count them and let myself feel just the edge of the pain they signaled for someone, somewhere. But the siren wasn't tolling for me. Not my turn. This time.

Now when I hear a siren, I say a prayer. I know there is a story, and I pray for strength for all the people involved. I know how much strength they might need.

I also pray that the ambulance gets there in time to be of help. Not too late, not too late. That's because fifteen minutes didn't used to seem like a lot of time to me. Now I know fifteen minutes can be filled with no heartbeat, little breathing, blue lips, and people standing in terror, waiting.

When my brown phone rings in my cozy downstairs office, especially if I have to hurry to reach it in time, I can feel my heart beating in my chest, and I breathe shallowly. I remember his words, "Is anyone there with you? I have some bad news about Katie."

Katie giggled as she walked out the door the other day, and I almost cried. I had never realized how many magical things are contained in a giggle: delight, humor, aliveness, connection, warmth, love. And personality. I would recognize my girl's giggle in a crowd with no problem.

My goal now is to say to myself: "Every day is a gift." Every day that has Katie in it is a gift. Every day with Martin or Murray in it is rich beyond measuring. So what if someone is offended by the lyrics of one of my songs? So what if we can't find friends to spend some time with us in the mountains? I will not let little disappointments drown my gratitude for the simple act of waking up with love in my life.

And so I think of my troubles differently now. Even during those first awful days in the hospital, I would say to myself, "Well, I could be planning Katie's funeral now, or I could be here exhausted and scared. I will gladly take exhausted and scared."

I hear my heart differently now. Anyone's heart could be harboring the quirk that almost killed my daughter. My heart could. Lisa Marie, who sits across from me at this table in our favorite coffee shop for writing—Lisa Marie could have a heart ready to stop or a blood vessel ready to burst or a clot ready to get stuck in some vital spot.

I don't want to be ghoulish about this, concentrating on death every moment, but I want to look at my precious daughter differently, at everyone differently. I want to put my arms around each moment of my life. Every time a young man takes my cappuccino order or a clerk checks my groceries, I want that interaction to have its own poetry, its own meaning.

I want each day of my life to be a series of connections, of tiny meaningful adventures, that add up to a deep appreciation for the everyday things of life as well as the big miracles, such as my daughter's giggle.

Five Years Later

Katie and I celebrated her fifth "rebirthday," as I call it, by having incredibly decadent and wonderful facials. We've decided that facials are a great idea, and we will have them every year to celebrate her "rebirthday."

Katie is not one to deal with her emotions, although she gets better as she gets older. She has not read this chapter, for example. On her first "rebirthday," I asked her if I could hold her hand during those five minutes her brain had been deprived of oxygen. She reluctantly agreed.

As the Cosmic Jokster would have it, I was getting my hair colored during those five minutes, so Katie agreed to come to the beauty salon and hold my hand. While she was there, I had a helium-filled balloon delivered. This ritual was for me, not her, and I felt she owed it to me. She has no memory of those first five days of her hospitalization, but I do! I assure her that when she is a mother, she will understand.

Katie has had her defibrillator go off only once in five years. Her heart rate got too high, and it shocked her. She did not go into v-fib, so she didn't lose her license for six months as she did when she almost died. She is healthy and strong, a college graduate in four years, even though she lost a term recuperating from her near fatal "cardiac event."

I am proud of her, proud beyond words.

Song: Repo Man
(from the CD *Daring to Sing*)

I *started writing this song in the Albany General Hospital Intensive Care Unit. I was sitting with my girl during that first night, and the song started coming to me. I had no paper or tape recorder with me, so I called home and left the song on voice mail.*

Chorus:
He sees you when you're sleeping. He knows when you're awake.
He knows just what you love the most, and that's what he's gonna take.

Cuz he's the Repo Man. He's the Repo Man.
You can run as fast as you can. You can't outrun the Repo Man.
You can't outrun the Repo Man.

You can try to shrink. You can try to be small.
The Repo Man will still take it all.
You can try to be good, do everything just right.
The Repo Man will still come get you in the night.

He sees you when you're sleeping. He knows when you're awake.
He knows just what you love the most, and that's what he's gonna take.

Don't dare to dance. Don't dare to sing.
Don't dare to write. Don't dare to dream.
Don't dare to love. Don't dare to even breathe.
The Repo Man will never set you free.

He sees you when you're sleeping. He knows when you're awake.
He knows just what you love the most, and that's what he's gonna take.

He feeds on your fear. He thrives on your doubt.
If you want any joy in your life, there's only one way out:

It's called courage, "just" courage. Take a deep breath.
It's called courage, only courage. Take the next step.

Then when he sees you when you're sleeping and knows when you're awake,
when he knows just what you love the most,
that's when you'll have faith.

Then the Repo Man, the Repo Man, he can run as fast as he can.
You have dissolved the Repo Man. You have dissolved the Repo Man.

Poem: Grizzly Mother

When Katie almost died, her dad's wife, a nurse who had known Katie only three years, presented herself to the hospital staff as if she were Katie's mother. Worse than that, at least in my mind, she continued to act as if she were Katie's mother even when I was there. She took the lead in conversations with the doctors and even took my place at the head of the bed when I got up to answer the phone and did not relinquish it when I finished my call.

To be as fair as I can be, her intention was to support her husband and Katie. She forgot that Katie needed me, her mother. But the fact that I had to fight for my rightful place as mother exacerbated my suffering. For months afterward, I could not let go of my rage. Poem Crazy, by Susan Wooldridge, came to my rescue.

In one chapter she suggests we write in hyperbole and bash our feelings right out of the ballpark. I jumped into this poem with all four paws. I became the grizzly bear mom out to protect her cub. I realize now that letting myself recreate the situation without worrying about being "nice" is a type of Do-Over. Allowing myself to write freely released my victimization and rekindled my compassion for Debbie. All good.

I include this with no apology. If you get between a mother and her cub, watch out!

She stands by the side of my baby's hospital bed,
this woman,
and claims the space of Mother.
Fool.

I lumber through the Emergency Room door,
pausing for exactly one heartbeat to assess the Situation.
I growl,
a low growl from the belly of Mother Earth.
Quick as a cat
I claw at her face,
leaving lines that quickly ooze with her red blood.
Drops splash and stain her clothes.
My giant, brown, hairy paw backhands her, and she flies across the room,
crashes into the wall, and slumps to the floor.
She doesn't stir.

I stand upright on my hind legs for a few moments and watch her stillness.
I wait in peace. I feel no pity.
She dared to try and take my place. Let her lie there and rot.
I have work to do.

I walk heavily on my claw-filled paws toward the blonde young woman
who is lying on the bed,
attached to life-giving tubes and needles.
My injured cub.

She makes noises strange to me. Her wounds are all inside her body.
She carries no sores for me to lick.

I curl around her and make sounds from deep in my belly,
wordless mother bear sounds, overflowing with comfort, ripe with strength.

My baby stirs and then settles into her limp sheets.
She surrenders to her need for help, softening in her fragility.

I stand guard,
the growl from my belly heard by anyone approaching my cub.

No one dares disturb me as I heal my child.
People crawl into my presence, making sure they are welcome before they touch her wounds.

I have the power of all mothers charging through my body.
I am the mountain. I am the core of the planet.
I am the galaxies beyond the galaxies.
I am connected to all that is real and alive and vital.

Beware of me.
Respect the power of mother that surges through me.
I will not hesitate to kill you if you get between me and my cub who needs me.

Poem: Before and Now

Here is the poem that pulls the whole experience together.

Before,
I used to think I loved my daughter.
That was before she almost died.
Now,
her smile warms me like the sun
breaking through layers of stubborn, soul-numbing clouds.
Every cell of my being absorbs so much joy when I see her
I think I might crack wide open,
splattering my gratitude all over the trees and flowers,
covering the faces of the people I love.

Before,
I used to worry about her character.
Now,
I spoil her.
But now she is almost unspoilable.
She is grateful, feels spoiled,
looks around her and counts her blessings.

Ninety-nine out of one hundred mothers went to a funeral.
I got to go to the hospital
and watch my twenty-year-old regress to an infant
and fight to pull the needles from her arms and the tube from her throat.
The panic in her eyes quivered through my body.

I covered her bare chest with her gown,
knowing how much she would hate that all eyes could see her nakedness,
knowing, too, how beautiful and whole her nakedness was.
Her heart was beating, and she was breathing.
What else mattered?

We were lucky.
If she had reached the bathroom down the hall from the college library,
she would have died on the cold tile floor
with bits of toilet paper and scuff marks to keep her company.

We were lucky.
If her boyfriend hadn't heard her fall,
if he hadn't rushed to her collapsed body,
already blue from lack of oxygen,
if the paramedics hadn't been reassigned
so they were only five minutes away
instead of a brain-damaging twelve,
if she hadn't been surrounded by so many angels,
we would have lost her forever.

Where are those ninety-nine other mothers, I think,
the ones visiting graves a year later
instead of celebrating "re-birthday" parties with helium balloons?
How are they today?
Who are they today?
Who would I be today if my daughter had been one of the ninety-nine?

Sometimes I imagine myself following all of those caskets,
walking with my sunshine girl,
holding her hand,
radiant in my joy,
surrounded in the deep sorrow of all those other devastated mothers.

Why did all those others die while Katie lives?
Her life is a gift almost too big to receive,
and yet I clasp my precious baby and the rest of her life to my breast greedily.
"Please, don't ever take her away from me!"
I plead to the forces that pick the ones who live and the ones who die.

Before,
she walked through her days with a heart that could kill her
while she was sleeping
or while she was driving her car to work.
Now,
a computer angel stands guard,
a lump of metal and wires tucked inside a surgeon-made pocket over her heart.
A beautiful scar that will save her life
and save me the mother's agony of burying a child.

I am living a miracle I don't deserve and didn't earn.
I am bathed daily in the wonder of my daughter's life.
How many troubles can I have
when Katie's giggles sound like symphonies
and touching my cheek to her face
feels like I'm touching the center of everything important,
everything sacred,
everything most Real?

Before,
I used to count the tragedies in my life.
Now,
I count the miracles.

Letter: Katie Turns Twenty-One

> *"Child of mine. You are the sweetest song and the greatest gift
> I will ever know."*
> —from a Bill Staines song

To Kathleen Rebecca on her 21st Birthday
Darling Girl,

You have not been an easy child to raise. You have wanted to be on your own from the moment of your birth. You didn't like cuddling, and you had definite ideas about what you wanted to wear from the time you could toddle to the dresser.

Your spirit of independence made me gnash my teeth some days, but I always knew that the qualities that made you a challenge to raise would serve you well in adulthood. I did my best to give you lots of room to grow into who you would become.

You have grown into everything I could have hoped for. You are strong and beautiful, and you have the courage to stand up for what you feel is right. You let me kiss and hold you now in ways you wouldn't when you were little. Now you know you have your own space, and you don't have to fight for it anymore.

There is no way to describe how a mother feels for her children. I love many people—Murray, Mom, Sadie, your dad—but you and Martin are in my heart in ways no one else ever will be. You are a part of my biology. I love you to madness and always will.

We almost lost you this year. For the rest of my life I will live inside the miracle of your resurrection. How bad can any day be if you are alive in it?

Loving you has helped me touch the scariest places inside myself. You are my heart out there in the world, wandering around. What happens to you happens to me. You are not me and should not be. I shouldn't try to stop my pain by limiting your life. That is a mother's toughest task, I think. Giving your children the space to become who they are is so invisible, but it is the most important part of loving your children into healthy adults.

You have a great, magical life ahead of you. Your heart will be broken because that is the nature of living and loving. I don't know the specific events that will break your heart, but I do know that you will live through them and be stronger and more loving because of them. That is what you have done with your near-death experience, and that is what you will do with all the trials that come your way.

I am so proud of you, and I love you so much. We are going to have such great adventures together! The best is yet to come.

Your loving, very human mother

Poem: Sweet Agony

Katie had problems with anxiety after her near death experience. She has always been high strung. Even as an infant, she would howl and scream when startled. She is one sensitive girl.

I did not like the idea of Katie taking drugs to deal with her anxiety. She had grief work to do, and I was afraid if she were all drugged up she would continue her bad habit of avoiding painful feelings. I took her to my acupuncturist/MD, an amazing healer, to see if she could help Katie. I was amazed that Katie would even consider going.

It took about two needles, and Katie had had enough. (I usually had over thirty needles, six around each eye.) Watching her retreat into her fear and hold on to her anxieties caused me to feel a "sweet agony."

She lies on the table,
my beloved twenty-two-year-old daughter,
and cries quietly,
large tears splashing down her cheeks.

An acupuncture needle sticks out of her forehead,
the only one she can stand.
Her doctor holds one of her hands.
I hold the other.
We sing with our words
a duet of healing.

Katie is afraid,
her fear huge,
more real than her belief that this pain will set her free.

She is her pain now,
more than she is her wisdom,
more than she is her deep trust of herself.
Her pain is her truth at this moment,
more powerful than my love for her.

Love, you weakling!
You are the only reality,
the force of creation and transformation.
You have the power to heal and delight,
to bridge black holes,
and, as I stand here,
watching my child drown in her fear,
you seem impotent,
disgustingly impotent.

If a human can love perfectly,
if a mother can love perfectly,
then I am close to loving my daughter perfectly at this moment.
As I hold her beautiful hand,
she decides to trust her fear more than an elusive freedom she merely senses.
No words of faith can be bigger than her fear now,
no past healing matters.

I hold her hand and tell her what I know to be true,
that I trust pain more than she does,
that if I know anything, I know that the only way out is through pain.
I know the freedom at the other end.
Her doctor says she will start singing when she quits crying;
she will start humming as she does the dishes.
She'll sing along with the radio.

I want to hear Katie's song.
I want her to hear her own song.
I know that until she can bear the sound of her own tears
she will never be free enough to allow the flow of her sweet song through
    her body.
She must trust this pain first.
Her crying needs to sound beautiful in her ears
instead of sounding "hysterical,"
an endless cacophony
that will never bring her any peace or joy.

I must stand here,
hip deep in my pool of love, and wait for her.
I must sing my siren song of joy,
of life overflowing.
I must trust my pain over and over
and show her the beauty of an unfolding life.

That is the most perfect love I have to give my daughter,
and right now it doesn't seem like enough.

Letter: A Challenge

Katie messed up. This was my response. And, just to keep the record straight, she was in debt, not in jail.

Kathleen, my beloved daughter,

You have integrity built into your genes.
You cannot violate what you know to be right with impunity.
The integrity that calls you from your belly will not be denied.

You are out of integrity, and no amount of distractions can hide you from you.
No amount of spending will bury the gnawing in your belly. It will only make it worse.
No amount of connection with a man, any man, will distract you for long
from the courageous acts your belly calls you to perform.
No drug, no antidepressant, no anxiety pill, no amount of alcohol
will relieve you of your responsibility to the truth inside you.

You have been practicing giving in to impulses,
and you have gotten very good at it.
When "I want!" cries in you
like a hungry bird,
you feed it.
You cannot bear to listen to its pleading.
But this little bird is really a raptor,
and it will devour you
and everyone you love
if you keep trying to feed its insatiable "I want!"

You have been practicing being a coward,
and you have gotten very good at it.
When you feel uncomfortable,
even just a little uncomfortable,
you run to bury your pain.
You drink.
You buy something.
You take a pill.

You find a man to hold you.
And in this running and burying,
you avoid your real work in the world.
You drown out the subtle call of all that is best within you.

The more you practice giving in to urgent impulses and running from discomfort,
the more problems you will have,
the blacker your despair will become.

There is only one way out,
oh, most beloved child of mine.
You must practice courage.
You must practice integrity.
You must not make promises lightly
and then follow up with excuses and reasons and more promises you don't keep.

You must face discomfort head on.
You must be willing to let discomfort run through you,
as it will,
and then do what needs doing.
You must be intrepid enough to find, nurture, and follow your bliss.

When you were in the hospital,
I learned something I already knew about myself:
I would gladly give my life for you.
In a heartbeat.

When you were in the hospital,
I learned something about you I already knew:
you are strong enough to do what needs to be done.
In every beat of your heart.

Kathleen, I love you completely and forever,
no matter what you choose to do.
I pray, though, that you will choose wisely
soon.

Now.
Mom

Poem: My Daughter Left Today

Katie got a job and moved to Los Angeles after she graduated.

My daughter left today,
though not for the first time.

She left for Montessori school when she was four,
then for elementary school at six,
and then on to junior high and high school.

She moved five hundred miles away
for her first semester of college,
then moved back to her home town
until she graduated six months ago.

She left for Portland to be a sports marketing intern,
then moved home for the holidays.

But today she left,
really left,
for the first time.

She was almost casual with me,
"It's not hard leaving you.
You are my Mommy!"
she said,
after telling me she sobbed
saying good-bye to her boyfriend's parents.

But I understood.
Her boyfriend and his family,
as compelling as their belonging and laughter is,
are temporal.
I am her mother and I am eternal.
I am in her DNA,
in her bones.
She smells my thoughts,
calls out a "What's wrong?"
when I haven't moved or spoken,
only shifted a vision in my head
that I imagined was private.

We are great Charades partners
because we only have to hint at clues.
We are both efficient and quick,
so we make a great traveling team.
She is the only person I know who can exit a car as fast as I can.

My daughter left today for her first grown-up job.
It's in L.A.,
her dream city.
She was born to be a California girl,
born with a fierce independence
and a deep fear of change.
An interesting combination.

She left today,
this daughter of mine,
whose stubborn unwillingness to meet my expectations
drove me to therapy and freedom—

This beloved, difficult-to-raise daughter of mine
left today
to drive the thousand miles she will live away from me,
to make more money in her first year out
than I have ever made in one year in my life.

She left today to find her life as an adult.
She left to start paying her own way.
She dove into the sea of life,
and now she will have to develop her own strokes
and find her own islands.
She will have to find her own remedies
for drowning
and sunburn
and dehydration.

She will have to figure out what to do about sharks
and stingrays.

And, though I love her to madness,
she will have to do
the deepest,
tallest,
widest parts
of this journey for herself.

My daughter left today
to grow up,
to grow away,

to grow separate,
to grow imperfect,
to make some of the same mistakes I've made
and to make some she invents for herself.

My daughter left today,
if it's possible,
for anyone whose connection
is buried so deeply in my heart,
to ever leave.

Letter: Mother's Day

If you have not yet experienced what it feels like to have one of your children going out with someone you don't like—well, you just have not suffered yet. Imagine that your beloved daughter goes out with someone for two years who does not want to be in your home, will not let you get to know him, and is not interested in getting to know you. Then imagine that he does not treat your beloved daughter well. No, don't. It's too painful.

I did the best I could through all of this, and in spite of my best, Katie and I had our worst fights over this young man. Katie spent the last Christmas my mother was alive with him instead of her family.

> Dear Katie,
> I need to say this to you, but I will only say it this once, and you don't need to respond. I would appreciate it, though, if you would read what I have to say.
> I know you want everyone to be happy, especially Jason. You just wish everyone got along great. You wish it were easy, and that no one ever felt like they didn't get enough of you. I know you try to make everyone happy, and I know how difficult it is to do that. I know you love me and care about me. I never doubt that. You try to make it all good for everyone, and I know that causes you stress sometimes.
> Here is what I need to say: I see a pattern that worries me. You want to make everyone happy, and as far as that goes, that is not a

bad thing. But the fact is, you can never make everyone happy, and by trying to make everyone happy, you sometimes make more people unhappy, especially yourself.

When you were with your last boyfriend, Josh, you let him treat you disrespectfully. You wanted to make him happy. You spent way more time with his family because that was the path of least resistance. I don't blame you for that. I understand, believe me. And that is what bothers me.

You come from a line of women who don't want to rock the boat, women who want to make everyone happy. My mom stayed with a brutal alcoholic, a selfish narcissist, because she wanted everyone to be happy.

I used to be a pleaser, too, although I was very clear about physical abuse in my life. I was never with anyone who treated me the way Josh treated you. He disrespected you repeatedly, and you just took it. That worries me.

Jason feels more comfortable around his own family. Of course he does. But there is no way in the world, if the situation were reversed, that you would expect him to desert his mother on Mother's Day. If he rarely saw his family, you would want him to see them. If his grandmother were very ill, you would want him to see her. You would be gracious and thoughtful because that is what you are like—when you are not with Jason.

I raised you to be thoughtful and considerate. But I also raised you to take a stand for what is right. It is wrong of Jason to ask this of you.

I'm assuming you would really rather be with your grandmother and me on Mother's Day, but maybe I am wrong about that. If you really want to be around his family more than us, then do it with my blessing. You would at least be taking a stand for honesty, and I could respect that even if I didn't like it.

But right now you are dishonest. You say you and Jason are coming over for brunch and you will call and then you don't call. You stroll in late in the morning, saying you can only stay for ten minutes because you "have" to get to Jason's family, which you spent the whole afternoon with and had dinner with last night. Sadie spent hours shopping and cooking, looking forward to a good visit. To say you will come over and then act with such thoughtlessness is unkind.

I'm worried about your submissiveness. You might get involved with someone who would really isolate you from your family, and you might want to please him so much you would let him do it. It has happened to many women.

Now you are probably really angry with me, or crying. It scares me to write this boldly to you, but I know the only path that works out in the end is the path of truth and character.

My phoniness detector works great, and so does yours. This is a good thing in the long run. Sometimes not being able to pretend is uncomfortable in the short run, but it is the only way to live that is sustainable. Nothing else works.

Just so I'm clear: If you are coming, tell me when you will be here. Then stick to it. This is all I want. I will not argue with you about it. Just don't offer a gift, like time for Mother's Day, and then snatch it away. That feels really bad.

Okay, so I'm not an easy mother sometimes. I'm not an easy wife or friend either. But I am as true and deep as they get. I am committed to loving whomever you love. But don't ask me to pretend. I gave that up long ago.

I will not refer to this letter. You tell me when you'll be around, and I will be cheerful and grateful. I will treat Jason with graciousness and warmth as I always have done. I love you to pieces!

Sigh,
Mom

Letter to the Boyfriend

All I can say is, considering how I felt about this guy, I must be a saint to have been able to write this letter.

Dear Jason,

I admire your incredible dedication, how hard you worked in a vacuum. With no financial aid and, I would say, no emotional support from your coach, you kept working hard, giving 100 percent, even when you were denied playing time, over and over again. You stayed in there and stuck with it. I didn't have that kind of intrepidness at your age, and I still don't when it comes to physical challenges. That you now have a full scholarship and high rankings in the conference are icing on the cake. You invested so much for years with no guarantees of reward. Truly amazing.

Not only that, but unlike many college athletes, you will graduate with a double major in business and engineering and with a high GPA. That task, without football, would be quite an accomplishment, but add it to football, and I'll bet there are few college players in the country who could match it.

Then along comes my daughter, and you cry when she tells you about how she almost died. Thank you for that.

She tells me how you snuck money into her purse and paid her bills secretly when she was struggling for cash. Thank you for caring that much about her.

You have a great giggle, and even I can see you smile. Come and eat pizza with us more often, cheer for your favorite team. I can't see sports even on TV, and, truth to tell, I don't care about them much. But I love my daughter to distraction, and she loves you. Therefore, there is more than enough room in my heart to love you as well.

You are always welcome in our home. Come more often and let us get to know you, let us all get more comfortable and natural around each other.

And treat my daughter well, or I'll kick your ass!

Vicki

Jason broke up with Katie on New Year's Day, affirming my opinion of him.

Epilogue

Katie and I are on a great adventure, which, if I am lucky, will continue until I die (first)!

While many of these writings make it appear that Katie and I have lots of conflict, nothing could be further from the truth. Even though I wrote to Katie in times of celebration and times of trial, writing to her was more effective than talking in times of stress, so I have more of a record of our problems. But Katie and I travel together well and play games with cutthroat efficiency. Our minds work much the same. We share honesty, laughter, and love, and we are very good friends.

I will be glad, though, when she learns how to manage her money better, gets a job she loves, meets a man she adores and who adores her, has a baby or two, and lives happily, no, make that, authentically ever after.

Your Turn

So how is your relationship with your daughter? Is she fulfilling your every fantasy? I hope not. Or has your daughter not yet (or maybe never) manifested on the physical plane known as planet Earth? Write it all out. Confess. Make wishes. Write a letter to your daughter-of-the-flesh or your spirit daughter or to the female energy known as Gaia. Let 'er rip!

Chapter 27

Martin James

*Martin James playing at the
National Ultimate Frisbee Championship Game.
Photo by Scobel Wiggins*

Well done, son. Well done.
I love who you've become.
You're just the way I hoped you'd be.
I love the man in you I see.
Well done, son. Well done.

My son, Martin, is an amazing human being. As I write this, he has completed his first year of grad school at the University of Colorado in Boulder. He is on scholarship, so he no longer accepts much financial help from his father or me. He is on an Ultimate Frisbee team that won first place at the national tournament in 2004. He is a mensch, and I am enormously proud of him.

My First Poem to Martin

This is a poem to my son, Martin,
who, from the moment he was born,
has been a solid, loving, giving child,

whose ability and desire
to nurse hourly caused me to weep in frustration,
who still knows how to fly
and be a puppy
(his vacuous puppy imitation makes me smile),

whose soft little body curls into mine,
sometimes putting his little arm
around my shoulders,
returning comfort.

His solid gentleness,
so like his father's,
bathes me in wholeness,
goodness.

I write to you, Martin,
gift of God,
pretender extraordinaire,
my I-do-it-myselfer,
my baby,
my son,
two years old,
soon to be three.

Story: Martin and Self-Esteem

Here is my definition of self-esteem.

My mother used to recount a story about Martin when he was about five. She and her husband, Marvin, had taken Martin and Katie bowling, one of their favorite things to do together. This was in the days when no one had thought of bumper guards and young children threw mostly gutter balls.

My children would struggle up to the line with a ball that was much too heavy for them. They would carefully set the ball in the center of the lane, then give it a good push. Their "good push" usually resulted in a painfully slow journey down the lane for a few feet and then a slow roll into the gutter. Hitting any pins was a big deal. Strikes sometimes happened, but spares were pretty much nonexistent, as aiming at a few pins left over from the first throw was way beyond their skill level.

About two-thirds of the way through the game, Martin had knocked down a few pins, but he had thrown mostly gutter balls, and his sister had a higher score.

Then he walked up to the lane, set the ball down between his legs, and pushed as usual. This time, instead of going directly to the gutter, his ball wobbled down the center. Both grandparents got excited. The ball stayed in the center, going so slowly that Mom said she wasn't sure it wouldn't just stop before it reached the pins.

When the ball hit the head pin, everyone stood as if pulled by an invisible cord from the sky. Slowly, one by one, the head pin struck the next two pins, which struck the next pins until all that was left was the ten pin circling leisurely on its bottom. That stubborn ten pin finally fell, and the grandparents, his sister, and Martin cheered. A strike!

Martin turned, smiling, and said, "Well, I guess I'm a good bowler after all!"

That's self-confidence.

Most of us don't have Martin's sense of self-esteem. He had a big space for mistakes and "failure." He wasn't going to give up his sense of himself as a bowler without a fight.

He carried this trait into his teens. Much to my surprise, and without any managing from me or his father, Martin became an award-winning tuba player. He was in every band and symphony our college town offered. He played in a student-directed quintet. He was good.

But he also joined the swim team, where, as he put it, he "sucked." He didn't take up competitive swimming until he was a sophomore in high school, and I'm not sure why he wanted to add this sport. Swim practices are grueling. He would drag himself home five nights a week and then often go to a meet on Saturday, this along with playing in all of his bands and sometimes acting in plays.

He was not concerned with winning. He didn't care if I came to watch him or not. He swam for himself. He would tell me not where he placed in the meet, but rather of how he had improved his "PR" or personal record. He was competing against only himself, and he was willing to work extremely hard with no hope of becoming a star.

I admire my son for his string of straight A semesters and for being the best tuba player in six northwestern states. I admire him for being hysterically funny as the Beast of Yugoslavia in Kurt Vonnegut's *Happy Birthday, Wanda June*.

But I think I admire Martin most for the quality in him that gets him to work hard for his swim team even though he is not a good swimmer. He can enjoy improving without needing to be the best.

I wasn't like that as a child or even as an adult, until the last few years. I was good at many things, and I stuck with those. I was too insecure to do something I wasn't good at immediately. One try, one failure, one negative comment from someone and I would erase a possible talent from the blackboard in my mind. I gave myself no space to make mistakes and learn.

The vast majority of us are not born with Martin's inherent sense of self. We have to work at it. Martin has been a great teacher for me. I have seen, for the first time in my life, what it is like to have perfect self-esteem pitch. He has helped tune me to my own inner song, and for that gift I will always be grateful.

Letter: Martin's 14th Birthday

Dear Martin,

I've given you the material things for your birthday I wanted to—a wet suit and dinner. But more importantly, I want to say some things to you and have them recorded.

I am proud to have you as my son. Every year I enjoy you more: your sense of humor, your intelligence, your heart, and your wit continue to mature. You can't imagine how delightful it is to be able to observe this process in someone you love, someone you've known since birth, someone who grew inside you.

You are growing into a wonderful man. This summer when I hurt my knee on the rafting trip, you helped me up the hill to the disgusting-smelling toilet. You lifted my arm and put it around your shoulder, even as you were giving me a hard time about being such a "wuss."

You are learning to take responsibility for your behavior, making excuses less often, owning up to and accepting the consequences of your choices with humor and grace.

You are one of the most fun people I know. I just love it that we will know each other all of our lives, that I will get to know your children if you have them. I get to play with you forever. Major cool.

Your sense of fun and fair play, your rebellious spirit (I don't know where you got that), will continue to be a part of the basic material that makes you you.

I look forward with delight to knowing you as a man of 24, 34, and 44 (That's how old I'll be next Saturday). But I promise you this: If you EVER become an old fart, crabby and critical, I will take you down, even if I have to hire help to do it.

I love you very much, dear son.
Well done.

Love,
Mom

Martin and the Piano Picture

Martin James, age three
Photo by Vicki Hannah Lein

I wrote this when Martin was still in high school. His dad and I were divorced, and he lived with each of us for several weeks at a time.

I have a picture of Martin playing the piano in is underwear. He was about three, sitting on the piano bench, deep in concentration. He was plunking on the keys, totally unaware of anything else. It is one of my all-time favorite photos, and it is on my refrigerator.

Martin is six foot three inches tall now. He still loves music, still gets completely absorbed in what he is doing. But he doesn't end his days on my lap anymore, sucking his two fingers, all snuggly in his yellow sleeper pajamas.

Now he sleeps at his dad's or his friends' houses. Sometimes at my house, when he is with me, he will go to bed early with a "goodnight" as he walks down the hall. Or he'll be playing Play Station Football downstairs and holler a "goodnight" through the door distractedly.

I fear the little boy sitting on the piano bench in his underwear is gone from me forever. I fear I will never again feel the closeness I felt with him then, never have the simple pleasure of mother and son just living together easily and naturally. He is a young man now, and young men must leave their mothers to be healthy.

I know that.

Even so, separating from him hurts and tears more than I ever dreamed it would. I didn't plan on this kind of pain when he was sixteen. I didn't plan on losing my beloved little boy.

But I have lost my little boy, and I must learn to love this new young man, learn how to be his mother in a new way, learn to support him differently than I did when he was four.

I must learn to live with this empty lap until it is filled with a grandchild or two. I will love my son through his child, a double love made special by the deep knowing in my body that this time with young children is fleeting, these warm moments of snuggling gone all too soon. The cycle of mother's laps filling and emptying is completely human and timeless.

Now my lap is empty. I will sit with that.

Story: Martin and Hypocrisy

Red Ribbon week came to Martin's high school his junior year, as it did every year. Red Ribbon week is designed to help students stay off drugs. Drug-free students are asked to wear a little red ribbon. Schools usually produce an assembly and lots of hoopla.

The leadership class had been ordered to wear red ribbons. They were not all drug/alcohol free, and everyone in the school knew it.

Martin and a pal, during their free period, went out to a local T-shirt shop and had T-shirts made that said, "I smoke crack." Martin put on a red ribbon and went back to school.

While studying in the library later that afternoon, he was summoned to the vice principal's office. Martin was asked to explain his t-shirt with its unusual, and ridiculous, claim.

"I understand why you did this Martin, but this was not the way to handle the situation," the vice principal said. "You could have been sent home for three days for pulling this stunt, but I will just have you turn your T-shirt inside out. Don't let this happen again."

Martin told me this story with trepidation. His father had agreed with the vice principal. I laughed. "I think it was brilliant!" I said. "It was poetic and articulate, and you were exercising your right of free speech. I think the way the school dealt with this is an example of everything that is wrong with education today."

Martin was delighted and pleasantly surprised by my response.

During his graduation from the University of Puget Sound, Martin received the math award. When the professor was paying tribute to my son, he said that Martin was well-known as someone who has his feet on the ground and has no time for academic pretenses or pomposity. I cheered from the crowd. There is nothing he could have said that could have made me prouder.

Story: "Martin, It Works Both Ways"

Martin and I were great pals until he became a teenager. When he was 16 he started lecturing me about my inappropriate behavior. He said his friends thought that he was "way out," but that I was even further out than he. In short, I embarrassed him. Surprise, surprise. (I once asked him if anyone in his group was proud of their mother. He paused for a moment and said, "Well, there are guys who are proud of their fathers." "Yes, I know that. But are any of your friends proud of their mothers." "No," he finally admitted. "Fine, then," I said. "If I am in the file marked 'Unacceptable Mothers' but I am with all of your friends' mothers, I won't worry so much.")

Even knowing this, my patience was rubbed raw. I was feeling uncomfortable living under his critical scrutiny. I had culled out the people in my life who made me feel inadequate and here I was living with one, and, even worse, he was my beloved son.

Giving birth to my children was like giving strangers a six-lane freeway through my heart. The minute Katie and Martin were born, I was completely defenseless in my love for them, completely vulnerable. When they were born, death became real for me, and I've been recovering ever since.

Now this boy suddenly turned into a man. This six-foot-three-inch testosterone-wielding critical science nerd, my son, was a stranger to me, and a hostile one at that.

I talked to my friends with sons. They assured me that this was normal. Sons had to separate from their mothers in order to be healthy.

One friend said that if it didn't feel as if a serrated knife were cutting through my flesh, Martin wasn't doing it right.

Martin was doing it right.

Our difficulties came to a head on a trip to California to visit my ailing mother and her husband. Martin, Katie, and I drove down together, a rare treat. Since the divorce four years earlier, the three of us had not been alone often. I looked forward to our trip, not only for a chance to have the three of us together, but also for the chance to reconnect with my son.

On the trip down, Martin continued his sarcastic comments about my behavior. Nothing downright disrespectful, just the rolling of eyes, and a quiet withdrawal of his approval.

When we got to my mother's and entered the living room, I couldn't see the left half of the coffee table. I was even thinking to myself, "I thought this coffee table was bigger," when I walked right into it and fell over onto the couch.

My shins were both bruised and my toes scraped, and I felt like a fool. Martin and Katie both laughed, and laughed, and laughed.

Martin, I knew, was using this as a chance to vent his anger at me for my being such an unacceptable mom. Katie shoe-horned in her ridicule, more for the enjoyment of ganging up on the adult than for any specific grievance against me.

I didn't think my pain was funny, and I didn't think their laughing at me was funny. I told them so. They laughed anyway.

Later, sitting out on the patio, Martin explained to me again about how I talked about inappropriate things and didn't act as a mother should.

"Martin," I said, "I know I say and do things that embarrass you, but please make sure you let me know if I ever get cruel." He knew I was referring to his laughing at me when I got hurt.

He became quiet.

In that moment, I had decided that even though I loved this child of mine, this bright, talented man, to madness, I would not allow him to mistreat me. If that meant he left me—oh, well. I have lost significant men in my life: my father, my brother. Losing Martin would rip my heart out, but letting him pour his disapproval all over my exuberance would kill my soul.

In that instant, I let him go.

On the trip home, I started a conversation that I knew I wouldn't be able to have any other time. Martin was driving, trapped in the car, and we had to get to Oregon. We would finish this talk no matter how much he might want to avoid it.

"Martin, I've been thinking about our relationship a lot and talking to a lot of people. I've realized something on this trip." Martin kept driving, staring at the road, and didn't comment.

"When I was looking through all those old photos at Mom's, the ones of you when you were little, I realized something. You remember that picture of you when you were about four, standing in your bathrobe? Your little legs sticking out? You were so cute. In some crazy mom part of my brain, I wanted you to stay four forever.

"One of my main jobs as a mother, though, is letting go of that picture. My idea of who you are needs to constantly change as you change and grow. This sounds easy to do, but, trust me, it isn't.

"Katie's changes have been more gradual," I said, glancing at Katie in the back seat, "but with you it seems that all of a sudden you are this different person, and I am having a difficult time keeping up with who you really are.

"But I think this work goes both ways. I think kids need to work at changing their ideas of who their parents are, too. I am not who you thought I was when you were four years old, either.

"Here is my request: I will work hard to change my idea of who you are and to keep up with the man you are becoming. In exchange, I would like you to try to change your ideas about who I am from what you thought when you were four years old."

Martin didn't say anything, but I took this as a good sign.

He hasn't corrected me since this conversation. He did say later, after we got home, that many of my comments were funny and were probably okay except that I was his mother. Maybe Martin has decided to let me grow up, too.

A few days after our trip, I listened to my e-mail. I heard the first line of a message to Martin before I realized it was not for me. The e-mail was in response to a previous e-mail Martin had sent, and it said: "Thank you, Martin, for your appreciative e-mail. It's been a long time since anyone thanked me so sweetly. You made my day."

I don't remember why I got the e-mail. I didn't know the person Martin sent the e-mail to. Martin had initiated a gracious thank you note, and some computer angel let me see my son at his best.

He is still my little boy, I thought after reading this email. His legs aren't as knobby as they were when he was four, but his heart is as grand. I finally recognized my little boy in the big hunk of a man he was now. Maybe he remembers the comfort he got in my lap as I read him dinosaur books when he was two.

At any rate, we are both working now to give each other the space to be who we really are and who we might become. That's as good as it gets.

Poem: Martin, It's Finally Your Turn

Am I too proud of you,
dear son?
Do I enjoy your brain
and your heart
and your laughter
too much?

Does your sister suffer in comparison?
Does she suffer?
Have I held back my love for you
to protect her?

Have you lost out on your rightful attention,
as you did that day she closed the heavy car door on your leg
by "accident"?
She was in sixth grade,
you in fourth,
and I ran after her,
afraid she would wallow in shame,
and left you in the back seat
with a near broken shin.

"What about me?" you cried
when I finally returned to you,
still writhing in pain in the back seat of Mom's old Buick.
Your outrage at the injustice
brought me to my senses
and filled me with my own shame.
The squeaky wheel gets greased,
and Katie has always been a squeaky wheel.

Here it is,
your poem,
and she has wiggled her way in.
This poem is supposed to be your turn.

What if you had been my first child,
the older brother?
What if you had been the child
to break trail into my heart?

I loved you too much when you were a baby,
needed your healthy maleness to heal me.
I squeezed you too tightly,
and you banished me and my neediness
for months.
No hugs for me.

Even when you weren't quite two years old,
your center was strong and true.
One of my greatest gifts to you as a mother
was giving you the space you demanded as a toddler.

And I ached every time I gave it to you.
I suffered,
knowing I deserved this punishment,
knowing that I was bigger than you
and could break you to my will if I wanted.

But I knew that forcing you to succumb to my hugs
would be a form of spiritual abuse
from which you might never recover.

You had a problem with arrogance for a while
and a tough time learning how to
"ride the beast" of your intellect and your talents,
but now I see your compassion growing
with an accompanying tenderness.
I can see the full, good man you are becoming.

You have helped break my stubborn heart,
held together my whole life by scars
and the glue of self-will.

You have filled my heart so full that
it shattered,
as it needed to.

And now I hold my love for you gently,
with more air and light
and less desperation.

You are a powerful being on this earth, Martin,
and you have just begun to shine.

Love,
Mom

Martin's Poem for Me

This is Martin's response to Martin, It's Finally Your Turn.

Mom,
You certainly don't beat around the bush, do you? To be honest, I hadn't thought about the relationship between Katie, you, and myself

all that much. Perhaps this is a compliment to you, Mom; your mediation was so successful that I hardly even noticed there was a problem! There were, of course, times when something clearly was going on that required more careful scrutiny than what was immediately apparent (the slamming of the car door comes to mind).

Here is my poem for you:

Dear Mom,

Sometimes I wonder
how everything worked out.
You know?

You had no easy task,
coming from your "family" of five.
Then things had to be sorted out
after the divorce,
and after you lost most of your vision.
We were just kids
and it was also
not easy.

But here we are!
You, the master of your own destiny!
Katie, well, at least she's paying off her debt.
And I, an up-and-coming professional student.
Doesn't it make you wonder?

How did we get from point A to point B?
Well, the core of the thing is
in no small part because of you.
Perhaps your biggest obstacle was that
you loved too much,
and we were incapable
of dealing with that.

Your desire to do us good
is so transparent.
Your thirst for our energy
is so unveiled.

And you held us when we were weak
or lying unconscious in a hospital.
And step-by-step
we walked together.

And here we are!
At the next leg of the journey!
But not without a thank you,
Mom.

P.S. Do not expect me to read this to you aloud or even acknowledge its existence outside of a small group of people.

Your Turn

Do you have a letter or a card you would like to send to some male in your life? It is never too late or too early. We need to celebrate great males wherever we find them.

You could write a letter to your son as he is now or as a man, the kind of man you want him to become. If you don't have a son, you can make up your own or write to mine. I can't guarantee he will read it, though.

Chapter 28

Shirley May

July 29, 1926—April 2, 2003

Shirley May, cutthroat card player
Photo by Dale Haslem

Some of the following poems and stories I shared with my mother; some I did not. Almost all of these writings happened in the last five years of Mom's life. I knew she was dying and I wanted to make sense of her life and mine. In my song *Mommy is an Angel*, which I include later in this chapter, I wrote: "I spent the first half of my life wanting to be anyone but my Mom. Now I would gladly settle for being half as strong." I think these two lines sum up my journey. I hope it doesn't take Katie as long as it took me to get to this understanding, but I have a feeling it might. Sigh.

Poem: Beatrice Lela

My grandmother died when my mother was fifteen. Mom lamented her entire life about how "selfish" she was while her mother was dying. "I was only thinking of myself," she told me over and over, as if some other abandoned teenager would have behaved differently.

I imagine it is early summer
and my grandmother,
Beatrice Lela,
is leaning against a fence,
waiting for a friend to meet her
to go for a walk
or go to the malt shop for root beer floats.

The year is 1923,
and my grandmother Beatrice is only seventeen,
living at home with her family,
solid Midwesterners.
She might even have some of those Norwegian, bachelor farmers for uncles.

I imagine her leaning against a fence,
wearing a dress that drapes well below her knees,
a shirtwaist dress,
I think you call it.
She has long, dark hair
and a firm, athletic body.
She was a basketball player—
a good one.
She is innocent,
unsophisticated,
alive and happy,
secure in the bosom of her family.

I imagine,
as she is standing there so fresh and lovely,
watching puppies wrestling in the grass
and fingering the white ribbons in her hair,
that a young man saunters up to her.
He is handsome,
a few years older than she.

He is the most charming man she has ever met.

I imagine he makes her laugh,
fills her with an excitement she has not known before,
sends shivers through her body
that are unfamiliar
and yet fill her with an urgency for more.

I imagine he looks at her with an intensity
that tilts her world,
makes her feel everything she has known
up to this moment in time
is not quite real.

Her hardworking family of farmers and housewives—
people who pay their debts,
sweep the porches in front of their cozy little homes,
and take tuna noodle casseroles to church potlucks—
these people she has loved and who have loved her all of her life up to
    this moment
now seem a little dull,
like a photograph that has faded in the sun.

She doesn't know quite who she is with this man,
my grandfather.

She has no idea that falling in love
with this exciting stranger from Iowa,
getting pregnant and then married when she is seventeen,
will send her across country to Oregon,
where she will bear him two daughters,
where she will live for only seventeen more years,
years of fights and beatings and unpaid bills.

She would never have been able to imagine
on that sunny day years ago
that she would die a slow, painful death from uterine cancer,
at home,
lying on the couch,
nursed by her abusive husband's lover.

She could never imagine on that sweet day of her youth
that she would be ripped forever from the support of her family
and that she would leave two unloved, unprotected daughters
to make their own way in the world.

And she wouldn't know
because she died before it happened to her,
that she would pass on a gene for blindness to you, Mom,
and that you would pass it on to me.

Grandma Beatrice loved my mother
and that love filled her up and spilled out onto me,
saving my life.

Gramma's House

After Beatrice died, my grandfather, who always insisted we call him "George," never "Grandpa," sent my mother and her sister to live with one of his drinking buddies, his wife, and their five children. Mom fell in love with the youngest and married him when she was seventeen and he eighteen.

My dad's mother, Gramma, loved my mother as a daughter, even after Mom and my dad divorced. Thank God for the solid, Iowa-farm-girl love of my grandmother Inda.

Gramma's house was full of mysteries: dark recesses under the stairs where boxes of comic books lived, narrow doors that open to windowless passageways which led nowhere, and an attic full of old furniture and memories. She had a wringer/washing machine in her entry way and a real wood stove to cook on in her kitchen. Her garden was full of secret places where elves lived and cowboys and Indians hid among the branches that touched the ground.

I loved the sound of the squeaky screen door banging behind Gramma as she smiled her welcoming hello. We would greet each other, hugging as we did with no one else in my family, and climb the cement steps to the back porch. The porch floor tilted slightly due to the sinking of the foundation, but I did not know that then. All I noticed were the shelves for storing canned goods, a small pantry at the far right, and an opening to the internal woodshed. The smell of the firewood seeping from the woodshed, a dank sanctuary for spiders, filled me with a deep sense of home.

Gramma's pantry was always filled with canned peaches, cherries, tomatoes, beans, corn, and pickles. Sometimes I would help her can in the summer, jars lining the counters and covering her dinette set. Once the shelves were full, Gramma started filling her chest freezer, which also lived on the porch.

Gramma's freezer held magic: homemade bread, jam, and frozen corn from her brother's fields. Plus scrapple, venison, and the salmon one of her grandsons had given her from his last fishing trip. She could literally feed a dozen people, probably twenty, with no notice. The first words she uttered, after the smile and "hellloooo!" were always, "Have you eaten?" I don't know why she asked because it didn't matter what you answered. She always started putting out food anyway.

If she knew you were coming, she always had your favorite foods ready. I loved her chicken and noodles made from scratch and her chocolate, chocolate cake in an eight-by-eleven pan. She always baked a sugarless apple pie for my diabetic step-dad and a cherry pie for my husband, Will.

She loved us all with her food.

Some of my fondest memories are of eating her homemade bread, fresh from the oven, with homemade strawberry jam. Or drinking hot chocolate through a glass straw—chocolate made from scratch with Hershey's cocoa.

My Gramma's house was the one place where no one misbehaved. No one swore, got drunk, or made cruel comments. Gramma's house was an emotional DMZ in my life. My mother's gentle love grew there, and I was always safe sitting in Gramma's kitchen, seeing the best of my family—everyone who crossed her doorway.

Story: Still Mom

When my Mom was forty she lost her central vision in one eye before she even noticed she had a problem. Actually, that's not exactly true: she'd noticed signs—not being able to see under her left arm as she shaved, seeing Venetian blinds as wavy lines—but she'd ignored these signs. The doctors didn't tell her after she lost the vision in one eye that the chances were good it would happen within five years in her other eye, as well. She says now if she'd known she might go blind, she would have made some changes in her life. I'm not so sure that's true. Mom wasn't a WarriorBabe back then.

Quite suddenly, though, she did lose the central vision in her other eye, and she was legally blind, no longer able to read or drive. I hadn't known there was anything wrong with even one eye, so her sudden blindness took me by surprise.

I was fifteen and, although I was afraid for my mom, I have to admit I almost liked the drama of having a blind mother. I thought perhaps having a blind mother would make me seem more mysterious. It would make my life a real, understandable tragedy. People would feel sorry for me, and I would be healed by their care and concern. I would be a little heroine in my own play, getting the applause and the attention without all that messy pain.

I was ashamed of these feelings, never sharing them with anyone. I was sorry for Mom, tried always to be more sorry, at least as sorry as I thought I should be, but I couldn't imagine what being blind would be like. I kept thinking of blind people in the movies—how exotic they seemed, how they seemed to have a special aura.

My Mom didn't seem special. Her vision loss was mostly irritating. It got in the way. She didn't hold her head in that funny half-cocked way people in the movies do. Her sense of hearing didn't improve. She was still just my Mom, only now I had to drive her to the store to buy groceries, reading the labels and prices, carrying the sacks, putting the food away. I felt like a housewife at fifteen, and I hated it.

Helping Mom interfered with my life. I resented her dependence, especially her dependence on me. I was fifteen, and I wanted to be left alone to be a star at school, occasionally telling people about my blind mother and watching their shocked faces. I enjoyed their discomfort, and I enjoyed secretly knowing that my mom wasn't a "blind person;" she was just my Mom who couldn't see.

She made me drive to the store to buy her cigarettes, which, when you live in rural California, could mean a twenty-five mile drive on a 100-degree day in a car without air-conditioning. Her new husband had an air-conditioned car, but he wouldn't let me drive it, even to take Mom to buy groceries, because it put miles on the car and would lower its resale value. So when she had to be taken to the emergency room because she couldn't breathe, I thought it quite clever to say, "That will teach you to smoke."

Barely able to walk, Mom turned her face to me as her husband hustled her out the door into the garage to take her to the hospital. The expression of terror and amazement in her eyes forced me to feel my callousness. She looked at me, a look of surprise, hurt, betrayal. She looked at me not as a mother looks at her child, but as one human, in misery, looks at another, not seeking pity or even understanding.

I didn't know what she was seeking; all I know is that whatever it was, I didn't give it to her. Instead, I gave her pain. I spoke to her with cruelty when she wasn't even asking for anything except to be left alone. All she needed was the tiniest bit of human compassion as her husband helped her get to the emergency room to find her lost breath. But I was too busy with my life to give her even a little kindness.

When she paused in her panic to look at me, she asked a question with her eyes, a question I couldn't or wouldn't answer. There I was, sprawled on the couch, watching some inane TV show in the middle of the afternoon on a hot summer day, and I couldn't bother to get up and see my gasping, wheezing mother to the hospital—to the car door, even.

How can I excuse this behavior? I can't. I did it. The fear and bewilderment in Mom's eyes forced me to acknowledge a cold place in me, a place that felt huge and mean. I was ashamed. But I kept watching my TV show, slightly troubled, but not troubled enough to get me to get up off the couch to comfort my terrified mother.

We did not speak of this moment for years and when we did Mom made excuses for me and I gave myself no quarter. (I am my mother's daughter, after all.)

Even through my self-centered adolescent haze, I could see that my Mom was a hero to many people. On several bowling teams, her average for many years was about 165. Even though she couldn't see the pins, she knew where they were. She would line up using the spots on the lane to guide her and then give it her best shot. If any pins were left, a teammate would tell her and she would know exactly where to stand and throw to knock down the pins she couldn't see. When she tore her rotator cuff in her right shoulder, she switched to bowling with her left arm until her emphysema stopped her bowling, and her life, all together.

What goes around, comes around. When I was forty-three I lost my central vision, too. My daughter was fifteen, the same age I was when my mother lost her vision. I was recently divorced, as my mother had been, and it seemed as if the wheel of fate had turned and crushed me under its weight.

That I seemed to be retracing my mother's footsteps terrified me. I had spent the last twelve years in therapy, working hard to create my own life and not relive my mother's and here I was: blind, and divorced with a 15-year-old daughter who now had to drive me to buy groceries as I had driven Mom. Was I going to get her breast cancer, too?

Our mutual blindness united us. When I called Mom to tell her I had her disease, she was the only person in the world I wouldn't have wanted to smack with a big stick when she said, "It's not so bad." The way she embraced life became a model for how I wanted to deal with my own challenges.

My mother was a hero, but she was still my mom, my fabulous mom. She loved me well as she lay dying and she loves me now from wherever she is.

Poem: What Kind of a Mother Have You Been?

Murray read this to Mom the last time we visited her in California before she got bronchitis and died ten days later. As he read the title, "What Kind of a Mother Have You Been?" she groaned.

What kind of a mother have you been?
Not a perfect one—
you'd be the first to tell me that.
You would be the one to bring up
how you should have stayed home more
and not gone drinking with Dad.
You would be the one to say
you should have cooked more,
less often bringing home finger steaks
and deep fried chicken from Dad's bar.

So what kind of a mother have you been?
You have been a miracle mother, that's all.
You have given in abundance
what you were never given yourself,
that's all.
You have made me feel loved every day of my life,
that's all.
You have fanned every spark of creativity and imagination in me,
while denying your own genius,
that's all.

You filled me with enough unconditional love,
so I could go out into the world and break trails
you couldn't break for yourself:
graduate from high school and college,
earn a Master's degree,
write songs,
produce a CD
and speak at international conferences.

People tell me I am inspirational.
They look at what I have accomplished,
being blind and all,
and some inchoate spark in them is brightened.

But I can give to others, Mom,
only what I got from you.
That you were able to tend your little flame
against all the winds in your life that tried to blow it out,
that you could nurture this flame against all odds
and then throw kindling on the flame you saw in me—
well,
this is a miracle.
You are a miracle.

I love you, Mom,
for now and forever.
Everything I am able to give others
you started in me.
Every dream I've encouraged,
every act of courage I have attempted or inspired
can be traced directly back to you.

May you breathe this truth with each breath you take.
May the knowledge of the obstacles you have overcome
and the love and hope you have spawned in the world
fill your lungs with life.

What kind of a mom have you been?
The best kind:
my mom.

From your grateful daughter,
Vicki

Story: The Breaking of a Family

I wrote this piece during the last four years of my mother's life.

My blind mother, who is seventy-two, and has been recently hospitalized with emphysema, has just divorced her husband of thirty-one years. I couldn't be happier for her.

I was grateful for my mother's first divorce from my father, too. I was fourteen at the time and couldn't understand all the grim faces and woeful whispers about divorce. My parents' divorce was the best thing that had ever happened to me. That divorce didn't break my home: my parents' divorce kept my spirit from breaking and allowed for the possibility of a new home, one that could replace the "home" that was already badly broken.

My parents' divorce meant that I knew when I went to sleep at night I would be able to sleep undisturbed until morning. No screaming, no broken beer bottles, no shaming and swearing. Just blissful silence from the time I drifted off to sleep until I woke up in the morning. This is a blessing easily taken for granted.

When my parents separated for the last time, (I had lost count of how many other separations we endured), Mom, David, my younger brother by three years, and I moved into a small house Mom bought for eight thousand dollars. My older sister, Lee, had moved out by this time, and we were left with a congenial family trio.

I loved our little house, although it was much less fancy than the one Mom and Dad had redecorated in a vain attempt to create so much debt they would have to stay together. The Christmas before we moved out, they bought me a four-poster bed and a lace turquoise bedspread with a matching canopy. I loved the bedroom set but felt uneasy, knowing even at thirteen, money didn't buy happiness. A turquoise shell over a sick relationship wasn't going to cover their problems for long.

After the divorce, the three of us thrived in the precious home of ours that sat on its own little hill in a neighborhood close to school. I called it the "Fairy Tale House" because of its curving walk of red steps to the front porch and because of the arched doorways.

I didn't care that it was heated by a sawdust furnace or that it needed painting. I loved my attic bedroom with its slanted roof and window seat. I used to sit in that window seat for hours and watch the cars drive down the street, listening to the Beach Boys, especially, "In My Room." I was happy and at peace for the first time in a long time, and it was because I now lived in a "broken" home.

Mom could still read and drive then. She had already lost the central vision in her right eye, but I didn't know that at the time. We had a wonderful summer together, and then Mom had to be hospitalized because she was starting to lose the central vision in her other eye. She was going blind.

I remember being scared, but being fourteen and believing that my mother was invincible and could handle anything that wasn't drunk and screaming at her, I didn't worry too much about our future.

Mom fell apart, though, and moved down to California with my brother to live with her sister. I stayed and lived with a Catholic family on a dairy farm, one of seven teenagers still living at home. I finished out my sophomore year in high school and then moved down to live with Mom and my brother.

By then Mom had met and fallen in love with a charming salesman. I liked him. He was funny and generous and very kind to my mother, my brother, and me.

He remained this way all through the building of their new house out in the country by a lake. We were in posh circumstances now, a far cry from my brother having to put cardboard in his shoes to make them last.

But everything changed after Mom and Marvin's wedding. My new stepfather lost his charm and generosity. He never spent more on us than my father's child support payments, and he begrudged every penny, even for the dentist. We only got new clothes for birthday or Christmas presents.

We were much happier, though, than we had been with my father. We could sit down at dinner and know with certainty we would be able to finish the meal without violence. We had dinners regularly, which was a new experience for us. In the last years of my parents' marriage, dinners were rarely attempted because they were usually miserable failures. Who could eat heartily in the midst of all that tension?

My new family didn't fight: no more yelling and swearing. But there wasn't any affection, either, except with my mother. I settled for the peace and quiet, and so did my mom—for thirty-one years.

My mom could have divorced my stepfather many years ago. They had been living on investments, and nothing had changed much for them financially for over twenty years. Mom stayed with her husband not because she was blind and developing emphysema, but because she felt responsible for him.

He was "helpless" without her—couldn't even get himself a bowl of cereal. When he retired from his sales job, he retired from any work around the house except for his woodworking hobbies.

It irked me to see my mother wait hand and foot on this man who sat and let his legs atrophy watching golf on TV. I resented the fact that she couldn't come and visit me very often or for long because he got so "lonely." I was bitter when he forced her to come home from blind school, where she was happier than she had been in her entire life, because he "missed her."

She longed to buy her children presents, but he limited her to birthday and Christmas gifts of twenty-five dollars each. The only money she could spend without his inspection was the allowance of twenty-five dollars a month he gave her when she quit smoking thirty years ago.

So now, at seventy-two, my mother has had enough and has moved out. For the first time in her life, she is on her own with some money to play with. Not much money (she lives in senior low income housing,) but enough that she can buy a little gift for her children if she likes or go for a plane ride to visit relatives in Minnesota anytime she wants.

She waits on no one now but herself, and for a change, has all day to think about what she wants. I visit her more often because her home has more life in it now that it is full of her sparkly, fun energy. I hope she meets some lively man in his seventies who likes to dance and go to musicals and play cards. I hope she is still healthy enough to do some traveling.

I hope these last years of her life are her best years. There is no way my mother broke anything when she decided to divorce her second husband except maybe the bonds of guilt that had kept her trapped with him for so many years.

A Little Self-Indulgence from my Soapbox

We romanticize families in this country. Any intact family is better than a "broken" home. I know this isn't true, not only for my mother and myself, but for countless children I have worked with over my years as a teacher and counselor.

There are many reasons for divorce, and many of them are great reasons that lead to a healthier, stronger life. Instead of labeling all children of divorce as survivors of a broken home, we would do better to celebrate those heroes, such as my mother, who have the courage to leave an abusive situation.

I have attended several fifty-year wedding anniversaries, and, while I could respect their longevity, I could see nothing in their relationship to emulate. Just the fact that people were married fifty years is nothing to celebrate. Have they been happy and honest and growing and true to themselves? Or have they been conventional, frightened of change, willing to gloss over abuse and dysfunction because they didn't have the courage to deal with life as it really is? Were they really married for fifty years, soul partners and life mates, or were they merely colluding in a convenient lie?

My mom has been married more than fifty years, if you count both marriages. Most of those years she has compromised herself right out of the best that is in her.

So here's to you, Shirley May, getting a divorce at seventy-two. Go girl!

Poem: Sitting by the Fire

On March 22, 2003, Mom was admitted to intensive care with bronchitis. She had been in the hospital several times and had recovered, so I wasn't terribly worried. When I called her, she sounded fairly good, so I decided to wait a while and see if I needed to go to California to be with her. If so, I would need to arrange for the five-hundred-mile trip.

My mother lies in a hospital bed, barely able to breathe,
and I am here by the fire writing poetry.
I want to be with her, and I don't.

I want to be with her because I would love
to hold her hand and make her laugh,
read her books, feed her,
or drive to pick up her friends who want to visit.
I would love to make her less afraid.

But I am here by the fire writing poetry instead of helping my mom
because part of me doesn't want to be there.
I would have to take a bus, and someone would have to come and get me,
and I would have to wear a mask because I have a cold,
and I couldn't read to her or help her with her medicines,
and I might spill food on her as I tried to feed her.

And I can't bear being in the middle of my own disability
as I try to help her die with grace.

If I knew for sure she were dying,
I would get myself there no matter what,
but I know she will make it through this bout of bronchitis.
Next time she won't.
Next time,
I will make sure I am with her to share in the poem of her death.

Poem: Shirley Living and Dying

Mom didn't get better as I thought she would. She got worse, so I flew down to California to be with her. My brother, my nephew, my mom, and I all decided going to rehabilitation was worth a try, so I helped make that happen and then flew home. Mom hated rehab and was afraid she might die there. I needed to return and help her move home to die.

"If you want to see your grandmother alive one more time, you had better see her now," I told my children. "Next weekend would be better," Martin said. "Next weekend she might be gone," I told him. So Murray, Katie, Martin, and I drove down to visit Mom for the last time.

The ten-hour drive to say goodbye to Mom was full of laughter and camaraderie, though none of us ever forgot our mission. When we got to the rehab center, I knew Katie, especially, would be freaked out by the sounds and smells and the overriding atmosphere of despair and death. She was. That was on a Thursday. We got Mom home on Saturday and drove back to Oregon on Sunday. My brother called Sunday night and said, "The hospice nurse says Mom could go any minute. You need to come back." So, for the third time in a week, I traveled to see my dying mother.

If I had known the timeline, I would have just stayed, but we thought she might get better. We thought she would be in rehab for two weeks and then come home. Even after she was at home, we thought she might linger for weeks or for months. I do not castigate myself for my coming and going that last week of Mom's life. I did the best I could based upon the information I had at the time, and that is the best any of us can do. I am grateful I was with her the last morning she woke up and could talk and the last night of her life. It was one of the most exquisite, sacred moments of my life and always will be a cherished memory.

Shirley dying
was the best of Shirley living.

Shirley dying
was efficient.
Her goal had been to take care of herself
and then keel over.

But she did better than that.
She gave her family two weeks to gather around her.
And in those last few days, at home, in her own bed,
she gave us time
to laugh with her,
love her,
and say goodbye.

Shirley dying
was full of gratitude.
"I . . . am . . . so . . . lucky," she gasped to me when she was back in the intensive care unit.
"I don't know where all this faith has come from lately, but I have plenty of it."
On the phone just a few weeks before her death, she said to me,
"I am not at all afraid to die."

Shirley dying
was full of love.
"I love you" poured from her lips,
as the oxygen tube in her nose filled her lungs with enough air to linger.
"I'm going to miss you all so much," she told us,
as we lay on her bed or stood by the tanks of oxygen
by the pictures of all of us,
too many for anyone but a proud mother and grandmother.

"You'd better haunt me!" I told her,
after she told me no one could ever love me as much as she did.
"You'd better believe it!" she exclaimed.
Exclaimed,
when she didn't have the strength to scratch her itchy head.

Shirley dying
was exquisite.
I wasn't there when she got agitated and banished everyone from her bedroom,

and I would not have enjoyed her being distraught,
but I would have loved her fire.
She was an angel,
but she wasn't a saint.
She could hurl it when she needed to.

Shirley dying
was full of humor.
Wiggling her finger at Murray,
she had him lean down over her so he could hear her whisper,
"I love you, f-head."

"Mom, it's Martin," I told her,
as my six-foot-four son stood next to her bed.
"Tell me a joke," she commanded.
"Okay," said Martin, not missing a beat.
"A minister, a rabbi, and a monk walked into a bar.
The bartender said, 'What is this? Some kind of joke?'"
We all laughed, except Mom.

Mom lay quietly propped up by a half dozen pillows.
"Tell it again!" she said.
Martin,
cheerfully obedient,
launched into his joke once again.
This time she laughed.
Did she raise herself up out of her bed a bit,
doubling over?
It seems to me she did.

But did she tilt her head?
Could she have?
Was there just so much of her personality left
that I could feel her movements even if she wasn't making them?

Maybe Mom should have protected her sacred space better.
She was so good at turning a molecule of consideration
into a mountain of love.
She did this with me,
repeatedly.
"Did you hear that Vicki can sit and cross her ankles? Isn't that amazing?"
All of my slightest accomplishments were astounding,
and all of my defects brushed away as nothing.

"I don't need anything for my apartment," she would say
when she got only a phone call from me for Mother's Day.
It was true. She didn't need any more stuff,
and I loved my mother well.
Buying things for people doesn't prove how much you love them.
Mom taught me that love is a steady, warm beam of faith,
a beam just like the one she shone on me,
the one that nourished my spirit
and guarded my soul
all my life.

Shirley dying
was the best of Shirley living.

The last time she woke up was Tuesday morning when I played her my song,
"My Mommy is an Angel,"
"I really like that!" Mom had said,
cocking her head with delight.
These were about the last words she said,
certainly the last words she said with all of herself in them.
These were her last words,
except,
of course,
for her chant to everyone who came to hold her hand and say goodbye:
"I love you. I love you so much . . ."

I guess I will have to be like Dumbo
and learn that it isn't the magic feather that gives me the power to fly.
My mother doesn't have to be alive
for me to be able to fly.
I hope.

Poem: The Breathing

Why didn't anyone tell me about this breathing,
this loud,
wet,
raspy breathing
that is being wrestled out of my sweet, dying mother
breath by strangled breath?

The hospice nurse told us about the fluid buildup on Mom's chest,
had us put a patch behind her ear to try and minimize it.
Why, then, am I caught so off guard by this sound?

I have slept beside her the last two nights,
with the oxygen machine churning,
Mom struggling for breath,
snoring and gasping.
Then blessed apnea,
quiet moments of peace,
a deep sucking gasp,
then the battle for breath returns.

But tonight,
her last, though of course I don't know it yet,
I cannot bear to sleep with her.
This unearthly sound,
this dying sound,
is coming from my mother,
and it is rattling my courage.

I fear listening to this sound
will shake me from my composure.
I feel hysteria nudging me,
and I know I cannot sleep with my mother tonight.

I feel cowardly,
but I have no choice.
Now I must take care of me.

I stand at the door of Mom's bedroom and ask her silently
if I can step twenty feet into the living room
of her one-bedroom senior apartment,
the first home of her own,
the first home she created with herself at the center,
instead of some abusive or selfish man.

I hold her hand.
She is dying at home
in her bed she loved so much,
surrounded by loving friends and family.
She has met her goal.

My children and my husband have been here:
Katie rubbing her feet,
Martin feeding her pudding,
Murray crawling onto the bed with her and whispering in her ear.
Laughter, gratitude, love and light pour from my dying mother.
Her dying is exquisite, and I am honored to be a part of such a gift.

Then this breathing starts.
Mother is working her way out of this world,
hard work,
like laboring me into life.
It is her journey, not mine.
I feel I *should* be right next to her,

should be holding her hand,
should be earning my gold medal in grieving,
should be proving my daughter love.

I have to trust that this, too, is perfect,
trust that honoring this need of mine
to step away from my mother's death bed
is somehow perfect.
Maybe if I stayed with her,
next to her as I feel I *should*,
I would make it harder for her to go.
Sometimes what looks like love isn't.
Sometimes what looks like selfishness
is an even sweeter love.

I will have to trust.
I will have to trust this breathing that scares and revolts me.

I will have to trust this dying.

Poem: The Delivery

Several months after Mom died I received her ashes in the mail.

My Mom came to our house the other day.
In a box.

My mom in a box.

I don't know quite what this means.
The grief counselor,
in a condescending way, I thought,
suggested that I might want to consider the idea
that my mom wasn't really in the box.

Duh.

WOMAN WITH A VOICE

But what is in the box?

Are they her ashes even, I wonder,
thinking about the scandals.
Could all of my mom's ashes really be in that small box?
Did they crush her bones after they incinerated her?
A Pulverizer,
maybe the machine is called—
huge, loud, dark, and ominous—
crushing the bones of dead people,
beloved or forgotten.

Murray took the box from the delivery man
and set it on the custom-made bookshelf he had loved into existence.
I picked it up and knew I could not hold it long.
With the irresistible knowing that comes from my bones,
I knew I needed to get that box out of my hands.

I walked over to our living room fireplace and set her on the tile,
feeling just a little guilty that I couldn't hold the box
or say something loving or profound.

So there the box of Mom, or whatever is in it,
waits,
in our living room,
next to the stereo speakers,
behind the fan.

I don't know yet what I want to do with what is in the box.

When Mom lay on her death bed,
I asked her if she wanted me to put the ashes
around my garden, and she said yes.
David, my brother, suggested he could put them around his chicken coop,
kidding, of course.
Mom did not like the idea of being split up.

But now I don't know what to do.

When Murray
cuddled on her death bed with her,
whispered in her ear that she would always be in his heart,
Mom had gotten that distressed,
panicked look she got those last few days and said,
"I'm in your yard?"

We all laughed.

I've thought of getting a stone plaque that says:
"Shirley May, Forever in Our Yard,"
but I'm not sure that's a good idea.

I do know I want a place to visit Mom,
whether she is really in the box or not.
I don't want her in a river or in the ocean,
but I don't think I want her in this yard,
this house where we may not live out our lives.
I don't want part of her in a bottle around my neck either.
Do I want her in a vase in my house?
I don't know.

For now I will wait
and listen,
while Mom's ashes hide behind the fan
on the fireplace.

Mom donated her blind eyes to science.
When the men from the crematorium covered her face
with two small white cloths
and then zipped up the bag,
I knew her ashes would be a little incomplete.

Donating her eyes was a generous act, though.
Someone might benefit from her struggle with blindness.
Her retinas were her final gift to the world.

Now it is summer.
I water our garden with the quick-connect hose,
listen to our new fountain,
drink coffee and
listen to books on tape,
as Mom did.

I don't hear her yet,
don't feel her presence,
her guidance,
even though she promised to haunt me.

I have plenty of time,
the rest of my life without her,
to listen for what I need to do
with The Delivery.

Guided Writing: Is This Heaven?

I share these two guided writings because they uncover the process of my grief in a way no other kind of writing can. Every time I write I am guided a little further on the path of healing. I am always amazed how these writings give me exactly what I need at the moment I am writing.

I am walking through a field of white flowers,
a field of giant alyssum.
The hills undulate under the white carpet of blossoms,
and I almost feel seasick,
as if my body is gently rolling amid this ship of flowers.
I don't have my sea legs.

The flowers smell sweet, dainty—their aroma almost palpable.
I twirl in the path and dance in delight.

How did I get here?
Where is here?

The undulating hills of white flowers flow into the horizon.
Am I in heaven? I wonder.
Is Mom here?

Mom loved flowers, mostly Gramma's flowers:
blood red dahlias, purple peonies.
Unpretentious flower arrangements
would grace Gramma's worn laminate counter
and sit quietly on her dinette table in the kitchen.

Mom would be happy if this were heaven.
I would be happy if she were here and this were heaven.

Can Mom romp through fields like this now,
a young carefree girl as she never was in life?

I want to lie down and roll in this carpet of life.
I want white flower juice sticking to my hair
and running down my clothes.
I want this smell of living flowers to remove forever the smell of death.
I want this field of flowers to replace the memory
of my mother in a death bag
with her white hair and face,
her mouth frozen open,
cloth fragments placed on each side of her face
just before the bag is zipped up.

Good-bye, Mom.

I leave the trail now and dance in this dainty white life.
I worry about smashing them,
but they are resilient and bounce back as soon as my foot leaves them.

I see something shiny,
a piece of broken glass maybe? Or a mirror?
It is a mirror, though it is not broken.
It is an exquisite, little framed mirror,
lying amid the sweet flora.
Such a happy mirror!
It is precious. I can't believe my luck.
The mirror feels like Mom, though I'm not clear why.
I love mirrors, and Mom loved clowns,
but this delicate mirror seems just right.
It wants to live with me and be a smiling reminder of Mom.

I dance and frolic through the flowers some more,
singing now at the top of my lungs,
singing better than I have ever sung,
singing songs of joy and gratitude,
songs of wisdom and deep seeing,
songs that reflect back to people their majesty and magic.

A bird comes swooping by my ear.
Not a gentle, tame bird, I think.
A wild, joy-bird.
A coyote bird.
A songster: white and blue and orange and purple.

What is this bird doing here?
What kind of bird is this?
I am not to know.
This is a bird of life, a wild, magical bird
that I cannot control and can never fully know.

We dance together, and the bird becomes iridescent,
like a glass bird with swirls of colors that keep changing.
We sing a duet, a song of life.

I begin to tire, and I'm afraid the bird will leave me.
I'm afraid that if I end this dance I will curl up in a ball of sorrow,
and all the flowers will disappear.
I'm afraid I will be alone. I will be in a field of mud.

My song turns to a wail of pain and loss,
and I fall into a bed of flowers.

For a while all is still.
I can hear nothing but the silence of the dirt.

The scent of the blossoms covers me like a fuzzy blanket.
The wild bird's song changes into a river of melody.
It sounds like a rainbow.
I feel it flowing through me,
through every cell,
marinating my DNA,
and I know that I have become the field of blossoms,
the mirror in my pocket,
and the bird of joy and changing colors.

I fall into a restful, peaceful, deep sleep.

Guided Writing: Heaven: This Time for Sure

I am walking along a trail bathed in a white mist. As I look around I realize I am completely surrounded, cuddled even, by puffy, friendly cumulous clouds. I can see no trail and I wonder where the steadiness I am feeling beneath my feet comes from.

Then I remember *Pilgrim's Progress* by John Bunyan. Just as the hero, Christian, is starting his journey, only a few steps along the path, he falls in the Slough of Despond. He is immediately engulfed, splashing and flailing about, trying to save himself. He has barely begun and already he feels defeated. Then he stops his frantic fight for survival, surrenders a bit, and his feet touch a solidity he never could have found if he had kept struggling. Immediately after his surrender Hope ambles down the path, reaches into the Slough, and gives him a hand up. Maybe I have quit wrestling with the Angel of Death long enough to surrender a little myself.

This billowy peacefulness must be heaven, I think. Mom has just died, and here I am dreaming about a classical cloudy heaven. I smile to myself.

I am happy here, serene. Then I feel a little tired and the clouds immediately rise up to support me, molding a chair around me. My needs are met before I feel them, just as when I was in Mom's womb.

What object will I find? I wonder. (I have experienced this guided writing many times.) The object is my breath. I stop and fill my lungs with sweet oxygen. I remember how much breathing helped me when I was in labor with Katie and then Martin. I was amazed at how much something as simple as breath could help. I gave birth without medication, natural childbirth, and I was a bit too stubborn about it, I realized later. That Darvon drip might have helped a lot.

I feel grateful for my ability to breathe and for the reminder that I always have my breath with me. Now that Mom is gone forever, I feel comforted by this simple truth. Mom died of lack of breath, struggled for years, continually losing her ability to fill her lungs and nourish her blood and her brain. So breath is not so simple, after all.

What animal will meet me, I wonder, and then I hear the answer: it is my music. My music is alive within and around me, but I have never thought of it as a life force that accompanies me.

I am feeling loved and at peace, abundant with my breath and my music. What obstacle could possibly befall me?

As soon as I have this thought, I am plummeting through space, my warm safety replaced by cold uncertainty. The clouds have given way beneath me suddenly and I am out of control, falling into the unknown. Usually I would panic at such a sudden loss, trying to slow it down and make sense of it.

But this time I remember my breath and my music and I surrender to the fall. I breathe deeply and feel my body. I sing and feel my soul. I know that it is not the outcome but the journey that matters. I learn that I have all I need to support me through any loss or disappointment. My job is to remember what I know, breathe, and sing.

How wise my Muse is, I think, leading me on this Guided Writing. My prodigious brain never could have engineered this solution, never could have discovered the wisdom to know how to comfort me so deeply and succinctly. My mother is dead forever and yet I am alive now, in each moment, full of breath and song. I have never been alone and I need never be alone again.

Song: My Mommy is an Angel
(from the CD *Daring to Sing*)

Mom flew up to Oregon for her last Christmas. This song was in progress but it would not be rushed. I told her the first verse, and she asked, "Are you going to put in a verse about my bleeding hemorrhoids?" The last morning of her life I played her a tape of this song with piano accompaniment and harmony.

My mother had polyps on her colon,
and her rotator cuff was torn as well.
She took prednisone for her polymyalgia,
and it made her sweet face swell.

My mother inherited a small gene
from her mother, who was so kind.
My grandma died when she was thirty-four,
never knowing her daughter would go blind.

Chorus:
My mother was an angel with inhalers,
and her cholesterol was too high.
But my mommy, she is an angel,
and we all know that angels never die.

Twenty years ago my mother had one breast removed,
but the cancer wouldn't leave her alone.
So resilient, it returned four more times.
and then it settled in her bones.

But my mom's greatest challenge was emphysema.
It stole her life more every year.
Sometimes she'd call and say, "Vicki it's getting too hard,"
and I'd say, "I know, sweet Mommy dear."

Chorus

Bridge:
I spent the first half of my life wanting to be anyone but my mom.
Now I would gladly settle for being half as strong.

Chorus

Epilogue

We now have a bench in our back yard with the inscription "Shirley May, forever in our yard." Her ashes are in the legs of the bench. Mom would love to know that she is still giving us comfort and support. Bless her.

Shirley May's stone bench under our magnolia tree
Photo by Jan Bateman

Your Turn

Do you have anything you need to write to your mother, to the mother you wish you had or you wish you were? It doesn't matter if your mother is living or dead. If you feel your muse tugging at you, do it now! Split your mother in two if you like and write one letter to the mom who loved you well and the one who couldn't. Write a letter from your mom to you, a letter she might not be able to write in this lifetime, but the letter she would write if she could set aside her shame and fear for a moment.

Biologically speaking, no human parent sets out to destroy her young, but some do. If your mother was unusually toxic, what gifts have you received? You must have an inordinate amount of perseverance to be reading these words right now. Your compassion for others is probably well-developed. Maybe you can turn more of that love light back on yourself and love yourself the way your mother didn't.

Chapter 29

My Daddy is a Stranger

Telling the Truth

My father is not responsible for the pain I still carry. It is my job and mine alone to have the courage to let myself completely feel my pain and allow it to heal, as it will.

I want to make this point clear before I continue writing about my dad because it is too easy to get lost in blame. We are all victims and perpetrators. We all have to get honest about the damage we do to ourselves and to others if we want to set ourselves free to love.

My dad is still living, though I have no contact with him. I am including a chapter about him because to leave him out would feel, well, weird. He is my dad, I do love him, and if he called and asked me to attend an AA meeting with him, I would go in a heartbeat.

How does one have an authentic relationship with someone who practices an addiction? It ain't easy. We all must find our own way, always refusing to pretend that we don't see what we see and know what we know. At the same time, we need to protect ourselves as the sacred space we are.

I did not sever my relationship with my dad—he disconnected from me. In fact, it was I who last invited him to lunch. That was in 1992. We ate in a deli I had chosen, probably a mistake on my part. I think he would have been more comfortable in a Denny's. I gave him pictures of my children, whom he had not seen for years. I also gave him tapes of songs I had written and recorded. I thought he would be interested because he was a singer himself. He accepted my gifts without comment.

After about thirty minutes of my happy sharing about my life and my children, Dad abruptly said, "Are we done?" I guess we were.

I saw him for five minutes at a wedding a few years later, but this lunch was our last conversation. My theory is that it is just too painful for Dad to be around me. I think seeing me makes him realize all he has lost, and it is too painful for him to bear.

Many of my best qualities I inherited from my dad: my love of performing and singing, my gregariousness. Mom was a shy, non-singer. I can truthfully sing "Well Done" to my dad: "Well done, Dad. Well done. You helped me to become the best I could be. You set me free. I love the you I see in me."

It took me a long time to get to the place where I could sing those words and mean them. I had to get to the point where I had forgiven my dad. I had to get to the point where forgiveness was no longer an issue. There was nothing to forgive. Perhaps now is a good time to revisit the notion of forgiveness.

Level Three Forgiveness

Level One forgiveness sounds like: "Oh, that's okay. It doesn't bother me!" or something to that effect. We want to pretend that we have gone through the pain and let go because that is the loving thing, the Christian thing, the Zen thing to do. But forced or faked forgiveness is not forgiveness at all. It is denial, and it is an unsatisfying meal, indeed.

I could forgive my dad when I allowed myself to feel compassion for him and for myself. He has every right to be an alcoholic. He grew up in a culture that knew nothing about alcoholism and other addictions. He was genetically and socially wired to become an addict. Mom said he gave up his heavy drinking for her, and that was when he was fifteen.

Yet his predisposition to become an alcoholic does not absolve him from the pain he has caused me and others. He is responsible for his choices.

Aye, there's the rub! Finding this balance between compassion and responsibility is an art. I make no excuses for my father, but I do not feel any anger either. I feel sadness for all we have lost. But there is nothing to forgive. I would not be who I am today if I had grown up in a stable family. My wounds have deepened me, and I would not change anything in my past.

But I am sacred space, and I will not for a moment tolerate being treated as anything less than that. True forgiveness must be in balance with a commitment to the sacredness of each of us.

Story: "Dad, Are You an Alcoholic?"

When I was in seventh grade, I asked my dad if he were an alcoholic. We were in the kitchen of our home on Villard Street. I was sitting on a stool at the breakfast counter. Dad was standing by the sink, fixing himself some crackers and milk.

We weren't often alone. He worked at his bar until three or four o'clock in the morning, and when I came home from school, if he were home, most often he'd be asleep on the couch. We didn't have little chats; we didn't often speak directly to each other. Thinking back, I can't believe I ever had the nerve to ask him the question.

He laughed, as he crunched the saltine crackers in the glass with a spoon, and said no, he wasn't an alcoholic. "But you have some of the symptoms," I said. (We'd just finished a unit in health class about alcoholism.)

"I know I'm not an alcoholic because I don't drink in the morning," he said, almost bored. I knew that he didn't drink in the morning, and I didn't want to think he was an alcoholic, so I accepted his answer, feeling vaguely foolish about asking it in the first place.

About ten years later, I started to refer to my dad as an alcoholic. Even so, I worked in his tavern as a singing waitress. We used to sing duets when it wasn't busy. Dad sang harmony, while I strummed chords on the guitar. When I was off work he used to fill my glass . . . with Green Hungarian wine. Glassful after glassful—I'd drink what he poured, not wanting to waste "expensive" wine, not wanting to refuse my father's gift.

I drank more than I wanted, more often than was good for me. I drank uneasily. I remembered Dad during my childhood, the violent drunk, the man who kicked in doors and didn't apologize. But I didn't see that side of him at work, so it was easier to pretend. Yes, I thought he was an alcoholic, but I didn't have any sense of what that meant except that he drank too much sometimes and hurt people.

When I was about thirty I finally went to listen to a talk about alcoholism at my church. Until then, I thought I knew all I needed to know about the subject. I was an expert because of my experience. Learning that my family behaved as a typical alcoholic family and that I was a typical "hero" child of an alcoholic relieved me of a great burden and was the beginning of my recovery. This journey, though, has had its share of bumps.

Sitting on that worn plaid couch at that first lecture about alcoholism, I could almost imagine the teenager my father had been, almost feel love for him again. And that made me mad. I didn't want alcoholism to be a disease; if it were a disease, my dad might be blameless, and I'd just have to forget all the pain he caused me because he wasn't responsible for his behavior anymore.

Letter to My Dad, 1989

I wrote this letter to my dad after I had been in counseling for several years. My counselor suggested that it would be a good idea to invite my dad to a session or two. "You're kidding," I responded. "My dad will never come."

My counselor wasn't kidding, and my dad, much to my amazement, did come. He assured me he was happy to talk with my counselor and me, stressing the fact that this was about me and not him.

Before the session we met in the parking lot in front of my counselor's office, and to say it was awkward would be a gross understatement. Dad and I had had almost no contact since I stopped him from telling me a racist joke. We did not call each other, or get together for meals or holidays.

My counselor had Dad tell his version of my childhood, and I sat in shocked silence. His version bore absolutely no resemblance to my memories. He, as it turned out, was the victim! He did not mention his numerous affairs, putting Mom in the hospital, his drunk driving near-fatal accident, or breaking down the door to Mom's bedroom. Sheesh! My counselor had to gently nudge me with the toe of his shoe to keep me from jumping up and screaming.

When Dad finished telling his version of our family history, my counselor asked if I had any questions. Did I! "What about all the violence?" I asked, this question escaping from my mouth like toxic fumes from a volcano. "What about kicking down the bedroom door and forcing Mom to have sex?"

"I don't remember that," he said calmly, "but if you say it happened, it happened. She was my wife, and I had my rights."

I sat in an even deeper shocked silence.

Dad stood to leave, then turned and wrapped his arms around me and cried. I put one arm around him but kept one in my pocket. I had compassion for him, but I also was not going to pretend that pulling your wife across the kitchen floor by her hair is any man's "right."

Confronting my father face-to-face helped me enormously, even though he did not accept any responsibility for his behavior. My counselor had been right, and after this session, I started reclaiming my power in the world. I no longer equated anger with violence or strength with abuse.

As you'll see in the following letter, when I accepted my anger and started recovering my power, I also recovered my joyful memories as well.

> Dear Dad,
>
> I am disappointed that you don't want to come and talk with my counselor and me anymore. I know it was really scary for you and that we talked about things you'd rather forget. I'd like to put those things in the past, too, but pretending they didn't happen doesn't work for me. I was hoping we might be able to meet at a restaurant with the kids. But I don't want to do that until we've had a chance to work through more of our past.
>
> Even if we don't see each other again outside of chance meetings at Gramma's, I'm glad we had one session because I've recovered the memory of the good dad I had long ago. I'd lost that. I remember when we lived in North Bend how you used to read me stories when I went to bed and how you sometimes helped me relax and go to sleep.
>
> When Mom was gone, you would fix whatever we wanted for breakfast and make cleaning the kitchen fun. I liked you best. You seemed more cheerful than Mom.
>
> Then we moved to McMinnville, and I didn't see so much of you anymore. You and Mom fought with increasing violence. I

remember eating a lot of Casey's Bar chicken, but I don't remember playing with you anymore.

You got horses for me at Bellview, and that meant a lot to me. I would have liked it more had you taught me about the horses and ridden with me (you took me on a ride only once that I remember), but I appreciate the effort you took. Those horses were a refuge for me, especially when we moved to Villard Street. That's when the fighting got really bad, and the image I have of you there is either screaming at Mom and beating down doors or sleeping on the couch.

I liked it when you would move out or when Mom, David, and I moved that once to the apartment. I liked the peace and quiet, knowing dinner would be at the same time every day and no one would get mad. I didn't want to move back. Lee said I was being selfish, and Mom said I'd have a whole new bedroom set, but I still didn't want to go. It's not that I didn't want to live with you. It's just that I hated not knowing what was going to happen around home. Some of my friends couldn't spend the night with me because of the fighting. I don't blame their parents. I wouldn't let Katie and Martin spend the night in a home where fighting might break out in the middle of the night.

You have no idea how scary it was for me, lying in my bed, listening to you and Mom and Lee fight. You have no idea how much damage it did to me to have Mom crawl into my bed for safety and have you drag her out screaming. I can't bear the thought of Katie or Martin witnessing such a scene. I've been afraid of men all my life because I was so afraid of you. I was always afraid I'd be next—that you'd hurt me the way you hurt Mom.

I've also thought, in my little girl mind that remains a part of me, that if I'd been a better daughter, you wouldn't have stayed out so late or drunk so much or yelled so much. If I'd been a better daughter, maybe you would have wanted to stay home and pay attention to me. I've always wanted your approval, but I don't like it when you brag about me, when you take a little piece of one of my accomplishments and pretend you know all about me.

I always wanted your time and listening. Just that. Just looking at me and listening, trying to understand what I was saying or thinking, helping me learn what I needed to learn to be successful in this world. A girl needs her daddy to tell her about the world, to make her feel safe. She needs a daddy to help shape her femininity. You could have been that daddy. You had the ability. But you drank instead and stayed out late and had affairs.

You see—we have a lot to talk about.

I used to be really angry; I'm not so much anymore. But I'm not willing to pretend all is well, that there aren't things to talk about between us. It's important for me to have you know you hurt me. I want you to be sorry for what you have done. A sincere apology would help me feel I'd been listened to. And seen. And cared about. I know you have cared about me in your own way, but for a long time, you haven't shown it in a way I could feel.

I had surgery on my right eye again. I'm not driving at night, I need a magnifying glass to read sometimes, and I don't know if I'll be able to hang on to the vision I have left very much longer. I could use some support from you—a card asking how I am or just telling me you're thinking about me—it doesn't have to be much. I've come to not count on you for anything. Because of this, I have a hard time asking anyone for help. So asking now feels like a courageous reaching out.

Again, I appreciate that you came to therapy with me even once. Some part of you still cares enough to risk and to hurt for me. I think you would have been a better dad if you'd known how and if you hadn't drunk so much. I know you don't see alcohol as an issue in your life, but I introduce myself as an adult child of an alcoholic at the treatment center where I work. I give talks on what it's like to be a child of an alcoholic. If you ever want to work on this, I am more than willing to help. I know you won't like hearing this, but I need to say it. I'm tired of pretending.

Who knows where we'll go from here, Dad. If you change your mind and want to talk with my therapist and me, let me know.

I wish you well.

Love,
Vicki

Dad never responded to this letter.

Another Letter to My Dad, 1991

Dear Dad,

I'm having my 40th birthday party tonight, and I wish you could be here. I wish we had a relationship, so we could celebrate our mutual birthdays together. You'll be 66 on Monday, right? I'm not even sure of your age.

I'm sad about all that we have missed, all that we don't know about each other. We're very different, and yet I know much of my passion for living comes from you. We both love to sing. We were able to share that once when I worked at your tavern in southern Oregon. Singing with you, our voices blending, you singing harmony—those were special moments. More special, maybe, because we could have had so many other shared moments together, and we haven't.

You would have made a great actor, and I love being in plays. I'm sorry you haven't been a part of that. Did you know I was the lead in a play at Linn Benton Community College a few years ago? I wish we could have been in plays together.

I probably get my writing ability from you. I remember you used to tell great stories. Did you know I wrote a few columns for our local newspaper before I wrote one that angered so many people the paper wouldn't publish me anymore?

I'm having a children's book published in January: *My Daddy Is a Stranger*. The music teacher at school and I are producing a book and a tape of songs I wrote for our school. I wish you could have been part of that.

When you called last February, I hardly knew what to say. You know so little about me anymore, and I know so little about you. Your version of our life was so different from my memories, when you talked with my counselor and me, that I hardly know where to make a connection.

I blame alcoholism for stealing you from me. When I was growing up, I'd see glimpses of what kind of a dad you could have been if you hadn't drunk so much. Losing you to alcohol wounded me for many years. Your violent temper when you'd been drinking frightened me, robbed me for years of my own anger because I was afraid I'd get mean the way you did.

I've reclaimed my life now, and I don't know that I would change anything in my past. What happened to me is part of who I am. I wrote the poem I've enclosed, "Sometimes My Daddy Is . . ." as a way of filling myself up with daddies. I see so many children who are daddy-hungry. I want to do what I can to give them the vision, the taste of what having a daddy is like. Many of the images in the story I got from you—cowboy, comedian, truck driver, and singer. I tasted what kind of a terrific dad you could have been.

I haven't figured out a way to be with you and still maintain my integrity. That is a failing on my part. I may be able to figure it out. I might not. Right now, being with you hurts me too much.

I wish you well. I pray for you almost every day. I am grateful for what you have given me. If you wrote to me and said, "Vicki, tell me about who you are. I want to know," I would answer. If you would like to write to Katie and Martin and tell them about who you are, your history—anything—that would be great.

Happy Birthday, Dad.

Love,
Vicki

Poem: Sometimes My Daddy Is . . .

Sometimes my daddy is a cowboy.
He has a cowboy hat, a shirt with snaps,
and dust on his jeans.
He knows how to dig postholes
all day long in the hot sun without fainting.
Some of his best friends are horses
because he knows they shouldn't be broken—
they should be gentled.
He takes his time with them,
helping them find their courage.

He talks softly to his horses,
patting them on their necks,
scratching them behind their ears.
When they are finally peaceful,
he sets his boot in the stirrup,
throws his leg over the saddle,
and the horse only swishes her tail
because she feels safe and loved.
Sometimes my daddy is a cowboy.

Sometimes my daddy is a storyteller.
I sit in his lap at night before bed.
We rock together in Grandpa's old chair.
Back and forth, my head leaning against his chest,
feeling his heartbeat against my cheek,
rocking back and forth,
back and forth.
He tells me stories.

Stories of when he was a little boy.
Stories about heroes in real life, his heroes.
Stories about how he met Mom and fell in love.
Stories about what a fine, strong grownup I will become.

And I believe him,
every word.
Sometimes my daddy is a storyteller.

Sometimes my daddy is a truck driver.
He drives down the road,
two trailers filled with logs following behind his cab,
headed for the mill.
His strong fingers grip the steering wheel.
He lets me ride with him sometimes.
I even get to shift gears
or sit in his lap and steer down one-track gravel roads.

We stop at restaurants along the highway,
the ones with lots of room
for eighteen wheelers to line up side by side.
He waves as we drive in.
Everyone knows my dad.
His truck is the shiniest and the safest, they all say.
He is a hard worker,
a dependable man, they all say.
Sometimes my daddy is a truck driver.

Sometimes my daddy is a singer.
He can sing anything, and he does—
songs with yodeling,
or songs about little lost sheep.
Sometimes I sing the melody
and he sings harmony.
We sound like angels.

He sings to me, odes he made up
about something funny I've done.
I have a hard time looking in his eyes
as he sits beside me strumming his guitar.
I am too embarrassed.

When I look in his eyes,
I love him so much it hurts my chest.
Sometimes my daddy is a singer.

Sometimes my daddy is a doctor.
He saves lives.
People come to him afraid,
and he talks softly and touches them gently on the arm.
He catches babies when they are born
and digs gravel out of little boys' knees.
He stitches up little girls' heads
when they've jumped too hard on a bed
and fallen backwards onto the edge of a dresser.

Some people think he knows everything,
but I know he can never find his keys in the morning.
Some people think he is always strong,
but I saw him cry when our dog got hit by a car and died.
He couldn't save our Shep, and he was sad.
Sometimes my daddy is a doctor.

Sometimes my daddy is a scientist.
He can see adventure everywhere,
even under the boat docks at the coast.
I lean over the side, almost falling in,
except his strong hands hold me steady.
"Just a bunch of gunk," I think,
until he shows me
the magic of the tube worms and barnacles.

Down by the ocean,
he points out limpets grazing like cows
on the green algae growing on the rocks.
Who ever would have thought
those little shells sticking to the rocks could act like cows?

He asks me questions that make me think,
helping me connect what I know
with what I am trying to understand.
Sometimes my daddy is a scientist.

Sometimes my daddy is a comedian.
Nobody ever pays him for his jokes,
but he sure makes us laugh.
At the dinner table,
in between the carrots
(that he sometimes eats like Bugs Bunny,)
and dessert,
(his favorite is cherry pie,)
he gets us laughing so hard
sometimes we choke and spit our food out on our plates.
He can make any old boring job, like washing dishes,
almost a party.
I am never sure just how he does that.
Sometimes my daddy is a comedian.

Sometimes my daddy is a potter.
He can magically transform the wet clay in his hands
from a lump
into a delicate vase
or a mask with holes where the eyes should be.
I sit on his lap, and he holds my hands
as the potter's wheel turns and turns.
My daddy's hands hold mine
as we shape the clay together.
Sometimes my daddy is a potter.

Sometimes my daddy is anything I need him to be.

My Last Letter to My Dad, 1992

Dear Dad,

I'm sending you this book *My Daddy Is a Stranger*, because I love you. I wrote it because I deal with so many children who literally have never seen their fathers or don't know where they are. I also wrote it because you have felt like a stranger to me for years, and I wanted to write something that would help fill me up with "daddy" strength.

I'm still searching and praying for ways to have you in my life. I've encouraged you to write me, and the offer still stands. I will write back. I want you to know what is going on in our lives, and I want to know what is going on in yours.

Martin is in 5th grade and growing into a fine young man. He assigns himself homework. He's working hard at learning how to play basketball even though he gets discouraged sometimes. He has a great sense of humor and a kind heart. He's smart, too.

Katie is enjoying middle school. She's a great friend. She enjoys the social scene and still does well in school. She and I belong to a group with five other pairs of moms and daughters. We meet once a month and go on beach retreats twice a year. The group gives us a chance to talk over the tough decisions we are all facing, plus we get to know other moms and daughters. It's great fun.

Besides my book, the music teacher and I have published our own book and tape of songs we wrote for our school assemblies last year. We sent one song to a music publishing company, but we haven't heard back from them yet. I've presented to counselors in Eugene about our assembly program and have been accepted to present at the American School Counselor Association national conference this June in Albuquerque. So, professionally, things are going extremely well for me.

A few weeks ago, I had more eye trouble. I lost the central vision in my left eye several years ago, and now I've had six laser surgeries in my right eye. The doctor says there is a ridge running under my central vision in my right eye that he can't treat if it erupts. I will be legally blind if that ridge blows up. I'm working on healing with some friends on Wednesday nights at 9:00. I'd like you to take a few moments then to think of me, if you can do that comfortably.

I'm sorry we aren't closer, Dad. I wish we were. We're very different in some ways, but I think we share a lot of common passions. Who would have ever thought I'd be singing solos in front of five hundred people (most of them children, of course).

Love and Best Wishes,
Vicki

Guided Writing: A Walk with My Wound

My Muse is smarter than I am and it was in one of my guided writings that I made peace with my pain of not having the family I wanted.

In my waking dream, I walk along a spring stream, swollen with fresh melted snow. It is cold, clear, and pure. I yearn to feel purity flowing through me.

A huge open wound exposes my chest, the wound of not having a loving birth family. I have carried this wound since I was a small child, living in a chaotic, dangerous home. I made peace with my mother, whose love saved me, twenty years ago, but now she is dead.

My wound is a cavern from sternum to collarbone, breast to breast. My heart lies unsafe beneath it. Open and red and deep, my wound is so tender that any feeling of loss, like a tiny piece of shrapnel, infects the sore, filling me with despair.

"Have I done something to deserve this wound? Will it ever heal? Have I ever given it a chance to heal?" I wonder, as I breathe the fresh, snow-scented air along the stream.

I do not believe I have ever let myself walk in peace with this open wound. I have tried to hold the sides of the gaping sore together with clumsy fingers, and I have distracted myself from its raw vulnerability by talking too much or trying too hard, but I do not believe I have ever just "let it be."

I thought I had healed this wound by forgiving my family. But the wound is still with me, easily irritated when I am around big family gatherings like my ex-husband's.

I was never a part of his family the way I longed to be. My wound ached for me to belong, to let me believe that Will's dad could be my dad, could be a spiritual mentor for me and champion my magnificence. He could not do this for me, even though I think some part of him may have wanted to.

There I would sit at Will's family reunions, the little fatherless girl, wanting a dad to love me and care for me as I had not been cared for.

"Can I ever heal this wound?" I wonder. "Am I a cripple? Will this pain last my whole life? I am fifty-two. When will enough be enough already? When will I get over it and go on? Where is the gift in this wound? Is there a gift?"

As I sit by the cold stream, so alive with the season, something floats by and is stopped by a rock. I bend down and pick it up, my hand instantly frozen in the water. The object is small and round. It is a ball, a globe of clear glass.

I once had one of these, and some child I was working with in a school stole it from me. This pure glass crystal has no chip in it. How could that be, tumbled by the water as it has been?

Could I also be pure with no chip in me? Is this wound not a deformity after all? Is my chest open to the world in a way that it would not be without this wound?

Yes, it is.

Is my heart open to the world in a way that it would not be without this wound?

Yes.

Can I heal this wound?

Yes. I will walk with my gash open to the world, protecting myself from infection as best I can, but I will never again avoid the power and gift of my painful history.

A bird lands on my shoulder, a songbird. "Oh, wise one," I say to the bird, "be with me in the journey with my wound, please. I do not want to be alone."

"Vicki," the bird sings to me, "you are never alone, and you know that. I am the melodies flowing through you, the hope in you that never dies. 'Hope is a thing with feathers that perches in the soul and sings the tune without the words and never stops at all.'" (How wonderful to meet a bird who quotes Emily Dickinson!)

I heal in the sun next to a stream that is cold and clean from melted snow, and I am full of gratitude. This path I have taken is my path, no one else's. It is for me to find my way, to find my companions, to sing my songs and dance my dances and have faith that my life is as it should be.

When my wound hurts, I will allow myself to feel the pain, keeping my injury in the open for healing. I will not pretend I am not wounded, but I will not let my wound prevent my laughter or compassion. I will love people as much as they will let me, and I will let them love me as best they can.

My wound and I have become friends, finally.

Poem: A Few Good Men

My dad could have been a good man. When my mother fell in love with him, he was handsome and charming and he had ideals. He was smart and ambitious. After many years of marriage which ended in divorce, three children, broken bottles and broken doors, my father confessed that if he had treated my mother as he had wanted, instead of feeling compelled to prove his manhood by drinking and carousing, they might still be happily married.

I think we should all do a better job of teaching what manhood is really about. I also believe if all the good men decided to make this their mission, violence in the world might almost disappear.

We only need a few good men,
and most of the men in the world are good, I believe.

We only need a few of these good men
to become willing to say, "No,"
"No" to all jokes that demean women,
"No" to all acts of violence against women and children.

That's all.

All we need is a few good men,
like the men who knew OJ was beating Nicole,
to say, "No. That is not cool.

Only cowards beat women and children.
It's that simple.
Stop it.
Stop it now and forever."

That's all we need,
just a few good men:
policemen
who don't write off violence and harassment of women
as merely another domestic matter, private.
Violence is violence,
and rape is rape,
whether you are married to the bully or not.

Women are raised to be victims,
taught not to be too loud (called strident),
or too assertive (called ball-busting).
Women are taught not to speak of their accomplishments (called bragging),
while men are taught to hold center stage,
tell the jokes,
and shout their achievements.
In a man this is confidence.
In a woman it's pushy bitchiness.

So don't shake your heads
at the stupid women who stay with men who beat them
or revile them.
We are taught to seek strong men who will protect us.
If we get confused about what is strong
and what is abusive,
how can you blame us?
You are confused about manhood, too.

But we sometimes pay for our confusion with our lives,
staying with men until they beat us to death.
Or we might pay with the lives of our children,

killed by the men their mothers "loved,"
women who couldn't tell the difference between a strong, interesting man
and a sociopathic, narcissistic coward
who feels powerful only when he is dominating.

So don't hesitate to speak up!
We only need a few of you,
you good men out there,
most of the men I have ever known in my life.

Most of you are good,
but you are too,
too,
too,
too
silent.

Poem: Ju-Ju's Daddy is Not a Stranger

While I am on the subject of finding good men, I include a poem which proves there are miracles in the world. Sometimes love will grow through heaviness and darkness, as a flower finds the crack in a sidewalk and blossoms in spite of its surroundings. My mother gave me more than she was given, and this daddy repeats that blessing.

She's too young to know what "daddy" means,
but she is old enough to be comforted by his male smell
and his smiling, "goo-gooing," undefended face.

His heartbeat sings her to sleep,
and he is intent on cracking the code of her gurgles and cries.
He has put his prodigious brain to work,
creating a world worthy of his brand new daughter.

She's too young to know what "daddy" means,
but she's learning to trust the world,
a world infinitely safer than the one her daddy knew.

Ju-Ju's daddy has surrounded her with more love and security than he was ever given.
And that is as good as it gets.

Ju-Ju does not yet know what "daddy" means,
but she knows all the way into her DNA what a daddy is.

Your Turn

Do you have any appreciations you would like to share with your father? Even if your father has died, you can still write him a letter and let him know how much he added to your life.

Got any father issues you would like to write about? It is okay to tell the whole truth about your relationship. In fact, it is imperative that you tell the truth if you want to be the author of your life. I have heard too many lies about parents: "I adore my mother!" ("You mean the one who beat you?") "My dad and I are really close!" (You mean the one who never defended you from your crazy mother?") Telling hard truths opens us up to feeling the gratitude and compassion that will enrich our lives and set us free. Give truth a chance to help you find peace.

Do you have any response to A Few Good Men? Want to mail it to anyone? Read it at a fundraiser? Let me know if you use this poem—you have my permission. I hope it travels all over the world inspiring people to take a stand for true manhood. A good man who owns his power with humility resonates like a clear bell and changes the world just by breathing.

Chapter 30

Friends: Our Family of the Heart

"A friend is someone who leaves you with all your freedom intact but who, by what he thinks of you, obliges you to be fully what you are."

J.L. Heureux

"She is a friend of mind. She gather me, man. The pieces I am, she gather them and give them back to me in all the right order. It's good, you know, when you got a woman who is a friend of your mind."

Toni Morrison, *Beloved*

As the saying goes, your family is chosen for you, but you choose your friends. The friends I have chosen have saved my spirit all of my life. What each of us brings to the party of a friendship is unique. No recipe exists for what being a good friend should look or sound like. I think there is an alchemy of personalities and experience that can make a friendship exciting, nourishing, and challenging. An authentic friendship is a delicious transformation that occurs when two spirits meet, mingle, and then call themselves friends.

I have a few dear friends, some friends to play with, and many other acquaintances whose friendship I enjoy for five minutes when we see each other at the Saturday market or at art fairs during the summer. Friends of all shapes and flavors are one of my greatest delights.

Our deep friendships, though, require authenticity and hard work. If you get into the real stuff of who you are and who they are, you will probably run into shame and jealousy and other difficult bits of soul. If you can stick with it, your friendship will be even stronger. But sticking with it, through all of the muck, requires grit.

Needless to say, people this hearty are somewhat rare. You might have to clear the space around you of "crazymakers" so your new friends can find you. This may require patience, but friends such as these are well worth the wait.

This chapter is dedicated to all those friends who have touched my soul for years or for only a few hours. I treasure these connections, whether long-lasting or fleeting.

On Friendship

What I want in a friendship:

I like friendships with people who dream big for their lives and dream
big for mine.

I like friendships where our foibles make us laugh from our bellies
until we cry and almost pee our pants.

I like friendships where we reflect back to each other our greatest glory.

I like friendships with flawed people who love from generous hearts,
people who will admit their own mistakes
and be gentle with mine.

I like friendships with people who make mistakes,
apologize,
and then change their behavior.

I like having friendships with people who keep their promises
and hold me to mine.

I like having friendships with people who aren't afraid to work at our
friendship,
people who understand the pacing and tribulations of a true friendship
and can give us time for understanding and healing.

I like having friendships with people who are creative in the same way
    I am
and people who are creative in completely different ways.

I like having friendships with people who define the area outside their
    comfort zone
as adventure,
not so scary they want to stay safe all the time.

I like having friendships with people who like me,
who get me,
who will give me space to be too intense
or too self-absorbed,
trusting I will come back.
I want friends who remember that I am a fine listener, as well as a
    prolific talker.

I like having friendships with people who are hooked on growing
instead of making excuses,
people who know how to settle in deep to a learning.

I have fallen in love with truth
and I love being around people who are also in love with truth.
I love being around people who can help me see patterns in my behavior
I can't see.

I love equal friendships where we take turns being the sad one,
or the helpless one,
or the cheerful one,
or the wise one.

Being my friend is not always easy,
especially if you want to hang on to an illusion or an addiction
and you want someone to pretend you aren't.

What I give in a friendship:

I used to cook some, but now I rarely even boil water.
You most likely will never get a batch of homemade cookies from me
if you are sad or hurt or celebrating.
I am not my Gramma,
who could feed a dozen people who dropped in.

I have never liked buying, sending, or receiving cards much,
so you might not ever get a card from me.
I might bring you some flowers plucked out of my yard,
but that will never be my truest gift to you.

My truest gift,
the best gift of myself,
will be my listening.
Sometimes I can reflect back to you more of your glory
than you might be able to see for yourself.
Maybe I can hear your story and shape it,
retelling your life to you
in a way that helps you treasure your experience with a new appreciation.

When I am at my best,
when my ears and heart are in tune with the secret song of you,
a glorious explosion can startle us both out of our assumptions
and into an overwhelming appreciation of the deliciousness of just
    being alive.

When I am at my best
I give from my unique palate of talents,
give freely,
without counting.

One spirit having a human experience
touches another spirit having a human experience.
This delightful collision of souls is what I call **friend**.

Friendship Chronicles

The next section of this chapter chronicles my friendship with Jan Bateman—confidant, editor, and writing buddy. As our stories mingle, Jan and I "pull back the curtain" on our friendship in a way I have not seen in any other book. Jan and I belong to a mutual admiration society, which will become evident. As Toni Morrison puts it, we are "friends of mind."

In contrast, the second half of this chapter is devoted to the dissolution of a treasured friendship. While not nearly as sunny, I think revealing the bones of a broken friendship can shed light on the value of loving like we'll never get hurt, even when we know loving inevitably opens us to loss and pain.

Poem: A Funny Story

The following is the first poem I wrote which included Jan. We were teaching in the same high school, but it wasn't until we took a class called Journal Writing for Teachers that our friendship deepened. Many years later we started writing together in a coffee shop.

"I've got a funny story for you, Jan," I said,
as she wandered into my classroom for a friendly chat.
"It was my birthday yesterday
and a bouquet of flowers came.
The note said 'Mom and Dad.'

"That's funny because I don't have a mom and dad.
I have
a MomandMarvin and DadandThelma
and JamesandElvira, my in-laws,
but I don't have a Mom and Dad,
so *I* don't know who sent me flowers on my birthday."

I laughed.

She laughed.

Then—
"That's not funny.
That's not funny at all,"
she said.
"My folks have tackled tough challenges,
and unpredictable ups and downs,
but for fifty-four years
they have stayed married
and I might get flowers from them anytime—
and I'll know who sent the flowers
if the card says:
'Love,
Mom and Dad'."

"I guess it isn't a funny story after all," I said,
and laughed, burying my tears—a bad habit.

It isn't a funny story.

Poem: Belaboring the Obvious

Too much of the time many of us are blind to our own beauty and the beauty in others. Maybe if we practice speaking what is obvious to us, our speaking will be like adding bits of colored glass to a window which reveals and celebrates the glory of those we love. Reflecting the magnificence we see is one of the great gifts of friendship.

Obviously, Jan,
you are a great writer
with a gift for storytelling
that fills me with awe
and joy
and sadness.

Obviously,
you have a responsibility
to write the poem of your life,
to weave your exquisite stories
into a tapestry of meaning
and honoring
and hope.

This is so obvious to me;
it must be obvious to you.

What? You say this isn't obvious to you at all?
This talent and love and wisdom you are packing around with you
and have been packing around with you your entire life
is not obvious to you?
Wow.

So who is blind here anyway?

All of us.

Tell you what.
I'll make a deal with you.
I'll keep sharing what is obvious to me,
keep crafting the poem that I am,
trusting that the sharing is good,
if you will keep writing your stories
about what is obvious to you,
not so special,
and surely not important enough
to write about
or read aloud to me.

Let's keep up this
chronicling of the obvious.

Maybe if we do this long enough it will become obvious to us that nothing is obvious.

Obviously.

Embracing the "Obvious"
By JKB

    Vicki takes me out of my comfort zone on occasion. But the "whys of it" invariably reveal themselves. On a day when I was especially concerned that my elderly dad was still driving, I mentioned it to Vicki. I had no time to duck when she snapped, "Why don't you ask him what he's going to wear to the funeral of the kid he runs over and kills." Slam dunk. Vicki is really easy, except when she is not—but I could count on her being purposeful.

    In twenty some years I have lost not a syllable of that comment. But it plays very differently now. Of course, I did not intend to use her script, but it certainly helped me get braced for the responsibility I knew I would have to take soon. Dad made it easy. He knew. And one day, without a word from me, he just handed me his license and said, "You'd better turn this in for me." And that was that. Had I needed to convince him to stop driving, Vicki had given me the strategy, if not the words to use.

    I believe our friendship was sealed right then, over "Dad and his driving." Out there, open, honest, trust-full. Not risk-free. Neither of us played that way.

    After ten years teaching in our high school, Vicki sought new challenges. I spent another ten years teaching right there and during that time Vicki and I saw each other only occasionally. Soon after I retired, we reconnected. In the summer of 1997 we both showed up at the wedding of a young man who had been one of our all-time most delightful and amazing students. We were proud to have developed adult friendships with our Andy.

    Sometime later, Vicki and I went for coffee, pretty stoked to finally share old and new times. And we definitely had something to offer each other. For starters, I was eager for her insights and she had use for my eyesight (and maybe wit and wisdom, in moderation).

Eventually our writing sessions began. Some results of those sharing, growing and energizing times appear in these pages. "Writing with Vicki" is the best club I ever joined.

Poem: Why I Like You, Jan Bateman

This was one of those poems where the title took me everywhere I wanted to go. It is a great question to hang out in: why do I like you anyway?

Here is one reason I like you:
I like the way you like me.

Here is another reason I like you:
I like the way you like other people:
Joyce, Barby, Denny, Rayma, Matt, Susan, Andy, the Baileys—
anyone who has touched your life.

Here is another reason I like you:
You live inside a poem and you know it.
You are open to wonder and connection,
and you laugh with the giant cosmic joke
of being alive and being human.

Another reason I like you
is the way you read my poems,
as if they matter,
as if each image I chose is precious
and should be held and honored.
I like the way you put yourself inside my poems,
the way you wrestle with meaning
and let yourself surf in delight.

I feel honored and cherished when you read my poetry
and I know this is your habit in the world:
to honor and cherish.
I like it that I'm in a big crowd of people you honor and cherish.

I like the way you say "Joyce,"
every time,
as if you have been given this incredible blessing,
and can't believe your luck.

Did you learn how to love people so well from your big brother, Denny?
Yup.
But I'm guessing you have your original "Jan spin"
to the way you connect the dots of people's souls.

I like the way you tell a story,
and I don't know how much longer I will be patient,
waiting for you to write your book.
As soon as you realize what a gift your book will be
to the people you love
you will do it.
You will write every day,
Your love going onto the computer screen
or on your notebook paper.
Line after line of love remembered and reflected.

Precious,
you are,
dear friend.

Being Friends with Purpose
By JKB

Want to hear about nurturing a friendship? I can tell you about that. And Vicki, my friend, ours will be the friendship in the focus.

I pull up your steep driveway in "Taco," my little red truck. It's a '95 Toyota Tacoma, and I love it, but I don't care much about the details—except when the teenager working at the gas station wonders if it belongs to my grandson. Never happen.

You bound, yes bound, down your steep front steps. You swing into the truck and tuck your briefcase ala laptop beside you. God, you move fast. You pat the top of your hat. It's still there. I see which textures and deep, rich tones define your outfit of the day. I don't think you pay much attention to which flannel shirt and Birkenstocks I'm wearing.

"How are you today?" We almost always ask, especially if I'm a little late. (I know if I'm not a little late, you aren't quite sure who may be out there in your driveway.) That question, that social nicety, launches us into communicating about real stuff. And we talk and talk until we've driven downtown to the Sunnyside Up Café and we're still talking while we order our coffee and bagels and then we sit down and talk some more. Often, we laugh or cry, or both. Heartfelt reactions. Over time, we've had much to ponder. We've had grieving to do. And we've had ideas to plant for projects and products.

Our friendship is a fine fit. Our many similarities and vast differences make for a creative complement. We savor language and enjoy its many flavors. We both delight in exploring human communication, and noting both the bold strokes and the subtleties of relationships. We grow from talking to or about just about anybody. And we can actually write together. As I wind down telling you yet another story from my past, you often suggest—in fact, more than often—that I get it on paper. "You need to write it, Jan. "Okay Vicki, when I do, it will be with mighty thanks to you."

Mornings at the friendly little eatery happen every week or two. We usually have some writing project to bring into focus, but not being agenda-bound is great. If we get "visited out," we move on to our writing, you on your laptop, I on a yellow legal pad. A year or so ago, you would bring your poems, both old and new, and let me read them aloud to us. Now many of those poems, old friends to me, appear in *Woman with a Voice*.

As your book has progressed, we have learned that much of the best editing would come via the phone. That way we could both be computer-assisted and connected. What a process. How better to affirm the respect, strength, trust of a friendship. Grooming a friend's writing has to be right up there with criticizing her children. If either of us flinched, we recovered. Being able to edit for you has been absolutely affirming for me.

Vicki, when your good things happen, you do not chalk it up to luck, but to preparation and determination. When bad things happen, you work with what is. I never forget that what you can see is not what I can see. But it's often hard to remember that you "have a visual disability"—you "see" into the important places, you perceive with such clarity. Physically, you have accommodated. You walk the walk every bit as much as you talk the talk. That can be confusing sometimes. I don't know how to explain you to others. "She's legally blind; her vision failed about ten years ago due to a hereditary disease, she can't drive or read regular print, but she seems to do everything. Sometimes, like with cashiers, she has to tell them she can't see. They certainly cannot notice it on their own." I hope it's okay to be proud of a friend's abilities. I know I speak proudly of you.

Even mishaps have turned into memories to treasure. We were in a parking garage in downtown Portland, and I cut a corner too close, scraping Taco's side on a pillar. The noise was frightening; the damage assessment would have to wait. In the moment, you said, "I should have warned you, I could tell you were too close." Yep, we laughed—the blind woman seeks responsibility for the driver's mistake. Why not? It didn't hurt to laugh.

Here's a flat out irony. You have embraced my photography endeavors and I feel so honored. I cannot know what you see as you struggle to get a photo print in the light and at an angle that works for you. But your comments always work for me. You are leading me toward images for the book and photos for other projects I may find.

Vicki, you are the quintessential MMM—Magical Motivation Machine! (I needed to get quintessential into this.) People want to do what's good for them, and you certainly know how to spell out what that might be and how they can do it. You don't make them want to write; you have them *begging to get to write*. I have watched you light up third graders, high school students, and adults. And I've heard about sessions with ages in between. Your knowledge feeds your enthusiasm. Your style engages the willing and converts the skeptics. You rarely have to employ it, but your ability to take a dig and turn it into dignity is amazing. This is not a testimonial—this is a friend sharing admiration.

I think you have become comfortable in the light, actually, in many lights. You have earned that comfort and have made the stage your zone. Any stage. You may be sharing tears and coffee. You may be responding on the phone. You may be leading a writing workshop for a school district. You may be wired up for a Head Start program audience. Or you may be leaning into a Free Range Chix microphone.

One of your times on stage that will always be very special to me came when you and a cast were performing "Six Women with Brain Death," at the Albany Civic Theater. We got to share that with my brother Den. May 2002. He would live only three months longer. Having you two meet, amazing souls that you are, was such a gift for me. He got another piece to the Vicki puzzle, this friend I so often mentioned. And you felt his gentle spirit.

I believe all of the above represents "how to nurture a friendship." What do you think, Vicki? We've become richer—and it is free.

Poem: What She Knew Without Being Told

During one of the writing sessions Jan just described, she talked about her love of baseball as a young girl. When she shared this story with me, a poem started singing in my head. You will be able to read her version of this story in the book I am bullying her into writing, but for now, you will have to settle for mine.

She knew without being told
that she wanted to play baseball.

She was only eight
and a lefty,
but she knew without being told
that she wanted to play second base.

She knew without being told
that the two older girls on the team
were worth emulating.

And she knew without being told
that putting her entire heart
and spirit
on the line for a baseball game
was what she was destined to do.

She knew without being told
she would have to start at the bottom and work her way up.
Her first jersey read "0"
and that was just fine with her.

Two years later,
wearing a jersey which now bore a huge "2,"
she knew without being told
she would be a starter.
She was an important member of the team.
She knew that,
in the deepest part of her being,
without being told.

But that was the season she would be told,
by adamant boys and firm-browed coaches,
that she was off the team.

She had to be told,
as she grasped the chicken wire fence defining the baseball field,
she wouldn't be a starter this year after all.
No girls allowed in PeeWee ball anymore.
New league rules.
The other two girls were too old for PeeWee League now,
so it hardly mattered to them.

Jan would have to be told more than once that she was not a baseball
    player any longer.
"What do these words mean?
Off the team?" she wondered.
She couldn't quite get her mind around her dismissal from the team.

She had to be told
that her anatomy made her ineligible.
New rules.

Ovaries make it harder to catch a grounder.
No, that wasn't it.
Fallopian tubes make it harder to smack a line drive.
No, that wasn't it either.

She didn't have to be told
that it was her femaleness,
her double X chromosomes
that eradicated her as a ball player.

She didn't have to be told
by anything more than the smug tone
and the offhanded cruel delivery
that being a girl
meant you could get stepped on in this world
by any male,
anytime,
and no jury would convict
or even indict it as a crime.

She didn't have to be told
she had a crucial life decision to make:
would this cheap dismissal
of her passion and courage and talent and glory
define her forever?

Yes,
in a way it would.

That day
as her ten-year old fingers crooked
through the holes in the chicken wire fence,
refused access to the playing field,
an indelible vow was planting itself in her.
you can burn me, assault me, dismiss me
if you choose,

but you will never touch the core of me,
never be granted entrance into the sanctuary
of my magnificence.

She knew this finally and forever
without being told

From JKB: Of course, these scars are a part of forever. In the first two years the wounds just did not heal—I was angry, frustrated and embarrassed. But then I found a great diversion—women's fast pitch softball. I could not wait to become the young 'un on the team. They gave me a uniform the day before my thirteenth birthday. Throughout my teen years, I lived for those Girls of Summer months with the Rogue Valley Dairy Maids. And I did become a left-handed second baseman.

Poem: For Denny Bateman of the Great Heart

October 8, 1937-August 22, 2002

Diamond Lake doe with Den
Photo by Rayma Bateman

After six years of living with melanoma, Denny's life on this Earth ended. Jan read a version of this poem to her brother during his last days.

When Jan told me this I cried and made another vow to listen to my Muse and not let my Dinosaur stop me from writing by convincing me that I am self-indulgent and narcissistic.

    To Denny of the Great Heart:

You have two unique sisters.
I have the privilege of knowing the younger one,
the one I'm told you call "Carrot,"
the one who joins me in writer-joy every week.

I hear from the melody of the words she uses
when she speaks of you
that you are a cuddly guy
and a brave one,
though you pooh-pooh how much courage it took
to walk into the room where a disturbed high school student
held a loaded gun.
You don't want to waste our time talking about your heroism.

You've loved your little sister well.
I know because I can see it.
You get at least some credit for her incredible heart,
don't you?
Weren't you always there for her
as she challenged her way in a world
that tried so hard to confound her?
She needed you to be a big heart
where she could rest in your safe love
You have given your love
to Janny K. Carrot
every day of her life.

And now your cancer is taking more and more from you.
You can't drive.
You need help putting on your socks and tying your shoes,

But you have always been the helper, the problem-solver, the rock.
Where do you find the courage to accept this gift of love
your grown-up little sister
needs to give you now?

You are being asked to give by receiving,
a humbler, gentler gift.
Yet receiving opens us
in ways giving never can.
When we receive we are not in control.
We must surrender
and open to our vulnerability.

To give is human,
but to receive connects us with the Divine.

All my life I had told myself the story that I hadn't been loved enough.
Where was the love I deserved?
Where could I find the strength, support, and nurturing I so desperately
    needed?

All around me,
all the time,
was the unexpected answer.

There was always plenty of love around.
my receptor cells were clogged,
that's all.

After my first keynote speech,
People literally lined up to love me.
I wanted to close down,
and shut my heart against their appreciation.

What was this sudden numbness about? I wondered.
I,
the starved one,
saying no to love?

Yup.

How about that?

I meditated,
I opened my arms and my heart,
and promised myself that I would never again
shut out the love people gave me,
in response to the love I gave them.

Who would have thought
that receiving would be harder than giving?
Who would have thought
that when we give we are in control
and when we receive,
when we open to this magnificent accepting,
we are vulnerable to our core?

You know that now, Denny,
don't you?
Soon, when your wife leaves on a long-planned trip,
you will have your beloved sisters, Jan and Barby,
come and stay with you.
Even though it makes your dependence more stark,
even though your losses are mounting up,
no kidding.

You will have to receive this gift of tender care,
or your sisters will not have one moment's peace,
thinking of you alone,

trying to pull up your suspenders by yourself.
If you wanted to torture them,
you would say, "No. That's okay. I can handle my illness without your help."

But you won't be able to hurt them,
so you will say "Yes."
And your receiving of their gift
will be one of the greatest gifts you have ever given them.
And it may turn out to be one of the greatest gifts you have ever given yourself.
You may receive the gift of knowing,
once and for all,
finally and deeply,
that just being around the essence of you,
Denny of the Great Heart,
is all the gift you have ever needed to give.

Thank you for the plant stand
made with such loving hands.
I will treasure the green life it supports,
as I treasure your sister,
forever.

—Vicki

From JKB: Receiving this poem from Vicki was overwhelming; sharing it with Denny was reassuring and confirming. His understanding ran so deep. His appreciation was so open. A few days later, I read the poem to Rayma, Den's wife, and she absorbed it quietly. Too soon, Denny was into his final days. As if Rayma had been waiting for the time she knew was right, she asked me to read "Denny of the Great Heart" to him again. I felt absolutely blessed that I had Vicki's message to share, once more, with my brother. Thank you for the comfort, Vicki.

Letter to Vicki: Adventuring through the Book
By JKB

Dear Vicki,

    Woman with a Voice prepares to "Power Up!" Take off is eminent. The test flights have been rich in discovery and contemplation—served with an abundance of complimentary joy. Thank you for letting me ride along on this most credible journey.

    And Vicki, already another book (at least), is revving on the runway of your mind. Venture on, Brave Woman. Sign me up, if there's room. I'm taking from this experience a backpack chock full of incentives, blessings, scripts, directions, and strategies. I will treasure them and, more importantly, exercise them.

    This book has given voice and substance to special people in your life. Thank you for sharing your Murray. The Cosmos certainly has aligned the two of you. Thank you for introducing Katie and Martin and chronicling their growth from wee ones to the adults they have become. Each time I revisit your mom's life, I wish so much I could have known her. By your words, I have seen her soul.

    You have depicted folks of many stripes—and your intersections with them. You brush, with strong strokes, the power and responsibility of honest communication. But on the flip side of that brush is an absorbent layer, the sponge. Listening is the essence of your magic, is it not? You are a collector of spirits.

    Time and space seem so unimportant when the business of thinking and sharing and spinning goes on. For however long it's been, thank you for hearing me and valuing my experiences. So often over coffee, I would prattle on and then on the spot or overnight you would create poetry that captured those moments I had lived. I am honored to have you include selected "JKB" entries herein.

    And thank you for letting your words return to you from my voice. It was often with disbelief that I would hold your manuscript and read it like I truly knew it. Must be because you had invited me to know you. And you invited me to share some of my words in your book.

The invitation challenged me to use my Muse, amuse, astound, find ground, stand on it and hear myself. Thank you. I needed that. And your patience. It is beyond remarkable, my friend, that you, who seems always ready, can wait in grace while others trail. (Specifically, this *other*)

Thanks for the trip.

With love and admiration,

Jan

The Dissolution of a Friendship

I am including the following material after much deliberation, because I would feel dishonest if I only told the story of a deep friendship that is still working.

Sadie and I were great friends for fourteen years. We haven't spoken in almost two. She lived with Murray and me for four years and then moved out to go on a sabbatical. We had a few e-mail conversations and one phone call after she moved out and that has been it. This breakup is told from my point of view, so I have taken pains to try not to put Sadie in a bad light. I want to validate the challenges of a close friendship without diminishing either person in any way.

The breakup of a deep friendship can be devastating. While my divorce from my children's father will be a source of pain for many years to come, the loss of a best friend has been painful in a different way. If Sadie and I had children together, the loss of love and connection probably would be as difficult as a divorce. But if we had children together, if friends were as deeply entangled with financial, familial, and social connections as a married couple, we might have gone to counseling and worked it out. We got to know each other extremely well, got too close, I'm afraid, and too much of our personal baggage tripped us up, despite our best intentions.

Poem: Sadie, A Friend Worth Having

I wrote this poem before Sadie moved out, before I knew she would ask for a complete cessation of communication. I was still hoping we could find a way to stay connected. In fact, it had never occurred to me that we would ever have no contact with one another. I thought she was family and that she would be family forever.

No matter what she is doing,
she does it pedal to the metal.
A trip to the store,
a walk in the woods,
or debriefing of the day can all be magical events
because Sadie makes them so.
Sometimes her intensity causes her to crash along the roadside
or into other travelers,
but there is something brilliant
about her full-throttled living into any situation.

When I met Sadie, I had turned down the pilot light of my being so much
my fire was in danger of going out.
Graduate school was my attempt to rekindle my life force.
It was a great adventure into the unknown,
away from the predictable and safe world of a small Oregon working-class town.

When I started working on my Master's degree in counseling,
I was sure I would finally be with my tribe:
people who cared about feelings and deeper meanings,
people who wouldn't tell me I analyzed things too much
or that I was too sensitive
or that childhood trauma didn't affect them or me.

I wanted friends who defined the area outside their comfort zone as
    adventure
instead of terror.
I wanted my new friends to be people who lived in the present,
people who spoke their truth
and weren't afraid to shatter conventionalities.

But I didn't find my tribe in graduate school.
I did not find integrity.
I did not find much understanding,
only enough to keep me afloat until a Ph.D. student
whispered to me that I was a star
and shouldn't let any of the professors
try to bully my brilliance out of me.

And I found Sadie.

Sadie did not need rescuing, but I thought I did.
She seemed to have more than enough sparkle for both of us.
If I could hang around her enough,
Maybe her gift for turning assumptions inside out,
her artistic eye, and her talent for making lifelong friends easily would
    rub off on me.

She wasn't very interested in me
when we first met in graduate school,
so I was the one who called.
What an alive life she had.
I wanted some of that.
I wanted some of her.

Well do I remember how she took my neat, tidy, and matching housewife
    persona
and "funked me up."
We spent hours in The Golden Crane shopping.
She pulled me away from pre-planned outfits

and taught me how to combine colors and fabrics in ways I had never
  imagined.
I spent five hundred dollars,
More than I had ever spent for clothes in one setting,
and I have never looked the same since.
I trusted her opinion,
submitted to her opinion,
didn't have my own opinion,
and that was just fine with me.

Not even letting myself have an opinion, though,
turned out to be a bad idea.
I had no sense of my own belly when it came to fashion,
or buying furniture,
or making friends.
I wanted Someone Who Knew For Sure
about all kinds of things I didn't know about.
Sadie seemed to be Someone Who Knew.

She would take my breath away when she would ask questions,
which seemed very bold to me at the time,
questions such as:
"You never talk about your husband, Will.
What is it that keeps you together?"
And I told her,
believing it myself,
"He takes care of my shoes."
(When I fell in Wallowa Lake,
Will carefully moved my wet shoes on the porch
so they would stay in the sun and dry.
His tender care warmed me as well.)

"What kind of an answer is that?" she asked.
My best answer, I said,
but her question had taken me into my marriage
in a way that forced me to wake up to truths I had avoided.

Will loved me the best he could and received love from me the best he could,
but it wasn't enough for either one of us.

I was so hungry for her insights
that I took responsibility for keeping in touch
by calling and being readily available for any of her invitations.
Sadie rarely called me or initiated any connection.

I considered her one of my best friends
and saw myself as only one of millions to her.
She picked up new friends like pennies on a sidewalk.

Then Katie almost died,
and I called Sadie.
She was great in an emergency
and coming a hair's breath away from losing my girl
constituted the biggest emergency of my life.
She told me later it was my calling her
that woke her up to how important she was to me.
That was in April.

The next Memorial Day I asked her to come to our house
and help us create beauty in a cement corner in our yard.
During that weekend, sunny and full of laughter and art,
she sat on our garden-house deck and mused, "I can imagine living here."
"Really?" I said. "That would be a dream come true for me.
Living with a great man and a close woman friend? What could be better?"
She would move in for only a year, she said,
but one year turned into two, then three, then four.

Now Sadie is moving out.
It is a good thing.

Murray and I are ready to have our physical and psychic space back.
Sadie is heading off on an amazing Adventure of a Lifetime,

a journey where she might be able to find out who she deeply is,
away from family,
and work,
and friends,
and me.
The truth is
it is not good for Sadie to be around me
or for me to be around Sadie anymore.

Maybe that will change as she travels through the third world.
Maybe not.
It doesn't really matter.
We have been on a grand adventure together.
I have become stronger,
learning how to set boundaries and limits and stay clear.
She has been listened to and loved well.

Sadie brought many good flavors into my life,
but now our friendship has changed forever.

Vicki and Sadie's Friendship Repair Kit

I wrote this after Sadie moved out, but before she broke off all contact with me. I was searching for a Level Three shift. I did not want to be stuck in being right and making Sadie wrong. I wanted to call us both to the center of love and compassion that had dominated our friendship for so many years.

I never sent this to her because she asked for a complete break from me for an indefinite amount of time and I wanted to honor her request. I include it here, though, because I hope this Repair Kit might be useful for someone else.

In order to honor all the years of their friendship, which began in 1987, and in order to honor the four-year creative living arrangement they had with Murray, Vicki and Sadie do hereby agree to use the strategies here listed to repair their damaged friendship.

Both parties agree to:

1. Hold a space for the possibility that their friendship could become light and easy again, mutually fulfilling and stimulating. Our friendship will have to be better than ever, or it will have to be just a memory.
2. Be impeccable about keeping agreements. This is to avoid either having to say or hear "I'm sorry."
3. Be impeccable about admitting our mistakes.

Vicki's Commitments to Sadie:

1. I will continue to send my poetry and other writing to help you know what is going on with me. Communicating this way doesn't involve conversation, which is difficult for us right now.
2. I will continue to imagine that you are with us at holiday times when our relationship was at its best.
3. I will commit to releasing all unforgiveness by giving unconditional love to myself and to you. I will practice this every day.

Sadie's Commitments to Vicki:

(Sadie to fill in her commitments.)

Sadie and Vicki wish each other only happiness, joy, and the satisfaction of living out their own, individual truth.

Namaste.

Poem: Sadie and Vicki: A Celebration

When Sadie requested an end to any contact between us, she also told me she had given me more than she had any other person. Despite all she had given, it seemed she continually let me down, she said. She needed space, she didn't know for how long, to get stronger in herself before we renewed contact.

Her comment about giving me more than she had given anyone else hurt and upset me. Did I ever ask her to do more than she wanted? No. Was there any way I could have prevented her from giving too much and trying to please me? No. This was the heart of our problem, I felt, but I was powerless to solve it by myself.

Not wanting to end on this note, I waited a few days and sent what follows. She responded with a celebratory list of her own, which I am not sharing here because I do not have her permission. It was full of love and appreciation, though, and helped me live more peacefully with the abruptness of her disconnection.

Our coming together was perfect,
giving each of us the teacher we needed,
and our separation is perfect as well.

We survived a psycho supervisor and professors who didn't ever come clean.
You changed the way I dress forever
after only one afternoon of shopping at The Golden Crane.
I got you into public schools,
and you pulled back the curtain on the magic of play therapy for me.

You let me stay with you when I needed a safe harbor for a trial separation.
You came and slept with me when I was terrified after I finally moved
    into a duplex.
You were there completely when Katie almost died,
ready to do anything I needed.
You were at Artichoke Music when I bought my Martin guitar,
sitting on the floor in the corner,
crying over your breakup with your lover of two years.

We camped together,
swam in the summer Santiam River,
and watched your grown niece pout as she went to get firewood and
    gave up.

You scooped me off to the beach when I was drowning in my hormonal
    madness.
You saw and loved the glory of Murray
and drank in the majesty of him as he taught us Aikido on the beach.

We taught college classes in the summer together,
summer after summer.
We collaborated at your elementary school,
spending many hours driving and talking,
some of our best times.

We holidayed together,
sumptuous dinners you cooked and my family ate with delight.

We gardened together,
planting pots of flowers and building a pond,
shovelful by shovelful.

We partied together,
crafts and food and laughing and music.

We danced, created,
laughed and cried,
yelled and then made up.

Your art continues to feed us:
your gorgeous mosaics,
sprung from your soul.
The Sedona Room,
the garden mural in the bathroom downstairs,
the mosaic birdbath you made for my fiftieth birthday,
the one that still isn't quite sure where it wants to live.

We lived together for four years,
an amazing experiment in intimacy.
Murray and I are stronger for it,
more appreciative because of your reflecting back to us
our remarkably rich interconnection.

We have been intimacy warriors ourselves,
you and I,
have had a relationship unlike any I have known or will probably know again.

You gave your best to us,
and we gave our best to you.

You and I are forever changed,
forever better,
forever connected,
whether we ever hear each other's voice again or not.

Blessings to you.

Epilogue

Several months after Sadie returned from her sabbatical in Central America, she came and got the rest of her belongings from our house, garden, and garage. I chose not to be present when she came through our home for the last time.

I doubt we have a future as friends on the physical plane, as they say. I am no longer the Little Girl in Gray and she needs space to find solidity away from me. We learned from each other and our friendship was perfect for both of us. The perfection didn't always feel good for either of us, but I think Sadie would agree that it was well worth the ride.

Your Turn

Do you have any friend from any time in your life you would like to honor with a letter such as the one Jan wrote for me? Write it and send it, if possible. If your friend has died, it is never too late to send such an epistle to someone who loved your friend as you did. Love and friendship are so precious—let us leave markers on this most remarkable, human journey.

Have you had a friendship you valued end in divorce? Are you satisfied with how you handled it? Would a letter of apology help? How about writing a letter of appreciation of all you received from the friendship, without mentioning the problems? Are you still hurt? You might want to write a "How Could You?" letter for yourself to help purge you of the debris left in your heart.

You might want to start some conversations about broken friendships with the friends you have now. We don't talk about this much, so we don't have the skills and perspective to deal with our pain. Pull back the curtain and see what happens.

Part IV

Saying Aloha

"Whatever you can do or dream you can, begin it; boldness has genius, power and magic in it. Begin it NOW."
—Goethe

Chapter 31

That's All For Now!

I hope this book has been as much fun to read as it has been to write. My Dinosaur has fought with me throughout the process, but the fact that you are reading this means it did not win.

I do not know if this book is any good. I hope it will be helpful, and I do know that my intention was to be honest to the bone. I am acting on faith, hoping that by sharing myself honestly and deeply I can make a difference for myself and others.

But whether this book is any good or not, does not really matter. If I sell no books, it does not matter. Whether *Woman with a Voice* becomes a *New York Times* best seller for 68 weeks does not matter, either. The money would be nice, to be sure. Having a best seller would enable me to continue singing, speaking, and writing, which would be great. But I have to trust my angels here. Whatever happens is perfect.

So, Bethany, Shaen, and everyone else who has joined me in the adventure of this book, take the gifts that resonate for you and live your lives as fully and as beautifully as you can. Thank you for letting me be a part of your journey.

Blessings,
Vicki Hannah Lein
March 2005

Story: The Joy of Writing?
By Effie I. Clendenon

Effie took a class from me the summer before I finished this book. I include her essay, which I "forced" her to read to the rest of the class, because her experience so clearly illustrates what happens when we surround ourselves with people who encourage us. Her Muse came out to visit, big time, and I am delighted to be able to share the results of that visit with you.

I was a first grade teacher and I needed a pay increase. Scanning through the catalog from the educational company I prefer, I was trying to fit in 12 college credits that would be accepted by my district into a summer already full with family obligations. Try as I might, I could not avoid a class that sounded particularly distasteful to me, if I wanted that coveted pay increase. Teaching Students the Joy of Writing, UGGHH! How could you ever *teach* JOY of writing if you found no joy in writing yourself?

So afraid that a class on teaching the JOY of writing would hold the expectation that I actually write something, I was sick to my stomach. Several times that summer I toyed with the idea of dropping the class before it started, but I needed that raise. I have always been a "good" student, able to please instructors, act appropriately, and hand over products that met teachers' expectations. I decided I would just have to grit my teeth, jump through the appointed hoops and suffer through the class silently. Keeping my eye on the prize should enable me to do so.

Still, my fear of writing for an audience forced me to devise a means of protection. The night before the class began, I chose two topics to have on hand for those dreaded words, "Now, it's your turn to write something so we can see how you do and give you any required help." The translation would go something like this, "Now it's time to show us how awful and inept you actually are at writing and let us rip you to shreds."

I was completely unprepared for what, or should I say, who, was waiting for me in that class! Vicki Hannah Lein! Completely charming and disarming, Vicki is a master at her craft. Her style, sense of serious humor, and ability to make the environment so open, unrestricted, and safe cracked my armor just enough to let out my secret. I had always wanted to write books for children.

As a youngster, I was open and proud of my desire. Offering innocently to all who inquired, "What do you want to be when you grow up?" that I wanted to be an author. The admission was almost always met with laughter. It only served to make me more determined. That is, until the seventh grade.

Mr. Duncan had us disclose what we hoped to be as adults. When my turn came, I proclaimed that I wanted to be an author. Somehow the combined laughter of 24 classmates served to melt that dream, pour the molten liquid into a bottle, and seal it tight. A time or two I dared to unseal the bottle just a little, but feeling burned when I attempted to reveal the contents, I sealed it even tighter.

Halfway through that first day of Vicki's class, without even realizing it was slipping out of my mouth, I offered that I always had wanted to write children's books. The class seized upon that dream, encouraging me and helping me to believe that perhaps I could write something worth reading.

That night I had to fight back tears. Why had I opened my big fat mouth! What made me think I could write books! I must think I was really something, an author? Right! Several times that night, and during my shower the next morning I had to spit on my Dinosaur. "Ptooie! I spit on you!" I said aloud dozens of times. I felt foolish, but it made me feel better, safer, stronger. Vicki had said it would.

On the second day, Vicki asked how we had felt the evening before. When it was my turn, I confessed that I had had Dinosaur trouble and had to say, "Ptooie! I spit on you!" a number of times. The whole class laughed. This time, however, the laughter was not directed at my destiny, but at the Dinosaurs we were all battling—the whisperings that tell us we are not good enough, not smart enough, not whatever enough to have and do wonderful things. This time, the laughter was empowering, like Vicki herself—fun and freeing and fresh.

I left the second day knowing not only that I could write, but that I would write. I have to write. It is the purpose of my being. Perhaps my writing will not be well received by any but my closest family and friends. Perhaps not even by them. It no longer matters. The bottle has lost its ability to be sealed. Its contents, kept silent so long, now boil over and spill onto paper. That is enough.

From Vicki: Isn't Effie amazing? Isn't her Muse patient and determined? Isn't this process awesome?

Poem: What If?
By Karen Bowers

    A teacher from an elementary school I worked with wrote this poem. Since it embodies so much of what this book is about, I just had to include it.

I want to begin pondering new possibilities . . . what if?

What if I were 100% me—
not afraid of the judgment that comes from others,
from their eyes, their body language,
their whispers,
even when they don't say it to my face?

What if I could internalize the idea that I AM EQUAL?

What if I could live the idea that different is OK?
What is "different" anyway?
Aren't we all different?
Maybe everyone is actually running scared,
afraid that someone will discover their differences.
Maybe I'll celebrate my differences,
announce them to the world,
standing firm and tall and proud.

Maybe I'll turn my face to the sun and stand with my arms open wide,
pulling in energy and then pouring it back out into the universe.

Maybe, just maybe,
my courage will be a beacon that calls others home as well,
and then we could just be different together,
instead of the same
and oh, so alone.

What if new possibilities begin now?

What if?

Story: Creating the Song *Beauty Like a Rock*

Julia Cameron, in her book *The Artist's Way*, writes about taking yourself and your inner artist on a weekly "date." You can go anywhere on these dates—to a grocery store, to an art gallery, to a craft store, or for a walk. The goal is to let your artist lead.

My woman's group had gone through *The Artist's Way* once, and we had all benefited. Because I couldn't drive, I had a hard time arranging artist dates. What I wanted to do required vision, and we were supposed to do these dates alone.

The second time I went through the book, I decided I would be very intentional about my artist dates. Rather than just taking a few hours of a day, I would, in fact, give the whole day to my inner artist. I called them my Genius Days.

On my first Genius Day, I woke up with "WarriorBabe" in my head. I looked forward with great anticipation to my second Genius Day, hoping I would hit pay dirt again. Alas, Murphy's Law prevailed. I woke up tired and lethargic. All I really wanted to do was lie by the fire and listen to a book on tape.

Because my only rule on a Genius Day is that I do only what I feel like doing, I honored my desire to sleep and curled up by the fire and napped.

I was listening to a book of essays by Alice Walker, author of *The Color Purple* and *Possessing the Secret of Joy*. I fell asleep as I listened to her, not because the book was at all boring, but because the lyrical nature of her writing lulled me to sleep.

I wondered, as the day progressed, how this would be a Genius Day if I didn't produce anything. Then I would stop worrying and say to myself, "I guess this is what this particular Genius Day looks like," and then I'd nap some more, sacred napping I know now.

I was drowsily listening to one of Alice Walker's essays when I heard the phrase "beauty like a rock." I sat bolt upright, turned off the tape recorder and wrote the song. The song landed on me, complete—a grand gift indeed. (Boy do I love taking dictation from my Muse.)

"Oh," I thought to myself, "This is how this Genius Day looks.

How interesting. This day was perfect as it was. If I had given in to my shame and doubt and forced myself to 'get productive,' I would have stopped before I got to the phrase 'beauty like a rock.' I would have missed my chance, my Muse, and my song."

I love this story because it reminds me how important it is to trust what happens—to not get caught up in thinking my experience "should" be different. If I just relax into what is before me in the moment and see where it leads, I stumble into these amazing, angelic gifts. I couldn't have set a goal to write "Beauty Like a Rock." I hadn't heard the phrase. I wasn't listening to Alice Walker to find a song. I was listening to Alice Walker only because I felt like listening to her.

Actually, I had meant to order something from the Library for the Blind by Alice Hoffman but accidentally said Alice Walker instead. My subconscious knew what I needed, or someone or something did.

Maybe this was all accidental, but I find it curious that when I call forth a Genius Day, wonderful accidents happen to me. (My third Genius Day culminated in "Come to the Cliff.")

I have beauty, strong as stone, growing in me. Wasn't it clever of my beauty to get me napping and listening to Alice Walker? Haven't I tried to shame myself out of my beauty or to organize it or to pretty it up, and hasn't it successfully resisted all my attempts to fix it or control it?

Hasn't my beauty been there since I was five, singing into the record maker my dad had for a few weeks? Or when I tried out for a talent show in third grade, singing "Blue Moon" a cappella? And when I kept on singing even when I didn't make it into the talent show? Hasn't the beauty and fire in me stubbornly outlived all of my attempts to snuff it out or bend it to my will?

Doesn't the eternal whisper of my inner beauty help me see beauty in every child I meet? And in adults? I see it even when they can't. Isn't this what has blessed me and driven me crazy all my life?

Don't I have this beauty like a rock growing in me and isn't it growing in you and in everyone else as well?

Song: Beauty Like a Rock
(from the CD *Alive, Alive*)

> *Imagine five-year-olds singing this with joyful abandon. Kindergarteners can be very earnest, especially when they are looking into another child's eyes, singing:* "You've got this beauty like a rock growing in you."

Got this beauty like a rock growing in me.
Got this beauty like a rock growing in me.
It is tough. It is forever. It is real, and it is clever.
Got this beauty like a rock growing in me.

You've got this beauty like a rock growing in you.
You've got this beauty like a rock growing in you.
It is tough. It is forever. It is real, and it is clever.
You've got this beauty like a rock growing in you.

Gonna honor the beauty growing in me.
Gonna honor the beauty growing in me.
Gonna save it. Gonna share it. But I never will compare it.
Gonna honor the beauty growing in me.

You've gotta honor the beauty growing in you.
You've gotta honor the beauty growing in you.
You can save it. You can share it. But please, never do compare it.
You've gotta honor the beauty growing in you.

Gonna follow the beauty growing in me.
Gonna let my beauty set me free!
Gonna listen and obey. Gonna let my beauty show me the way.
Gonna follow the beauty growing in me.

You've gotta follow the beauty growing in you.
You've gotta follow the beauty growing in you.
Please listen and obey; let your beauty show you the way.
You've gotta follow the beauty growing in you.

We've got this beauty like a rock growing—it's true!
We've got this beauty like a rock growing—it's true!
It is tough. It is forever. It is real, and it's clever.
We've got this beauty like a rock growing—it's true!

Poem: Africa Singing

In November of 2004 a miracle occurred: I was invited to present at the Association of International Schools in Africa in Dakar, Senegal. Never could my nine-year-old self have dreamed she would make such a trip.

The second day of the conference I was asked to lead the participants in a song at the opening plenary session. I had worked with a group of twenty-five the day before and ended the session with raucous laughter, receiving a standing ovation as thanks. (Just for the record, I like standing ovations just fine.) I stepped up on the platform, a little nervous, and said, "Could my group from yesterday give me a wave?" On the right side of the room about a third of the way back a group of arms waved with enthusiasm. I was home. Encouraged, I taught the words and the accompanying sign language of Beauty Like a Rock.

The joyful energy of the group almost knocked me to the ground. Beauty *is a gospel song and I had always dreamed of teaching it to a group with gospel in their bones, but I had never before had such an opportunity. Yet here I was, in a city I had to look up on the map, on a continent I had never known I wanted to visit, leading this group in a song they sang as if they had been waiting to sing it their whole lives. I started to cry. This was even better than being on Oprah!*

I am singing in Africa.
I am singing in Africa in color.
I am singing from my belly,
and my toes,
and my heart,
singing from the Source
to the Source,
surrounded by the Source,
singing to the stars

And I will never be the same.

"We've got this Beauty like a rock growing in US!" we thunder
and the stars lean toward us to listen,
the magma at the center of the Earth smiles.

We will never be the same.

A Final Poem: As It Turns Out

Well.
As it turns out,
I am not alone.

As it turns out,
I have two children who are bonded to me by blood, and history, and love.

As it turns out,
I have a husband
who is bonded to me by vows, and history, and love.

As it turns out,
I have friends
who are bonded to me by history and love.

As it turns out,
I have people in my life
who are willing to hang out in subtleties with me,
willing to experience every crack and sharp edge of my soul.
I have people in my life who are willing to play with me—
laughing at inside jokes,
dancing in the kitchen,
and gorging on the deliciousness of Jon Stewart and The Daily Show.

As it turns out,
I am rich beyond my wildest imagination:
rich in garden
and harmony,
creativity and audience.

As it turns out,
all my wishes have come true.
Well, how about that?

Your Turn

What beauty in you needs to be honored and followed? When do you practice denying your genius and when are you going to stop? Do you commit the "little murder" of comparing yourself to others? Stop it, already!

Are you the same person you were when you started reading this book? I know I am not the same person I was when I started writing it. How have you changed? What promises have you made to yourself? Are you going to sign up for that art class? Do you want to take singing lessons? (I highly recommend Claude Stein, who teaches a Natural Singer workshop. You can reach him at vocalsman@aol.com.)

Whatever musings you choose to follow, bless you, and may the world be a little better because you have lived.

Remember: Muse it or lose it!

Glossary

Murray and I have developed our own language over the years based on our partnering exploits. I have included some of our code words and phrases here in case I didn't explain myself clearly in the text.

"Actually, This is a Good Thing!"

To shift a situation instantaneously, just say, "Actually, this is a good thing!" when something goes wrong. For example, "Actually it is a good thing that I am stuck in this traffic jam! Now I have time to think about everything I am grateful for in my life."

"Are We Having a Fight I Don't Know About?"

Murray said this to me once when I was going on and on about something. I thought I was having a nice Level Two discussion, when really I was nailing him for some behavior he had done or failed to do. His question brought me to my senses and helped me own up to my anger.

Bellytime

For years it has been our practice to have bellytime every day when Murray comes home from work. I lie on the couch and he lies on top of me and I stroke his hair as we talk about our day. We use no structure, just stream of consciousness. This is one of our best practices. It keeps us connected and allows for random thoughts to surface.

Big Rocks

I heard once of a speaker who brought out a large jar and filled it with big rocks. "Is this full?" he asked his audience? "No." So he poured in pea gravel. "Is it full now?" he asked. "No." He poured in sand, then water. "What is the message here," he asked. "It is not that we can always fit something else in. The message is that if we want the important things to be in our lives, like exercise and love maintenance, then we have to put those 'big rocks' in first or they won't fit in at all."

Bitch of the North

This is what I am afraid I will become if I allow myself to be angry or take a stand for my sacredness. My Dinosaur Voice threatens me with this all the time. "If you get too ugly, people will leave you and you will be all alone," it says with a heartless glee. I have learned to say, "Maybe so," to this voice and plod on anyway.

Cosmic Teat

The giant rescuer in the sky. We hate to admit it, but sometimes we want all of our challenges to go away so we can suckle on the Cosmic Teat of All-Accepting Love. When we try to force another living, breathing human being to be our Cosmic Teat, we are in big trouble and so are they.

The Couple's (or Friend's or Family's) Coupon Book

Create a coupon book of gifts of time and attention for your sweetie, your children, your parents, or your friends.

Some examples:

This coupon entitles you to:

- One hour of being right.
- Three free complaints.
- One half hour of massage.
- One afternoon of "honey-doing."
- An Authentic Listening session where I go first.

Courage Muscle

Muscles atrophy without use and if we practice being cowards, our courage muscles will shrivel. No matter how weak our muscles are to start with, we can begin a daily practice of getting braver. Small steps taken regularly lead to big results.

Coyote or The Trickster

Coyote wants to help us let go of our stubbornness and set us free. His "gifts" don't always feel good. He will trick us sometimes, making us laugh at ourselves. I think Coyote helped me walk off the dock of Wallowa Lake when I believed I could control the pain in my life if I were extra careful. It takes a big splash to wake us up sometimes.

Default Outcome

This is what happens if you just lift up your feet and let your life happen to you. If you grew up in an alcoholic home, for example, just lift up your feet and you will have an addiction or marry someone who does.

Dinosaur Voice

This is the voice inside us that steals our joy, our hope, and our right to inhabit a space on the planet. This is the voice that says, "That is a stupid idea!" or "Who do you think you are?" Every bad evaluation or critical comment is fodder for the Dinosaur Voice inside us. The voice can be loud and bullying or it can be sneaky, like a snake hissing in our ears, "You are a fraud," it whispers. "You are being found out."

I teach people to turn to this voice and say "Ptooie! I spit on you!" This must be done, for some reason, with a French accent.

Do-Overs

Do-Overs are fun and instantly shift negative energy. Very simply, when you realize you have blown it, ask for a Do-Over, just as you would in a volleyball game when no one is sure whether the ball was in or out. Let go of being right and just get back into the game with what you wish you had said or done.

Down Time

Unless we make down time a Big Rock, we will be pulled into busyness and away from our knowing center. Murray and I have down time together when we do bellytime, but we also have down time alone to just "veg." People often say to me, "Where do you get your energy?" or "What vitamins are you taking?" I respond by saying, "You should see me nap!"

Entertaining a New Idea

When you invite a new idea, no matter how outrageous, into your mind for a congenial visit and a cup of tea, you aren't committing to letting this idea move in with you; you are just giving your unemotional attention to a new possibility. It can't hurt to entertain a new idea. You can always throw it out.

Finger-Holding Confessions

A method of getting those thoughts out of your head that won't go away, the thoughts you aren't proud of and don't really believe. Announce that you have a confession and ask if now is a good time. If it is, have your beloved hold your index finger as you spew out your "horrible" feelings and thoughts, clearing out your belly. The **only** response your beloved can have at this time is "I love you."

Ginger Pig

This phrase comes from a Japanese lunch date where a dear friend of mine accidentally ate most of the pickled ginger. She felt horrible and called a few days later to apologize for her "crime." We started laughing and since then "being a ginger pig" reminds us that we do not need to take ourselves so seriously or to take care of everyone else's needs all the time, for crying out loud!

"Help Me Understand"

What you say when you are ready to really listen. This is a Level Three shifting comment. Stay put in your listening until you are sure you do understand, and then you can ask if you might be understood as well.

"How Many Stops Do We Have to Make?"

If men aren't careful, they can become old farts. Early in our relationship, Murray and I were on our way to Portland and had stopped a few times for various reasons. When I suggested we stop at a little store to pick up some bottled water, he said irritably, "How many stops do we have to make?" Crabby, crabby, crabby. "What difference does it make," I replied. "So we get there a few minutes later."

Murray came to his senses, laughed, and now if either one of us drops into "old fartedness" the other will cheerfully say, "How many stops do we have to make?"

"Huh"

What you say when someone offers a comment that is insulting, inappropriate, or inciting. It is a response that is not a response. You don't invite an argument, but you don't let the comment take on momentum. You can also try "That's an interesting perspective" if you think you can get away with it.

Intimacy Warriors

Intimacy Warriors will settle for nothing less than the real thing. No pretending is tolerated. We want only the truth, whether it is pretty or not. "I let you in and you let me in" is our motto.

"Is There a Request Buried in There Somewhere?"

Another brilliant Murray intervention. As I was airing a laundry list of complaints, Murray asked this question and again shifted me out of Level One into Level Two. Switching from complaining to requesting changed the entire nature of our conversation and helped me stop practicing a bad habit and start practicing a relationship-enhancing one.

Level One Responses/Reactions

Responses require using our wisdom, caring, and courage. So technically, Level One responses are reactions. We do them without thinking, even though we may justify them with slogans that might sound "logical." "He hit me first!" may sound reasonable, but it is really an excuse to do what feels good in the moment. "Everyone else is doing it" is an excuse to be dishonest or mean, but it does not involve wisdom, caring, or courage.

These reactions come from the Dinosaur part of our brain and are based on fear. We want to be right. We want to avoid shame. We want to have power over others. We want revenge. Level One reactions are addictive and perpetuate and exacerbate our problems. All addictions live here as does our need to control.

Level Two Responses

Only when we realize that Level One responses are making our life worse, do we turn to Level Two. At this Level we do not care who is right anymore. We want to find a win/win solution, and we are willing to do the work to get there. This Level does not have any emotional jolt to it.

Level Three Responses

Now we have entered the land of mystery where obstacles are transformed into gifts. We forgive, feeling that delicious release of true forgiveness. We feel compassion. We listen deeply. There is a Level Three response to any situation, but they are not always easy to find. Knowing that a Level Three is out there somewhere, though, helps me not drown too long in the self-indulgence of my Level One reactions.

"Maybe So"

What you say to the Dinosaur Voice in your head or to someone who is imitating the Dinosaur Voice in your head.

Murphy and His Law

I think Murphy's Law (If anything can go wrong, it will go wrong) is fairly hysterical. When I make friends with Murphy, knowing that he will show up whether we're friends or not, then it gets to be funny when the third electronic device in my home breaks in a week. Time to pick up my feet, point myself downstream, and ride the rapids because I am not going to be able to control anything anyway. Murphy and Coyote are cousins.

The Muse

The Muse is in all of us, it is always full, and it is full of more than we could ever imagine or control. We need to practice listening to it, listening for its subtle urgings and nudges, and our lives will be instantaneously transformed. We need to have the courage to do what it asks: "If you build it, he will come." We need to be willing to look like idiots, if need be. If we practice, we will hear this call more often and we will get used to living with its wild, alive energy running through us. We will be "bemused," full of humor and perspective, and life will never be quite the same. (If you are hearing in your head that you do not have a Muse inside you, that is your Dinosaur talking. Ptooie!)

"Ow!"

What to say when someone says or does something that hurts. Giving an "I message," (I feel hurt when you speak to me in that tone) works well, but sometimes our brains just can't process that fast. "Ow!" says it all without blaming.

Owning Your Own Farts

The habit of admitting your mistakes quickly and completely

Pop-Up Timer

You know those timers in turkeys that pop out when the turkey is done? Murray coined this phrase when we were out having a lot of fun, but he was done. His pop up timer was out. That says it all.

Power Rock

In the first few months we were together, Murray helped me understand, in a humorous way, how I was taking responsibility for everything. He called this bad habit my "power rock." We were walking on a beach in Mexico and he said, "Well, if you are going to be carrying such a heavy load, why don't you carry this rock so you can feel it?" He handed me a BIG rock and I carried it for a while, laughing. He was so right! He had caught me, setting me free from my self-imposed delusional sense of responsibility. I fell even more in love with him. What a man! This metaphor has helped me ever since.

Progress, Not Perfection

This is a term from drug and alcohol recovery that helps remind me to celebrate my little triumphs instead of focusing on what might possibly be improved. This is sanity medicine.

"Ptooie! I Spit on You!"

What we can say to the Dinosaur Voice in our heads that tells us our ideas are bad or that we are getting too big for our britches. Must be spoken with a French accent.

Receptor Cells

If we find ourselves feeling neglected, it is because our receptor cells are clogged. When this happens, we refuse to let other people contribute to us. We need to be open to receiving, so we can accept and be grateful for the gifts we are given all day long. Refusing to let people help us can be a selfish act, even though we tell ourselves we are being generous. This is tricky. When someone is sick, for example, people feel better when they can do something concrete to help. If we refuse to graciously receive the love people are offering us, we may be unintentionally "hogging the giving." We need to look those gift hogs in the mouth, especially when we are the pig.

Repo Man

A friend of mine used to be afraid that the "Repo Man" would come and take away everything she loved. When my daughter Katie almost died, the words to the song Repo Man came to me as I sat with her in the emergency room that first night. The only way to deal with the Repo Man is to have faith, take a deep breath, and take the next step right in front of us.

Sacred Napping

It is hard to take the rest time we need. I always need more rest than I think I "should." It helps me to tell myself that my napping is sacred. The research on napping is clear: we are more energized and more productive when we take the time to nap for twenty minutes every day.

I also know that when everyone is in a tizzy, it is important that someone is in the corner breathing, holding a serene center. My friend Lena helped me figure out this one.

Sacred Space

What we all are all of the time. If we practice honoring our sacred space and the sacred space of others, life can only get richer.

Suck of the Muck

The term I use to describe those addictive tendencies that will pull us down if we are not diligent and mindful. If we grew up in the muck, the muck is our default outcome.

Taking Turns Being Right

Sometimes Murray will say, "I just need to be right for a little while!" This lets me know I have fallen into a micromanaging bad habit or that I have not been listening well. "You are so right!" I will say and the game has begun.

"That Would be a Brave Thing to Do"

This is what our courage lion whispers in our ear when he is urging us to live a life of more grandeur. Its promptings are subtle, but if we ignore the call to take a risk to become what we were meant to be, we will suffer a "courage hangover." This is unpleasant, indeed.

"This is Perfect!"

A cousin of "Actually, this is a good thing!." Saying "This is perfect" reminds me to look for the perfection in whatever is happening to me.

"What Can I Say to Help You Stop Being Mad at Me?"

This question invites us to experiment with creativity and humor to help us shift out of a sticky self-righteousness. Once, when I still harbored bad feelings toward Murray even though our problem had been resolved, Murray asked me what I needed to hear to get him out of the doghouse. "I want you to say you were bad," I said to him. "I was bad," he replied. This felt so good, I asked him to repeat "I was bad" several times until we were both laughing and the fight was truly over.

"What DID You Do to the Thermostat?"

If I say something with a disrespectful tone in my voice, Murray will respond with "What DID you do to that thermostat?" to gently remind me to knock it off.

"You Are Not on My Committee!"

When I decided I wanted to lose some weight, Murray rushed in with advice. Since I knew he had some issues with "fat," his comments felt like Level One pokes disguised as Level Two "suggestions." I told him I had not put him on my Losing Weight Committee and that if he really wanted to help me, he could stop buying junk food and cook more vegetables. Turn about is fair play and Murray has had to fire me from his Making His Job More Efficient Committee, as well as others. Even if you have requested help, placing someone on one of your Committees, you can release them from this responsibility at any time. You hired them and you can fire them. It feels great.

"You Do Not Have My Permission to Build My Character Right Now"

When someone offers you unsolicited advice or comments on your behavior in order to get you back in line, say this to them and see what happens. If the person laughs, then you will know you are with someone who will respect your boundaries. If they hype up their attack, then you know you are with someone who does not respect your boundaries.

"You're Not the Boss of Me!"

What you say to the Voice inside you that wants you to avoid taking a risk because it might be embarrassing. Embarrassment is just a feeling and if you don't cling to it, it will go away and another feeling will come along. Embarrassment will never kill you but it might steal your life if you let it.

Soul Resources

Black, Claudia. 1981. *It Will Never Happen to Me.*

Bradshaw, John. 1988. *Healing The Shame That Binds You.*

Bronson, Po. 2002. *What Should I Do with My Life.*

Cameron, Julia. 1992. *The Artist's Way.*

Campbell, Joseph with Bill Moyers. 1988. *The Power of Myth.*

Canfield, Jack and Hansen, Mark Victor. 1993. *Chicken Soup for the Soul.*

Covey, Stephen. 1989. *Seven Habits of Highly Effective People.*

Frankl, Viktor. 1959. *A Man's Search for Meaning.*

Glickstein, Lee. 1998. *Be Heard Now.*

Goleman, Daniel. 1995. *Emotional Intelligence.*

James, Jennifer. 1993. *Defending Yourself Against Criticism: The Slug Manual.*

James, Jennifer. 1986. *Success is the Quality of Your Journey.*

Keirsey, David and Bates, Marilyn. 1984. *Please Understand Me: Character and Temperament Types.*

Kingsolver, Barbara. 1995. *High Tide in Tucson: Essays from Now or Never.*

Lerner, Harriet. 1989. *Dance of Intimacy.*

Levine, Mel. 2002. *A Mind at a Time.*

Myss, Carolyn. 1997. *Anatomy of The Spirit.*

Peck, M. Scott. 1978. *The Road Less Traveled.*

Rainer, Tristan. 1978. *The New Diary.*

Roberts, Monty. 1997. *The Man Who Listens To Horses.*

Tannen, Deborah. 1990. *You Just Don't Understand.*

Thomas, Marlo, editor. 2002. *The Right Words at the Right Time.*

Ueland, Brenda. 1977. *If You Want To Write.*

Walker, Alice. 1982. *The Color Purple.*

Williams, Margery. 1922. *The Velveteen Rabbit.*

Williamson, Marianne, 1992. *Return to Love.*

Wooldridge, Susan. 1996. *Poem Crazy.*

More Soul Resources

from Vicki Hannah Lein

Web Sites

- www.womanwithavoice.com
- www.joyworks.us
- www.playgroundofthesoul.com
- www.warriorbabe.com
- www.freerangechix.net

Personal Coaching

Individual assistance in finding your voice and overcoming obstacles. Check—www.womanwithavoice.com for details.

CDs

Alive, Alive: Songs that Lift You Up, Dust You Off, and Set You Free (includes seven of the songs in this book)

Daring to Sing (includes more songs from this book)

Daring to be a Poet, poetry from *Woman with a Voice: Daring to Live Authentically Ever After*

Calling for the Best

All of the above are available at—
www.joyworks.us and www.womanwithavoice.com

Free Range Chix Unclogged
Available at—www.freerangechix.net

Printed in the United States
44437LVS00002B/358-360